Bible Stories And Religious Classics

by

Philip P. Walls

Bible Stories And Religious Classics
by Philip P. Walls

ISBN: 978-93-61155-37-6

Published by

DOUBLE 9 BOOKS

2/13-B, Ansari Road
Daryaganj, New Delhi – 110002
info@double9books.com
www.double9books.com
Tel. 011-40042856

ABOUT THE AUTHOR

American author, social reformer, and philanthropist Anson Phelps Stokes was well-known for his literary journey. Throughout his life, "Stokes" actively participated in several social and humanitarian activities. He hailed from a well-known family. Stokes was very interested in education and religious studies. He was a key figure in the founding of the Yale Divinity School and held the position of Secretary of the Yale University Corporation. Additionally, he was a key figure in the establishment of the Phelps-Stokes Fund, which sought to enhance Native American and African American education. Stokes was a writer who wrote many novels on social and religious subjects. His work "Bible Stories and Religious Classics" is one of note; it offers readers a compilation of biblical tales and spiritual lessons to enhance their comprehension of various religious beliefs. Stokes is still honoured for his contributions to social reform and philanthropy. His commitment to education and his initiatives to advance equality and understanding have had a long-lasting effect on society.

CONTENTS

INTRODUCTION

There never was a time when the demand for books for young people was so great as it is to-day or when so much was being done to meet the demand. "Children's Counter," "Boys' Books," are signs which, especially at the Christmas season, attract the eye in every large book shop. Tales of adventure, manuals about various branches of nature study, historical romances, lives of heroes—in fact, almost every kind of book—is to be found in abundance, beautifully illustrated, attractively bound, well printed, all designed and written especially for the youth of our land. It is indeed an encouraging sign. It means that the child of to-day is being introduced to the world's best in literature and science and history and art in simple and gradual ways.

In the Middle Ages stories of the martyrs and legends of the Church, along with some simple form of catechetical instruction, formed the basis of a child's mental and religious training. Later, during and after the Crusades, the stories of war and the mysteries of the East increased the stock in trade for the homes of Europe; but still the horizon remained a narrow one. Even the invention of printing did not bring to the young as many direct advantages as would naturally be expected. To-day, when Christian missionaries set up a printing press in some distant island of the sea, the first books which they print in the vernacular are almost invariably those parts of the Bible, such as the Gospels and the stories of Genesis, which most appeal to the young, and, what is of special importance, they have the young directly and mainly in mind in their publishing work. This was not true a few centuries ago. The presses were, perhaps naturally and inevitably, almost exclusively occupied with books for the learned world. To be sure, the Legenda Aurea, of which I shall speak later, although not intended primarily for children, proved a great boon to them. So did the Chap Books of England. But it was not until the middle of the eighteenth century, when John Newbery set up his book shop at St. Paul's Churchyard, London, that any special attention was given by printers to the publication, in attractive form, of juvenile books. Newbery's children's books made him famous in his day, but the world seems to have forgotten him. Yet he deserves a monument along with Æsop, and La Fontaine, and Kate Greenaway, and Andersen, and Scott and

Henty, and all the other greater and lesser lights who have done so much to gladden the heart and enlarge the mind of childhood and youth.

But from Newbery's day to this year of our Lord nineteen hundred and three is a very long jump in what we may call the evolution of juvenile literature, for the preparation of reading matter for young people seems now almost to have reached its climax. There is one field, however, and that the one which this volume tries to cover, which strangely enough seems to have been almost neglected. Of "goody-goody" Sunday School library books of an old-fashioned type, which are insipid and lacking both in virility of thought and literary form, there are, alas, already too many. What we need is something to take their place, something which will furnish real literature, and yet which from subject matter and manner of handling is specially adapted to what I still like to call Sunday reading, a phrase which unfortunately seems to mean little to most people to-day. Bearing this in mind, it is the purpose of this book to gather together, in attractive form, such religious classics as are specially fitted to interest and uplift young people.

There is a wide variety in so far as *subject matter, source* and *form* are concerned, but a certain unity is given to the contents of the volume by the religious note, which, whether brought prominently forward or not, is found alike in all the selections.

The Bible has furnished directly or indirectly most of the *subject matter* here used. The biographies of various Scripture characters appear in large numbers. Adam and Noah head the list, and Peter and Paul bring up the end of a procession of worthies whose heroic deeds as the servants of Jehovah will always appeal to the imagination of youthful minds. But it is not with Bible characters only that this book deals. The lives of Christian saints who entered upon their inheritance, such as Christopher and Sylvester and Francis of Assisi, also have their place, while yet more prominent are stories and poems based on some Bible incidents. Even selections such as Hawthorne's Great Stone Face or Wordsworth's Ode to Duty have their roots deep in the Bible, for they can be understood and explained only by those who know the Revelation it contains. In so far, then, as the subject matter of the volume is concerned, either it or its inspiration can always be traced back to the Bible.

When we turn from the Bible material which, as we have seen, supplies both subject and inspiration, to the *source* from which the selections in their literary form as here given are derived, we find that the old foundations have sufficed for many kinds of structure. Probably the source from which the editor has drawn most largely is the Golden Legend. This work, which was translated into English and printed by Caxton in 1483, although little heard of now, was for several centuries a household word in Christendom. It was the creation of a Genoese Archbishop, Jacobus de Voragine, and dates from about the middle of the thirteenth century. The good Archbishop, using the Bible and the Lives of the Saints as a basis, and as a sharer of the superstitions of the time having unbounded faith in every legend of the Church, put together in simple form for the edification of his flock the various stories about Jewish and Christian worthies which compose the original Legenda Aurea. This was translated into French by one Jean de Vignay in the fourteenth century, and the English version was in turn mainly made from this translation. In the simple, sturdy language of Caxton the book became a most popular one, being often read aloud in the Parish Churches of England, where it helped to familiarize the people, especially the young, with sacred story as represented by the heroes of the Old Testament and the saints of the Church. In Caxton's introduction there is a quaint sentence regarding the name of the book. After mentioning the Latin title, he adds "that is to say in Englyshe the golden legende for lyke as passeth golde in vallwe al other metallys, soo thys legende exedeth all other bokes." Whether the good printer's judgment be justified or no, it is not for us to say. It is true, however, that after the passing of over six centuries since its original production, the editor of this volume in looking for religious classics for young people has made more use of it than of any other collection. All honor, then, to the old Archbishop of Genoa and to William Caxton, who made his work accessible to the youth of England.

The only other work which deserves any special mention as a source for the contents of this volume, is the Stories and Tales of Hans Christian Andersen. If ever there was any one who deserved the title of the Children's Friend, surely this son of a poor Danish shoemaker is the man. His Tales have been translated into many languages, and because of their true imagination and their simplicity of expression they have appealed to all children. Ten or more of them appear in this volume. They are charming and wholesome reading, and their continued popularity makes us realize the truth of these closing lines in Andersen's The Old Grave Stones: "The good and the beautiful perish never; they live eternally in tale and song."

The other sources from which this collection has been made up are so varied as to require no mention aside from that given with each title. The Master Poets of English Literature have been freely drawn upon: Byron to tell of the Destruction of Sennacherib, Milton to sing of Christ's Nativity, Wordsworth to meditate aloud on Duty, and other great writers to emphasize various deep truths of life.

As we turn from subject matter and source to *form*, we again find great variety. Almost every kind of literature is represented. The early lengends of the Jewish people, told by the author of the Legenda Aurea almost in the words of Scripture, bring to young and old alike the same lessons about God and Duty. The fact that they are legends, rather than exact history, does not in any way lessen their religious value. Then, too, the book contains allegories, such as that of the Pilgrim's Progress, Christendom's greatest religious classic next to the Bible itself, and those of some of Andersen's Tales. Poetry also is well represented, the selections being in large part suggested by Scripture. There are in addition many stories in the ordinary sense of the word—tales which are entirely the fabric of the imagination, but which, like the selections from Hawthorne, have some great lesson to teach. In fact, the literary forms represented in this volume are almost as numerous as those of the Bible itself. The latter used to be looked upon merely as a storehouse of historic facts and devotional songs; now we see in it Legend, Oratory, Poetry, Allegory, History, Proverb and Prophecy; and we find that all of these forms are used by God's servants to teach His truth to men.

Sufficient has been said, I think, to show the purpose and scope of this volume and to introduce the reader to its contents. It is my hope and belief that the effort of my friend, Mr. Philip P. Wells, to make this a collection of religious classics in the full meaning of these words may prove successful. My highest wish, however, is that those who read these selections, with their great variety of source and form, may mark the inspiration of thought or incident common to them all, and may find an interest in refreshing what may be an old acquaintance with that Book of Books which gives with classic truth the fundamental subject matter for all deep thought and high aspiration.

ANSON PHELPS STOKES, JR.

THE LIFE OF ADAM

The Sunday of Septuagesima beginneth the story of the Bible, in which is read the legend and story of Adam which followeth

In the beginning God made and created heaven and earth. The earth was idle and void and covered with darkness. And the spirit of God was borne on the waters, and God said: Be made light, and anon light was made. And God saw that light was good, and divided the light from darkness, and called the light day and darkness night.

And thus was made light with heaven and earth first, and even and morning was made one day. The second day he made the firmament, and divided the waters that were under the firmament from them that were above, and called the firmament heaven. The third day were made on the earth herbs and fruits in their kind. The fourth day God made the sun and moon and stars, etc. The fifth day he made the fishes in the water and birds in the air. The sixth day God made the beasts on the earth, every one in his kind and gender. And God saw that all these works were good and said: Make we man unto our similitude and image. Here spake the Father to the Son and Holy Ghost, or else as it were the common voice of three persons, when it was said make we, and to our, in plural number. Man was made to the image of God in his soul. Here it is to be noted that he made not only the soul with the body, but he made both body and soul. As to the body he made male and female. God gave to man the lordship and power upon living beasts. Thus in six days was heaven and earth made and all the ornation of them. And then he made the seventh day on which he rested, not for that he was weary, but ceased his operation, and showed the seventh day which he blessed. Thus he shortly showed the generations of heaven and earth, for here he determined the works of the six days and the seventh day he sanctified and made holy. God had planted in the beginning Paradise a place of desire and delices. And man was made in the field of Damascus; he was made of the slime of the earth. Paradise was made the third day of creation, and was beset with herbs, plants and trees, and is a place of most mirth and joy. In the midst whereof be set two trees, that is the tree of life, and that other the tree of knowing good and evil. And there is a well, which casteth out water for to water the trees and herbs of Paradise. This well is the mother of all waters, which well is divided into four parts. One part is called Phison. This goeth about Inde. The second is called Gijon, otherwise Nilus, and that runneth about Ethiopia, the other two be called Tigris and Euphrates. Tigris runneth toward Assyria, and Euphrates is called fruitful, which runneth in Chaldea. These four floods come and spring out of the same well, and depart, and yet in some place some of them meet again.

Then God took man from the place of his creation and brought him into Paradise, for to work there, not to labor needily, but in delighting and recreating him, and that he should keep Paradise. For like as Paradise should refresh him, so should he labor to serve God, and there God gave him a commandment. Every commandment standeth in two things, in doing or forbidding, in doing he commanded him to eat of all the trees of Paradise, in forbidding he commanded that he should not eat of the tree of the knowledge of good and evil. This commandment was given to the man, and by the man it went to the woman. For when the woman was made it was commanded to them both, and hereto he set a pain, saying: Whatsoever day thou eatest thereof thou shalt die by death.

God said: It is not good a man to be alone, make we to him an helper like to himself for to bring forth children. Adam supposed that some helper to him had been among the beasts which had been like to him. Therefore God brought to Adam all living beasts of the earth and air, in which he understood them of the water also, which with one commandment all came tofore him. They were brought for two causes, one was because man should give to each of them a name, by which they should know that he should dominate over them, and the second cause was because Adam should know that there was none of them like to him. And he named them in the Hebrew tongue, which was only the language and none other at the beginning. And so none being found like unto him, God sent in Adam a lust to sleep, which was no dream, but as is supposed in an extasy or in a trance; in which was showed to him the celestial court. Wherefore when he awoke he prophesied of the conjunction of Christ to his church, and of the flood that was to come, and of the doom and destruction of the world by fire he knew, which afterward he told to his children.

Whiles that Adam slept, God took one of his ribs, both flesh and bone, and made that a woman, and set her tofore Adam. Which then said: This is now a bone of my bones and flesh of my flesh; and Adam gave her a name like as her lord, and said she should be called virago, which is as much as to say as made of a man, and is a name taken of a man. And anon, the name giving, he prophesied, saying: Because she is taken of the side of a man, therefore a man shall forsake and leave father and mother and abide and be adherent unto his wife, and they shall be two in one flesh; and though they be two persons, yet in matrimony and wedlock they be but one flesh, and in other things twain. For why, neither of them had power of his own flesh. They were both naked and were not ashamed, for they stood both in the state of innocence. Then the serpent which was hotter than any beast of the earth and naturally deceivable, for he was full of the devil Lucifer, which was deject and cast out of heaven, had great envy to man that was bodily in Paradise, and knew well, if he might make him to trespass and break God's commandments, that he should be cast out also.

Yet he was afeard to be taken or espied of the man, he went to the woman, not so prudent and more prone to slide and bow. And in the form of the serpent, for then the serpent was erect as a man. Bede saith that he chose a serpent having a maiden's cheer [face], for like oft apply to like, and spake by the tongue of the serpent to Eve, and said: Why commanded you God that ye should not eat of all the trees of Paradise? This he said to find occasion to say that he was come for. Then the woman answered and said: Ne forte moriamur, lest haply we die, which she said doubting, for lightly she was flexible to every part. Whereunto anon he answered: Nay in no wise ye shall die, but God would not that ye should be like him in science, and knowing that when ye eat of this tree ye shall be as gods knowing good and evil, he as envious forbade you. And anon the woman, elate in pride and willing to be like to God, accorded thereto and believed him. The woman saw that the tree was fair to look on, and clean and sweet of savor, took and ate thereof, and gave unto Adam of the same, happily desiring him by fair words. But Adam anon agreed, for when he saw the woman not dead he supposed that God had said that they should die to fear them with, and then ate of the fruit forbidden. And anon their sight was opened that they saw their nakedness, and then anon they understood that they had trespassed. And thus they knew that they were naked, and they took fig leaves and sewed them together for to cover their members in manner of breeches.

And anon after, they heard the voice of our Lord God walking, and anon they hied him. Our Lord called the man and said: Adam, where art thou? Calling him in blaming him and not as knowing where he was, but as who said: Adam, see in what misery thou art. Which answered: I have hid me, Lord, for I am naked. Our Lord said: Who told thee that thou wert naked, but that thou hast eaten of the tree forbidden? He then not meekly confessing his trespass, but laid the fault on his wife, and on him as giver of the woman to him, and said: The woman that thou gavest to me as a fellow, gave to me of the tree, and I ate thereof. And then our Lord said to the woman: Why didst thou so? Neither she accused herself, but laid the sin on the serpent, and privily she laid the fault on the maker of him. The serpent was not demanded, for he did it not of himself, but the devil by him.

And our Lord, cursing them, began at the serpent, keeping an order and congruous number of curses. The serpent was the first and sinned most, for he sinned in three things. The woman next and sinned less than he, but more than the man, for she sinned in two things. The man sinned last and least, for he sinned but in one. The serpent had envy, he lied, and deceived, for these three he had three curses. Because he had envy at the excellence of man, it was said to him: Thou shalt go and creep on thy breast; because he lied he is punished in his mouth, when it was said: Thou shalt eat earth all the days of thy life. Also he took away his voice and put venom in his mouth. And because he deceived, it was said: I shall put enmity between thee and woman, and thy seed and her seed. She shall break thy head, etc. In two things the woman sinned, in pride and eating the fruit. Because she sinned in pride, he meeked her, saying: Thou shalt be under the power of man, and he shall have lordship over thee, and he shall put thee to affliction. Now is she subject to a man by condition and dread, which before was but subject by love; and because she sinned in the fruit, she is punished in her fruit, when it was said to her: Thou shalt bring forth children in sorrow; in the pain of sorrow standeth the curse, but in bringing forth of children is a blessing. And so, in punishing, God forgat not to have mercy. And because Adam sinned but only in eating of the fruit, therefore he was punished in seeking his meat, as it is said to him: Accursed be the earth in thy work, that is to say for thy work of thy sin, for which is made that the earth that brought forth good and wholesome fruits plenteously, from henceforth shall bring forth but seldom, and also none without man's labor, and also sometime weeds, briars, and thorns shall grow. And he added: Thereto shalt thou eat herbs of the earth, as who saith thou shalt be like a beast or jument. He cursed the earth because the trespass was of the fruit of the earth and not of the water. He added thereto to him of labor: In the sweat of thy cheer [face] thou shalt eat thy bread unto the time thou return again into the earth; that is to say till thou die, for thou art earth, and into earth thou shalt go again.

Then Adam, wailing and sorrowing the misery that was to come of his posterity, named his wife Eve, which is to say, mother of all living folk. Then God made to Adam and Eve two leathern coats of the skins of dead beasts, to the end that they bare with them the sign of mortality, and said: Lo, Adam is made as one of us, knowing good and evil, now lest he put his hand and take of the tree of life and live ever, as who saith: beware and cast him out, lest he take and eat of the tree of life. And so he was cast out of Paradise, and set in the field of Damascus where as he was made and taken from, for to work and labor there. And our Lord set Cherubim to keep Paradise of delight with a burning sword and pliant, to the end that none should enter there ne come to the tree of life.

After then that Adam was cast out of Paradise and set in the world, he engendered Cain, the fifteenth year after he was made, and his sister Calmana; but after another fifteen years was Abel born, and his sister Delbora.

When Adam was an hundred and thirty years of age, Cain slew Abel his brother. Truth it is, after many days Cain and Abel offered sacrifice and gifts unto God. It is to be believed that Adam taught his sons to offer to God their tithes and first fruits. Cain offered fruits, for he was a ploughman and tiller of earth, and Abel offered milk and the first of the lambs, Moses saith, of the fattest of the flock. And God beheld the gifts of Abel, for he and his sacrifices were acceptable to our Lord; and as to Cain his sacrifices, God beheld them not, for they were not to him acceptable, he offered withies and thorns. And as some doctors say, fire came from heaven and lighted the sacrifice of Abel, and the gifts of Cain pleased not our Lord, for the sacrifice would not belight nor burn clear in the light of God. Whereof Cain had great envy unto his brother Abel, which arose against him and slew him. And our Lord said to him: Where is Abel thy brother? He answered and said: I wot never, am I keeper of my brother? Then our Lord said: What hast thou done? The voice of the blood of thy brother crieth to thee from the earth, wherefore thou art cursed, and accursed be the earth that received the blood of thy brother by his mouth of thy hands. When thou shalt work and labor the earth it shall bring forth no fruit, but thou shalt be fugitive, vagabond, and void on the earth. This Cain deserved well to be cursed, knowing the pain of the first trespass of Adam, yet he added thereto murder and slaughter of his brother.

Then Cain, dreading that beasts should devour him, or if he went forth he should be slain of the men, or if he dwelt with them, they would slay him for his sin, damned himself, and in despair said: My wickedness is more than I can deserve to have forgiveness, whoso find me shall slay me. This he said of dread, or else wishing, as who said, would God he would slay me. Then our Lord said: Nay not so, thou shalt die, but not soon, for whosoever slayeth Cain shall be punished seven sithes more, for he should deliver him from dread, from labor and misery, and added that he should be punished personally sevenfold more. This punition shall endure to him in pain unto the seventh, Lameth, whosomever shall slay Cain shall loose seven vengeances. Some hold that his pain endured unto the seventh generation, for he committed seven sins. He departed not truly, he had envy to his brother, he wrought guilefully, he slew his brother falsely, he denied it, he despaired and damned, he did no penance. And after he went into the east, fugitive and vagabond. Cain knew his wife which bare Enoch, and he made a city and named it Enoch after the name of his son Enoch. Here it showeth well that this time were many men, though their generation be not said, whom Cain called to his city, by whose help he made it, whom he induced to theft and robbery.

He was the first that walled or made cities; dreading them that he hurted, for surety he brought his people into the towns. Then Enoch gat Irad, and Irad Mehujael, and he gat Methusael, and he gat Lameth, which was the seventh from Adam and worst, for he brought in first bigamy. This Lameth took two wives, Adah and Zilla; of Adah he gat Jabal which found first the craft to make folds for shepherds and to change their pasture, and ordained flocks of sheep, and departed the sheep from the goats after the quality, the lambs by themselves, and the older by themselves, and understood the feeding of them after the season of the year. The name of his brother was Jubal, father of singers in the harp and organs, not of the instruments, for they were found long after, but he was the finder of music, that is to say of consonants of accord, such as shepherds use in their delights and sports. And forasmuch as he heard Adam prophesy of two judgments by the fire and water, that all things should be destroyed thereby, and that his craft new found should not perish, he did do write it in two pillars or columns, one of marble, another of clay of the earth, to the end that one should endure against the water, and that other against the fire. Josephus saith that the pillar of marble is yet in the land of Syria. Of Zilla he begat Tubal-cain, which found first the craft of smithery and working of iron, and made things for war, and sculptures and gravings in metal to the pleasure of the eyes, which he so working, Tubal, tofore said, had delight in the sound of his hammers, of which he made the consonants and tunes of accord in his song. Noema, sister of Tubal-cain, found first the craft of diverse texture.

Lameth was a shooter, and used to shoot at wild beasts, for none use of the meat of them, but only for to have the skins for their clothing, and lived so long that he was blind and had a child to lead him. And on a time by adventure he slew Cain. For Cain was always afeard and hid him among bushes and briars, and the child that led Lameth had supposed it had been some wild beast and directed Lameth to shoot thereat, and so, weening to shoot at a beast, slew Cain. And when he knew that he had slain Cain, he with his bow slew the child, and thus he slew them both to his damnation; therefore as the sin of Cain was punished seven sithes, so was the sin of Lameth seventy sithes and seven. That is to say, seventy-seven souls that came of Lameth were perished in the deluge and Noah's flood; also his wife did him much sorrow, and evil-entreated him. And he being wroth said that he suffered that for his double homicide and manslaughter, yet nevertheless he feared him by pain, saying: Why will ye slay me? he shall be more and sorer punished that slayeth me, than he that slew Cain.

Josephus said that when Abel was slain and Cain fled away, Adam when he was one hundred and thirty years old engendered Seth like to his similitude, and he to the image of God. This Seth was a good man, and he gat Enos, and Enos Cainan, and Cainan begot Malaleel, and Malaleel Jared, and Jared Enoch, and Enoch Methuselah, and Methuselah Lamech, and Lamech Noah. And like as in the generation of Cain the seventh was the worst, so in the generation of Seth the seventh was the best, that was Enoch whom God took and brought him into Paradise, unto the time that he shall come with Elias for to convert the hearts of the fathers into the sons. And Adam lived after he had begotten Seth eight hundred years, and engendered sons and daughters. Some hold opinion thirty sons and thirty daughters, and some fifty of that one and fifty of that other. We find no certainty of them in the Bible. But all the days of Adam living here in earth amount to the sum of nine hundred and thirty years. And in the end of his life when he should die, it is said, but of none authority, that he sent Seth his son into Paradise for to fetch the oil of mercy, where he received certain grains of the fruit of the tree of mercy by an angel. And when he came again he found his father Adam yet alive and told him what he had done. And then Adam laughed first and then died. And then he laid the grains or kernels under his father's tongue and buried him in the vale of Hebron; and out of his mouth grew three trees of the three grains, of which trees the cross that our Lord suffered his passion on was made, by virtue of which he gat very mercy, and was brought out of darkness into very light of Heaven. To the which he bring us that liveth and reigneth God, world without end.

HERE BEGINNETH THE HISTORY OF NOAH

The First Sunday in Sexagesima

After that Adam was dead, died Eve and was buried by him. At the beginning, in the first age, the people lived long. Adam lived nine hundred and thirty years, and Methuselah lived nine hundred and sixty-nine years. S. Jerome saith that he died the same year that the flood was. Then Noah was the tenth from Adam in the generation of Seth, in whom the first age was ended. The seventy interpreters say that this first age dured two thousand two hundred and forty-four years. S. Jerome saith not fully two thousand, and Methodius full two thousand, etc.

Noah then was a man perfect and righteous and kept God's commandment. And when he was five hundred years old, he gat Shem, Ham, and Japhet. This time men began to multiply on the earth, and the children of God, that is to say of Seth, as religious, saw the daughters of men, that is to say of Cain, and took them to their wives. This time was so much sin on the earth, wherefore God was displeased and determined in his prescience to destroy man that he had made, and said: I shall put man away that I have made, and my spirit shall not abide in man for ever, for he is flesh. As who said, I shall not punish man perpetually as I do the devil, for man is frail, and yet ere I shall destroy him I shall give him space and time of repentance and to amend him, if he will. The time of repentance shall be one hundred and twenty years. Then Noah, righteous and perfect, walked with God, that is in his laws, and the earth was corrupt by sin and filled.

When God saw the earth to be corrupt, and that every man was corrupt by sin upon the earth, he said to Noah: The end of all people is come tofore me except them that shall be saved, and the earth is replenished with their wickedness. I shall destroy them with the earth, id est [that is], with the fertility of the earth. Make to thee an ark of tree, hewn, polished, and squared. And make there divers places, and lime it with clay and pitch within and without, that is to wit with glue which is so fervent, that the timber may not be loosed. And thou shalt make it three hundred cubits of length, fifty in breadth, and thirty of height. And make therein divers distinctions of places and chambers and of wardrobes. And the ark had a door for to enter in and come out, and a window was made thereon, which that the Hebrews say was of crystal. This ark was on making, from the beginning that God commanded first to make it, one hundred and twenty years. In which time Noah oft desired the people to leave their sin, and how he had spoken with God, and that he was commanded to make the ship, for God should destroy them for their sin, but if they left it. And they mocked him and said that he raved and was a fool, and gave no faith to his saying and continued in their sin and wickedness. Then, when the ark was perfectly made, God bade him to take into it of all the beasts of the earth, and also of the fowls of the air, of each two, male and female, that they may live. And also of all the meats of the earth that be comestible, that they may serve and feed thee and them. And Noah did all that our Lord commanded him. Then said our Lord to Noah: Enter thou and all thy household into the ark, that is to say thou and thy wife and thy three sons and their three wives. I have seen that thou art rightful in this generation. Of all beasts that be clean thou shalt take seven, and of unclean beasts but only two. And of the birds seven and seven, male and female, that they may be saved on the face of the earth. Yet after seven days I shall rain upon the earth forty days and forty nights, and shall destroy all the substance that I made on the earth. And Noah did all things that our Lord commanded him.

He was six hundred years old when the flood began on the earth. And then Noah entered in and his sons, his wife, and the wives of his sons, all into the ark to eschew the waters of the flood. Of all the beasts and the fowls, and of all that moved and had life on earth, male and female, Noah took in to him as our Lord had bidden. And seven days after they were entered, the water began to increase. The wells of the abysms were broken, and the cataracts of heaven were opened, that is to say the clouds, and it rained on the earth forty days and forty nights. And the ark was elevate and borne upon the waters on height above the mountains and hills, for the water was grown higher fifteen cubits above all the mountains, that it should purge and wash the filth of the air. Then was consumed all that was on the earth living, man, woman, and beast and birds. And all that ever bare life, so that nothing abode upon the earth, for the water was fifteen cubits above the highest mountain of the earth. And when Noah was entered he shut the door fast without forth, and limed it with glue.

And so the waters abode elevate in height an hundred and fifty days from the day that Noah entered in. And our Lord then remembered Noah and all them that were in the ark with him, and also on the beasts and fowls, and ceased the waters. And the wells and cataracts were closed, and the rains were prohibited, and forbidden to rain no more. The seventh month, the twenty-seventh day of the month, the ark rested on the hills of Armenia. The tenth month, of the first day of the month, the tops of the hills appeared first. After these forty days after the lessing of the waters, Noah opened the window and desired sore to have tidings of ceasing of the flood. And sent out a raven for to have tidings, and when he was gone he returned no more again, for peradventure she found some dead carrion of a beast swimming on the water, and lighted thereon to feed her and was left there. After this he sent out a dove which flew out, and when she could find no place to rest ne set her foot on, she returned unto Noah and he took her in. Yet then were not the tops of the hills bare. And seven days after he sent her out again, which at even returned, bearing a branch of an olive tree, burgeoning, in her mouth. And after other seven days he sent her again, which came no more again.

Then in the year of Noah six hundred and one, the first day of the month, Noah opened the covering of the ark and saw that the earth was dry, but he durst not go out, but abode the commandment of our Lord. The second month, the twenty-seventh day of the month, our Lord said to Noah: Go out of the ark, thou and thy wife, thy sons and the wives of thy sons. He commanded them to go conjointly out which disjointly entered, and let go out with them all the beasts and fowls living, and all the reptiles, every each after his kind and gender, to whom our Lord said: Grow ye and multiply upon the earth. Then Noah issued out and his wife, and his sons with their wives, and all the beasts, the same day a year after they entered in, every one after his gender. Noah then edified an altar to our Lord and took of all the beasts that were clean and offered sacrifice unto our Lord; and our Lord smelled the sweetness of the sacrifice and said to Noah: From henceforth I shall not curse the earth for man, for he is prone and ready to fall from the beginning of his youth. I shall no more destroy man by such vengeance. And then our Lord blessed them and said: Grow ye and multiply the earth and be ye lords of all the beasts of the earth, of the fowls of the air, and of the fishes. I have given all things to you, but eat no flesh with the blood. I command you to slay no man, nor to shed no man's blood. I have made man after mine image. Whosomever sheddeth his brother's blood, his blood shall be shed. Go ye forth and grow and multiply and fill the earth. This said our Lord to Noah and his sons: Lo! I have made a covenant with you and with them that shall come after you, that I shall no more bring such a flood to slay all people, and in token thereof I have set my rainbow in the clouds of heaven, for who that trespasseth I shall do justice otherwise on him. Noah lived after the flood three hundred and fifty years. From the time of Adam until after Noah's flood, the time and season was alway green and tempered; and all that time men ate no flesh, for the herbs and fruits were then of great strength and effect, they were pure and nourishing. But after the flood the earth was weaker and brought not forth so good fruit, wherefore flesh was ordained to be eaten. And then Noah began to labor for his livelihood with his sons, and began to till the earth, to destroy briars and thorns and to plant vines. And so on a time Noah had drunk so much of the wine that he was drunk, and lay and slept. Ham, his middlest son, laughed and scorned his father, and called his brethren to see, which rebuked Ham of his folly and sin. And Noah awoke, and when he understood how Ham his son had scorned him, he cursed him and also his son Canaan, and blessed Shem and Japhet. All the days of Noah were nine hundred and fifty years and then he died. And after his death his sons dealed all the world between them, Shem had all Asia, Ham Africa, and Japhet all Europe. Thus was it departed. Asia is the best part and is as much as the other two, and that is in the east. Africa is the south part, and therein is Carthage and many rich countries, therein be blue and black men. Ham had that to his part Africa. The third part is Europe which is in the north and west, therein is Greece, Rome, and Germany. In Europe reigneth now most the christian law and faith, wherein is many a rich realm. And so was the world departed to the three sons of Noah.

THE RAINBOW

Triumphal arch, that fill'st the sky
  When storms prepare to part,
I ask not proud Philosophy
  To teach me what thou art.

Still seem, as to my childhood's sight,
  A midway station given,
For happy spirits to alight,
  Betwixt the earth and heaven.

Can all that optics teach, unfold
  Thy form to please me so,
As when I dreamt of gems and gold
  Hid in thy radiant bow?

When science from creation's face
  Enchantment's veil withdraws,
What lovely visions yield their place
  To cold material laws!

And yet, fair bow, no fabling dreams,
  But words of the Most High,
Have told why first thy robe of beams
  Was woven in the sky.

When o'er the green undeluged earth
  Heaven's covenant thou didst shine,
How came the world's gray fathers forth
  To watch thy sacred sign!

And when its yellow lustre smiled
  O'er mountains yet untrod,
Each mother held aloft her child
  To bless the bow of God.

The earth to thee her incense yields,
  The lark thy welcome sings,

When, glittering in the freshen'd fields,
  The snowy mushroom springs.

How glorious is thy girdle, cast
  O'er mountain, tower, and town,
Or mirror'd in the ocean vast
  A thousand fathoms down!

As fresh in yon horizon dark,
  As young thy beauties seem,
As when the eagle from the ark
  First sported in thy beam.

For, faithful to its sacred page,
  Heaven still rebuilds thy span;
Nor lets the type grow pale with age
  That first spoke peace to man.

T. CAMPBELL.

HERE FOLLOWETH THE LIFE OF ABRAHAM

The Sunday called Quinquagesima is read in the church the history of the holy patriarch Abraham which was the son of Terah. This Terah was the tenth from Noah in the generation of Shem. Japhet had seven sons and Ham four sons. Out of the generation of Ham Nimrod came, which was a wicked man and cursed in his works, and began to make the tower of Babel which was great and high. And at the making of this tower, God changed the languages, in such wise that no man understood other. For tofore the building of that tower was but one manner speech in all the world, and there were made seventy-two speeches. The tower was great, it was ten miles about and five thousand and eighty-four steps of height. This Nimrod was the first man that found mawmetry and idolatry, which endured long and yet doth. Then I turn again to Terah which had three sons, which was Abram, Nahor, and Haran. Of Nahor came Us, Bus, and Batuel. Of Us came Job, of Bus came Balaam, and of Batuel Rebekah and Laban. Of Haran came Lot and two daughters, Melcha and Sara.

Now I shall speak of Abram of whom our blessed lady came. He wedded Sara, daughter of his brother Haran. Abram was ever faithful and true, he was sixty-five years old when his father died, for whom he mourned till our Lord comforted him, which said to Abram: Abram, make thee ready and go out of thy land and kindred, and also from the house of thy father, and come into the land that I shall show to thee. I shall make thee grow into much people; I shall bless thee and magnify thy name, and thou shalt be blessed, and I shall bless them that bless thee, and curse them that curse thee, and in thee shall be blessed all the kindreds of the earth.

Abram was seventy years old when he departed from the land of Haran, and he took with him Sara his wife, and Lot the son of his brother, and their meiny [company], and his cattle and his substance, and came into the land of Canaan, and came into the vale of Sichem, in which were ill people which were the people of Canaan. And our Lord said to Abram: I shall give to thee this land and to thine heirs. Then Abram did raise an altar on which he did sacrifice, and blessed and thanked our Lord. Abram beheld all the land toward the south, and saw the beauty thereof, and found it like as our Lord told him. But he had not been long in the land but that there fell great hunger therein, wherefore he left that country and went into Egypt and took with him Sara his wife. And as they went by the way Abram said to his wife: I fear and dread sore that when we come to this people, which be lawless, that they shall take thee for thy beauty and slay me, because they would use thee. Wherefore say thou art my sister, and I thy brother, and she agreed thereto. And when they were come in to that country the people saw that she was so fair, and anon they told the king, which anon commanded that she should be brought into his presence. And when she was come, God of his good grace so purveyed for her, that no man had power to do her villany. Wherefore the king was feared that God would have taken vengeance on him for her, and sent for Abram and said to him that he should take his wife, and that he had evil done to say, that she was his sister, and so delivered her again, and gave him gold and silver, and bade that men should worship him in all his land, and he should freely at his pleasure depart with all his goods. Then after this Abram took his wife Sara and went home again, and came unto Bethel, and set there an altar of stone, and there he adored and worshipped the name of God. His store and beasts began to multiply, and Lot with his meiny was also there. And their beasts began so sore to increase and multiply, that unnethe [hardly] the country might suffice to their pasture, in so much that rumor and grudging began to sourde and arise between the herdmen of Abram and the herdmen of Lot. Then Abram said to Lot: Lo! this country is great and wide, I pray thee to choose on which hand thou wilt go, and take it for thy meiny and thy beasts. And let no strife be between me and thee, ne between my herdmen ne thy herdmen. Lo! behold all the country is tofore thee, take which thou wilt; if thou go on the right side, I shall go on the left side, and if thou take the left, I will go on the right side. Then Lot beheld the country and saw a fair plain toward flom Jordan, which was pleasant, and the flood ran toward Sodom and Gomorrah, which was like a paradise, and took that part for him. And Abram took toward the west, which was beside the people of Canaan at the foot of mount Mamre. And Lot dwelled in Sodom. The people of Sodom were worst of all people.

Our Lord said to Abram: Lift up thine eyes and see directly from the place that thou art now in, from the north to the south, and from the east to the west. All this land that thou seest I shall give thee, and to thy seed for evermore. I shall make thy seed as powder or dust of the earth, who that may number the dust of the earth shall number thy seed. Arise therefore and walk the land in length and in breadth, for I shall give it to thee. Abram moved then his tabernacle and dwelled in the valley of Mamre, which is in Hebron, and set there his tabernacle. It happened soon after that there was a war in that land, that four kings warred again other five kings, which were of Sodom, Gomorrah and other. And the four kings overthrew the five and slew them, and spoiled and took all the substance of the country and took also with them Lot and all his goods. And a man gat away from them and came to Abram, and told him how that Lot was taken and led away. And then anon Abram did do gather his people together, the number of three hundred and eighteen. And followed after, and departed his people in two parties because they should not escape. And Abram smote in among them, and slew the kings, and rescued Lot and all his goods, and delivered the men of Sodom that were taken and the women. And they of Sodom came against him, and Melchisedech came and met with him, and offered to him bread and wine. This Melchisedech was king and priest of Jerusalem and all the country, and blessed Abram. And there Abram gave to him the tythes of all he had. And the king of Sodom would that Abram should have had such prey as he took, but he would not have as much as the latchet of a shoe, and thus gat Abram much love of all the people.

After this our Lord appeared to Abram in a vision and said: Abram, dread thee nothing, I am thy protector, and thy reward and meed shall be great. Abram answered: Lord God, what wilt thou give me? Thou wottest well I have no children, and sith I have none I will well that Eleazar the son of my bailiff be my heir. Nay, said our Lord, he shall not be thine heir, but he that shall issue and come of thy seed shall be thine heir. Our Lord led him out and bade him behold the heaven, and number the stars if thou mayst, and said to him, so shall thy offspringing and seed be. And Abram believed it and gave faith to our Lord's words, and it was reputed to him to justice. And our Lord said to him, I am the Lord that led thee out of the land of Ur of the Chaldees for to give to thee this land into thy possession. And Abram said: Lord, how shall I know that I shall possess it? A voice said to Abram: Thy seed shall be exiled into Egypt by the space of four hundred years, and shall be there in servitude, and after, I shall bring them hither again in the fourth generation. Thou shalt abide here unto thy good age, and shalt be buried here, and go with thy fathers in peace. Sara was yet without child, and she had a handmaid named Hagar, an Egyptian, and she on a day said to Abram her husband: Thou seest I may bear no child, wherefore I would thou took Hagar my maid, that thou might get a child which I might keep and hold for mine. And ten year after that Abram had dwelled in that land, he took Hagar, and anon she despised her mistress. Then Sara said to Abram: Thou dost evil. My servant now hath me in despite, God judge this between thee and me. To whom Abram answered: Thine handmaid is in thine hands, chastise her as it pleaseth thee. After this Sara chastised Hagar and put her to so great affliction that she went away; and as she went an angel met with her in the wilderness by a well, and said: Hagar, whence comest and whither goest thou? She answered: I flee away from the face of my lady Sara. To whom the angel said, return again and submit thee by humbleness unto thy lady, and I shall multiply thy seed, and so much people shall come of it that it cannot be numbered for multitude. And he said furthermore: Thou shalt bear a child and shalt call him Ishmael. He shall be a fierce man, he shall be against all men, and all men against him. Then Hagar returned home and served her lady, and soon after this she was delivered of Ishmael. Abram was eighty-six years old when Ishmael was born.

When Abram was ninety-nine years, our Lord appeared to him and said: Abram, lo! I am the Lord Almighty, walk thou before me and be perfect, and I shall keep covenant between me and thee and shall multiply thy seed greatly. And Abram fell down lowting low to the earth and thanked him. Then our Lord said I AM, and my covenant I shall keep to thee, thou shalt be father of much people. Thou shalt no more be called Abram, but Abraham, for I have ordained thee father of much people. I shall make thee to increase most abundantly; kings and princes shall come of thee, and shall stablish my covenant between me and thee, and thy seed in thy generations. I shall give to thee and to thy seed after thee the land of thy pilgrimage, all the land of Canaan, into their possession and I shall be their God. Yet said God to Abraham: And thou shalt keep thy covenant to me, and thine heirs after thee in their generations, and this shall be the covenant that ye shall keep and thine heirs after thee. Every child masculine that shall be born shall be circumcised when he is eight days old. And see that the men in your generation be circumcised, begin at thyself and thy children. And all that dwell in thy kindred, who of you that shall not be circumcised shall be cast and put out for ever from my people, because he obeyeth not my statute and ordinance. And thy wife Sara shall be called no more Sara but she shall be called Sarah, and I shall bless her, and shall give to thee a son of her, whom I shall bless also. I shall him increase into nations, and kings of peoples shall come of him. Abraham fell down on his face toward the earth and laughed in his heart, saying: May it be that a woman of ninety years may bear a child? I beseech thee, Lord, that Ishmael may live before thee. Our Lord said to Abraham, Sarah shall bring forth a son whom thou shalt name Isaac, and I shall keep my covenant to him for evermore, and to his heirs after him. And I have heard thy request for Ishmael also. I shall bless him and increase, and shall multiply his seed into much people, twelve dukes shall come of him. I shall keep my covenant to Isaac, whom Sarah shall bring forth the next year.

After this on a time, as Abraham sat beside his house in the vale of Mamre in the heat of the day, and as he lift up his eyes, he saw three young men coming to him, and anon as he saw these three standing by him he ran to them and worshipped one alone; he saw three and worshipped but one. That betokeneth the Trinity, and prayed them to be harboured with him, and took water and washed their feet: and prayed them to tarry under the tree, and he would bring bread to them for to comfort them. And they bade him do as he had said, he went and bade Sarah to make three ashy cakes and sent his child for a tender fat calf, which was sodden and boiled. And he served them with butter and milk, and the calf, and set it tofore them. He stood by them, and when they had eaten they demanded him: Where is Sarah thy wife? And he said: Yonder in the tabernacle. And he said, I shall go and come again, and Sarah thy wife shall have a child. And she stood behind the door and heard it and laughed, and said softly to herself: How may it be that I should bear a child? She thought it impossible. Then said our Lord to Abraham: Why laugheth Sarah thy wife, saying in scorn, Shall I bear a child? but as I said to thee before, I shall return and come again, and she shall have a child in that time. And he asked Sarah why she smiled in scorn, and she said she smiled ne laughed not, and our Lord said, It is not so, for thou laughedst.

When they had rested Abraham conveyed them on the way. And our Lord said to Abraham: I have not hid from thee what I purpose to do. The cry of Sodom and Gomorrah is multiplied and their sin is much grievous. I shall descend and see if the sin be so great, the stench thereof cometh to heaven, I shall take vengeance and destroy them. Then Abraham said: I hope, Lord, thou wilt not destroy the just and righteous man with the wicked sinner. I beseech thee, Lord, to spare them. Our Lord said: If there be fifty good and righteous men among them, I shall spare them. And Abraham said: Good Lord, if there be found forty, I pray thee to spare them. Our Lord said: If there be forty, I shall spare them, and so from forty to thirty and from thirty to twenty and from twenty to ten, and our Lord said: If there be found ten good men among them, I shall not destroy them. And then our Lord went from Abraham, and he returned home again. That same eventide came two angels into Sodom, and Lot sat at his gate, and when he saw them he went and worshipped them and prayed them to come and rest in his house, and abide there and wash their feet. And they said: Nay, we shall abide here in the street, and Lot constrained them and brought them into his house and made a feast to them. Then said the angels to Lot: If thou have here of thy kindred, sons or daughters, all them that long to thee, lead out of this city, we shall destroy this place, for the cry thereof is come to our Lord, which hath sent us for to destroy them. Lot went unto his kinsmen and said: Arise and take your children, and go out of this city, for our Lord shall destroy it. And they supposed that he had raved or japed [jested]. And as soon as it was day the angels said to Lot: Arise, and take thy wife and thy two daughters, and go out of this town lest ye perish with them. Yet he dissimuling, they took him by the hand and his wife and two daughters, because that God should spare them, and led them out of the city. And there they said to him: Save thy soul and look not behind thee lest thou perish also, but save thee in the mountain. Lot said to them: I beseech thee, my Lord, forasmuch as thy servant hath found grace before thee, and that thou hast showed thy mercy to me, and that peradventure I might take harm on the hill, that I may go into the little city hereby and may be saved there. He said to Lot: I have heard thy prayers, and for thy sake I shall not subvert this town for which thou hast prayed, hie thee and save thyself there, for I may do nothing till thou be therein. Therefore that town is called Zoar. So Lot went in to Zoar; and the sun arose, and our Lord rained from heaven upon Sodom and Gomorrah sulphur and fire, and subverted the cities and all the dwellers of the towns about that region, and all that was there growing and burgeoning. Lot's wife turned her and looked toward the cities, and anon she was turned into a statue or image of salt, which abideth so unto this day. Abraham arose in the morning early, and looked toward the cities, and saw the smoke ascending from the places, like as it had been the light of a furnace. What time our Lord subverted these cities he remembered Abraham, and delivered Lot from the vengeance of the cities in which he dwelled. Then Lot ascended from Zoar and dwelled in the mountain, and his two daughters with him. He dreaded to abide any longer in the town, but dwelled in a cave, he and his two daughters with him.

Abraham departed from thence and went southward and dwelled between Kadesh and Shur, and went a pilgrimage to Gerar. He said that his wife was his sister. Abimelech the king of Gerar sent for her and took her. God came to Abimelech in his sleep and said: Thou shalt be dead for the woman that thou hast taken, she hath an husband. Abimelech said: Lord, wilt thou slay a man ignorant and rightful? She said that she was his sister, in the simpleness of my heart and cleanness of my hands I did this. And God said to him: I know well that with a simple heart thou didst it, and therefore I have kept thee from her, now yield the woman to her husband, and he shall pray for thee, he is a prophet and thou shalt live. And if thou deliver her not, thou shalt die, and all they that be in thy house. Abimelech arose up the same night and called all his servants, and told them all these words. All they dreaded sore. Also Abimelech called Abraham and said to him: What hast thou done to us, that we have trespassed to thee? Thou hast caused me and my realm to sin greatly. Thou hast done that thou shouldst not have done. What sawest thou for to do so? Abraham said: I thought that the dread of God was not in this place, and that ye would slay me for my wife; and certainly otherwise she is also my sister, the daughter of my father but not of my mother, and I have wedded her. And after that I went from the house of my father, I said to her: Wheresomever we go say thou art my sister.

Then Abimelech took sheep and oxen and servants and maidens, and gave to Abraham, and delivered to him Sarah his wife, and said: Lo! the land is here tofore thee, wheresoever thou wilt, dwell and abide. And he said to Sarah: Lo! I have given to thy brother a thousand pieces of silver, this shall be to thee a veil of thine eyes, and wheresomever thou go, remember that thou wert taken. Abraham prayed for Abimelech and his meiny [company] and God healed him, his wife and all his servants. Our Lord then visited Sarah, and she brought forth a son in her old age, that same time that God had promised. Abraham called his son that she had borne, Isaac, and when he was eight days old he circumcised him as God had commanded, and Abraham was then an hundred years old. Then said Sarah: Who would have supposed that I should give suck to my child, being so old? I laughed when I heard our Lord say so, and all they that shall hear of it may well laugh. The child grew and was weaned, and Abraham made a great feast at the day of his weaning. After this, on a day when Sarah saw the son of Hagar her handmaid play with her son Isaac, she said to Abraham: Cast out this handmaid with her son, the son of the handmaid shall not be heir with my son Isaac. Abraham took this word hard and grievously for his son. Then said God to him: Let it not be hard to thee for thy son and handmaid, whatsomever Sarah say to thee hear her voice, for in Isaac shall thy seed be called. Yet shall I make the son of the handmaid grow into great people, for he is of thy seed. Abraham rose early in the morning, and took bread and a bottle of water, and laid it on her shoulder, and gave to her the child and let her go, which, when she was departed, erred in the wilderness of Beersheba. And when the water was consumed that was in the bottle, she left the child under a tree that was there and went thence as far as a bow shot and sat her down, and said: I shall not see my son die, and there she wept. Our Lord heard the voice of the child, and an angel called Hagar saying, What doest thou, Hagar? Be not afeard, our Lord hath heard the voice of the child from the place which he is now in. Arise and take the child and hold him by the hand, for I shall make him to increase into much people. God opened her eyes and she saw a pit of water, and anon she went and filled the bottle, and gave the child to drink, and abode with him, which grew and dwelled in the wilderness, and became there a young man and an archer, and dwelled also in the desert of Paran. And his mother took to him a wife of the land of Egypt.

That same time said Abimelech, and Phicol the prince of his host, unto Abraham: Our Lord is with thee in all things that thou doest. Swear thou by the Lord that thou grieve not me, ne them that shall come after me, ne my kindred, but after the mercy that I have showed to thee, so do to me and to my land in which thou hast dwelled as a stranger. And Abraham said, I shall swear. And he blamed Abimelech for the pit of water which his servants had taken away by strength. Abimelech answered: I know not who hath done this thing, and thou toldest me not thereof, and I never heard thereof till this day. And then after this they made covenant together, and promised each to other to be friends together.

After all these things God tempted Abraham, and said to him: Abraham, Abraham. He answered and said: I am here, and he said to him: Take thou thine only son that thou lovest, Isaac, and go into the land of Vision and offer him in sacrifice to me upon one of the hills that I shall show to thee. Then Abraham arose in the night, and made ready his ass, and took with him two young men and Isaac his son. And when they had hewn and gathered the wood together to make sacrifice, they went to the place that God commanded him. The third day after, he lift up his eyes and saw from afar the place, and he said to his children: Abide ye here with the ass, I and my son shall go to yonder place, and when we have worshipped there we shall return to you. Then he took the wood of the sacrifice and laid it on his son Isaac, and he bare in his hands fire and the sword. And as they went both together, Isaac said to his father: Father mine. What wilt thou, my son? said Abraham, and he said: Lo! here is fire and wood, where is the sacrifice that shall be offered? Abraham answered: My son, God shall provide for him a sacrifice well enough. They went forth and came to the place that God had ordained, and there made an altar, and laid the wood thereon, and took Isaac and set him on the wood on the altar, and took his sword and would have offered him up to God. And lo! the angel of God cried to him from heaven saying: Abraham, Abraham, which answered: I am here, and he said to him: Extend not thy hand upon my child, and do nothing to him, now I know that thou dreadest God, and hast not spared thine only son for me. Abraham looked behind him, and saw among the briars a ram fast by the horns, which he took, and offered him in sacrifice for his son. He called that place: The Lord seeth. The angel called Abraham the second time saying: I have sworn by myself, saith the Lord, because thou hast done this thing, and hast not spared thine only son for me, I shall bless thee and shall multiply thy seed as the stars of heaven, and like the gravel that is on the seaside, thy seed shall possess the gates of their enemies, and in thy seed shall be blessed all the people of the earth, for thou obeyedst to me. Abraham then returned to his servants, and went into Beersheba and dwelled there. Sarah lived an hundred and twenty-seven years and died in the city of Arba, which is Hebron in the land of Canaan; for whom Abraham made sorrow and wept, and bought of the children of Heth a field, and buried her worshipfully in a double spelunke.

Abraham was an old man, and God blessed him in all his things. He said to the eldest and upperest servant in all his house: I charge and conjure thee by the name of God of heaven and of earth that thou suffer not my son Isaac to take no wife of the daughters of Canaan amongst whom I dwell, but go into the country where my kindred is, and take of them a wife to my son. And the servant answered: If no woman there will come with me into this country, shall I bring thy son into that country from whence thou earnest? Abraham said: Beware that thou lead not my son thither. The Lord of heaven and of earth, that took me from the house of my father and from the place of my nativity, hath said and sworn to me, saying: To thy seed I shall give this land. He shall send his angel tofore thee, and thou shalt take there a wife for my son. If no woman will come with thee thou shalt not be bounden by thine oath, but in no wise lead my son thither. His servant then swore and promised to him that he would so do.

He took ten camels of the flock of his lord, and of all his goods bare with him, and went in to Mesopotamia unto the town of Nahor. And he made the camels to tarry without the town by a pit side at such time as the women be wont to come out for to draw water. And there he prayed our Lord, saying: Lord God of my lord Abraham, I beseech thee to help me this day, and do mercy unto my lord Abraham. Lo! I stand here nigh by the well of water, and the daughters of the dwellers of this town come hither for to draw water, therefore the maid to whom I say: Set down thy pot that I may drink, and then she set down her pot and say: I will give to thee drink, and to the camels, that I may understand thereby that she be the maid that thou hast ordained to thy servant Isaac, and thou showest thy mercy to my lord Abraham. He had not fully finished these words with himself, but that Rebekah, daughter of Bethuel, son of Milcah wife of Nahor, brother of Abraham, came out of the town, having a pot on her shoulder, which was a right fair maid, and much beauteous and unknown to the man. She went down to the well and filled her pot with water and returned. The servant of Abraham ran to her and said: I pray thee to give me a little of the water in thy pot for to drink. Which said: Drink, my lord, and lightly took the pot from her shoulder, and held it, and gave him drink. And when he had drunk she said: Yet I shall give to thy camels drink, and draw water for them till all have drunken; and she poured out the water into a vessel that was there for beasts to drink, and ran to the pit and drew water that every one drank his draught. He then thought in himself secretly that God had made him to have a prosperous journey.

After they had drunk, he gave her two rings to hang on her ears weighing two shekels, and as many armlets weighing ten shekels, and asked her whose daughter she was, and if there were any room in her father's house to be lodged. And she answered: I am daughter to Bethuel, Nahor's son, and in my father's house is place enough to lodge thee and thy camels, and plenty of chaff and hay for them. And the man inclined down to the ground and worshipped God saying: Blessed be the Lord God of my lord Abraham, which hath not taken away his mercy ne his truth from my lord, and hath brought me in my journey right into the house of my lord's brother. The maid Rebekah ran and told at home all that she had heard. Rebekah had a brother named Laban, which hastily went out to the man where as he was when he had seen the rings in his sister's ears and her poinettes or armlets on her hands; and had heard her say all that the man said. He came to the man that stood by the well yet, and said to him: Come in, thou blessed of God, why standest thou without? I have made ready the house for thee, and have ordained place for thy camels. And brought him in, and strawed his camels, and gave them chaff and hay, and water to wash the camels' feet, and the men's feet that came with him.

And they set forth bread tofore him, which said: I shall not eat till I have done mine errand and said wherefore I am come. And it was answered to him, say on, and he said: I am servant of Abraham, and God hath blessed and magnified him greatly and hath given to him oxen and sheep, silver and gold, servants men and women, camels and asses. And Sarah his wife hath brought him forth a son in her old age, and he hath given to him all that he had. And my lord hath charged and adjured me saying: In no wise let my son Isaac have no wife of the daughters of Canaan in whose land he dwelleth, but go unto the house of my father and of my kindred, and of them thou shall take a wife to my son, wherefore I am come hither. And told all how he prayed God of some token, and how Rebekah did to him, and in conclusion desired to have Rebekah for his lord Isaac; and if he would not, that he might depart and go into some other place, on the right side or on the left, to seek a wife for his lord's son. Then Bethuel and Laban said to him: This word is come of God, against his will we may nothing do. Lo! Rebekah standeth tofore thee, take her and go forth that she may be wife unto the son of thy lord, as our Lord hath said. Which words when Abraham's servant had heard, he fell down to the ground and thanked our Lord, and anon took forth silver vessels and of gold and good clothes and gave them to Rebekah for a gift. And to her brethren and mother he gave also gifts, and anon they made a feast, and ate and were joyful together. On the morn betimes, the servant of Abraham arose, and desired to depart and take Rebekah with him and go to his lord. Then the mother and her brethren said: Let the maid abide with us but only ten days, and then take her and go thy way. I pray you, said he, retain ne let [hinder] me not, our Lord hath addressed my way and achieved my errand, wherefore let me go to my lord. And they said: We shall call the maid and know her will; and when she was demanded if she would go with that man, she said: Yea, I shall go with him. Then they let her go, and her nurse with her, and so she departed, and they said to her: Thou art our sister, we pray God that thou mayst increase into a thousand thousand, and that thy seed may possess the gates of their enemies. Then Rebekah and her maidens ascended upon the camels, and followed the servant of Abraham which hastily returned unto his lord.

That same time, when they were come, Isaac walked by the way without forth and looked up and saw the camels coming from far. Rebekah espied him and demanded of the servant who that he was that came in the field against them. He answered and said: That is my lord Isaac, and anon she took her pall or mantle and covered her. The servant anon told unto his lord Isaac all that he had done; which received her and led her into the tabernacle of Sarah his mother and wedded her, and took her in to his wife, and so much loved her, that the love attempered the sorrow that he had for his mother. Abraham after this wedded another wife, by whom he had divers children. Abraham gave to Isaac all his possessions, and to his other children he gave movable goods, and departed the sons of his concubines from his son Isaac whilst he yet lived. And all the days of the life of Abraham were one hundred and seventy-five years, and then died in good mind and age, and Isaac and Ishmael buried him by his wife Sarah in a double spelunke [cave].

HERE BEGINNETH THE LIFE OF ISAAC

WITH THE HISTORY OF ESAU AND OF JACOB

Which is read in the Church the Second Sunday in Lent

Isaac was forty years old when he wedded Rebekah and she bare him no children. Wherefore he besought our Lord that she might bring forth fruit. Our Lord heard his prayer, and she had twain sons at once. The first was rough from the head to the foot, and he was named Esau; and the other was named Jacob. Isaac the father was sixty years old when these children were born. And after this, when they were grown to reasonable age, Esau became a ploughman, and a tiller of the earth, and an hunter. And Jacob was simple and dwelled at home with his mother. Isaac the father loved well Esau, because he ate oft of the venison that Esau took, and Rebekah the mother loved Jacob.

Jacob on a time had made a good pottage, and Esau his brother had been an hunting all day and came home sore an hungred, and found Jacob having good pottage, and prayed him to give him some, for he was weary and much hungry. To whom Jacob said: If thou wilt sell to me thy patrimony and heritage I shall give thee some pottage. And Esau answered, Lo! I die for hunger, what shall avail me mine inheritance if I die, and what shall profit me my patrimony? I am content that thou take it for this pottage. Jacob then said: Swear that to me thou shalt never claim it, and that thou art content I shall enjoy it, and Esau sware it, and so sold away his patrimony, and took the pottage and ate it, and went his way, setting nothing thereby that he had sold his patrimony. This aforesaid is to bring in my matter of the history that is read, for now followeth the legend as it is read in the church.

Isaac began to wax old and his eyes failed and dimmed that he might not clearly see. And on a time he called Esau his oldest son and said to him: Son mine, which answered: Father, I am here ready, to whom the father said: Behold that I wax old and know not the day that I shall die and depart out of this world, wherefore take thine harness, thy bow and quiver with tackles, and go forth an hunting, and when thou hast taken any venison, make to me thereof such manner meat as thou knowest that I am wont to eat, and bring it to me that I may eat it, and that my soul may bless thee ere I die. Which all these words Rebekah heard. And Esau went forth for to accomplish the commandment of his father, and she said then to Jacob: I have heard thy father say to Esau, thy brother: Bring to me of thy venison, and make thereof meat that I may eat, and that I may bless thee tofore our Lord ere I die. Now my son, take heed to my counsel, and go forth to the flock, and bring to me two the best kids that thou canst find, and I shall make of them meat such as thy father shall gladly eat, which when thou hast brought to him and hast eaten he may bless thee ere he die: To whom Jacob answered: Knowest thou not that my brother is rough and hairy and I am smooth? If my father take me to him and taste me and feel, I dread me that he shall think that I mock him, and shall give me his curse for the blessing. The mother then said to him: In me, said she, be this curse, my son, nevertheless hear me; go to the flock and do that I have said to thee. He went and fetched the kids and delivered them to his mother, and she went and ordained them into such meat as she knew well that his father loved, and took the best clothes that Esau had, and did them on Jacob. And the skins of the kid she did about his neck and hands there as he was bare, and delivered to him bread and the pulment that she had boiled. And he went to his father and said: Father mine, and he answered: I am here; who art thou, my son? Jacob said: I am Esau, thy first begotten son, I have done as thou commandedst me, arise, sit and eat of the venison of my hunting that thy soul may bless me. Then said Isaac again to his son: How mightest thou, said he, so soon find and take it, my son? To whom he answered: It was the will of God that such thing as I desired came soon to my hand. Isaac said to him: Come hither to me, my son, that I may touch and handle thee, that I may prove whether thou be my son Esau or not. He came to his father, and when he had felt him, Isaac said: The voice truly is the voice of Jacob, but the hands be the hands of Esau. And he knew him not, for his hands expressed the likeness and similitude of the more brother. Therefore blessing him, he said to him: Thou art then my son Esau? He answered and said: I am he. Then said Isaac: Bring to the meat of thine hunting, my son, that my soul may bless thee; which he offered and gave to his father, and also wine. And when he had eaten and drunken a good draught of the wine, he said to Jacob: Come hither to me, my son, and kiss me; and he went to him and kissed him. Anon as he felt the sweet savour and smell of his clothes, blessing him he said: Lo! the sweet odour of my son is as the odour of a field full of flowers, whom our Lord bless. God give to thee of the dew of heaven, and of the fatness of the earth, abundance of wheat, wine, and oil, and the people serve thee, and the tribes worship thee. Be thou lord of thy brethren, and the sons of thy mother shall bow down and kneel to thee. Whosomever curseth thee, be he accursed, and who that blesseth thee, with blessings be he fulfilled.

Unnethe [hardly] had Isaac fulfilled these words and Jacob gone out, when that Esau came with his meat that he had gotten with hunting, entered in, and offered to his father saying: Arise, father mine, and eat of the venison that thy son hath ordained for thee, that thy soul may bless me. Isaac said to him: Who art thou? To whom he answered, I am thy first begotten son Esau. Isaac then was greatly abashed and astonied, and marvelled more than can be thought credible. And then he was in a trance, as the master of histories saith, in which he had knowledge that God would that Jacob should have the blessing. And said to Esau: Who then was he that right now a little tofore thy coming brought to me venison? And I have eaten of all that he brought to me ere thou camest. I have blessed him, and he shall be blessed. When Esau heard these words of his father, he cried with a great cry, and was sore astonied and said: Father, I pray thee bless me also. To whom he said: Thy brother germain is come fraudulently, and hath received thy blessing. Then said Esau: Certainly and justly may his name be called well Jacob, for on another time tofore this he supplanted me of my patrimony, and now secondly he hath undernome from me my blessing. And yet then he said to his father: Hast thou not reserved to me one blessing? Isaac answered: I have ordained him to be thy lord, I have subdued all his brethren to his servitude. I have stablished him in wheat, wine and oil. And after this what shall I do to thee, my son? To whom Esau said: Hast thou not, father, yet one blessing? I beseech thee to bless me. Then with a great sighing and weeping Isaac moved said to him: In the fatness of the earth and in the dew of heaven shall be thy blessing, thou shalt live in thy sword, and shalt serve thy brother. Then was Esau woebegone, and hated Jacob for supplanting him of his blessing that his father had blessed him with, and said in his heart: The days of sorrow shall come to my father, for I shall slay my brother Jacob. This was told to Rebekah, which anon sent for Jacob her son, and said to him: Lo! Esau thy brother threateneth to slay thee, therefore now my son hear my voice and do as I shall counsel. Make thee ready and go to my brother in Aran, and dwell there with him unto the time that his anger and fury be overpast, and his indignation ceased, and that he forget such things that thou hast done to him, and then after that I shall send for thee, and bring thee hither again. And Rebekah went to Isaac her husband and said: I am weary of my life because of the daughters of Heth, if Jacob take to him a wife of that kindred, I will no longer live. Isaac then called Jacob and blessed him and commanded to him saying: I charge thee in no wise to take a wife of the kindred of Canaan, but go and walk into Mesopotamia of Syria, unto the house of Bethuel, father of thy mother, and take to thee there a wife of the daughters of Laban thine uncle. God Almighty bless thee, and make thee grow and multiply, that thou mayst be increased into tourbes of people, and give to thee the blessings of Abraham, and to thy seed after thee, that thou mayst possess and own the land of thy pilgrimage which he granted to thy grandsire. When Isaac had thus said, and given him leave to go, he departed anon, and went into Mesopotamia of Syria to Laban, son of Bethuel, brother of Rebekah his mother. Esau seeing that his father had blessed Jacob and sent him into Mesopotamia of Syria to wed a wife there, and that after his blessing commanded to him saying: Take thou no wife of the daughters of Canaan; and he obeying his father went into Syria, proving thereby that his father saw not gladly the daughters of Canaan, he went to Ishmael, and took him a wife beside them that he had taken tofore, that was Melech, daughter of Ishmael, son of Abraham.

Then Jacob departed from Beersheba and went forth on his journey toward Aran. When he came to a certain place after going down of the sun and would rest there all night, he took of the stones that were there and laid under his head and slept in the same place. And there he saw in his sleep a ladder standing on the earth, and the upper end thereof touched heaven, and angels of God ascending and descending upon it, and our Lord in the midst of the ladder saying to him: I am the Lord God of Abraham thy father, and of Isaac; the land on which thou sleepest I shall give to thee and to thy seed, and thy seed shall be as dust of the earth; thou shalt spread abroad unto the east and unto the west, and north and south, and all the tribes of the earth shall be blessed in thee and in thy seed. And I shall be thy keeper wheresoever thou shalt go, and shall bring thee again into this land, and I shall not leave till I have accomplished all that I have said. When Jacob was awaked from his sleep and dreaming, he said: Verily God is in this place, and I wist not of it. And he said dreadingly: How terrible is this place, none other thing is here but the house of God and the gate of heaven. Then Jacob arose early and took the stone that lay under his head, and raised it for witness, pouring oil thereon, and called the name of the place Bethel which tofore was called Luza. And there he made a vow to our Lord, saying: If God be with me and keep me in the way that I walk, and give me bread to eat, and clothes to cover me, and I may return prosperously into the house of my father, the Lord shall be my God, and this stone that I have raised in witness, this shall be called the house of God. And the good of all things that thou givest to me, I shall offer to thee the tithes and tenth part. Then Jacob went forth into the east, and saw a pit in a field and three flocks of sheep lying by it, for of that pit were the beasts watered. And the mouth thereof was shut and closed with a great stone, for the custom was when all the sheep were gathered, they rolled away the stone, and when they had drunken they laid the stone again at the pit mouth. And then he said to the shepherds: Brethren, whence are ye? Which answered: Of Aran. Then he asking them said: Know ye not Laban, son of Nahor? They said: We know him well. How fareth he, said he, is he all whole? He fareth well, said they; and lo! Rachel his daughter cometh there with her flock. Then said Jacob: It is yet far to even, it is yet time that the flocks be led to drink, and after be driven to pasture, which answered: We may not so do till all the beasts be gathered, and then we remove the stone from the mouth of the pit and water our beasts. And as they talked, Rachel came with the flock of her father, for she kept that time the beasts. And when Jacob saw her and knew that she was his erne's [uncle's] daughter, and that they were his erne's sheep, he removed the stone from the pit's mouth, and when her sheep had drunken, he kissed her, and weeping he told her that he was brother to her father and son of Rebekah. Then she hied her and told it to her father, which when he understood that Jacob, his sister's son, was come, he ran against him and, embracing, kissed him, and led him into his house. And when he had heard the cause of his journey he said: Thou art my mouth and my flesh.

And when he had been there the space of a month, he demanded Jacob if he would gladly serve him because he was his cousin, and what hire and reward he would have. He had two daughters, the more was named Leah, and the less was called Rachel, but Leah was blear-eyed, and Rachel was fair of visage and well-favored, whom Jacob loved, and said: I shall serve thee for Rachel thy younger daughter seven years. Laban answered: It is better that I give her to thee than to a strange man; dwell and abide with me, and thou shalt have her. And so Jacob served him for Rachel seven years, and him thought it but a little while, because of the great love that he had to her. And at the end of seven years, Jacob said to Laban: Give to me my wife, for the time is come that I should have her. Then Laban called all his friends and made a feast for the wedding, and at night he brought in Leah, the more daughter, and delivered to her an handmaid named Zilpah. Then Jacob, when the morning came, saw that it was Leah. He said to Laban her father: What hast thou done? Have I not served thee for Rachel, why hast thou brought Leah to me? Laban answered: It is not the usage ne custom of our country to give the younger first to be wedded, but fulfil and make an end of this marriage this week, and then shall I give to thee Rachel my daughter for other seven years that thou shalt serve to me. Jacob agreed gladly, and when that week was passed, he wedded Rachel to his wife. To whom Laban her father gave an handmaid named Bilhah. Nevertheless when the wedding of the younger was finished, because of the great love that he had to her, him thought that the other seven years were but short.

[And Jacob while he served Laban had these sons: Reuben, Simeon, Levi, Judah, Dan, Naphtali, Gad, Asher, Issachar, Zebulon, Joseph.] When Joseph was born, Jacob said to Laban his wives' father: Give me leave to depart that I may go in to my country and my land; give to me my wives and children for whom I have served thee that I may go hence. Thou knowest what service I have served thee. Laban said to him: I have founden grace in thy sight; I know it by experience that God hath blessed me for thee; I have ordained the reward that I shall give to thee. Then Jacob answered: Thou knowest how I have served thee, and how much thy possession was in my hands. Thou hadst but little when I came to thee, and now thou art rich, God hath blessed thee at mine entry; it is now right that I provide somewhat toward mine house. Laban said: What shall I give to thee? Jacob answered: I will nothing but that thou do that I demand. I shall yet feed and keep thy beasts, and depart asunder all the sheep of divers colors. And all that ever shall be of divers colors and spotty, as well in sheep as in goats, let me have them for my reward and meed, and Laban granted thereto. Then at time of departing, Laban took them of two colors, and Jacob them that were of one color. Thus was Jacob made much rich out of measure, and had many flocks, and servants both men and women, camels and asses.

After that Jacob had heard Laban's sons say: Jacob hath taken all that was our father's from him, and of his faculty is made rich, he was abashed and understood well by Laban's looking that he was not so friendly to himward as he had been tofore. And also our Lord said to him that he should return into the land of his fathers and to his generation, and that he would be with him. He then called Rachel and Leah into the field whereas he fed his flocks, and said to them: I see well by your father's visage that he is not toward me as he was yesterday or that other day; forsooth the God of my father was with me, and ye know well how I have served your father with all my might and strength, but he hath deceived me, and hath changed mine hire and meed ten times, and yet our Lord hath not suffered him to grieve me. When he said the beasts of party color should be mine, then all the ewes brought forth lambs of variable colors. And when he said the contrary they brought forth all white. God hath taken the substance of your father and hath given it to me. And now God hath commanded me to depart, wherefore make you ready and let us depart hence. Then answered Rachel and Leah: Shall we have nothing else of our father's faculty and of the heritage of his house? Shall he repute us as strangers, and he hath eaten and sold our goods? Sith God hath taken the goods of our father and hath given it to us and to our children, wherefore all that God commanded to thee, do it.

Jacob arose and set his children and his wives upon his camels, and went his way and took all his substance, and flocks, and all that he had gotten in Mesopotamia and went toward his father Isaac into the land of Canaan. That time was Laban gone to shear his sheep, and Rachel stole away the idols of her father. Jacob would not let Laban know of his departing, and when he was departed with all that longed to him of right, he came to the mount of Gilead. It was told to Laban, the third day after, that Jacob was fled and gone, who anon took his brethren and pursued him by the space of seven days and overtook him in the mount of Gilead. He saw our Lord in his sleep saying to him: Beware that thou speak not angrily ne hard words to Jacob. That time Jacob had set his tabernacle in the hill, and when he came thither with his brethren, he said to Jacob: Why hast thou done thus to me to take away my daughters as prisoners taken by sword? Why fleddest thou from me and wouldst not let me have knowledge thereof? Thou hast not suffered me to kiss my sons and daughters, thou hast done follily. Now may I do thee harm and evil, but the God of thy father said to me yesterday: Beware that thou speak no hard words against Jacob. Thou desirest to go to the house of thy father, why hast thou stolen my gods? Jacob answered: That I departed thee not knowing, I dreaded that violently thou wouldst have taken from me thy daughters. And where thou reprovest me of theft, whosoever have stolen thy gods let him be slain tofore our brethren. Seek and what thou findest that is thine, take with thee.

He, saying this, knew not that Rachel had stolen her father's gods. Then Laban entered the tabernacle of Jacob and Leah, and sought and found nothing. And when he came into the tabernacle of Rachel, she hied her and hid the idols under the litter of her camel and sat upon it. And he sought and found nought. Then said Rachel: Let not my lord be wroth for I may not arise to thee, for sickness is fallen to me, and so she deceived her father. Then Jacob, being angry and grudging, said to Laban: What is my trespass and what have I sinned to thee that thou hast pursued me, and hast searched everything? What hast thou now founden of all the substance of thy house? Lay it forth tofore my brethren and thy brethren, that they judge between me and thee. I have served thee twenty years and have been with thee, thy sheep and thy goats were never barren. I have eaten no wethers of thy flock, nor beast hath destroyed none. I shall make all good what was stolen. I prayed therefore day and night, I labored both in heat and in cold, sleep fled from mine eyes. Thus I served thee in thy house twenty years, fourteen for thy daughters and six for thy flocks. Thou hast changed mine hire and reward ten times. But if the God of my father Abraham and the dread of Isaac had been with me, haply thou wouldst now have left me naked. Our Lord God hath beholden mine affliction and the labor of mine hands and reproved thee yesterday. Laban answered to him: My daughters and sons, and thy flocks, and all that thou beholdest are thine, what may I do to my sons and nephews? Let us now be friends, and make we a fast league and confederacy together. Then Jacob raised a stone, and raised it in token of friendship and peace, and so they ate together in friendship, and sware each to other to abide in love ever after. And after this Laban arose in the night, and kissed his daughters and sons, and blessed them, and returned into his country.

Jacob went forth in his journey that he had taken. Angels of God met him, which when he saw, he said: These be the castles of God, and called that place Mahanaim. He sent messengers tofore him to Esau his brother in the land of Seir, in the land of Edom, and bade them say thus to Esau: This saith thy brother Jacob: I have dwelled with Laban unto this day, I have oxen and asses, servants both men and women. I send now a legation unto my lord that I may find grace in his sight. These messengers returned to Jacob and said: We came to Esau thy brother, and lo! he cometh for to meet thee with four hundred men. Jacob was sore afraid then, and divided his company into twain turmes [two troops], saying: If Esau come to that one and destroy that, that other shall yet be saved. Then said Jacob: O God of my father Abraham, and God of my father Isaac, O Lord that saidst to me, return into thy land and place of thy nativity, and saidst I shall do well to thee, I am the least in all thy mercies, and in thy truth that thou hast granted to thy servant, with my staff I have gone this river of Jordan, and now I return with two turmes. I beseech the Lord keep me from the hands of my brother Esau, for I fear him greatly lest he come and smite down the mother with the sons. Thou hast said that thou shouldest do well to me and shouldest spread my seed like unto the gravel of the sea, and that it may not be numbered for multitude. Then when he had slept that night, he ordained gifts for to send to his brother, goats two hundred, kids twenty, sheep two hundred, and rams twenty; forty kine and twenty bulls, twenty asses and ten foals of them. And he sent by his servants all these beasts; and bade them say that Jacob his servant sent to him this present and that he followeth after. And Jacob thought to please him with gifts.

The night following, him thought a man wrestled with him all that night till the morning, and when he saw he might not overcome him, he hurted the sinew of his thigh that he halted thereof, and said to him: Let me go and leave me, for it is in the morning. Then Jacob answered: I shall not leave thee but if thou bless me. He said to him: What is thy name? he answered: Jacob. Then he said: Nay, said he, thy name shall no more be called Jacob, but Israel, for if thou hast been strong against God, how much more shalt thou prevail against men? Then Jacob said to him: What is thy name? tell me. He answered, Why demandest thou my name, which is marvellous? And he blessed him in the same place. Jacob called the name of that same place Penuel, saying: I have seen our Lord face to face, and my soul is made safe. And anon as he was past Penuel the sun arose. He halted on his foot, and therefore the children of Israel eat no sinews because it dried in the thigh of Jacob. Then Jacob lifting up his eyes saw Esau coming and four hundred men with him, and divided the sons of Leah and of Rachel, and of both their handmaidens, and set each handmaid and their children tofore in the first place, Leah and her sons in the second, and Rachel and Joseph all behind. And he going tofore kneeled down to ground and, worshipping his brother, approached him. Esau ran for to meet with his brother, and embraced him, straining his neck, and weeping kissed him, and he looked forth and saw the women and their children, and said: What been these and to whom longen they? Jacob answered: They be children which God hath given to me thy servant and his handmaidens, and their children approached and kneeled down, and Leah with her children also worshipped him, and last of all Joseph and Rachel worshipped him. Then said Esau: Whose been these turmes [troops] which I have met? Jacob answered: I have sent them to thee, my lord, unto the end that I may stand in thy grace. Esau said: I have many myself, keep these and let them be thine. Nay, said Jacob, I pray thee to take this gift which God hath sent me that I may find grace in thy sight, for meseemeth I see thy visage like the visage of God; and therefore be thou to me merciful, and take this blessing of me. Unnethe [hardly] by compelling he taking it, said: Let us go together, I shall accompany thee and be fellow of thy journey. Then said Jacob: Thou knowest well, my lord, that I have young children and tender, and sheep and oxen, which, if I over-labored, should die all in a day, wherefore please it you, my lord, to go tofore, and I shall follow as I may with my children and beasts. Esau answered: I pray thee then let my fellows abide and accompany thee, whatsoever need thou have. Jacob said: It is no need, I need no more but one, that I may stand in thy favor, my lord. And Esau returned then the same way and journey that he came into Seir. And Jacob came to Succoth and builded there an house, and from thence he went in to Shalem, the town of Shechem which is in the land of Canaan, and bought there a part of a field, in which he fixed his tabernacles, of the sons of Hamor father of Shechem for an hundred lambs. And there he raised an altar, and worshipped upon it the strongest God of Israel.

After this our Lord appeared to Jacob and said: Arise and go up to Bethel and dwell there, and make there an altar to the Lord that appeared to thee in the way when thou fleddest from thy brother Esau. Jacob then called all them of his house and said: Cast away from you all your strange gods that be among you, and make you clean and change your clothes; arise and let us go into Bethel, and make we there an altar to our Lord that heard me in the day of my tribulation, and was fellow of my journey. Then they gave to him all their strange gods, and the gold that hung on their ears, and he dalf a pit behind the city of Shechem and threw them therein. And when they departed, all the countries thereabout were afraid and durst not pursue them. Then Jacob came to a place called Luz which is in the land of Canaan, and all the people with him, which otherwise is called Bethel. He edified there an altar to our Lord, and named that place the House of God. Our Lord appeared to him in that place when he fled from his brother Esau. That same time died Deborah, the nurse of Rebekah, and was buried at the root of Bethel under an oak. Our Lord appeared again to Jacob after that he was returned from Mesopotamia of Syria, and was come into Bethel, and blessed him saying: Thou shalt no more be called Jacob but Israel shall be thy name, and called him Israel, and said to him: I am God Almighty, grow and multiply, folks and peoples of nations shall come of thee, kings shall come of thy loins. The land that I gave to Abraham and Isaac I shall give to thee and thy seed; and vanished from him.

He then raised a stone for a remembrance in the place where God spake to him, and anointed it with oil, calling the name of the place Bethel. He went thence and came in veer time unto the land that goeth to Ephrath, in which place Rachel bare a son. And the death drawing near, she named him Benoni, which is as much to say as the son of my sorrow. The father called him Benjamin, that is to say the son of the right hand. There Rachel died and was buried in the way toward Ephrath, that is Bethlehem. Jacob raised a title upon her tomb; this is the title of the monument of Rachel unto this present day. Jacob went thence and came to Isaac his father into Mamre the city of Arbah, that is Hebron, in which dwelled Abraham and Isaac. And all the days of Isaac were complete, which were an hundred and fourscore years, and he consumed and died in good mind, and Esau and Jacob his sons buried him.

Thus endeth the history of Isaac and his two sons Esau and Jacob.

HERE BEGINNETH THE HISTORY OF JOSEPH AND HIS BRETHREN

Which is read the Third Sunday in Lent

Joseph when he was sixteen years old began to keep and feed the flock with his brethren, he being yet a child, and was accompanied with the sons of Bilhah and Zilpah, wives of his father. Joseph complained on his brethren, and accused them to their father of the most evil sin. Israel loved Joseph above all his sons for as much as he had gotten him in his old age, and made for him a motley coat. His brethren then seeing that he was beloved of his father more than they were, hated him and might not speak to him a peaceable word. It happed on a time that Joseph dreamed, and saw a sweven [dream], and told it to his brethren, which caused them to hate him yet more. Joseph said to his brethren: Hear ye my dream that I had; methought that we bound sheaves in the field, and my sheaf stood up and yours standing round about and worshipped my sheaf. His brethren answered: Shalt thou be our king and shall we be subject and obey thy commandment? Therefore this cause of dreams and of these words ministered the more fume of hate and envy. Joseph saw another sweven and told to his father and brethren: Methought I saw in my sleep the sun, the moon, and eleven stars worship me. Which when his father and his brethren had heard, the father blamed him, and said: What may betoken this dream that thou sawest? Trowest thou that I, thy mother and thy brethren, shall worship thee upon the earth? His brethren had great envy hereat.

The father thought and considered a thing secretly in himself. On a time when his brethren kept their flocks of sheep in Shechem, Israel said to Joseph: Thy brethren feed their sheep in Shechem, come and I shall send thee to them, which answered: I am ready, and he said: Go and see if all things be well and prosperous at thy brethren and beasts, and come again and tell me what they do. He went from the vale of Hebron and came unto Shechem. There a man found him erring in the field, and asked him what he sought, and he answered: I seek my brethren, tell me where they feed their flocks. The man said to him: They been departed from this place, I heard them say Let us go in to Dothan. Which then when his brethren saw him come from far, tofore he approached to them they thought to slay him, and spake together saying: Lo! see the dreamer cometh. Come and let us slay him and put him into this old cistern. And we shall say that some wild evil beast hath devoured him, and then shall appear what his dreams shall profit him. Reuben hearing this, thought for to deliver him from their hands, and said: Let us not slay him ne shed his blood, but keep your hands undefouled. This he said, willing to keep him from their hands and render him again to his father. Anon then as he came they took off his motley coat, and set him into an old cistern that had no water. As they sat for to eat bread they saw Ishmaelites coming from Gilead, and their camels bringing spices and raisins into Egypt. Then said Judah to his brethren: What should it profit us if we slew our brother and shed his blood? It is better that he be sold to Ishmaelites and our hands be not defouled, he is our own brother and our flesh. His brethren agreed to his words, and drew him out of the cistern, and sold him to the Midianitish merchants passing forth by to Ishmaelites for thirty pieces of silver, which led him into Egypt. At this time when he was sold Reuben was not there, but was in another field with his beasts. And when he returned and came unto the cistern and found not Joseph, he tare his clothes for sorrow, and came to his brethren and said: The child is not yonder, whither shall I go to seek him? He had supposed his brethren had slain him in his absence. They told him what they had done, and took his coat, and besprinkled it with the blood of a kid which they slew, and sent it to their father saying: See whether this be the coat of thy son or not, this we have found. Which anon as the father saw it said: This is my son's coat, an evil wild beast hath devoured him, some beast hath eaten him; and rent his clothes and did on him a sackcloth, bewailing and sorrowing his son a long time. All his sons gathered them, together for to comfort their father and assuage his sorrow, but he would take no comfort, but said: I shall descend to my son into hell for to bewail him there. And thus, he abiding in sorrow, the Midianites carried Joseph into Egypt, and sold him to Potiphar, eunuch of Pharaoh, master of his knights.

Thus was Joseph led into Egypt, and Potiphar, prince of the host of Pharaoh, an Egyptian, bought him of the hands of Ishmaelites. Our Lord God was always with Joseph, and he was wise, ready, and prosperous in all manner of things. He dwelled in his lord's house and pleased so well his lord, that he stood in his grace that he made him upperest and above all other, and betook him the rule and governance of all his house, which well and wisely governed the household and all that he had charge of. Our Lord blessed the house of Egypt for Joseph's sake, and multiplied as well in beasts as in fields all his substance. Joseph was fair of visage and well favored.

After many days the lady, his master's wife, beheld and cast her eyes on Joseph, and tempted him to sin. He refused that, and would not attend ne listen to her words, ne would not consent to so sinful a work, and said to her: Lo! hath not my lord delivered to me all that he hath in his house? and he knoweth not what he hath, and there is nothing therein but that it is in my power and at my commandment except thee, which art his wife. How may I do this evil and sin to my lord? Such manner, or semblable words, he said daily to her, and the woman was the more desirous and grievous to the young man, and he always forsook and refused the sin. And when the lady saw that she was refused, she cried and called the men of the house and accused Joseph falsely. When the lord heard this, anon he gave faith and believed his wife, and being sore wroth, set Joseph in prison where the prisoners of the king were kept and he was there fast set in. Our Lord God was with Joseph, and had mercy on him, and made him in the favor and grace of the chief keeper of the prison, in so much that he delivered to Joseph the keeping of all the prisoners, and what he did was done, and the chief jailer was pleased with all. Our Lord was with him and directed all his works.

After this it fell so that two officers of the king's trespassed unto their lord, wherefore he was wroth with them and commanded them to the prison whereas Joseph was. That one of them was the butler, and that other the baker; and the keeper betook them to Joseph to keep, and he served them. After a while that they had been in prison they both saw on one night a dream of which they were astoned and abashed, and when Joseph was come in to serve them, and saw them heavy, he demanded them why they were heavier than they were wont to be, which answered: We have dreamed and there is none to interpret it to us. Joseph said to them: Suppose ye that God may not give me grace to interpret it? Tell to me what ye saw in your sleep. Then the butler told first and said: Methought I saw a vine had three branches, and after they had flowered the grapes were ripe, and then I took the cup of Pharaoh in my hand, and took the grapes and wrang out of them wine into the cup that I held, and presented it to Pharaoh to drink. Joseph answered: The three branches be yet three days, after which Pharaoh shall remember thy service and shall restore thee into thy foremost office and gree, for to serve him as thou wert wont to do. Then I pray thee to remember me when thou art at thine above, and be to me so merciful to sue unto Pharaoh that he take me out of this prison, for I was stolen out of the land of Hebrews and am innocently set here in prison. Then the master baker saw that he had wisely interpreted the butler's dream; he said: Methought that I had three baskets of meat upon my head, and in that one basket that was highest methought I bare all the meat of the bakehouse and birds came and ate of it. Joseph answered: This is the interpretation of the dream; the three baskets be three days yet to come, after which Pharaoh shall smite off thy head and shall hang thee on the cross, and the birds shall tear thy flesh. And the third day after this Pharaoh made a great feast unto his children, and remembered him, among the meals, on the master butler and the master baker. He restored his butler unto his office, and to serve him of the cup, and that other was hanged, that the truth of the interpreter was believed and proved. Notwithstanding the master butler in his wealth forgat Joseph his interpreter.

Two years after Pharaoh saw in his sleep a dream. Him thought he stood upon the river, from which he saw seven oxen ascend to the land which were fair and right fat, and were fed in a fat pasture; he saw other seven come out of the river, poor and lean, and were fed in places plenteous and burgeoning. These devoured the other that were so fat and fair. Herewith he started out of his sleep, and after slept again, and saw another dream. He saw seven ears of corn standing on one stalk, full and fair of corns, and as many other ears void and smitten with drought, which devoured the beauty of the first seven. In the morning Pharaoh awoke and was greatly afeard of these dreams, and sent for all conjectors and diviners of Egypt, and wise men; and when they were gathered he told to them his dream, and there was none that could interpret it. Then at last the master butler, remembering Joseph, said: I knowledge my sin, on a time the king being wroth with his servants, sent me and the master of the bakers into prison, where we in one night dreamed both prodigies of things coming. And there was a child of the Hebrews, servant to the jailer, to whom we told our dreams and he expounded them to us and said what should happen; I am restored to mine office and that other is hanged on the cross.

Anon, by the king's commandment, Joseph was taken out of prison and shaved, bathed, and changed his clothes, and brought tofore Pharaoh, to whom he said: I saw a dream which I have showed unto wise men, and there is none that can tell me the interpretation thereof. To whom Joseph answered: God shall answer by me things prosperous to Pharaoh. Then Pharaoh told to him his dreams, like as is tofore written, of the seven fat oxen and seven lean, and how the lean devoured the fat, and in likewise of the ears. Joseph answered: The king's dreams are one thing which God hath showed to Pharaoh. The seven fat oxen and the seven ears full, betoken seven years to come of great plenty and commodious, and the seven lean oxen, and the seven void ears smitten with drought, betoken seven years after them of great hunger and scarcity. Lo! there shall come first seven years of great fertility and plenty in all the land of Egypt, after whom shall follow other seven years of so great sterility, barrenness, and scarcity, that the abundance of the first shall be all forgotten. The great hunger of these latter years shall consume all the plenty of the first years. The latter dream pertaineth to the same, because God would that it should be fulfilled. Now therefore let the king provide for a man that is wise and witty, that may command and ordain provosts and officers in all places of the realm, that they gather into garners and barns the fifth part of all the corn and fruits that shall grow these first seven plenteous years that be to come, and that all this wheat may be kept in barns and garners in towns and villages, that it may be made ready against the coming of the seven scarce years that shall oppress by hunger all Egypt, to the end that the people be not enfamined. This counsel pleased much to Pharaoh and to all his ministers. Then Pharaoh said to his servants: Where should we find such a man as this is, which is fulfilled with the spirit of God? And then he said to Joseph: Forasmuch as God hath showed to thee all that thou hast spoken, trowest thou that we might find any wiser than thou or like to thee? Thou shalt be upperest of my house, and to the commandment of thy mouth all people shall obey. I only shall go tofore thee and sit but one seat above thee. Yet said Pharaoh to Joseph: Lo! I have ordained thee above and master upon all the land of Egypt. He took a ring from his hand and gave it into his hand, and clad him with a double stole furred with bise; and a golden collar he put about his neck, and made him to ascend upon his chair; the second trumpet crying that all men should kneel tofore him, and that they should know him upperest provost of all the land of Egypt. Then said the king of Egypt to Joseph: I am Pharaoh, without thy commandment shall no man move hand nor foot in all the land of Egypt. He changed his name and called him in the tongue of Egypt: The saviour of the world. He gave to him a wife named Asenath, daughter of Poti-phera, priest of Eliopoleos.

Joseph went forth then into the land of Egypt. Joseph was thirty years old when he stood in the favor and grace of Pharaoh. And he went round about all the region of Egypt. The plenteousness and fertility of the seven years came, and sheaves and shocks of corn were brought in to the barns; all the abundance of fruits was laid in every town. There was so great plenty of wheat that it might be compared to the gravel of the sea, and the plenty thereof exceedeth measure. Joseph had two sons by his wife ere the famine and hunger came, which Asenath the priest's daughter brought forth, of whom he called the name of the first Manasseh, saying: God hath made me to forget all my labors, and the house of my father hath forgotten me. He called the name of the second son Ephraim, saying: God hath made me to grow in the land of my poverty.

Then passed the seven years of plenty and fertility that were in Egypt, and the seven years of scarcity and hunger began to come, which Joseph had spoken of tofore, and hunger began to wax and grow in the universal world; also in all the land of Egypt was hunger and scarcity. And when the people hungered they cried to Pharaoh asking meat, to whom he answered: Go ye to Joseph, and whatsoever he saith to you do ye. Daily grew and increased the hunger in all the land. Then Joseph opened the barns and garners, and sold corn to the Egyptians, for the hunger oppressed them sore. All provinces came into Egypt for to buy meat to them, and to eschew the hunger.

Jacob, father unto Joseph, heard tell that corn and victuals were sold in Egypt, and said to his sons: Why be ye negligent? I have heard say that corn is sold in Egypt; go ye thither and buy for us that is necessary and behoveful, that we may live, and consume not for need. Then the ten brethren of Joseph descended into Egypt for to buy wheat, and Benjamin was left at home with the father, because whatsoever happed to the brethren in their journey. Then they entered into the land of Egypt with others for to buy corn. There was great famine in the land of Canaan, and Joseph was prince in the land of Egypt, also by his commandment wheat was sold unto the people. Then when his brethren were come and had adored and worshipped him, he anon knew them, and spake to them, as to strangers, hard words, demanding them saying: Whence be ye? Which answered: Of the land of Canaan, and come hither to buy that is necessary for us. And though he knew his brethren, yet was he unknown of them. He remembered the dreams that he sometime had seen, and told them and said: Ye be spies and be come hither for to espy the weakest places of this land, which said to him: It is not so, my lord, but we thy servants be come for to buy victuals. We be all sons to one man, we come peaceably, ne we thy servants think ne imagine none evil. To whom he answered: It is all otherwise, ye be come for to espy and consider the secretest places of this realm. Then they said: We are twelve brethren, thy servants, sons of one man in the land of Canaan, the youngest is at home with our father, and that other is dead. That is, said he, that I said; ye be spies. Now I have of you the experience. I swear to you by the health of Pharaoh ye shall not depart till that your youngest brother come. Send ye one of you for him to bring him hither. Ye shall abide in fetters in prison till the truth be proved whether the things that ye have said be true or false, else, by the health of Pharaoh, ye be spies. And delivered them to be kept three days. The third day they were brought out of prison, to whom he said: I dread God, if ye be peaceable as ye say, do as ye have said, and ye shall live. Let one brother be bounden in prison, and go ye your way, and lead home the wheat that ye have bought into your houses, and bring to me with you your youngest brother, that I may prove your words, that ye die not. They did as he said, and spake together: We be worthy and well deserved to suffer this, for we have sinned in our brother, seeing his anguish when he prayed us and we heard him not, therefore this tribulation is fallen upon us. Of whom Reuben said: Said not I to you, in no wise sin not ye in the child, and ye would not hear me? Now his blood is wroken. They knew not that Joseph understood them, forasmuch as he spake alway to them by an interpreter. Then Joseph turned him a little and wept. After he returned to them, and took Simeon in their presence and bound him, and sent him to prison, and commanded to his ministers to fill their sacks with wheat, and to put each man's money in their sacks, and above that to give them meat to spend in their way; which did so. And they took their wheat and laid it on their asses and departed on their way. After, one of them, on the way, opened his sack for to give his beast meat, and found his money in the mouth of his sack and said to his brethren: My money is given to me again, lo! I have found it in my sack. And they were all astonied: What is this that God hath done to us? Then they came home to their father in the land of Canaan and told to him all things that was fallen to them, saying: The lord of the country hath spoken hard to us and had supposed that we been spies of that province, to whom we answered that, we were peaceable people ne were no such spies, and that we were twelve sons gotten of one father, one is dead and the youngest is with our father in the land of Canaan. Which then said to us: Now shall I prove whether ye be peaceable or no. Ye shall leave here one brother with me, and lead home that is necessary for you, and go your way and see that ye bring with you your youngest brother that I may know that ye be none espies and that ye may receive this brother that I hold in prison, and then forthon what that ye will buy ye shall have license. And this said, each of them poured out the wheat, and every man found his money bounden in the mouth of every sack. Then said Jacob their father: Ye have made me without children. Joseph is gone and lost, Simeon is bounden in prison, and Benjamin ye will take away from me, on me come all these evils. To Reuben answered: Slay my two sons if I bring him not again to thee; deliver him to me in my hand, and I shall restore him again to thee. The father said: My son shall not go with you, his brother is dead and he is left now alone, if any adversity should hap to him in the way that ye go into, ye shall lead my old hairs with sorrow to hell.

In the meanwhile famine and hunger oppressed all the land greatly. And when the corn that they brought from Egypt was consumed, Jacob said to his sons: Return ye into Egypt and buy for us some meat, that we may live. Judah answered: That man said to us, under swearing of great oaths, that: Ye shall not see my face ne come into my presence, but if ye bring your youngest brother with you. Therefore if thou wilt send him with us, we shall go together and shall buy for us that shall be necessary, and if thou wilt not we shall not go. The man said as we oft have said to thee, that if we bring him not we shall not see his visage. Israel said to them: This have ye done into my misery, that ye told to him that ye had another brother. And they answered: The man demanded of us by order our progeny, if our father lived, if we had any brother. And we answered him consequently after that he demanded, we wist not what he would say, ne that he said bring your brother with you. Send the child with us that we may go forth and live, and that we ne our children die not for hunger. I shall receive thy son, and require him of my hand. If I lead him not thither and bring him again, I shall be guilty to thee of the sin ever after. If there had been no delay of this, we had been there and come again by this time.

Then Israel their father said to them: If it be so necessary as ye say, do ye as ye will; take with you of the best fruits of this land in your vessels, and give ye and present to that man gifts, a little raisins, and honey, storax, stacten, terebinthe, and dates, and bear with you double money, and also the same money that ye found in your sacks, lest there be any error therefore; and take with you Benjamin, your brother. My God, that is almighty, make him pleasant unto you, and that ye may return in safety with this your brother and him also that he holdeth in prison; I shall be as a man barren therewhiles, without children. Then the brethren took the gifts and double money and Benjamin, and went forth into Egypt, and came and stood tofore Joseph; whom when he had seen, and Benjamin, he commanded to the steward of his house that he should do slay sheep and calves and make a feast, for these brethren shall dine with me this day. He did as he was commanded and brought the men unto his lord's house.

Then were they all afeard and said softly together: Because of the money that we had in our sacks we be brought in that he take us with the default, and shall by violence bring us and our asses into servitude. Wherefore they said to the steward of the house, in the gate of the house ere they entered, saying: We pray thee to hear us: the last time that we came to buy victual, which when we had bought and departed, and were on our way, for to give our beasts meat we opened our sacks, and we found in the mouth of our sacks our money that we had paid, which we now bring again of the same weight, and we have more other for to buy to us that shall be necessary. It is not in our conscience to have it, we weet never who put it in our sacks. He answered to him: Peace be among you, fear ye nothing, the God of your father hath given to you the treasure that ye found in your sacks, for the money that ye paid to me I have it ready. And then he brought in Simeon to them, and brought them into the house, and washed their feet, and gave meat to their asses. They made ready and ordained their gifts and presents against the coming of Joseph. They heard say that they should dine and eat there.

Then Joseph entered into the house, and they offered to him the gifts, holding them in their hands, and worshipped him falling down to the ground. And he debonairly saluted them and demanded them, saying: Is your father in good health of whom ye told me, liveth he yet? They answered: Thy servant our father is in good health and liveth yet, and kneeled down and worshipped him. Then, said he, casting his eyes on his brother Benjamin that was of one mother, and said: Is this your young brother of whom ye told me? And also said, God be merciful to thee, my son; he hied him from themward, for he was moved in all his spirits and wept on his brother, and went into his bedchamber. After this he washed his visage and came out making good countenance and commanded to set bread on the board, and after that he set his brethren in order, each after their age, and ate together, and Joseph sat and ate with the Egyptians. For it was not lawful to the Egyptians to eat with the Hebrews. And each of them were well served, but Benjamin had the best part, and they ate and drank so much that they were drunken.

Then Joseph commanded the steward of his house to fill their sacks with wheat as much as they might receive, and the money of the wheat put it into every man's sack, and take my cup of silver, and the money of the youngest, and put that in his sack. And all this was done. And on the morn betimes they were suffered to depart with their asses. And when they were gone out of the town and a little on their way, then Joseph said to his steward: Make thee ready and ride after, and say to them: Why have ye done evil for good? The cup that my lord is accustomed to drink in, ye have stolen, ye might not do a worse thing. He did as Joseph had commanded and overtook them, and said to them all by order like as he had charge, which answered: Why saith your lord so, and doth to us his servants such letting? The money that we found in our sacks we brought again to thee from the land of Canaan, and how may it follow that we should steal any gold or silver from the house of thy lord? Look! at whom it be found of us all thy servants, let him die. Which said to them: Be it after your sentence, at whom that it ever be found he shall be my servant and the others shall go free and be not guilty. Then he hied and set down all their sacks, beginning at the oldest unto the youngest, and at last found the cup in the mouth of the sack of Benjamin. Then they all for sorrow cut and rent their clothes, and laded their asses again, and returned all into the town again. Then Judah entered first with his brethren unto Joseph and all they together fell down platte to the ground. To whom Joseph said: Why have ye done thus? Know not ye that there is no man like to me in the science of knowledge? To whom Judah answered: What shall we answer to thee, my lord; or what shall we speak or rightfully desire? God hath found and remembered the iniquity of us thy servants, for we be all thy servants, yea, we and he at whom the cup was found. Joseph answered: God forbid that I should so do, whosoever stole the cup shall be my servant, and go ye your way, for ye shall be free and go to your father. Then Judah approached near him and spake with a hardy cheer to him and said: I beseech thee my lord to hear me thy servant that I may say to thine audience a word, and that thou wilt not be wroth to thy servant. Thou art next to Pharaoh; my lord, thou demandedst first of us thy servants: Have ye a father or brother? And we answered to thee, my lord: Our father is an old man and we have a brother a young child which was born to him in his old age, whose brother of the same mother is dead, and he is an only son whom the father loveth tenderly. Thou saidst to us thy servants: Bring him hither to me that I may see. We told to thee my lord for truth: our father may not forego the child, if he forego him certainly he shall die. And thou saidst to us, thy servants: But if ye bring him not with you, ye shall no more see my visage. Then when we came to our father and told him all these things, and our father bade us to return and buy more corn. To whom we said: We may not go thither but if our youngest brother go with us, for if he be absent we dare not approach, ne come to the presence of the man; and he answered to us: Ye know well that my wife brought to me forth but two sons, that one went out, and ye said that wild beasts had devoured him, and yet I heard never of him ne he appeared not. If now ye should take this my son and anything happened to him in the way ye should bring my hoar hair with sorrow to hell. Therefore if I should come home to my father and bring not the child with me, sith the soul and health of my father dependeth of this child, and see that he is not come with us, he shall die and we thy servants should lead his old age with wailing and sorrow to hell. I myself shall be thy proper servant which have received him upon my faith and have promised for him, saying to my father: If I bring him not again I shall be guilty of the sin to my father ever after. I shall abide and continue thy servant for the child in the ministry and service of thee my lord. I may not depart, the child being absent, lest I be witness of the sorrow that my father shall take. Wherefore I beseech thee to suffer this child to go to his father and receive me into thy service. Thus said Judah, with much more; as Josephus, Antiquitatum, rehearseth more piteously, and saith moreover that the cause why he did do hide the cup in Benjamin's sack, was to know whether they loved Benjamin or hated him as they did him, what time they sold him to the Ishmaelites.

Then this request made, Joseph might no longer forbear, but commanded them that stood by to withdraw them, and when all men were gone out sauf he and his brethren, he began to say to them weeping: I am Joseph your brother, liveth yet my father? The brethren were so afeard that they could not speak ne answer to him. Then he debonairly said to them: Come hither to me; and when they came near him he said: I am Joseph your brother that ye sold into Egypt; be ye not afeard nor think not hard unto you that ye sold me into these regions. God hath sent me tofore you into Egypt for your health. It is two years since the famine began, and yet been five years to come in which men may not ear, sow, ne reap. God hath sent me tofore you that ye should be reserved on the earth, and that ye may have meat to live by. It is not by your counsel that I was sent hither, but by the will of God, which hath ordained me father of Pharaoh, and lord of all his house, and prince in all the land of Egypt. Hie you, and go to my father, and say ye to him: This word sendeth thee thy son Joseph: God hath made me lord of the universal land of Egypt, come to me lest thou die, and thou shalt dwell in the land of Goshen. Thou shalt be next me, thou and thy sons and the sons of thy sons, and I shall feed thy sheep, thy beasts and all that thou hast in possession. Yet rest five year to come of famine, therefore come lest thou perish, thy house, and all that thou owest. Lo! your eyes and the eyes of my brother Benjamin see that my mouth speaketh these words to you. Show ye to my father all my glory and all that ye have seen in Egypt. Hie ye and bring him to me. This said, he embraced his brother Benjamin about his neck and wept upon each of them. After this they durst better speak to him. Anon it was told and known all about in the King's hall that Joseph's brethren were come. And Pharaoh was joyful and glad thereof and all his household. And Pharaoh said to Joseph that he should say to his brethren: Lade ye your beasts and go into the land of Canaan, and bring from thence your father and kindred, and come to me, and I shall give you all the goods of Egypt, that ye may eat the marrow of the earth. Command ye also that they take carriages of this land of Egypt, for the carriage of their children and wives, and say to them: Take your father and come as soon as ye may, and leave nothing behind you, for all the best things shall be yours. The sons of Israel did as they were commanded. To whom Joseph gave carriages after the commandment of Pharaoh, and meat to eat by the way. He commanded to give to every each two garments. To Benjamin he gave three hundred pieces of silver, with five garments of the best, and also he sent clothing to his father, adding to them ten asses which were laden with all riches of Egypt, and as many asses laden and bearing bread and victual to spend by the way. And thus he let his brethren depart from him saying: Be ye not wroth in the way. Then they thus departing came into the land of Canaan to their father, and showed all this to their father, and said: Joseph thy son liveth and he lordeth in all the land of Egypt.

When Jacob heard this he awoke as a man had been awaked suddenly out of his sleep, yet nevertheless he believed them not, and they told to him all the order of the matter. When he saw the carriage and all that he had sent, his spirit revived and said: It sufficeth to me if Joseph my son yet live, I shall go and see him ere I die. Then Israel went forth with all that he had and came to the pit where tofore he had sworn to God; and slew there beasts to make sacrifices to the God of Isaac his father. He heard God by a vision that same night saying to him: Jacob, Jacob, to whom he answered: I am here all ready. God said to him: I am strongest God of thy father Isaac, dread thee not, but descend down into Egypt. I shall make thee to grow there into great people. I shall descend with thee thither, and I shall bring thee again when thou returnest. Joseph soothly shall put his hands upon thine eyes. Jacob then arose on the morn early, and his sons took him with their children and wives and set them on the carriages that Pharaoh had sent to bring him and all that he had into the land of Canaan. And so came into Egypt with all his progeny, sons and children, etc.

These be the names of the sons of Israel that entered with him into Egypt. The first begotten Reuben with his children four. Simeon with his seven sons. Levi with his three sons. Judah and his sons three. Issachar and his four sons. Zebulon and his sons three. These were sons of Leah that Jacob gat in Mesopotamia, and Dinah his daughter. All these sons and daughters were thirty-three. Gad also entered with his children seven. Asher with his children five and of his children's children two. These were sons of Zilpah, in number sixteen. The sons of Rachel were Joseph and Benjamin. Joseph had two sons in the land of Egypt by his wife Asenath, Manasseh and Ephraim. The sons of Benjamin were ten. All these children that came of Rachel were in number fourteen. Dan entered with one son, and Naphtali with four sons. These were the children of Bilhah; they were in number seven. All the souls that were issued of his seed that entered into Egypt with him, without the wives of his sons, were sixty-six. The sons of Joseph that were born in Egypt twain. Summa of all the souls of the house of Jacob that entered into Egypt were in all seventy.

Jacob sent them tofore him Judah unto Joseph, to show to him his coming. And he came to Joseph in Goshen, and anon Joseph ascended his chariot and went for to meet his father, and when he saw him, he embraced him meekly and wept. And his father received him joyously and embraced also him. Then said the father to Joseph: Now shall I die joyously because I have seen thy visage. Then said Joseph to his brethren and to all the house of his father: I shall go and ascend to Pharaoh and shall say to him, that my brethren and the house of my father that were in the land of Canaan be come to me, and be men keeping sheep, and can the manner well for to keep the flocks of sheep, and that they have brought with them their beasts, and all that ever they had. When he shall call you and ask you of what occupation ye be, ye shall say: We be shepherds, thy servants, from our childhood unto now, and our fathers also. This shall ye say that ye may dwell in the land of Goshen, for the Egyptians have spite unto herdmen of sheep. Then Joseph entered tofore Pharaoh and said to him: My father, my brethren, their sheep and beasts be come from the land of Canaan, and be in the land of Goshen. And he brought five of his brethren tofore the king, whom he demanded of what occupation they were of. They answered: We be keepers of sheep, thy servants, we and our fathers, we be come to dwell in thy land, for there is no grass for the flocks of sheep of us thy servants, the famine is so great in the land of Canaan. We beseech thee that thou command us thy servants to dwell in the land of Goshen. Then said the king to Joseph: Thy father and thy brethren be come to thee, the land of Egypt is at thy commandment, make thou them to dwell in the best place, and deliver to them the land of Goshen. And if thou know them for conning, ordain they to be masters of my beasts. After this Joseph brought his father in, and made him stand tofore the king which blessed him, and was demanded of the king how old he was. He answered: The days of the pilgrimage of my life be an hundred and thirty years, small and evil, and yet I am not come unto the days of my fathers that they have lived. And he blessed the king and went out. Then Joseph gave to his father and brethren possession in Egypt in the best soil of Rameses like as Pharaoh had commanded, and there fed them, giving to each of them victual.

In all the world was scarcity of bread, and hunger and famine oppressed specially and most, the land of Egypt and the land of Canaan. Of which lands Joseph gat all the money for selling of wheat, and brought it into the king's treasury. When all people lacked money, all Egypt came to Joseph saying: Give us bread, why die we to the lacking money. To whom he answered: Bring to me your beasts and I shall give you for them victuals, if ye have no money: which when they brought, he gave to them victuals and food for horses, sheep, oxen and asses, and sustained them one year for changing of their beasts. Then came they again the second year and said: We hide not from thee our lord that our money is failed and also our beasts be gone, and there is nothing left but our bodies and our land. Why then shall we die in thy sight? And we ourselves and also our land shall be thine, buy us into bondship and servitude of the king, and give us seed to sow lest the earth turn into wilderness. Then Joseph bought all the land of Egypt, every man selling his possessions for the vehement hunger that they had. He subdued all unto Pharaoh, and all his people from the last terms of Egypt unto the utterest ends of the same, except the land longing to the priests, which was given to them by the king, to whom were given victuals openly out of all the barns and garners, and therefore they were not compelled to sell their possessions. Then said Joseph to all the peoples: Lo, now ye see and know that Pharaoh oweth and is in possession of you and of your land. Take to you seed and sow ye the fields that ye may have fruit. The fifth part thereof ye shall give to the king and four parts I promise to you to sow, and for meat to your servants and to your children. Which answered: Our health is in thine hand, let our lord only behold us and we shall gladly serve the king. From that time unto this present day, in all the land of Egypt the fifth part is paid to the king; and it is holden for a law, except the land longing to the priests which is free from this condition.

Then Israel dwelled in Egypt in the land of Goshen, and was in possession thereof. He increased and multiplied greatly, and lived therein seventeen years. And all the years of his life were an hundred and seven and forty years. When he understood that the day of his death approached, he called to him his son Joseph and said to him: If I may find so much grace in thy sight, do to me so much mercy as thou promise and swear that thou bury me not in Egypt, but that I may rest with my fathers, and take and carry me from this land, and lay me in the sepulchre of my forefathers. To whom Joseph answered: I shall do that thou hast commanded. Then said he: Swear to me, and so he swore. And then Israel adored and worshipped our Lord, and turned him toward his bed's head. Then this done, anon after it was told to Joseph that his father was sick and feeble; who anon took his sons Manasseh and Ephraim and came to his father. Anon it was told to the father: Lo thy son Joseph cometh to thee, which then was comforted, and sat up in his bed. And Joseph entered in, and Jacob said: Almighty God appeared to me in Luz which is in the land of Canaan, and he blessed me and said: I shall increase thee and multiply thee into tourbes of peoples, I shall give to thee this land and to thy seed after thee in sempiternal possession, therefore thy two sons that be born to thee in this land of Egypt tofore I came hither to thee, shall be my sons Ephraim and Manasseh, they shall be reputed to me as Simeon and Reuben. The other that thou shalt get after them shall be thine, and shall be called in the name of their brethren in their possessions. Then he, seeing Joseph's sons, said to him: Who be these children? Joseph answered: They be my sons which God hath given to me in this place. Bring them hither, said he, to me that I may bless them. Israel's eyes were dimmed and might not see clearly for great age. He took them to him and kissed them and said to Joseph: I am not defrauded from the sight of thee, and furthermore God hath showed to me thy seed. Then when Joseph took them from his father's lap, he worshipped him kneeling low to the earth, and set Ephraim on his right side, and on the left side of Israel, and Manasseh on the right side of his father Israel, which took his right hand and laid it on the head of Ephraim the younger brother, and his left hand on the head of Manasseh which was first born. Then Jacob blessed the sons of Joseph and said: God, in whose sight walked my fathers Abraham and Isaac, God that hath fed me from my youth unto this present day, the angel that hath kept me from all evil bless these children, and my name be called on them, and the names of my fathers Abraham and Isaac, and grow they into multitude upon earth. Then Joseph seeing that his father set his right hand upon the head of Ephraim the younger brother took it heavily, and took his father's hand and would have laid it on the head of Manasseh, and said to his father; Nay father, it is not convenient, that ye do, this is the first begotten son, set thy right hand on his head. Which renied that and would not do so, but said: I wot, my son, I wot what I do, and this son shall increase into peoples and multiply, but his younger brother shall be greater than he, and his seed shall grow into gentiles, and blessed them, saying that same time: In thee shall be blessed Israel, and shall be said: God make thee like to Ephraim and Manasseh. And he said to Joseph his son: Lo! now I die and God shall be with you, and shall reduce and bring you again into the land of your fathers; and I give to thee one part above thy brethren, which I gat and won from the hand of the Amorite with my sword and my bow. Then Jacob called his sons tofore him and said to them:

Gather ye altogether tofore me, that I may show to you things that be to come, and hear your father Israel. And there he told to each of them his condition singularly. And when he had blessed his twelve sons he commanded them to bury him with his fathers in a double spelunke which is in the field of Ephron the Hittite against Mamre in the land of Canaan which Abraham bought. And this said he gathered to him his feet and died. Which anon as Joseph saw, he fell on his visage and kissed him. He commanded to his masters of physic and medicines, which were his servants, that they should embalm the body of his father with sweet spices aromatic; which was all done, and then went they sorrowing him forty days. The Egyptians wailed him seventy days, and when the wailing was past, Joseph did say to Pharaoh how he had sworn and promised to bury him in the land of Canaan. To whom Pharaoh said: Go and bury thy father like as thou hast sworn. Which then took his father's body and went, and with him were accompanied all the aged men of Pharaoh's house, and the noblest men of birth of all the land of Egypt, the house of Joseph with his brethren, without the young children, flocks and beasts, which they left in the land of Goshen. He had in his fellowship chariots, carts and horsemen, and was a great tourbe and company, and came over Jordan where as they hallowed the exequies by great wailing seven days long. And when they of the country saw this plaint and sorrowing they said: This is a great sorrow to the Egyptians. And that same place is named yet the bewailing of Egypt.

The children of Israel did as they were commanded, and bare him into the land of Canaan, and buried him in the double spelunke which Abraham had bought. Then when Jacob the father was buried, Joseph with all his fellowship returned into Egypt. Then his brethren after the death of their father spake together privily, and dreading that Joseph would avenge the wrong and evil that they had done to him, came to him and said: Thy father commanded us ere he died that we should say thus to thee: We pray thee that thou wilt forget, and not remember the sin and trespass of thy brethren, ne the malice that they executed in thee. We beseech thee that thou wilt forgive to thy father, servant of God, this wickedness. Which when Joseph heard he wept bitterly, and his brethren came to him kneeling low to the ground and worshipped him, and said, We be thy servants. To whom he answered: Be ye nothing afeard ne dread you not, ween ye that ye may resist God's will? Ye thought to have done to me evil, but God hath turned it into good, and hath exalted me as ye see and know, that he should save much people. Be ye nothing afeard, I shall feed you and your children. And comforted them with fair words, and spake friendly and joyously to them. And he abode and dwelled still in Egypt with all the house of his father, and lived an hundred and ten years, and saw the sons of Ephraim in to the third generation. After these things he said to his brethren: After my death, God shall visit you and shall do you depart from this land unto the land that he promised to Abraham, Isaac, and Jacob. When that time shall come, take my bones and lead them with you from this place, and then died. Whose body was embalmed with sweet spices and aromatics and laid in a chest in Egypt.

HERE NEXT FOLLOWETH THE HISTORY OF MOSES

Which is read in-the Church on Mid-lent Sunday

These be the names of the children of Israel that entered into Egypt with Jacob, and each entered with their household and meiny. Reuben, Simeon, Levi, Judah, Issachar, Zebulon, Benjamin, Dan, Naphtali, Gad, and Asher; they were all in number that entered seventy. Joseph was tofore in Egypt. And when he was dead and all his brethren and kindred, the children of Israel grew and multiplied greatly, and filled the earth. Then was there a new king upon Egypt which knew nothing of Joseph, and said to his people: Lo! and see the people of Israel is great, and stronger than we be, come and let us wisely oppress them, lest they multiply and give us battle and fight with us and drive us out of our land. Then he ordained provosts and masters over them to set them awork and put them to affliction of burdens. They builded to Pharaoh two towns, Pithom and Raamses. How much more they oppressed them, so much the more they increased and multiplied. The Egyptians hated the children of Israel and put them to affliction, scorning and having envy at them, and oppressed bitterly their life with hard work and sore labors of tile and clay, and grieved all them in such works. Then Pharaoh commanded to his people saying: Whatsomever is born of males cast ye into the river, and what of women keep ye them and let ye them live.

After this was a man of the house of Levi went out and took a wife of his kindred, which conceived and brought forth a son, and he saw him elegant and fair, and hid him three months, and when he might no longer hide him, took a little crib of rushes and wickers and pitched it with glue and pitch, and put therein the child, and set it on the river, and let it drive down in the stream, and the sister of the child standing afar, considering what should fall thereof. And it happed that same time, the daughter of king Pharaoh descended down to the river for to wash her in the water, and her maidens went by the brink, which then, when she saw the little crib or fiscelle she sent one of her maidens to fetch and take it up, which so fetched and brought to her, and she saw therein lying a fair child; and she having pity on it said: This is one of the children of the Hebrews. To whom anon spake the sister of the child: Wilt thou, said she, that I go and call thee a woman of the Hebrews that shall and may nourish this child? She answered: Go thy way. The maid went and called his mother, to whom Pharaoh's daughter said: Take this child and nourish him to me, and I shall give to thee thy meed and reward. The mother took her child and nourished it, and when it was weaned and could go she delivered it to the daughter of king Pharaoh, whom she received and adopted instead of a son and named him Moses, saying that I took him out of the water. And he there grew and waxed a pretty child. And as Josephus, Antiquitatum, saith: This daughter of Pharaoh, which was named Termuthe, loved well Moses and reputed him as her son by adoption, and on a day brought him to her father, who for his beauty took him in his arms and made much of him, and set his diadem on his head, wherein was his idol. And Moses anon took it, and cast it under his feet and trod on it, wherefore the king was wroth, and demanded of the great doctors and magicians what should fall of this child. And they kalked on his nativity and said: This is he that shall destroy thy reign and put it under foot, and shall rule and govern the Hebrews. Wherefore the king anon decreed that he should be put to death. But others said that Moses did it of childhood and ought not to die therefore, and counselled to make thereof a proof, and so they did.

They set tofore him a platter full of coals burning, and a platter full of cherries, and bade him eat, and he took and put the hot coals in his mouth and burned his tongue, which letted his speech ever after; and thus he escaped the death. Josephus saith that when Pharaoh would have slain him, Termuthe, his daughter, plucked him away and saved him. Then on a time as Moses was full grown, he went to his brethren, and saw the affliction of them, and a man of Egypt smiting one of the Hebrews, his brethren. And he looked hither and thither and saw no man. He smote the Egyptian and slew him and hid him in the sand. And another day he went out and found two of the Hebrews brawling and fighting together; then he said to him that did wrong: Why smitest thou thy neighbor? which answered: Who hath ordained thee prince and judge upon us? wilt thou slay me as thou slewest that other day an Egyptian? Moses was afeard and said to himself: How is this deed known and made open? Pharaoh heard hereof and sought Moses for to slay him, which then fled from his sight and dwelled in the land of Midian, and sat there by a pit side. The priest of Midian had seven daughters which came thither for to draw water, and to fill the vessels for to give drink to the flocks of the sheep of their father. Then came on them the herdmen and put them from it. Then rose Moses and defended the maidens and let them water their sheep, which then returned to their father Jethro. And he said to them: Why come ye now earlier than ye were wont to do? They said that a man of Egypt hath delivered us from the hand of the herdmen, and also he drew water for us and gave to the sheep drink. Where is he, said he, why left ye the man after you? go call him that he may eat some bread with us. Then Moses sware that he would dwell with him. And he took Zipporah one of his daughters aad wedded her to his wife, which conceived and bare him a son whom he called Gershom, saying: I was a stranger in a strange land. She brought to him forth another son whom he named Eleazar, saying: The God of my father is my helper and hath kept me from the hand of Pharaoh.

Long time after this died the king of Egypt, and the children of Israel, wailing, made great sorrow for the oppression of their labor, and cried unto God for help. Their cry came unto God of their works, and God heard their wailing, and remembered the promise he made with Abraham, Isaac, and Jacob, and our Lord beheld the children of Israel and knew them.

Moses fed the sheep of Jethro his wife's father. When he had brought the sheep into the innermost part of the desert he came unto the mount of God, Oreb. Our Lord appeared to him in flame of fire in the midst of a bush, and he saw the fire in the bush, and the bush burned not. Then said Moses, I shall go and see this great vision why the bush burneth not. Our Lord then beholding that he went for to see it, called him, being in the bush, and said: Moses, Moses, which answered: I am here. Then said our Lord: Approach no nearer hitherward. Take off thy shoon from thy feet, the place that thou standest on is holy ground. And said also: I am God of thy fathers, God of Abraham, and God of Isaac, and God of Jacob. Moses then hid his face, and durst not look toward God. To whom God said: I have seen the affliction of my people in Egypt, and I have heard their cry of the hardness that they suffer in their works, and I knowing the sorrow of them am descended to deliver them from the hand of the Egyptians, and shall lead them from this land into a good land and spacious, into a land that floweth milk and honey, unto the places of Canaanites, Hittites, Amorites, Perizzites, Hivites and Jebusites. The cry of the children of Israel is come to me, I have seen their affliction, how they be oppressed of the Egyptians. But come to me and I shall send thee unto Pharaoh that thou shalt lead the children of Israel out of Egypt. Then Moses said to him: Who am I that shall go to Pharaoh and lead the children out of Egypt? To whom God said: I shall be with thee, and this shall be the sign that I send thee. When thou shalt have led out my people of Egypt, thou shalt offer to God upon this hill. Moses said unto God: Lo! if I go to the children of Israel and say to them: God of your fathers hath sent me to you; if they say: What is his name? what shall I say? Our Lord said to Moses: I am that I am. He said: Thus shalt thou say to the children of Israel: He that is, sent me to you, and yet shalt thou say to them: The Lord God of your fathers, God of Abraham, God of Isaac, and God of Jacob, hath appeared to me saying: This is my name for evermore, and this is my memorial from generation to generation. Go and gather together the seniors and aged men of Israel, and say to them: The Lord God of your fathers hath appeared to me, God of Abraham, God of Isaac, and God of Jacob, saying: Visiting I have visited you, and have seen all that is fallen in Egypt, and I shall lead you out of the affliction of Egypt into the land of Canaan, Ethei, etc., unto the land flowing milk and honey, and they shall hear thy voice. Thou shalt go and take with thee the seniors of Israel to the king of Egypt, and shalt say to him: The Lord God of the Hebrews hath called us; we shall go the journey of three days in wilderness that we may offer to our Lord God. But I know well that the king of Egypt shall not suffer you to go but by strong hand. I shall stretch out my hand and shall smite Egypt in all my marvels that I shall do amid among them. After that he shall let you go. I shall then give my grace to this people tofore the Egyptians, and when ye shall go out ye shall not depart void, nor with nought, but every woman shall borrow of her neighbor, and of her hostess, vessels of silver and of gold, and clothes, and them shall ye lay on your sons, and on your daughters, and ye shall rob Egypt. Then Moses answered and said: They shall not believe me ne hear my voice, but shall say: God hath not appeared to thee.

God said then to him: What is that thou holdest in thine hand? He answered: A rod. Our Lord said: Cast it on the ground. He threw it down and it turned into a serpent, whereof Moses was afeard and would have fled. Our Lord said to him: Put forth thy hand and hold him by the tail; he stretched forth his hand and held him, and it turned again into a rod. To this, that they believe thee, that I have appeared to thee. And yet our Lord said to him: Put thy hand into thy bosom, which, when he hath put in, and drawn out again, it was like a leper's hand. Our Lord bade him to withdraw it into his bosom again, and he drew it out and it was then like that other flesh. If they hear not thee, and believe by the first sign and token, they shall believe thee by the second. If they believe none of the two ne hear thy voice, then take water of the river and pour on the dry ground, and whatsoever thou takest and drawest shall turn into blood. Then Moses said: I pray the Lord send some other, for I am not eloquent, but have a letting in my speech. Our Lord said to him: Who made the mouth of a man, or who hath made a man dumb or deaf, seeing or blind, not I? Go, therefore, I shall be in thy mouth and shall teach thee what thou shalt say. Then said Moses: I beseech thee Lord, said he, send some other whom thou wilt. Our Lord was wroth on Moses and said: Aaron thy brother deacon, I know that he is eloquent, lo! he shall come and meet with thee, and seeing thee he shall be glad in his heart. Speak thou to him and put my words in his mouth, and I shall be in thy mouth and in his mouth, and I shall show to you what ye ought to do, and he shall speak for the people, and shall be thy mouth, and thou shalt be in such things as pertain to God. Take with thee this rod in thine hand, by which thou shalt do signs and marvels. Then Moses went to Jethro his wife's father, and said to him, I shall go and return to my brethren into Egypt, and see if they yet live. To whom Jethro said: Go in God's name and place. Then said our Lord to Moses: Go and return into Egypt, all they be now dead that sought for to slay thee. Then Moses took his wife and his sons and set them upon an ass and returned in to Egypt, bearing the rod of God in his hand. Then our Lord said to Aaron: Go against Moses and meet with him in desert; which went for to meet with him unto the mount of God, and there kissed him.

And Moses told unto Aaron all that our Lord had said to him for which he sent him, and all the tokens and signs that he bade him do. They came both together and gathered and assembled all the seniors and aged men of the children of Israel. And Aaron told to them all that God had said to Moses, and made the signs and tokens tofore the people and the people believed it. They heard well that our Lord had visited the children of Israel, and that he had beholden the affliction of them, wherefore they fell down low to the ground and worshipped our Lord.

After this Moses and Aaron went unto Pharaoh and said: This saith the Lord God of Israel: Suffer my people to depart that they may sacrifice to me in desert. Then said Pharaoh: Who is that Lord that I may hear his voice and leave Israel? I know not that Lord, nor I will not leave Israel. They said to him: God of the Hebrews hath called us that we go the journey of three days in the wilderness and sacrifice unto our Lord God, lest peradventure pestilence or war fall to us. The king of Egypt said to them: Why solicit ye, Moses and Aaron, the people from their works and labor? Go ye unto your work. Pharaoh also said: The people is much, see how they grow and multiply, and yet much more shall do if they rested from their labor. Therefore he commanded the same day to the prefects and masters of their works saying: In no wise give no more chaff to the people for to make loam and clay, but let them go and gather stubble, and make them do as much labor as they did tofore, and lessen it nothing. They do now but cry: Let us go and make sacrifice to our God, let them be oppressed by labor and exercised that they attend not to leasings. Then the prefects and masters of their work said to them that Pharaoh had commanded to give them no chaff, but they should go and gather such as they might find, and that their work should not therefore be minished. Then the children were disperpled for to gather chaff, and their masters awaited on them and bade them: Make an end of your work as ye were wont to do when that chaff was delivered to you. And thus they were put to more affliction, and would make them to make as many tiles as they did tofore. Then the upperest of the children of Israel came to Pharaoh and complained saying: Why puttest thou thy servants to such affliction? He said to them: Ye be so idle that ye say ye will go and sacrifice to your God; ye shall have no chaff given to you, yet ye shall work your customable work and gather your chaff also.

Then the eldest and the upperest among the Hebrews went to Moses and Aaron and said: What have ye done? ye have so done that ye have made our odor to stink in the sight of Pharaoh, and have encouraged him to slay us. Then Moses counselled with our Lord how he should do, and said: Lord, why hast thou sent me hither? For, sith I have spoken to Pharaoh in thy name, he hath put thy people to more affliction than they had tofore, and thou hast not delivered them. Our Lord said to Moses: Now thou shalt see what I shall do to Pharaoh. By strong hand he shall let you go, and in a boistous he shall cast you from his land.

Yet said our Lord to Moses: I am the Lord God that appeared to Abraham, Isaac, and Jacob in my might, and my name is Adonai, I showed to them not that. I promised and made covenant with them that I should give to them the land of Canaan in which they dwelled. I now have heard the wailing and the tribulations that the Egyptians oppress them with, for which I shall deliver and bring them from the servitude of the Egyptians. Moses told all these things to the children of Israel, and they believed him not for the anguish of their spirits that they were in, and hard labor. Then said our Lord to Moses: Go and enter in to Pharaoh and bid him deliver my people of Israel out of his land. Moses answered: How should Pharaoh hear me when the children of Israel believe me not? Then our Lord said to Moses and Aaron that they both should go to Pharaoh and give him in commandment to let the children of Israel to depart. And he said to Moses: Lo! I have ordained thee to be God of Pharaoh, and Aaron thy brother shall be thy prophet. Thou shalt say to him all that I say to thee, and he shall say to Pharaoh that he suffer the children of Israel to depart from his land. But I shall enhard his heart, and shall multiply my signs and tokens in the land of Egypt, and he shall not hear ne believe you. And I shall lead the children of Israel my people. And shall show mine hand, and such wonders on Egypt, that Egyptians shall know that I am the Lord. Moses and Aaron did as our Lord commanded them. Moses was eighty years old when he came and stood tofore Pharaoh, and Aaron eighty-three years when they spake to Pharaoh. Then when they were tofore Pharaoh, Aaron cast the rod down, tofore Pharaoh, and anon the rod turned into a serpent. Then Pharaoh called his magicians and jugglers and bade them do the same. And they made their witchcraft and invocations and cast down their rods, which turned in likewise into serpents, but the rod of Aaron devoured their rods. Yet was the heart of Pharaoh hard and so indurate that he would not do as God bade. Then said our Lord to Moses: The heart of Pharaoh is grieved and will not deliver my people. Go to him to-morn in the morning and he shall come out, and thou shalt stand when he cometh on the bank of the river, and take in thine hand the rod that was turned into the serpent, and say to him: The Lord God of the Hebrews sendeth me to thee saying: Deliver my people that they may offer and make sacrifice to me in desert, yet thou hast no will to hear me. Therefore our Lord said: In this shalt thou know that I am the Lord: Lo! I shall smite with the rod that is in my hand the water of the flood, and it shall turn into blood; the fishes that be in the water shall die, and the Egyptians shall be put to affliction drinking of it. Then said our Lord to Moses: Say thou to Aaron: Take this rod and stretch thine hand upon all the waters of Egypt, upon the floods, rivers, ponds, and upon all the lakes where any water is, in that they turn to blood, that it may be a vengeance in all the land of Egypt, as well in treen vessels as in vessels of earth and stone.

Moses and Aaron did as God had commanded them, and smote the flood with the rod tofore Pharaoh and his servants, which turned into blood, and the fishes that were in the river died, and the water was corrupt. And the Egyptians might not drink the water, and all the water of Egypt was turned into blood. And in likewise did the enchanters with their witchcraft, and the heart of Pharaoh was so indurate that he would not let the people depart as our Lord had commanded, but he returned home for this time. The Egyptians went and dolven pits for water all about by the river, and they found no water to drink but all was blood. And this plague endured seven days, and whatsomever water the children of Israel took in this while was fair and good water. This was the first plague and vengeance. The second was that God sent frogs so many, that all the land was full, the rivers, the houses, chambers, beds, that they were woebegone, and these frogs entered into their meat, so many that they covered all the land of Egypt. Then Pharaoh prayed Moses and Aaron that God would take away these frogs, and that he would go suffer the people to do sacrifice; and then Moses asked when he would deliver them if the frogs were voided, and Pharaoh said: In the morn. And then Moses prayed, and they voided all. And when Pharaoh saw that he was quit of them, he kept not his promise and would not let them depart. The third vengeance that God sent to them was a great multitude of hungry horse-flies, as many as the dust of the earth, which were on men, and bit them and beasts. And then enchanters said then to Pharaoh: This is the finger of God. Yet would not Pharaoh let them depart. The fourth vengeance was that God sent all manner kind of flies and lice in such wise that the universal land of Egypt was full of all manner flies and lice, but in the land of Goshen were none. Yet was he so indurate that he would not let them go, but would that they should make their sacrifice to God in that land. But Moses would not so, but would go three days' journey in desert, and sacrifice to God there. Pharaoh said: I will that ye go into desert, but not far, and come soon again, and pray ye for me. And Moses prayed for him to our Lord, and the flies voided that there was not one left. And when they were gone Pharaoh would not keep his promise. Then the fifth plague was that God showed his hand upon the fields and upon the horses, asses, camels, sheep and oxen, and was a great pestilence on all the beasts. And God showed a wonder miracle between the possessions of the Egyptians and the possessions of his people of Israel, for of the beasts of the children of Israel there was not one that perished. Yet was Pharaoh so hard-hearted that he would not suffer the people to depart. The sixth plague was that Moses took ashes out of the chimney and cast on the land. And anon all the people of Egypt, as well men as beasts, were full of blotches, boils, and blains and wounds, and swellings in such wise that the enchanters could ne might not stand for pain tofore Pharaoh. Yet would not Pharaoh hear them, nor do as God had commanded. The seventh plague was a hail so great that there was never none like tofore, and thunder and fire that it destroyed all the grass and herbs of Egypt and smote down all that was in the field, men and beasts. But in the land of Goshen was none heard ne harm done. Yet would not Pharaoh deliver them. The eighth our Lord sent to them locusts, which is a manner great fly, called in some place an adder-bolte, which bit them and ate up all the corn and herbs that was left, in such wise that the people came to Pharaoh and desired him to deliver, saying that the land perished. Then Pharaoh gave to the men license to go and make their sacrifice, and leave their wives and children there still, till they came again, but Moses and Aaron said they must go all, wherefore he would not let them depart. The ninth plague and vengeance was that God sent so great darkness upon all the land of Egypt that the darkness was so great and horrible that they were palpable, and it endured three days and three nights. Wheresoever the children of Israel went it was light.

Then Pharaoh called Moses and Aaron and said to them: Go ye and make your sacrifice unto your Lord God, and let your sheep and beasts only abide. To whom Moses said: We shall take with us such hosties and sacrifices as we shall offer to our Lord God. All our flocks and beasts shall go with us, there shall not remain as much as a nail that shall be necessary in the honor of our Lord God, for we know not what we shall offer till we come to the place. Pharaoh was so indurate and hard-hearted that he would not let them go, and bade Moses that he should no more come in his sight. For when thou comest thou shalt die. Moses answered: Be it as thou hast said: I shall no more come to thy presence. And then our Lord said to Moses: There resteth now but one plague and vengeance, and after that he shall let you go. But first say to all the people that every man borrow of his friend, and woman of her neighbor, vessels of gold and silver, and clothes; our Lord shall give to his people grace and favor to borrow of the Egyptians; and then gave to them a commandment how they should depart. And our Lord said to Moses: At midnight I shall enter into Egypt and the first-begotten child and heir of all Egypt shall die, from the first-begotten son of Pharaoh that sitteth in his throne unto the first-begotten son of the handmaid that sitteth at the mill, and all the first-begotten of the beasts. There shall be a great cry and clamor in all the land of Egypt in such wise that there was never none like, ne never shall be after, and among all the children there shall not an hound be hurt, ne woman, ne beast, whereby ye shall know by what miracle God divideth the Egyptian and Israel. Moses and Aaron showed all these signs and plagues tofore Pharaoh, and his heart was so indurate that he would not let them depart. Then when Moses had said to the children how they should do, they departed, and ate their paschal lamb, and all other ceremonies as be expressed in the Bible, for a law to endure ever among them, which the children of Israel obeyed and accomplished, it was so that at midnight our Lord smote and slew every first-begotten son throughout all the land of Egypt, beginning at the first son and heir of Pharaoh unto the son of the caitiff that lay in prison, and also the first-begotten of the beasts. Pharaoh arose in the night and all his servants and all Egypt, and there was a great clamor and sorrowful noise and cry, for there was not a house in all Egypt but there lay therein one that was dead. Then Pharaoh did do call Moses and Aaron in the night, and said: Arise ye and go your way from my people, ye and the children of Israel, as ye say ye will, take your sheep and beasts with you like as ye desired, and at your departing bless ye me. The Egyptians constrained the children to depart and go their way hastily, saying: We all shall die. The children of Israel took their meal, and put it on their shoulders as they were commanded, and borrowed vessels of silver and of gold, and much clothing. Our Lord gave to them such favor tofore the Egyptians that the Egyptians lent to them all that they desired, and they spoiled and robbed Egypt.

And so the children of Israel departed, nigh the number of six hundred thousand footmen, besides women and children which were innumerable, and an huge great multitude of beasts of divers kinds. The time that the children of Israel had dwelt in Egypt was four hundred years. And so they departed out of Egypt, and went not the right way by the Philistines, but our Lord led them by the way of desert which is by the Red Sea. And the children descended out of Egypt armed. Moses took with him the bones of Joseph for he charged them so to do when he died. They went in the extreme ends of the wilderness, and our Lord went tofore them by day in a column of a cloud, and by night in a column of fire and was their leader and duke; the pillar of the cloud failed never by day, nor the pillar of fire by night tofore the people. Our Lord said to Moses, I shall make his heart so hard that he shall follow and pursue you, and I shall be glorified in Pharaoh, and in all his host, the Egyptians shall know that I am Lord. And anon it was told to Pharaoh that the children of Israel fled, and anon his heart was changed, and also the heart of his servants, and said: What shall we do, shall we suffer the children to depart and no more to serve us? Forthwith he took his chariot and all his people with him. He took with him six hundred chosen chariots, and all the chariots and wains of Egypt, and the dukes of all his hosts and he pursued the children of Israel and followed them in great pride. And when he approached, that the children of Israel saw him come, they were sore afraid and cried to our Lord God, and said to Moses: Was there not sepulchre enough for us in Egypt but that we must now die in wilderness? Said we not to thee: Go from us and let us serve the Egyptians: It had been much better for us to have served the Egyptians than to die here in wilderness. And Moses said to the people: Be ye not afraid, stand and see ye the great wonders that our Lord shall do for you this day. The Egyptians that ye now see, ye shall never see them after this day. God shall fight for you, and be ye still. Our Lord said then to Moses: What criest thou to me? Say to the children of Israel that they go forth. Take thou and raise the rod, and stretch thy hand upon the sea, and depart it that the children of Israel may go dry through the middle of it. I shall so indurate the heart of Pharaoh that he shall follow you, and all the Egyptians, and I shall be glorified in Pharaoh, and in all his host, his carts and horsemen. And the Egyptians shall know that I am Lord when I shall so be glorified. The angel of God went tofore the castles of Israel, and another came after in the cloud which stood between them of Egypt and the children of Israel. And the cloud was dark that the host of Israel might not come to them of all the night. Then Moses stretched his hand upon the sea, and there came a wind blowing in such wise that it waxed dry, and the children of Israel went in through the midst of the Red Sea all dry foot; for the water stood up as a wall on the right side and on the left side. The Egyptians then pursuing them followed and entered after them, and all the carts, chariots and horsemen, through the middle of the sea. And then our Lord beheld that the children of Israel were passed over and were on the dry land, on that other side. Anon turned the water on them, and the wheels on their carts turned up so down, and drowned all the host of Pharaoh, and sank down into the deep of the sea. Then said the Egyptians: Let us flee Israel; the Lord fighteth for them against us. And our Lord said to Moses: Stretch out thine hand upon the sea, and let the water return upon the Egyptians, and upon their chariots and horsemen. And so Moses stretched out his hand and the sea returned in to his first place. And then the Egyptians would have fled, but the water came and overflowed them in the midst of the flood, and it covered the chariots and horsemen, and all the host of Pharaoh, and there was not one saved of them. And the children of Israel had passed through the middle of the dry sea and came a-land.

Thus delivered our Lord the children of Israel from the hand of the Egyptians, and they saw the Egyptians lying dead upon the brinks of the sea. And the people then dreaded our Lord and believed in him, and to Moses his servant. Then Moses and the children of Israel sang this song to our Lord: Cantemus domino magnificatus est, Let us sing to our Lord, he is magnified, he hath overthrown the horsemen and carmen in the sea. And Miriam the sister of Aaron, a prophetess, took a timpane in her hand, and all the women followed her with timpanes and chords, and she went tofore singing Cantemus domino. Then Moses brought the children of Israel from the sea into the desert of Sur, and walked with them three days and three nights and found no water, and came into Marah, and the waters there were so bitter that they might not drink thereof. Then the people grudged against Moses, saying: What shall we drink? And he cried unto our Lord which showed to him a tree which he took and put into the waters, and anon they were turned into sweetness. There our Lord ordained commandments and judgments, and there he tempted him saying: If thou hearest the voice of thy Lord-God, and that thou do is rightful before him, and obeyest his commandments, and keep his precepts, I shall not bring none of the languors ne sorrows upon thee that I did in Egypt. I am Lord thy saviour. Then the children of Israel came in to Elim, where as were twelve fountains of water, and seventy palm trees, and they abode by the waters. Then from thence went all the multitude of the children of Israel into the desert of Sin, which is between Elim and Sinai, and grudged against Moses and Aaron in that wilderness, and said: Would God we had dwelled still in Egypt, whereas we sat and had plenty of bread and flesh; why have ye brought us into the desert for to slay all this multitude by hunger? Our Lord said then to Moses: I shall rain bread to you from heaven, let the people go out and gather every day that I may prove them whether they walk in my law or not; the sixth day let them gather double as much as they gather in one day of the other. Then said Moses and Aaron to all the children of Israel: At even ye shall know that God hath brought you from the land of Egypt, and to-morn ye shall see the glory of our Lord. I have well heard your murmur against our Lord, what have ye mused against us? what be we? and yet said Moses; Our Lord shall give you at even flesh for to eat and to-morn bread unto your fill, for as much as ye have murmured against him;

what be we? Your murmur is not against us but against our Lord. As Aaron spake to all the company of the children of Israel they beheld toward the wilderness, and our Lord spake to Moses in a cloud and said: I have heard the grudgings of the children of Israel; say to them: At even ye shall eat flesh and to-morn ye shall be filled with bread, and ye shall know that I am your Lord God. And when the even was come there came so many curlews that it covered all their lodgings, and on the morn there lay like dew all about in their circuit. Which when they saw and came for to gather, it was small and white like to coriander. And they wondered on it and said: Mahun, that is as much to say, what is this? To whom Moses said: This is the bread that God hath sent you to eat, and God commandeth that every man should gather as much for every head as is the measure of gomor, and let nothing be left till on the morn. And the sixth day gather ye double so much, that is two measures of gomor, and keep that one measure for the Sabbath, which God hath sanctified and commanded you to hallow it. Yet some of them brake God's commandment, and gathered more than they ate and kept it till on the morn, and then it began to putrify and be full of worms. And that they kept for the Sabbath day was good and putrified not. And thus our Lord fed the children of Israel forty years in the desert. And it was called Manna. Moses took one gomor thereof and put it in the tabernacle for to be kept for a perpetual memory and remembrance.

Then went they forth all the multitude of the children of Israel, in the desert of Sin in their mansions and came, to Rephidim, where as they had no water. Then all grudging they said to Moses, Give us water for to drink. To whom Moses answered: What grudge ye against me, why tempt ye our Lord? The people thirsted sore for lack and penury of water saying: Why hast thou brought us out of Egypt for to slay us and our children and beasts? Then Moses cried unto our Lord saying: What shall I do to this people? I trow within a while they shall stone me to death. Then our Lord said to Moses: Go before the people and take with thee the older men and seniors of Israel, and take the rod that thou smotest with the flood in thy hand, and I shall stand tofore upon the stone of Oreb, and smite thou the stone with the rod and the waters shall come out thereof that the people may drink. Moses did so tofore the seniors of Israel and called that place Temptation, because of the grudge of the children of Israel, and said: Is God with us or not? Then came Amalek and fought against the children of Israel in Rephidim. Moses said then to Joshua: Choose to thee men, and go out and fight against Amalek to-morrow. I shall stand on the top of the hill having the rod of God in my hand: Joshua did as Moses commanded him, and fought against Amalek. Moses, Aaron, and Hur ascended into the hill, and when Moses held up his hands, Israel won and overcame their enemies, and when he laid them down then Amalek had the better. The hands of Moses were heavy; Aaron and Hur took then a stone and put it under them, and they sustained his hands on either side, and so his hands were not weary until the going down of the sun. And so Joshua made Amalek to flee, and his people, by strength of his sword. Our Lord said to Moses: Write this for a remembrance in a book and deliver it to the ears of Joshua; I shall destroy and put away the memory of Amalek under heaven. Moses then edified an altar unto our Lord, and called there on the name of our Lord, saying: The Lord is mine exaltation, for this is the hand only of God, and the battle and God shall be against Amalek from generation to generation.

When Jethro the priest of Midian, which was cousin of Moses, heard say what our Lord had done to Moses and to the children of Israel his people, he took Zipporah the wife of Moses, and his two sons, Gershom and Eleazar and came with them to him into desert, whom Moses received with worship and kissed him. And when they were together Moses told him all what our Lord had done to Pharaoh and to the Egyptians for Israel, and all the labor that they endured and how our Lord had delivered them. Jethro was glad for all these things, that God had so saved them from the hands of the Egyptians and said: Blessed be the Lord that hath delivered you from the hand of the Egyptians and of Pharaoh, and hath saved his people; now I know that he is a great Lord above all gods, because they did so proudly against them. And Jethro offered sacrifices and offerings to our Lord. Aaron and all the seniors of Israel came and eat with him tofore our Lord. The next day Moses sat and judged and deemed the people from morning unto evening, which, when his cousin saw, he said to him: What doest thou? Why sittest thou alone and all the people tarry from the morning until evening? To whom Moses answered: The people came to me demanding sentence and the doom of God; when there is any debate or difference among them they come to me to judge them, and to show to them the precepts and the laws of God. Then said Jethro: Thou dost not well nor wisely, for by folly thou consumest thy self, and the people with thee; thou dost above thy might, thou mayst not alone sustain it, but hear me and do there after, and our Lord shall be with thee. Be thou unto the people in those things that appertain to God, that thou tell to them what they should do, and the ceremonies and rites to worship God, and the way by which they should go, and what work they shall do. Provide of all people wise men and dreading God, in whom is truth, and them that hate avarice and covetise, and ordain of them tribunes and centurions and deans that may in all times judge the people. And if there be of a great charge and weight, let it be referred to thee, and let them judge the small things; it shall be the easier to thee to bear the charge when it is so parted. If thou do so, thou shalt fulfil the commandment of

God, and sustain his precepts, and the people shall go home to their places in peace. Which things when Moses had heard and understood, he did all that he had counselled him, and chose out the strongest and wisest people of all Israel and ordained them princes of the people, tribunes, centurions, quinquagenaries, and deans, which at all times should judge and deem the people. And all the great and weighty matters they referred to him, deeming and judging the small causes. And then his cousin departed and went into his country.

The third month after the children of Israel departed out of Egypt, that same day they came into the wilderness of Sinai, and there about the region of the mount they fixed their tents. Moses ascended into the hill unto God. God called him on the hill and said: This shalt thou say to the house of Jacob and to the children of Israel. Ye yourselves have seen what I have done to the Egyptians, and how I have borne you on the wings of eagles and have taken you to me. If ye therefore hear my voice and keep my covenant, ye shall be to me in the reign of priesthood and holy people. These be the words that thou shalt say to the children of Israel. Moses came down and gathered all the most of birth, and expounded in them all the words that our Lord had commanded him. All the people answered: All that ever our Lord hath said we shall do,

When Moses had showed the people the words of our Lord, our Lord said to him: Now I shall come to thee in a cloud that the people may hear me speaking to thee, that they believe thee ever after. Moses went and told this to the people, and our Lord bade them to sanctify the people this day and to-morrow, and let them wash their clothes, and be ready the third day. The third day our Lord shall descend tofore all the people on the mount of Sinai. And ordain to the people the marks and terms in the circuit. And say to them: Beware that ye ascend not on the hill ne touch the ends of it. Whosoever touched the hill shall die by death, there shall no hand touch him, but with stones he shall be oppressed and with casting of them on him he shall be tolben; whether it be man or beast, he shall not live. When thou hearest the trump blown then ascend to the hill. Moses went down to the people and sanctified and hallowed them, and when they had washen their clothes he said to them: Be ye ready at the third day and approach not your wives; When the third day came, and the morning waxed clear, they heard thunder and lightning and saw a great cloud cover the mount, and the cry of the trump was so shrill that the people were sore afraid. When Moses had brought them forth unto the root of the hill they stood there. All the mount of Sinai smoked, for so much as our Lord descended on it in fire, and the smoke ascended from the hill as it had been from a furnace. The mount was terrible and dreadful, and the sound of the trump grew a little more and continued longer. Moses spake and our Lord answered him. Our Lord descended upon the top of the mount of Sinai, even on the top of it, and called Moses to him, which when he came said to him: Go down and charge the people that they come not to the terms of the hill for to see the Lord, for if they do, much multitude shall perish of them. The priests that shall come let them be sanctified lest they be smitten down. And thou and Aaron shall ascend the hill. All the people and priests let them not pass their bounds lest God smite them. Then Moses descended and told to the people all that our Lord hath said. After this our Lord called Moses and said: I am the Lord God that brought you out of Egypt and of thraldom. And gave him the Commandment first by speaking and many ceremonies as be rehearsed in the Bible, which is not requisite to be written here, but the ten commandments every man is bounden to know. And ere Moses received them written, he went up into the mount of Sinai, and fasted there forty days and forty nights ere he received them. In which time he commanded him to make many things, and to ordain the laws and ceremonies which now be not had in the new law. And also as doctors say, Moses learned that time all the histories tofore written of the making of heaven and earth, of Adam, Noah, Abraham, Isaac, Jacob, and of Joseph with his brethren. And at last delivered to him two tables of stone, both written with the hand of God, which follow.

The first commandment that God commanded is this. Thou shalt not worship no strange ne diverse gods.

The second commandment is this, that thou shalt not take the name of God in vain, that is to say, thou shalt not swear by him for nothing.

The third commandment is that thou have mind and remember that thou hallow and keep holy thy Sabbath day or Sunday. These three commandments be written in the first table and appertain only to God.

The fourth commandment is that thou shalt honor and worship thy father and mother, for thou shalt live the longer on earth.

The fifth commandment is that thou shalt slay no man.

The sixth commandment is, thou shalt not do adultery.

The seventh commandment is that thou shalt do no theft.

The eighth commandment is that thou shalt not bear false witness against thy neighbor.

The ninth commandment is that thou shalt not desire the wife of thy neighbor, nor shalt not covet her in thine heart.

The tenth commandment is that thou shalt not covet nothing that is, or longeth to, thy neighbor.

These be the ten commandments of our Lord, of which the three first belong to God, and the seven other be ordained for our neighbors. Every person that hath wit and understanding in himself, and age, is bound to know them and to obey and keep these ten commandments aforesaid or else he sinneth deadly.

Thus Moses abode in the hill forty days and forty nights and received of Almighty God the tables with the commandments written with the hand of God; and also received and learned many ceremonies and statutes that God ordained, by which the children of Israel should be ruled and judged. And whiles that Moses was thus with our Lord on the mount, the children of Israel saw that he tarried and descended not, and some of them said that he was dead or gone away, and would not return again, and some said nay; but in conclusion they gathered them together against Aaron, and said to him: Make to us some gods that may go tofore us, we know not what is befallen to Moses. Then Aaron said: Take the gold that hangeth in the ears of your wives and your children, and bring it to me. The people did as he bade, and brought the gold to Aaron, which he took and molt it and made thereof a calf. Then they said: These be thy gods, Israel, that brought thee out of the land of Egypt. Then the people made an altar tofore it, and made great joy and mirth, and danced and played tofore the calf, and offered and made sacrifices thereto. Our Lord spake to Moses, saying: Go hence and descend down, thy people have sinned whom thou hast brought forth from the land of Egypt. They have soon forsaken and left the way which thou hast showed to them. They have made to them a calf blown, and they have worshipped it, and offered sacrifices thereto, saying: These be thy gods, Israel, that have brought thee out of the land of Egypt, Yet said our Lord to Moses: I see well that this people is of evil disposition, suffer me that I may wreak my wrath on them, and I shall destroy them. I shall make thee governor of great people.

Moses then prayed our Lord God saying: Why art thou wroth, Lord, against thy people that thou hast brought out of the land of Egypt in a great strength and a boisterous hand? I beseech thee, Lord, let not the Egyptians say that their God hath locked them out for to slay them in the mountains. I pray thee Lord that thy wrath may assuage, and be thou pleased and benign upon the wickedness of thy people. Remember Abraham, Isaac, and Jacob thy servants, to whom thou promisedst and swaredst by thyself saying: I shall multiply your seed as the stars of heaven, and the universal, land of which I have spoken I shall give to your seed, and ye shall possess and have it ever. And with these words our Lord was pleased that he would do no harm as he had said unto his people; and Moses returned from the mount, bearing two tables of stone, written both with the hand of God. And the scripture that was in the tables were the ten commandments as fore be written. Joshua hearing the great noise of the children of Israel said to Moses: I trow they fight beneath, which answered and said: It is no cry of exhorting men to fight, ne noise to compel me to flee, but I hear the noise of singing. When he approached to them he saw the calf and the instruments of mirth, and he was so wroth that he threw down the tables and brake them at the foot of the hill, and ran and caught down the calf that they had made, and burnt and smote it all to powder, which he cast into water and gave it to drink to the children of Israel. Then said Moses to Aaron: What hath this people done to thee that thou hast made to sin grievously? To whom he answered: Let not my lord take none indignation at me, thou knowest well that this people is prone and ready to sin. They said to me: Make us gods that may go tofore us; we know not what is fallen to this Moses that led us out of Egypt. To whom I said: Who of you that hath gold give it me; they took and gave it to me, and I cast it into the fire, and thereof came out this calf. And then said Moses: All they that be of God's part and have not sinned in this calf let them join to me; and the children of Levi joined to him, and he bade each man take a sword on his side and take vengeance and slay every each his brother, friend, and his neighbor that have trespassed. And so the children of Levi went and slew thirty-three thousand of the children of Israel. And then said Moses: Ye have hallowed this day your hands unto our Lord, and ye shall be therefore blessed. The second day Moses spake to the people and said: Ye have committed and done the greatest sin that may be. I shall ascend unto our Lord again, and shall pray him for your sin. Then Moses ascended again, and received afterward two tables again, which our Lord bade him make. And therein our Lord wrote the commandments. And after, our Lord commanded him to make an ark and a tabernacle: in which ark was kept three things. First the rod with which he did marvels, a pot full of manna, and the two tables with commandments. And then after Moses taught them the law; how each man should behave him against other and what he should do, and what he should not do, and departed them into twelve tribes, and commanded that every man should bring a rod into the Tabernacle. And Moses wrote each name on the rod, and Moses shut fast the tabernacle. And on the morn there was found one of the rods that burgeoned and bare leaves and fruit, and was of an almond tree. That rod fell to Aaron.

And after this, long time, the children desired to eat flesh and remembered of the flesh that they ate in Egypt, and grudged against Moses, and would have ordained to them a duke for to have returned into Egypt. Wherefore Moses was so woe that he desired of our Lord to deliver him from this life, because he saw them so unkind against God. Then God sent to them so great plenty of curlews that two days and one night they flew so thick by the ground that they took great number, for they flew but the height of two cubits. And they had so many that they dried them hanging on their tabernacles and tents. Yet were they not content, but ever grudging, wherefore God smote them and took vengeance on them by a great plague and many died and were buried there. And then from thence they went into Hazeroth and dwelt. After this Miriam and Aaron, brother and sister of Moses, began to speak against Moses, because of his wife which was of Ethiopia, and said: God hath not spoken only by Moses, hath he not also spoken to us? Wherefore our Lord was wroth. Moses was the humblest and the meekest man that was in all the world. Anon then, our Lord said to him, and to Aaron and to Miriam: Go ye three only unto the tabernacle; and there our Lord said that there was none like to Moses, to whom he had spoken mouth to mouth, and reproved Aaron and Miriam because they spake so to Moses, and being wroth, departed from them, and anon, Miriam was smitten and made leper and white like snow. And when Aaron beheld her and saw her smitten with leprosy, he said to Moses: I beseech the Lord that thou set not the sin on us which we have committed follily, and let not this our sister be as a dead woman, or as born out of time and cast away from her mother, behold and see, half her flesh is devoured of the leprosy. Then Moses cried unto our Lord, saying: I beseech thee Lord that thou heal her; to whom our Lord said: If her father had spit in her face should she not be put to shame and rebuke seven days? Let her depart out of the castles seven days, and after she shall be called in again. So Miriam was shut out of the castles seven days, and the people removed not from the place till she was called again.

After this our Lord commanded Moses to send men into the land of Canaan that he should give them charge for to see and consider the goodness thereof, and that of every tribe he should send some. Moses did as our Lord had commanded, which went in and brought of the fruits with them, and they brought a branch with one cluster of grapes as much as two men might bear between them upon a colestaff. When they had seen the country and considered by the space of forty days they returned and told the commodities of the land, but some said that the people were strong, and many kings and giants, in such wise that they said it was impregnable and that the people were much stronger than they were. Wherefore the people anon were afeard, and murmured against Moses and would return again into Egypt. Then Joshua and Caleb, which were two of them that had considered the land, said to the people: Why grudge ye and wherefore be ye afraid? We have well seen the country, and it is good to win. The country floweth full of milk and honey, be not rebel against God, he shall give it us, be ye not afeard. Then all the people cried against them, and when they would have taken stones and stoned them, our Lord in his glory appeared in a cloud upon the covering of the tabernacle, and said to Moses: This people believeth not the signs and wonders that I have showed and done to them. I shall destroy them all by pestilence, and I shall make thee a prince upon people greater and stronger than this is. Then prayed Moses to our Lord for the people, that he would have pity on them and not destroy them, but to have mercy on them after the magnitude of his mercy. And our Lord at his request forgave them. Nevertheless our Lord said that all the men that had seen his majesty, and the signs and marvels that he did in Egypt, and in desert, and have tempted him ten times, and not obeyed unto his voice, shall not see ne come into the country and land that I have promised to their fathers, but Joshua and Caleb, my servants, shall enter into the land, and their seed shall possess it. Moses told all this unto the children and they wailed and sorrowed greatly therefore.

After this the people removed from thence and came into the desert of Sin; and then Miriam, sister of Moses and Aaron, died, and was buried in the same place. Then the people lacked water and came and grudged against Moses, and yet wished they had abided in Egypt. Then Moses and Aaron entered into the Tabernacle and fell down to the ground low, and prayed unto our Lord, saying: Lord God, hear the clamor of thy people, and open to them thy treasure, a fountain of living water, that they may drink and the murmuration of them may cease. Our Lord said to him then: Take the rod in thy hand, and thou and Aaron thy brother, assemble and gather the people and speak ye to the stone, and it shall give out water. And when the water cometh let all the multitude drink and their beasts. Moses then took the rod as our Lord bade, and gathered all the people tofore the stone and said to them: Hear ye rebels and out of belief; trow ye not that we may give you water out of this stone? And he lift up his hand and smote between the stone, and water came and flowed out in the most largest wise, in such wise that the people and beasts drank their fill. Then said God to Moses and Aaron: Because ye have not believed me and sanctified my name tofore the children of Israel, and given to me the laud, but have done this in your name, ye shall not bring this people into the land that I shall give to them. And therefore this water was called the water of contradiction, where the children grudged against God.

Anon after this, by God's commandment, Moses took Aaron upon the hill, and despoiled him of his vesture, and clothed therewith his son Eleazar, and made him upperest bishop for his father Aaron. And there Aaron died in the top of the hill, and Moses descended with Eleazar. And when all the multitude of people saw that Aaron was dead, they wept and wailed on him thirty days in every tribe and family.

After this the people went about the land of Edom, and began to wax weary, and grudged against our Lord and Moses, and said yet: Why hast thou led us out of the Land of Egypt for to slay us in this desert and wilderness? Bread faileth us, there is no water, and our souls abhor and loathe this light meat. For which cause God sent among them fiery-serpents, which bit and wounded many of them and slew also. Then they that were hurt came in to Moses and said: We have sinned, for we have spoken against our Lord and thee; pray for us unto God that he deliver from us these serpents. Then Moses prayed our Lord for the people. And our Lord said to him: Make a serpent of brass and set it up for a sign, and whosomever be hurt, and looketh thereon and beholdeth it, shall live and be whole. Then Moses made a serpent of brass, and set it up for a sign, and when they that were hurt beheld it they were made whole.

After this when Moses had showed to them all the laws of our Lord, and ceremonies, and had governed them forty years, and that he was an hundred and twenty years old, he ascended from the fields of Moab upon the mountain of Nebo into the top of Pisgah against Jericho, and there our Lord showed to him all the land of Gilead unto Dan, and the land of promise from that one end unto that other. And then our Lord said to him: This is the land that I promised to Abraham, Isaac, and Jacob, saying: I shall give it to thy seed. Now thou hast seen it with thine eyes, and shalt not enter ne come therein. And there in that place died Moses, servant of our Lord, as God commanded, and was buried in the vale of the land of Moab against Beth-peor. And yet never man knew his sepulchre unto this day. Moses was an hundred and twenty years old when he died, his eyes never dimmed, ne his teeth were never moved. The children of Israel wept and mourned for him thirty days in the fields of Moab. Joshua the son of Nun was replenished with the spirit of wisdom; for Moses set on him his hands, and the children obeyed him as our Lord had commanded to Moses. And there was never after a prophet in Israel like unto Moses, which knew and spake to God face to face in all signs and tokens that God did and showed by him in the land of Egypt to Pharaoh and all his servants.

THE BURIAL OF MOSES

By Nebo's lonely mountain,
  On this side Jordan's wave,
In a vale in the land of Moab
  There lies a lonely grave.
And no man knows that sepulchre,
  And no man saw it e'er,
For the angels of God upturned the sod,
  And laid the dead man there.

That was the grandest funeral
  That ever passed on earth;
But no man heard the trampling,
  Or saw the train go forth—
Noiselessly as the daylight
  Comes back when night is done,
And the crimson streak on ocean's cheek
  Grows into the great sun.

Noiselessly as the springtime
  Her crown of verdure weaves,
And all the trees on all the hills
  Open their thousand leaves;
So without sound of music,
  Or voice of them that wept,
Silently down from the mountain's crown
  The great procession swept.

Perchance the bald old eagle,
  On gray Beth-peor's height,
Out of his lonely eyrie
  Looked on the wondrous sight;
Perchance the lion stalking,
  Still shuns that hallowed spot,
For beast and bird have seen and heard
  That which man knoweth not.

But when the warrior dieth,
  His comrades in the war,
With arms reversed and muffled drum,
  Follow his funeral car;
They show the banners taken,
  They tell his battles won,
And after him lead his masterless steed,
  While peals the minute gun.

Amid the noblest of the land
  We lay the sage to rest,
And give the bard an honored place
  With costly marble drest,
In the great minster transept,
  Where lights like glories fall,
And the organ rings, and the sweet choir sings,
  Along the emblazoned wall.

This was the truest warrior
  That ever buckled sword;
This the most gifted poet
  That ever breathed a word.
And never earth's philosopher
  Traced with his golden pen
On the deathless page truths half so sage
  As he wrote down for men.

And had he not high honor?—
  The hillside for a pall,
To lie in state, while angels wait,
  With stars for tapers tall;
And the dark rock-pines, like tossing plumes,
  Over his bier to wave,
And God's own hand in that lonely land
  To lay him in the grave,—

In that strange grave without a name,
  Whence his uncoffined clay
Shall break again, O wondrous thought!
  Before the judgment day,
And stand with glory wrapt around
  On the hills he never trod;
And speak of the strife, that won our life,
  With the incarnate son of God.

O lonely grave in Moab's land!
  O dark Beth-peor's hill!
Speak to these curious hearts of ours,
  And teach them to be still.
God hath his mysteries of grace,
  Ways that we cannot tell;
He hides them deep, like the hidden sleep
  Of him He loved so well.

—*Cecil Frances Alexander.*

THE HISTORY OF JOSHUA

After Moses, Joshua was duke and leader of the children of Israel, and brought them into the land of behest, and did many great battles. For whom God showed many great marvels and in especial one; that was that the sun stood still at his request, till he had overcome his enemies, by the space of a day. And our Lord, when he fought, sent down such hail-stones that slew more of his enemies with the stones than with man's hand.

Joshua was a noble man and governed well Israel, and divided the land unto the twelve tribes by lot. And when he was an hundred and ten years old he died. And divers dukes after him judged and deemed Israel, of whom be noble histories, as of Jephthah, Gideon, and Samson, which I pass over unto the histories of the kings, which is read in holy church from the first Sunday after Trinity Sunday, unto the first Sunday of August.

THE HISTORY OF SAUL

The first Sunday after Trinity Sunday unto the first Sunday of the month of August is read the Book of Kings.

This history maketh mention that there was a man named Elkanah which had two wives, that one was named Hannah, and the name of the second Peninnah. Peninnah had children and Hannah had none but was barren. The good man at such days as he was bounden, went to his city for to make his sacrifice and worship God. In this time Hophni and Phineas sons of Eli, the great priest, were priests of our Lord. This Elkanah gave to Peninnah at such times as he offered, to her sons and daughters, certain parts, and unto Hannah he gave but one part. Peninnah did much sorrow and reproof to Hannah because she had had no children, and thus did every year, and provoked her to wrath, but she wept for sorrow and ate no meat. To whom Elkanah her husband said: Hannah, why weepest thou? and wherefore eatest thou not? Why is thine heart put to affliction? Am I not better to thee than ten sons? Then Hannah arose after she had eaten and drunk in Shilo and went to pray unto our Lord, making to him a vow if that she might have a son she should offer him to our Lord. Eli that time sat tofore the posts of the house of our Lord. And Hannah besought and prayed our Lord, making to him a vow, if that she might have a son she should offer him to our Lord. And it was so that she prayed so heartily in her thought and mind, that her lips moved not, wherefore Eli bare her on hand that she was drunk. And she said: Nay, my lord, I am a sorrowful woman, I have drunken no wine ne drink that may cause me to be drunken, but I have made my prayers, and cast my soul in the sight of Almighty God. Repute me not as one of the daughters of Belial, for the prayer that I have made and spoken yet is of the multitude of the heaviness and sorrow of my heart. Then Eli the priest said to her: Go in peace, the God of Israel give to thee the petition of thy heart for that thou hast prayed him. And she said: Would God that thy handservant might find grace in thy sight. And so she departed, and on the morn they went home again in to Ramatha.

After this our Lord remembered her, and she bare a fair son and named him Samuel for so much as she asked him of our Lord. Wherefore Elkanah, her husband, went and offered a solemn sacrifice and his vow accomplished, but Hannah ascended not with him. She said to her husband that she would not go till her child were weaned and taken from the pap. And after when Samuel was weaned, and was an infant, the mother took him, and three calves and three measures of meal, and a bottle of wine, and brought him unto the house of our Lord in Shilo and sacrificed that calf and offered the child to Eli, and told to Eli that she was the woman that prayed our Lord for that child. And there Hannah worshipped our Lord and thanked him, and there made this psalm which is one of the canticles: My heart hath rejoiced in the Lord, and so forth, all the remnant of that psalm. And then Elkanah with his wife returned home to his house. After this our Lord visited Hannah, and she conceived three sons, and two daughters, which she brought forth. And Samuel abode in the house of our Lord and was minister in the sight of Eli. But the two sons of Eli, Hophni and Phineas, were children of Belial, not knowing our Lord, but did great sins against the commandments of God. And our Lord sent a prophet to Eli because he corrected not his sons, and said he would take the office from him and from his house, and that there should not be an old man in his house and kindred, but should die ere they came to man's estate, and that God should raise a priest that should be faithful and after his heart.

Samuel served and ministered our Lord in a surplice before Eli. And on a time as Eli lay in his bed his eyes were so dimmed that he might not see the lantern of God till it was quenched and put out. Samuel slept in the temple of our Lord whereas the ark of God was, and our Lord called Samuel, which answered: I am ready, and ran to Eli and said: I am ready, thou callest me. Which said: I called thee not my son, return and sleep, and he returned and slept. And our Lord called him the second time, and he arose and went to Eli and said: Lo! I am here, thou calledst me, which answered: I called thee not, go thy way, and sleep. Samuel knew not the calling of our Lord yet, ne there was never revelation showed him tofore. And our Lord called Samuel the third time, which arose and came to Eli and said: I am here, for thou calledst me. Then Eli understood that our Lord had called him, and said to Samuel: Go and sleep, and if thou be called again thou shalt say: Speak, Lord, for thy servant heareth thee. Samuel returned and slept in his place, and our Lord came and called him: Samuel! Samuel! and Samuel said: Say, Lord, what it pleaseth, for thy servant heareth. And then our Lord said to Samuel: Lo! I make my word to be known in Israel that whoso heareth, his ears shall ring and sound thereof. In that day I shall raise against Eli that I have said upon his house. I shall begin and accomplish it. I have given him in knowledge that I shall judge his house for wickedness, forasmuch as he knoweth his sons to do wickedly, and hath not corrected them. Therefore I have sworn to the house of Eli that the wickedness of his house shall not be made clean with sacrifices ne gifts never.

Samuel slept till on the morn, and then he rose and opened the doors of the house of our Lord in his surplice; and Samuel was afeard to show this vision unto Eli. Eli called him and asked what our Lord hath said to him and charged him to tell him all: and Samuel told to him all that our Lord had said, and hid nothing from him. And he said: He is our Lord, what it pleaseth him, let him do. Samuel grew, and our Lord was with him in all his works. And it was known to all Israel from Dan to Beersheba that Samuel was the true prophet of our Lord. After this it was so that the Philistines warred against the children of Israel, against whom there was a battle, and the children of Israel overthrown and put to flight. Wherefore they assembled again, and took with them the ark of God which Hophni and Phineas, sons of Eli, bare, and when they came with a great multitude with the ark, the Philistines were afraid. Notwithstanding they fought against them manly and slew thirty thousand footmen of the children of Israel and took the ark of God. And the two sons of Eli were slain, Hophni and Phineas. And a man of the tribe of Benjamin ran for to tell this unto Eli which sat abiding some tidings of the battle. This man, as soon as he entered into the town, told how the field was lost, the people slain, and how the ark was taken. And there was a great sorrow and cry.

And when Eli heard this cry and wailing he demanded what this noise was and meant, and wherefore they so sorrowed. Then the man hied and came and told to Eli. Eli was at that tide ninety-eight years old, and his eyes were waxen blind and might not see, and he said: I am he that came from the battle, and fled this day from the host. To whom Eli said: What is there done, my son? He answered: The host of Israel is overthrown and fled tofore the Philistines, and a great ruin is made among the people, thy two sons be slain and the ark of God is taken. And when Eli heard him name the ark of God he fell down backward by the door and brake his neck and there died. He was an old man and had judged Israel forty years. Then the Philistines took the ark of God and set it in their temple of Dagon, by their god Dagon, in Ashdod. On the morn, the next day early, when they of Ashdod came into their temple, they saw their god Dagon lie on the ground tofore the ark of God upon his face, and the head and the two hands of Dagon were cut off. And there abode no more but the trunk only in the place. And God showed many vengeances to them of the country as long as the ark was with them, for God smote them with sickness, and wells boiled in towns and fields of that region, and there grew among them so many mice, that they suffered great persecution and confusion in that city.

The people seeing this vengeance and plague said: Let not the ark of the God of Israel abide longer with us, for his hand is hard on us and on Dagon our god, and sent for the great masters and governors of the Philistines, and when they were gathered they said: What shall we do with the ark of the God of Israel? And they answered: Let it be led all about the cities, and so it was, and a great vengeance and death was had upon all the cities, and smote every man with plague from the most to the least. And then they sent the ark of God into Acheron and when they of Acheron saw the ark, they cried saying: They have brought the ark of the God of Israel to us, for to slay us and our people. They cried that the ark should be sent home again, for much people were dead by the vengeance that was taken on them, and a great howling and wailing was among them. The ark was in the region of the Philistines seven months. After this they counselled with their priests what they should do with the ark, and it was concluded it should be sent home again, but the priests said: If ye send it home, send it not void, but what ye owe pay for your trespass and sin, and then ye shall be healed and cured of your sicknesses. And so they ordained after the number of the five provinces of the Philistines, five pieces of gold and five mice of gold, and led to a wain and put in it two wild kine, which never bear yoke, and said, Leave their calves at home and take the ark and set it on the wain, and also the vessels and pieces of gold that ye have paid for your trespass, set them at the side of the ark and let them go where they will, and thus they sent the ark of God unto the children of Israel.

Samuel then governed Israel long, and when he was old he set his sons judges on Israel, whose names were Joel and Abiah. And these two his sons walked not in his ways, but declined after covetise and took gifts and perverted justice and doom. Then assembled and gathered together all the greatest of birth of the children of Israel, and came to Samuel and said: Lo! thou art old and thy sons walk not in thy ways, wherefore ordain to us a king that may judge and rule us like as all other nations have. This displeased much to Samuel when they said, Ordain on us a king. Then Samuel counselled on this matter with our Lord, to whom God said: Hear the voice of the people that speak to thee: they have not cast only thee away, but me, that I should not reign on them, for they do now like as they ever have done sith I brought them out of Egypt unto this day; that is that they have served false gods and strange, and so do they to thee. Notwithstanding hear them, and tell to them tofore, the right of the king, and how he shall oppress them.

Samuel told all this to the people that demanded to have a king, and said: This shall be the right of a king that shall reign on you. He shall take your sons and make them his men of war, and set them in his chariots and shall make them his carters and riders of his horse in his chariots and carts, and shall ordain of them tribunes and centurions, earers and tillers of his fields, and mowers and reapers of his corn, and he shall make them smiths, and armorers of harness and cars, and he shall also take your daughters and make them his unguentaries [makers of perfumes], and ready at his will and pleasure; he shall also take from you your fields and vineyards and the best olives and give them to his servants, and he shall task and dime [tithe] your corn and sheaves, and the rents of your vineyards he shall value for to give to his officers and servants, and shall take from you your servants, both men and women, and set them to his works. And your asses and beasts he also shall take to his labor, your flocks of sheep he shall task and take the tenth or what shall please him, and ye shall be to him thrall and servants. And ye shall cry then wishing to flee from the face of your king, and our Lord shall not hear you nor deliver you because ye have asked for you a king. Yet for all this the people would not hear Samuel, but said: Give to us a king, for a king shall reign on us, and we shall be as all other people be. And our king shall judge us and go before us, and he shall fight our battles for us.

And Samuel heard all and counselled with our Lord. To whom God commanded to ordain to them a king, and so he did, for he took a man of the tribe of Benjamin whose name was Saul, a good man and chosen, and there was not a better among all the children of Israel, and he was higher of stature from the shoulder upward than any other of all the people. And Samuel anointed him king upon Israel, and said to him: Our Lord God hath anointed thee upon his heritage and ordained thee a prince, and thou shalt deliver his people from the hands of his enemies that be in the circuit and countries about, and so departed from him. And Samuel after this gathered the people together and said: Our Lord saith that he hath brought you from the land of Egypt, and saved you from the hands of all the kings that were your enemies and pursued you, and ye have forsaken our Lord God that hath only delivered you from all your evil and tribulations, and have said: Ordain upon us a king. Wherefore now stand every each in his tribe, and we shall lot who shall be our king. And the lot fell on the tribe of Benjamin, and in that tribe the lot fell upon Saul the son of Kish. And they sought him and could not find him, and it was told him that he was hid in his house at home, and the people ran thither and fetched him and set him amidst all the people. And he was higher than any of all the people from the shoulder upward. Then Samuel said to the people, Now ye see and behold whom our Lord hath chosen, for there is none like him of all the people. And then all the people cried: Vivat Rex, live the king. Samuel wrote the law of the realm to the people in a book, and put it tofore our Lord. Thus was Saul made the first king in Israel, and anon had much war, for on all sides men warred on the children of Israel, and he defended them, and Saul had divers battles and had victory.

Samuel came on a time to Saul and said God commanded him to fight against Amalek and that he should slay and destroy man, woman, and child, ox, cow, camel and ass and sheep, and spare nothing. Then Saul assembled his people and had two hundred thousand footmen and twenty thousand men of the tribe of Judah, and went forth and fought against Amalek and slew them, sauf he saved Agag the King of Amalek alive, and all other he slew, but he spared the best flocks of sheep and of other beasts, and also good clothes, and wethers, and all that was good he spared, and whatsomever was foul he destroyed. And this was showed to Samuel by our Lord, saying: Me forthinketh that I have ordained Saul king upon Israel, for he hath forsaken me, and not fulfilled my commandments. Samuel was sorry herefor, and wailed all the night. On the morn he rose and came to Saul, and Saul offered sacrifice to our Lord of the pillage that he had taken. And Samuel demanded of Saul what noise that was he heard of sheep and beasts, and he said that they were of the beasts that the people had brought from Amalek to offer unto our Lord, and the residue were slain. They have spared the best and fattest for to do sacrifice with unto thy Lord God. Then said Samuel to Saul: Rememberest thou not that whereas thou wert least among the tribes of Israel thou wert made upperest? And our Lord anointed thee, and made thee king. And he said to thee: Go and slay the sinners of Amalek and leave none alive, man ne beast; why hast thou not obeyed the commandment of our Lord? And hast run to robbery and done evil in the sight of God? And then said Saul to Samuel: I have taken Agag, king of the Amalekites, and brought him with me, but I have slain Amalek. The people have taken of the sheep and beasts of the best for to offer unto our Lord God. And then said Samuel: Trowest thou that our Lord would rather have sacrifice and offerings than not to obey his commandments? Better is obedience than sacrifice, and better it is to take heed to do after thy Lord than to offer the fat kidneys of the wethers. For it is a sin to withstand and to repugn against his Lord like the sin of idolatry. And because thou hast not obeyed our Lord, and cast away his word, our Lord hath cast thee away that thou shalt not be king. Then said Saul to Samuel: I have sinned for I have not obeyed the word of God and thy words, but have dreaded the people and obeyed to their request, but I pray thee to bear my sin and trespass and return with me that I may worship our Lord. And Samuel answered, I shall not return with thee. And so Samuel departed, and yet ere he departed, he did do slay [caused to be slain] Agag the king. And Samuel saw never Saul after unto his death.

Then our Lord bade Samuel to go and anoint one of the sons of Isai, otherwise called Jesse, to be king of Israel. And so he came into Bethlehem unto Jesse and bade him bring his sons tofore him. This Jesse had eight sons, be brought tofore Samuel seven of them, and Samuel said there was not he that he would have. Then he said that there was no more, save one which was youngest and yet a child, and kept sheep in the field. And Samuel said: Send for him, for I shall eat no bread till he come. And so he was sent for and brought. He was ruddy and fair of visage and well favored, and Samuel arose, and took an horn with oil and anointed him in the middle of his brethren. And forthwith the spirit of our Lord came directly in him that same day and ever after. Then Samuel departed and came into Ramah. And the spirit of our Lord went away from Saul and an evil spirit oft vexed him. Then his servants said to him: Thou oft art vexed with an evil spirit, it were good to have one that could harp, to be with thee when the spirit vexeth thee, thou shalt bear it the lighter. And he said to his servants: Provide ye to me such one. And then one said: I saw one of Jesse's sons play on a harp, a fair child and strong, wise in his talking and our Lord is with him. Then Saul sent messages to Jesse for David, and Jesse sent David his son with a present of bread, wine, and a kid, to Saul. And always when the evil spirit vexed Saul, David harped tofore him and anon he was eased, and the evil spirit went his way.

After this the Philistines gathered them into great hosts to make war against Saul and the children of Israel, and Saul gathered the children of Israel together and came against them in the vale of Terebinthe. The Philistines stood upon the hill on that other part, and the valley was between them. And there came out of the host of the Philistines a great giant named Goliath of Gath; he was six cubits high and a palm, and a helmet of brass on his head, and was clad in a habergeon. The weight of his habergeon was of five thousand shekels of weight of metal. He had boots of brass on his calves, and his shoulders were covered with plates of brass. His glaive was as a great colestaff, and there was thereon six shekels of iron, and his squire went tofore him and cried against them of Israel, and said they should choose a man to fight a singular battle against Goliath, and if he were overcome the Philistines should be servants to Israel, and if he prevailed and overcame his enemy, they of Israel should serve the Philistines, and thus he did cry forty days long. Saul and the children of Israel were sore afraid. David was at this time in Bethlehem with his father, and kept sheep, and three of his brethren were in the host with Saul. To whom Jesse said: David, take this pottage, ten loaves of bread, and ten cheeses, and go run unto the host to thy brethren, and see how they do, and learn how they be arrayed. David delivered his sheep to one to keep them, and bare these things unto the host. And when he came thither he heard a great cry, and he demanded after his brethren. And that same time came forth that giant Goliath and said, as he had done tofore, and David heard him speak. All they of Israel fled for fear of him, and David demanded what he was, and it was told him that he was come to destroy Israel, and also that what man that might slay him, the king should enrich him with great riches, and should give to him his daughter, and shall make the house of his father without tribute. And David said: What is this uncircumcised that hath despised the host of the God of Israel? And what reward shall he have that shall slay him? And the people said as afore is said. And when his oldest brother heard him speak to the people he was wroth with him, and said: Wherefore art thou come hither and hast left the few sheep in desert. I know well thy pride, thou art come for to see the battle. And David said: What have I done? Is it not as the people said? I dare fight well with this giant; and declined from his brother to other of the people. And all this was showed to Saul, and David was brought to him, and said to Saul: I, thy servant, shall fight against this giant if thou wilt. And Saul said to him: Thou mayst not withstand this Philistine nor fight against him, for thou art but a child; this giant hath been a fighter from his childhood. David said to Saul: I thy servant kept my father's sheep, and there came a lion and a bear and took away a wether from the middle of my flock, and I pursued after, and took it again from their mouths, and they arose and would have devoured me, and I caught them by the jaws and slew them. I thy servant slew the lion and the bear, therefore this Philistine uncircumcised shall be as one of them. I shall now go and deliver Israel from this opprobrium and shame. How is this Philistine uncircumcised so hardy as to curse the host of the living God? And yet said David: The Lord that kept me from the might of the lion and from the strength of the bear, he will deliver me from the power of the Philistine. Saul said then to David: Go, and our Lord be with thee.

Saul did do arm him with his armor, and girded his sword about him. And when he was armed, David said: I may not ne cannot fight thus, for I am not accustomed ne used, and unarmed him, and took his staff that he had in his hand, and chose to him five good round stones from the brook and put them in his bag, and took a sling in his hand, and went forth against the giant. And when Goliath saw him come, he despised him and said: Weenest thou that I am a hound that comest with thy staff to me? And he cursed David by his gods, and said to David: Come hither and I shall give thy flesh to the fowls of heaven and to the beasts of the earth. David said unto Goliath: Thou comest to me with thy sword and glaive, and I come to thee in the name of the Lord God of the host of Israel which thou hast this day despised; and that Lord shall give thee in my hand, and I shall slay thee and smite off thy head. And I shall give this day the bodies of the men of war of the Philistines to the fowls of heaven, and to the beasts of the earth. Then Goliath rose and hied toward David, and David on that other side hied, and took a stone and laid it in his sling, and threw it at the giant, and smote him in the forehead in such wise that the stone was fixed there, in that he fell down on his visage. Thus prevailed David against the Philistine with his sling and stone, and smote him and slew him. And he had no sword but he went and took Goliath's own sword and therewith smote off his head. And then the Philistines seeing this giant thus slain, fled, and the Israelites after followed, and slew many of them, and returned again and came into the tents, pavilions and lodgings of the Philistines, and took all the pillage.

David took the head of Goliath and brought it into Jerusalem, and his arms he brought into his tabernacle. And Abner brought David, having the head of Goliath in his hand, tofore Saul. And Saul demanded of him of what kindred that he was, and he said that he was son of Jesse of Bethlehem, and forthwith that same time Jonathan, the son of Saul, loved David as his own soul. Saul then would not give him license to return to his father, and Jonathan and he were confederate and swore each of them to be true to other, for Jonathan gave his coat that he was clad withal, and all his other garments, unto his sword and spear, unto David. And David did all that ever Saul bade him do wisely and prudently. And when he returned from the battle, and Goliath was slain, the women came out from every town singing with choirs and timpanes against the coming of Saul with great joy and gladness, saying: Saul hath slain a thousand and David hath slain ten thousand. And this saying displeased much to Saul, which said: They have given to David ten thousand and to me one thousand; what may he more have save the realm, and to be king? For this cause Saul never loved David after that day, ne never looked on him friendly but ever sought means afterward to destroy David, for he dreaded that David should be lord with him, and put him from him. And David was wise and kept him well from him. And after this he wedded Michal, daughter of Saul, and Jonathan made oft times peace between Saul and David, yet Saul kept no promise, but ever lay in wait to slay David. And Jonathan warned David thereof. And David gat him a company of men of war to the number of four hundred, and kept him in the mountains.

And on a time David was at home with his wife Michal, and Saul sent thither men of war to slay him in his house in the morning; and when Michal heard thereof, she said to David: But if thou save thyself this night, to-morn thou shalt die, and she let him out by a window by which he escaped and saved himself. Michal took an image and laid in his bed, and a rough skin of a goat on the head of the image, and covered it with clothes. And on the morn Saul sent spies for David, and it was answered to them that he lay sick in his bed. Then after this sent Saul messengers for to see David, and said to them: Bring him to me in his bed that he may be slain. And when the messengers came they found a simulachre or an image in his bed, and goats' skins on the head. Then said Saul to Michal his daughter: Why hast thou mocked me so, and hast suffered mine enemy to flee? And Michal answered to Saul and said: He said to me: Let me go or I shall slay thee.

David went to Samuel in Rama and told him all that Saul had done to him. And it was told to Saul that David was with Samuel, and he sent thither messengers to take him. And when they came they found them with the company of prophets, and they sat and prophesied with them. And he sent more. And they did also so. And the third time he sent more messengers. And they also prophesied. And then Saul being wroth asked where Samuel and David were, and went to them, and he prophesied when he came also, and took off his clothes and was naked all that day and night before Samuel. David then fled from thence and came to Jonathan and complained to him saying: What have I offended that thy father seeketh to slay me? Jonathan was sorry therefore, for he loved well David. After this Saul ever sought for to slay David. And on a time Saul went into a cave, and David was within the cave, to whom his squire said: Now hath God brought thine enemy into thine hand; now go and slay him. And David said: God forbid that I should lay any hand on him, he is anointed. I shall never hurt ne grieve him, let God do his pleasure. And he went to Saul and cut off a gobet [a small piece] of his mantle and kept it. And when Saul was gone out, soon after issued David out and cried to Saul saying: Lo! Saul, God hath brought thee into my hands. I might have slain thee if I had would, but God forbade that I should lay hand on thee, my lord anointed of God. And what have I offended that thou seekest to slay me? Who art thou? said Saul. Art thou not David my son? Yes, said David, I am thy servant, and kneeled down and worshipped him. Then said Saul: I have sinned, and wept and also said: Thou art rightfuller than I am, thou hast done to me good, and I have done to thee evil. And thou hast well showed to me this day that God had brought me into thine hand, and thou hast not slain me. God reward thee for this, that thou hast done to me; now know I well that thou shalt reign in Israel. I pray thee to be friendly to my seed, and destroy not my house, and swear and promise me that thou take not away my name from the house of my father; and David sware and promised to Saul. And then Saul departed and went home, and David and his people went in to surer places.

Anon after this Samuel died, and was buried in his house in Rama. And all Israel bewailed him greatly. Then there was a rich man in the mount of Carmel that hight Nabal, and on a time he sheared and clipped his sheep, to whom David sent certain men, and bade them say that David greeted him well, and whereas aforetimes his shepherds kept his sheep in desert, he never was grevious to them, ne they lost not much as a sheep as long as they were with us, and that he might ask his servants for they could tell, and that he would now in their need send them what it pleased him. Nabal answered to the children of David: Who is that David? Trow ye that I shall send the meat that I have made ready for them that shear my sheep and send it to men that I know not? The men returned and told to David all that he had said. Then said David to his men: Let every man take his sword and gird him withal, and David took his sword and girt him. And David went and four hundred men followed him, and he left two hundred behind him. One of the servants of Nabal told to Abigail, Nabal's wife, how that David had sent messengers from the desert unto his lord, and how wroth and wayward he was, and also he said that those men were good enough to them when they were in desert, ne never perished beast of yours as long as they were there. They were a wall and a shield for us both day and night all the time that we kept our flocks there, wherefore consider what is to be done. They purpose to do harm to him and to his house, for he is the son of Belial in such wise that no man may speak with him. Then Abigail hied her and took two hundred loaves of bread, one hundred bottles of wine, five wethers sodden, and five measures of pottage, and one hundred bonds of grapes dried, and two hundred masses of caricares, and laid all this upon asses, and said to her servants: Go ye tofore, and I shall follow after. She told hereof nothing to her husband Nabal.

Then she took an ass and rode after, and when she came to the foot of the hill, David and his men descended; to whom she ran, and David said: I have for naught saved all the beasts of this Nabal in desert, and there perished nothing of his that pertained to him, and he hath yielded evil for good. By the living God I shall not leave as much as his alive as one man. As soon as Abigail saw David she descended from her ass, and fell down tofore David, upon her visage and worshipped him on the earth, and fell down to his feet and said: In me, said she, my lord, be this wickedness, I beseech thee that I thine handmaiden may speak to thine ears, and that thou wilt hear the words of me thy servant. I pray and require thee my lord, let not thy heart be set against this wicked man Nabal, for according to his name he is a fool, and folly is with him. I thine handmaid saw not thy children that thou sendedst. Now, therefore, my lord, for the love of God and of thy soul, suffer not thy hand to shed no blood, and I beseech God that thine enemies may be like Nabal and they that would thee harm; and I beseech thee to receive this blessing and present which I thine handmaid have brought to thee, my lord, and give it to thy men that follow thee, my lord. Take away the wickedness from me thy servant, and I beseech God to make to thee, my lord, a house of truth, for thou, my lord, shall fight the battles of our Lord God; and let no malice be found in thee, never in all the days of thy life. If ever any man arise against thee or would pursue or would hurt thee, I beseech God to keep thee. And when our Lord God hath accomplished to thee, my lord, all that he hath spoken good of thee, and hath constituted thee duke upon Israel, let this not be in thy thought, ne scruple in thy heart that thou shouldest shed blood not guilty, ne be thou not now avenged. And when our Lord God hath done well to thee, my lord, have thou remembrance on me thine handmaid, and do well to me.

And David said to Abigail: Blessed be God of Israel that sent thee this day to meet me, and blessed be thy speech, and blessed be thou that hast withdrawn me from bloodshedding, and that I avenged me not on mine enemy with mine hand, else by the living God of Israel, if thou hadst not come unto me, there should not have blyven [been left] unto Nabal to-morn in the morning one man. Then David received all that she brought and said to her: Go peaceably into thine house, lo! I have heard thy voice and I have honored thy visage; and so Abigail came unto Nabal, and David returned into the place he came from. Nabal made a great feast in his house, like the feast of a king, and the heart of Nabal was jocund; he was drunken, and Abigail his wife told to him no word till on the morn, little ne much. On the morn when Nabal had digested the wine, his wife told him all these words. And his heart was mortified within him, and he was dead like a stone, for the tenth day after, our Lord smote him and he died. And when David heard that he was dead, he said: Blessed be the good Lord that hath judged the cause of mine opprobrium from the hand of Nabal, and hath kept me his servant from harm, and our Lord hath yielded the malice of Nabal on his own head. Then David sent to Abigail for to have her to his wife, and she humbled herself and said she his handmaid was ready to wash the feet of his servants. And she arose and took with her five maidens which went afoot by her, and she rode upon an ass, and followed the messengers, and was made wife to David. And David also took another wife called Ahinoam of Jezreel, and both two were his wives.

After this Saul always sought David for to slay him. And the people called Zyphites told to Saul that David was hid in the hill of Hachilah which was on the after part of the wilderness, and Saul took with him three thousand chosen men and followed and sought David. David when he heard of the coming of Saul went into the place whereas Saul was, and when he was asleep he took one with him and went into the tent where Saul slept, and Abner with him and all his people. Then said Abishai to David: God hath put thine enemy this day in thine hands, now I shall go and smite him through with my spear, and then after that we shall have no need to dread him. And David said to Abishai: Slay him not; who may extend his hand into the anointed king of God and be innocent? And David said yet more: By the living God, but if God smite him or the days come that he shall die or perish in battle, God be merciful to me, as I shall not lay my hand on him that is anointed of our Lord. Now take the spear that standeth at his head, and the cup of water, and let us go. David took the spear and the cup and departed thence and there was not one that saw them ne awaked, for they slept all. Then when David was on the hill far from them, David cried to the people and to Abner, saying: Abner, shalt not thou answer? And Abner answered: Who art thou that cryest and wakest the king? And David said to Abner: Art thou not a man and there is none like thee in Israel? why hast thou not therefore kept thy lord the king? There is one of the people gone in to slay the king thy lord; by the living Lord it is not good that ye do, but be ye worthy to die because ye have not kept your lord anointed of our Lord. Now look and see where the king's spear is, and the cup of water that stood at his head. Saul knew the voice of David and said: Is not this thy voice, my son David? And David said: It is my voice, my lord king. For what cause dost thou, my lord, pursue me thy servant? what thing have I done and what evil have I committed with my hand? Thou seest well I might have slain thee if I would; God judge between thee and me. And Saul said: I have sinned, return, my son; I shall never hereafter do thee harm ne evil, for thy soul is precious in my sight this day. It appeareth now that I have done follily, and am ignorant in many things. Then said David: Lo! here is the spear of the king, let a child come fetch it, our Lord shall reward to every man after his justice and faith. Our Lord hath this day brought thee into my hands, and yet I would not lay mine hand on him that is anointed of our Lord. And like as thy soul is magnified this day in my sight, so be my soul magnified in the sight of God and deliver me from all anguish. Saul said then to David: Blessed be thou, my son David. And David went then his way, and Saul returned home again.

And David said in his heart: Sometime it might hap to me to fall and come into the hands of Saul, it is better I flee from him and save me in the land of the Philistines. And he went thence with six hundred men and came to Achish king of Gath and dwelled there. And when Saul understood that he was with Achish he ceased to seek him. And Achish delivered to David a town to dwell in named Ziklag.

After this the Philistines gathered and assembled much people against Israel. And Saul assembled all Israel and came upon Gilboa; and when Saul saw all the host of the Philistines, his heart dreaded and fainted sore, he cried for to have counsel of our Lord. And our Lord answered him not, ne by swevens ne by priests, ne by prophets. Then said Saul to his servants: Fetch to me a woman having a phiton, otherwise called a phitoness or a witch. And they said that there was such a woman in Endor. Saul then changed his habit and clothing, and did on other clothing, and went, and two men with him, and came to the woman by night, and made her by her craft to raise Samuel. And Samuel said to Saul: Why hast thou put me from my rest, for to arise? And Saul said: I am coarted [constrained] thereto, for the Philistines fight against me, and God is gone from me, and will not hear me, neither by prophets, ne by swevens [dreams]. And Samuel said: What askest thou of me when God is gone from thee and gone unto David? God shall do to thee as he hath said to thee by me, and shall cut thy realm from thine hand, and shall give it thy neighbor David. For thou hast not obeyed his voice, ne hast not done his commandment in Amalek; therefore thou shalt lose the battle and Israel shall be overthrown. To-morrow thou and thy children shall be with me, and our Lord shall suffer the children of Israel to fall in the hands of the Philistines. Anon then Saul fell down to the earth. The words of Samuel made him afeard and there was no strength in him, for he had eaten no bread of all that day, he was greatly troubled. Then the phitoness desired him to eat, and she slew a paschal lamb that she had, and dighted and set it tofore him, and bread. And when he had eaten he walked with his servants all that night. And on the morn the Philistines assailed Saul and them of Israel, and fought a great battle, and the men of Israel fled from the face of the Philistines, and many of them were slain in the mount of Gilboa. The Philistines smote in against Saul and his sons, and slew Jonathan and Abinadab, and Melchi-shua, sons of Saul. And all the burden of the battle was turned on Saul, and the archers followed him and wounded him sore. Then said Saul to his squire: Pluck out thy sword and slay me, that these men uncircumcised come not and, scorning, slay me; and his squire would not for he was greatly afeard. Then Saul took his sword and slew himself, which thing when his squire saw, that is that Saul was dead, he took his sword and fell on it and was dead with him. Thus was Saul dead, and his three sons and his squire, and all his men that day together. Then the children of Israel that were thereabouts, and on that other side of Jordan, seeing that the men of Israel fled, and that Saul and his three sons were dead, left their cities and fled. The Philistines came and dwelled there, and the next day the Philistines went for to rifle and pillage them that were dead, and they found Saul and his three sons lying in the hill of Gilboa. And they cut off the head of Saul, and robbed him of his armor, and sent it into the land of the Philistines all about, that it might be showed in the temple of their idols, and unto the people; and set up his arms in the temple of

Ashtaroth, and hung his body on the wall of Bethshan. And when the men that dwelt in Jabesh-Gilead saw what the Philistines had done unto Saul, all the strongest men of them arose and went all that night and took down the bodies of Saul and of his sons from the wall of Bethshan and burned them, and took the bones and buried them in the wood of Jabesh-Gilead and fasted seven days.

Thus endeth the life of Saul which was first king upon Israel, and for disobedience of God's commandment was slain, and his heirs never reigned long after.

THE HISTORY OF DAVID

Here followeth how David reigned after Saul, and governed Israel. Shortly taken out of the Bible, the most historical matters and but little touched.

After the death of Saul David returned from the journey that he had against Amalek. For whilst David had been out with Achish the king, they of Amalek had been in Ziklag and taken all that was therein prisoners, and robbed and carried away with them the two wives of David, and had set fire and burned the town. And when David came again home and saw the town burned he pursued after, and by the conveying of one of them of Amalek that was left by the way sick, for to have his life he brought David upon the host of Amalek whereas they sat and ate and drank. And David smote on them with his meiny [company] and slew down all that he found, and rescued his wives and all the good that they had taken, and took much more of them. And when he was come to Ziklag, the third day after there came one from the host of Saul, and told to David how that Israel had lost the battle, and how they were fled, and how Saul the king and Jonathan his son were slain. David said to the young man that brought these tidings: How knowest thou that Saul and Jonathan be dead? And he answered it was so by adventure that I came upon the mount of Gilboa, and Saul rested upon his spear, and the horsemen and the chariots of the Philistines approached to himward, and he looked behind him and saw me, and called me, and said to me: Who art thou? And I said I am an Amalekite, and then he said: Stand upon me and slay me, for I am full of anguish, and yet my soul is in me. And I then standing on him slew him, knowing well that he might not live after the ruin. And I took the diadem from his head, and the armylle from his arm, which I have brought hither to thee, my lord. David took and rent his vestment, and all the men that were with him, and wailed and sorrowed much the death of Saul and Jonathan and of all the men of Israel, and fasted that day till even. And David said to the young man: Of whence art thou? And he said: I am the son of an Amalekite. And David said to him: Why dreadedst thou not to put thy hand forth to slay him that is anointed of God? David called one of his men, and bade him slay him. And he smote him and slew him. And David said: Thy blood be on thy head! thine own mouth hath spoken against thee, saying: I have slain Saul which was king anointed of our Lord.

David sorrowed and bewailed much the death of Saul and of Jonathan. After this David counselled with our Lord and demanded if he should go in to one of the cities of Judah. And our Lord bade him go, and he asked whither, and our Lord said: Into Hebron. Then David took his two wives and all the men that were with him, every each with his household, and dwelled in the towns of Hebron. And thither came the men of Judah and anointed David king to reign upon the tribe of Judah. And Abner prince of the host of Saul, and other servants of Saul, took Ishbosheth the son of Saul, and led him about, and made him king over Israel, except the tribe of Judah. Ishbosheth was forty years when he began to reign, and he reigned two years. The house of Judah only followed David. After this it happed that Abner, prince of the host of Ishbosheth, with certain men, went out of the castles, and Joab with certain men of David went also out and ran by the piscine [pool] of Gibeon. One party was on that one side, and that other on the other. And Abner said to Joab: Let our young men play and skirmish together, and Joab agreed. And there rose twelve of Benjamin, of the party of Ishbosheth, and twelve of the children of David; and when they met together each took other by the head, and roof their swords into each other's sides and were all there slain. And there arose a great battle, and Abner and his fellowship were put to flight by the men of David.

And among all other there was Asahel one of the brethren of Joab and was the swiftest runner that might be, and pursued Abner, and Abner looked behind him, and bade him decline on the right side or on the left side, and take one of the young men and his harness, and come not at me. Asahel would not leave him; yet Abner said to him: Go from me and follow not me lest I be compelled to slay thee, and then I may not make my peace with Joab thy brother. Which would not hear Abner, but despised him, and Abner then turned and slew him in the same place, and anon the sun went down and they withdrew. There were slain of the children of David nineteen men and of them of Benjamin three hundred and sixty were slain, and thus there was long strife and contention between the house of David and the house of Ishbosheth. After this Abner took a concubine of Saul and held her, wherefore Ishbosheth reproved him of it and Abner was wroth greatly thereof; and came to David and made friendship with him. Joab was not there when Abner made his peace with David; but when he knew it he came to Abner with a fair semblant and spake fair to him by dissimulation, and slew him for to avenge the death of Asahel his brother. And when David heard how Joab had slain Abner he cursed him, and bewailed greatly the death of Abner, and did do bury him [caused him to be buried] honorably, and David followed the bier himself. And when Ishbosheth, the son of Saul, heard that Abner was dead, he was all abashed and all Israel sore troubled.

There were two princes of thieves with Ishbosheth named Baanah and Rechab, which came on a day in to Ishbosheth where he lay and slept, and there they slew him, and took privily his head and brought it in to David in Hebron and said: Lo, here is the head of thine enemy Ishbosheth, that sought to slay thee; this day God hath given to thee my lord vengeance of Saul and of his seed. David answered to them: By the living God that hath delivered me from all anguish, him that told me that he had slain Saul, and had thought to have had a reward of me, I did do slay, how much more ye that be so wicked to slay him that is not guilty, in his house and upon his bed? Shall I not ask his blood of your hands, and throw you out of this world? Yes, certainly. And David commanded to his servants to slay them, and so they were slain, and cut off their hands and feet, and hung them on the piscine [pool] in Hebron, and took the head of Ishbosheth and buried it in the sepulchre of Abner. And then came all the tribes of Israel to David in Hebron, saying: We be thy mouth and thy flesh, when Saul lived and was king on us and reigned, thou wert coming and going; and because God hath said thou shalt reign upon my people and be their governor, therefore we shall obey thee. And all the seniors of Israel came and did homage to David in Hebron, and anointed him king over them.

David was thirty years old when he began to reign and he reigned forty years. He reigned in Hebron upon Judah seven years and six months, and in Jerusalem he reigned thirty-three years upon all Israel and Judah. David then made him a dwelling-place in the hill of Sion in Jerusalem. And after this the Philistines made war against him, but he oft overthrew them and slew many of them, and made them tributary to him, and after brought the ark of God in Jerusalem, and set it in his house. After this yet the Philistines made war again unto him and other kings were aiding and helping them against David, whom David overcame and slew and put under.

And on a time when Joab was out with his men of war lying at a siege tofore a city, David was at home, and walked in his chamber, and as he looked out at a window he saw a fair woman wash her and bain her in her chamber, which stood against his house, and demanded of his servants who she was, and they said she was Uriah's wife. And David sent letters to Joab and bade him to send home to him Uriah; and Joab sent Uriah to David, and David demanded how the host was ruled, and after bade him go home to his house and wash his feet. And Uriah went thence, and the king sent to him his dish with meat. Uriah would not go home, but lay before the gate of the king's house with other servants of the king's. And it was told to the king that Uriah went not home, and then David said to Uriah: Thou comest from a far way, why goest thou not home? And Uriah said to David: The ark of God and Israel and Judah be in the pavilions, and my lord Joab and the servants of thee, my lord, lie on the ground, and would ye that I should go to my house? By thy health and by the health of my soul I shall not do so. Then David said to Uriah, Abide here then this night, and to-morrow I shall deliver thee. Uriah abode there that day and the next, and David made him eat tofore him and made him drunk, yet for all that he would not go home, but lay with the servants of David. Then on the morn David wrote a letter to Joab, that he should set Uriah in the weakest place of the battle and where most jeopardy was, and that he should be left there that he might be slain. And Uriah bare this letter to Joab, and it was so done as David had written, and Uriah was slain in the battle. And Joab sent word to David how they had fought, and how Uriah was slain and dead. When Uriah's wife heard that her husband was dead, she mourned and wailed him; and after the mourning David sent for her and wedded her, and she bare him a son. And this that David had committed on Uriah displeased greatly our Lord.

Then our Lord sent Nathan the prophet unto David, which, when he came, said to him: There were two men dwelling in a city, that one rich and that other poor. The rich man had sheep and oxen right many, but the poor man had but one little sheep, which he bought and nourished and grew with his children, eating of his bread and drinking of his cup, and slept in his bosom. She was to him as a daughter. And on a time when a certain pilgrim came to the rich man, he, sparing his own sheep and oxen to make a feast to the pilgrim that was come to him, took the only sheep of the poor man and made meat thereof to his guest. David was wroth and said to Nathan: By the living God, the man that hath so done is the child of death, the man that hath so done shall yield therefor four times double. Then said Nathan to David: Thou art the same man that hath done this thing. This said the Lord God of Israel: I have anointed thee king upon Israel, and kept thee from the hand of Saul, and I have given to thee an house to keep in thine household and wives in thy bosom. I have given to thee the house of Israel and the house of Judah, and if these be small things I shall add and give to thee much more and greater. Why hast thou therefore despised the word of God and hast done evil in the sight of our Lord? Thou hast slain Uriah with a sword, and his wife hast thou taken unto thy wife, and thou hast slain him with the sword of the sons of Ammon. Therefore the sword shall not go from thy house, world without end, forasmuch as thou hast despised me and hast taken Uriah's wife unto thy wife. This said our Lord: I shall raise evil against thee, and shall take thy wives in thy sight and give them to thy neighbor. Thou hast done it privily, but I shall make this to be done and open in the sight of all Israel. And then said David to Nathan: Peccavi! I have sinned against our Lord. Nathan said: Our Lord hath taken away thy sin, thou shalt not die, but forasmuch as thou hast made the enemy to blaspheme the name of God, therefore the son that is born to thee shall die by death. And Nathan returned to his house. And for this sin David made this psalm: Miserere mei deus [Have pity on me, O God!], which is a psalm of mercy, for David did great penance for these sins of adultery and also of homicide.

Therefore God took away this sin, and forgave it him, but the son that she brought forth died. And after this Bathsheba, that had been Uriah's wife, brought forth another son named Solomon, which was well-beloved of God, and after David, Solomon was king.

After this David had much war and trouble and anger, insomuch that on a time Amnon, oldest son of David, loved Thamar his sister. David knew hereof, and was right sorry for it, but he would not rebuke his son Amnon for it, for he loved him because he was his first begotten son. Absalom hated Amnon ever after, and when Absalom on a time did do shear his sheep he prayed all his brethren to come eat with him, and made them a feast like a king's feast. At which feast he did do slay his brother Amnon; and anon it was told to the King David that Absalom had slain all the king's sons. Wherefore the king was in great heaviness and sorrow, but anon after it was told him that there was no more slain but Amnon, and the other sons came home. And Absalom fled into Geshur, and was there three years, and durst not come home. And after by the moyen of Joab he was sent for, and came into Jerusalem, but yet he might not come in his father the king's presence, and dwelled there two years, and might not see the King his father. This Absalom was the fairest man that ever was, for from the sole of his foot unto his head there was not a spot; he had so much hair on his head that it grieved him to bear, wherefore it was shorn off once a year, it weighed two hundred shekels of good weight. Then when he abode so long that he might not come to his father's presence he sent for Joab to come speak with him, and he would not come. He sent again for him and he came not. Then Absalom said to his servants: Know ye Joab's field that lieth by my field? They said yea. Go ye, said he, and set fire in the barley that is therein, and burn it. And Joab's servants came and told to Joab that Absalom had set fire on his corn. Then Joab came to Absalom and said: Why hast thou set fire on my corn! And he said, I have sent twice to thee, praying thee to come to me that I might send thee to the king, and that thou shouldst say to him why I came from Geshur; it had been better for me for to have abiden there. I pray thee that I may come to his presence and see his visage, and if he remember my wickedness let him slay me. Joab went in to the King and told to him all these words. Then was Absalom called, and entered in to the king, and he fell down and worshipped the king, and the king kissed him. After this Absalom did do make for himself chariots and horsemen and fifty men for to go before him, and walked among the tribes of Israel; and greeted and saluted them, taking them by the hand, and kissed them, by which he gat to him the hearts of the people; and said to his father that he had avowed to make sacrifice to God in Hebron, and his father gave him leave. And when he was there he gathered people to him, and made himself king, and did do cry that all men should obey and wait on him as king of Israel. When David heard this he was sore abashed and was fain to flee out of Jerusalem. And Absalom came with his people and entered into Jerusalem into his father's house, and after pursued his father to depose him. And David ordained his people and battle against him, and sent Joab, prince of his host, against Absalom, and divided his host into three parts, and would have gone with them, but Joab counselled that he should not go to the battle whatsomever happed, and then David bade them to save his son Absalom.

And they went forth and fought, and Absalom with his host was overthrown and put to flight. And as Absalom fled upon his mule he came under an oak, and his hair flew about a bough of the tree and held so fast that Absalom hung by his hair, and the mule ran forth. There came one to Joab and told him how that Absalom hung by his hair on a bough of an oak, and Joab said: Why hast thou not slain him? The man said: God forbid that I should set hand on the king's son; I heard the king say: keep my son Absalom alive and slay him not. Then Joab went and took three spears, and fixed them in the heart of Absalom as he hung on the tree by his hair, and yet after this ten young men, squires of Joab, ran and slew him. Then Joab trumped and blew the retreat, and retained the people that they should not pursue the people flying. And they took the body of Absalom and cast it in a great pit, and laid on him a great stone. And when David knew that his son was slain, he made great sorrow and said: O my son Absalom, my son Absalom, who shall grant to me that I may die for thee, my son Absalom, Absalom my son! It was told to Joab that the king wept and sorrowed the death of his son Absalom, and all their victory was turned into sorrow and wailing, insomuch that the people eschewed to enter into the city. Then Joab entered in to the king and said: Thou hast this day discouraged the cheer of all thy servants because they have saved thy life, and the lives of thy sons and daughters, of thy wives and of thy concubines, thou lovest them that hate thee, and hatest them that love thee, and showest well this day that thou settest little by thy dukes and servants; and truly I know now well that if Absalom had lived and all we thy servants had been slain, thou haddest been pleased. Therefore, arise now and come forth and satisfy the people; or else I swear to thee by the good lord that there shall not one of thy servants abide with thee till to-morrow, and that shall be worse to thee than all the harms and evils that ever yet fell to thee. Then David the king arose and sat in the gate, and anon it was shown to all the people that the king sat in the gate. And then all the people came in tofore the king, and they of Israel that had beerv with Absalom fled into their tabernacles, and after came again unto David when they knew that Absalom was dead.

And after, one Sheba, a cursed man, rebelled and gathered people against David. Against whom Joab with the host of David pursued, and drove him unto a city which he besieged, and by the means of a woman of the same city Sheba's head was smitten off and delivered to Joab over the wall, and so the city was saved, and Joab pleased. After this David called Joab, and bade him number the people of Israel, and so Joab walked through all the tribes of Israel, from Dan to Beersheba, and over Jordan and all the country, and there were founden in Israel eight hundred thousand strong men that were able to fight and to draw sword, and of the tribe of Judah fifty thousand fighting men. And after that the people was numbered, the heart of David was smitten by our Lord and was heavy, and said: I have sinned greatly in this deed, but I pray the Lord to take away the wickedness of thy servant, for I have done follily. David rose on the morn early, and the word of our Lord came to Gad the prophet saying: that he should go to David and bid him choose one of three things that he should say to him. When Gad came to David he said that he should choose whether he would have seven years hunger in his land, or three months he should flee his adversaries and enemies, or to have three days' pestilence. Of these three God biddeth thee choose which thou wilt; now advise thee and conclude what I shall answer to our Lord. David said to Gad: I am constrained to a great thing, but it is better for me to put me in the hands of our Lord, for his mercy is much more than in men, and so he chose pestilence.

Then our Lord sent pestilence the time constitute, and there died of the people from Dan to Beersheba seventy thousand men. And when the angel extended his hand upon Jerusalem for to destroy it, our Lord was merciful upon the affliction, and said to the angel so smiting: It sufficeth now, withdraw thy hand. David said to our Lord when he saw the angel smiting the people: I am he that have sinned and done wickedly, what have these sheep done? I beseech thee that thy hand turn upon me and upon the house of my father. Then came Gad to David and bade him make an altar in the same place where he saw the angel; and he bought the place, and made the altar, and offered sacrifices unto our Lord, and our Lord was merciful, and the plague ceased in Israel.

David was old and feeble and saw that his death approached, and ordained that his son Solomon should reign and be king after him. Howbeit that Adonijah his son took on him to be king during David's life. For which cause Bathsheba and Nathan came to David, and tofore them he said that

Solomon should be king, and ordained that he should be set on his mule by his prophets Nathan, Zadok the priest and Benaiah, and brought in to Sion. And there Zadok the priest and Nathan the prophet anointed him king upon Israel and blew in a trump and said: Live the King Solomon. And from thence they brought him into Jerusalem and set him upon his father's seat in his father's throne, and David worshipped him in his bed, and said: Blessed be the Lord God of Israel that hath suffered me to see my son in my throne and seat And then Adonijah and all they that were with him were afeared, and dreading Solomon ran away, and so ceased Adonijah. The days of David approached fast that he should die, and did do call Solomon before him, and there he commanded him to keep the commandments of our Lord and walk in his ways, and to observe his ceremonies, his precepts and his judgments, as it is written in the law of Moses, and said: Our Lord confirm thee in thy reign, and send to thee wisdom to rule it well. And when David had thus counselled and commanded him to do justice and keep God's law, he blessed him and died, and was buried with his fathers. This David was an holy man and made the holy psalter, which is an holy book and is contained therein the old law and the new law. He was a great prophet, for he prophesied the coming of Christ, his nativity, his passion, and resurrection, and also his ascension, and was great with God, yet God would not suffer him to build a temple for him, for he had shed man's blood. But God said to him, his son that should reign after him should be a man peaceable, and he should build the temple to God. And when David had reigned forty years king of Jerusalem, over Judah and Israel, he died in good mind, and was buried with his fathers in the city of David.

THE SONG OF DAVID

He sang of God, the mighty source
Of all things, the stupendous force
  On which all strength depends;
From whose right arm, beneath whose eyes,
All period, power, and enterprise
  Commences, reigns, and ends.

The world, the clustering spheres he made,
The glorious light, the soothing shade,
  Dale, champaign, grove, and hill:
The multitudinous abyss,
Where secrecy remains in bliss,
  And wisdom hides her skill.

Tell them, I AM, Jehovah said
To Moses: while Earth heard in dread,
  And, smitten to the heart,
At once, above, beneath, around,
All Nature, without voice or sound,
  Replied, "O Lord, THOU ART."

—C. Smart

THE STORY OF A CUP OF WATER

BY THEODORE T. MUNGER

[From "Lamps and Paths," by courtesy of Houghton, Mifflin & Co.]

Be noble! and the nobleness that lies
In other men, sleeping, but never dead,
Will rise in majesty to meet thine own.

> —James Russell Lowell: *Sonnet IV*

Restore to God his due in tithe and time:
A tithe purloined cankers the whole estate.
Sundays observe: think, when the bells do chime,
'Tis angels' music; therefore come not late.
God there deals blessings. If a king did so,
Who would not haste, nay give, to see the show?

> —George Herbert

O Lord, that lends me life,
Lend me a heart replete with thankfulness!

> —*King Henry VI.*, Part II.; i. I

"And David longed, and said, Oh that one would give me drink of the water of the well of Bethlehem, that is at the gate! And the three brake through the host of the Philistines, and drew water out of the well of Bethlehem, that was by the gate, and took it and brought it to David: but David would not drink of it, but poured it out to the Lord, and said, My God forbid it me, that I should do this thing: shall I drink the blood of these men that have put their lives in jeopardy? for with the jeopardy of their lives they brought it. Therefore he would not drink it." —I Chronicles xi. 17-19

If any of my young friends ask why I have read this long-time-ago Bible-story as a text for a sermon to-day, I will not only answer, but thank them for the question; for nothing helps a speaker at the start so much as a straight, intelligent question. I have read this story from the Chronicles, because I want to connect this beautiful occasion with some beautiful thing in the Bible; for beautiful things go together.

My main object and desire in this service is to have everything beautiful and pure and high. For I know how well you will remember this day in after years; I know how every feature and incident is imprinting itself upon your minds; I know how, twenty and forty years hence, when we older ones will be dead and gone, and you will be scattered far and wide, some in the great cities—New York, Chicago, St. Louis—some in California, and some further off still—I know how, on quiet June Sundays years hence, you will recall this Festival of Flowers in North Adams. You may be in some of the great cities, or on the broad prairies, or among the park-like forests of the Sierra, or in Puget Sound, but you will never forget this day. These familiar walls; this pulpit and font and chancel decked with flowers; this service, made *for* you and in part *by* you—you will never forget it. And because you will always remember it, I want to have it throughout just as beautiful, just as pure and inspiring, as possible. The flowers will do their part; they never fail to speak sweet, pure words to us. Your Superintendent always does his part well, and I hope you will all thank him in your hearts, if not in words, for his faithful and laborious interest in you. And your teachers and others who have brought together this wealth of beauty, this glory of color and perfume, this tribute of sweetness from mountain-side and field and garden—they have done well; and you will remember it all years hence, and when far away, and perhaps some tears will start for "the days that are no more."

But this occasion would not be complete to my mind if there were not linked with it some noble and inspiring truth. I want to make all these flowers and this music the setting of a truth, like a diamond set round with emeralds, or an opal with pearls. *You* have brought the pearls and the emeralds; *I* must bring a diamond or an opal to set in the midst of them. I am very sure that I have one in this old story—a diamond very brilliant if we brush away the old Hebrew dust, and cut away the sides and let in a little more light upon it. I am not sure, however, but I ought to call it a pearl rather than a diamond; for there is a chaste and gentle modesty about it that reminds one of the soft lustre of a pearl rather than of the flashing splendor of a diamond. St. John, in naming the precious stones that make the foundation of the heavenly city, omits the diamond—and for some good reason, I suspect—while the twelve gates were all pearls. Now, I think David stood very near one of those gates of pearl at the time of this story. To my mind, it is nearly the most beautiful in all this Book; and I know you will listen while I tell it more fully.

I have this impression of David—that if you had seen him when he was young, you would have thought him the most glorious human being you had ever looked on. He was one of those persons who fascinate all who come near them. He bound everybody to him in a wonderful way. They not only *liked* him, but they became absorbed in him, and were ready to obey him, and serve him, and to give themselves up to him in every way possible. I am not at all surprised that Saul's son and daughter and Saul himself fell in love with, and could hardly live without, him. It was so all along; and even after he became an old man everybody was fascinated by him—even his old uncles—and stood ready to do his bidding and consult his wishes.

It was somewhat so with Richard Coeur de Lion and Napoleon and Mary Stuart and Alexander and Julius Cæsar; but the personal fascination of none of these persons was so great as that of David. In some respects he was no greater than some of these; but he had a broader and more lovable nature than any of them, for he had what not one of them had in anything like the same degree—a great and noble generosity. David deserved all the love that was lavished upon him, because—let men love him ever so much—he loved more in return.

There was not apparently, at this early time of his life, one grain of selfishness about him. You know that the word *chivalry* was not used till about a thousand years back, while David lived almost three times as long ago; but he was one of the most *chivalrous* men that ever lived. By chivalry I mean a union of honor, purity, religion, nobleness, bravery, and devotion to a cause or person. David excited this chivalric devotion in others because he had so much of it in himself. And here I will stop a moment just to say that if you want to awaken any feeling in another toward yourself, you must first have it in yourself. I think there is a very general notion that in order to awaken admiration and love and regard in others one must have a fine appearance. There is a great deal of misplaced faith in fine clothes and bright eyes and clear complexions and pretty features; but I have yet to learn that these ever win genuine love and admiration. And so far as I have observed, a true sentiment only grows out of a corresponding sentiment; feeling comes from feeling; in short, others come at last to feel toward us just about as we feel toward them. And I never knew a person, young or old, to show a kind, generous, hearty disposition to others who was not surrounded by friends. And I have seen—I know not how many—selfish and unobliging and unsympathetic persons go friendless all their days in spite of wealth and fine appearance. Now, put this away in your memory to think of hereafter.

It was David's great-heartedness that bound others to him. At the time of this story he was a sort of outlaw, driven without any good reason from the court of Saul. But he was a man of too much spirit to allow himself to be tamely killed, and he loved Saul and his family too well to actually make war upon him, and he was too good a patriot to give trouble to his country—a pretty hard place he had to fill, I can assure you. But he was equal to it, and simply bided his time, drawing off into the wild and rocky regions where he could hide and also protect himself. But he was not a man whom people would leave alone. The magnetic power that was in him drew kindred spirits, and some that were not kindred who found it pleasanter to follow a chief in the wilds than to live in the dull quiet of their homes. But the greater part of them were brave, generous, devoted souls, who had come to the conclusion that to live with David and fight his battles and share his fortunes was more enjoyable than to plod along under Saul and his petty tyrannies. There were, in particular, eleven men of the tribe of Gad—mountaineers—fierce as lions and swift as roes, terrible men in battle, and full of devotion to David. In this way he got together quite a little army, which he used to defend the borders from the Philistines, who were a thieving set, and also to defend himself in case Saul troubled him. It was not exactly the best sort of a life for a man to live; and had not David been a person of very high principles, his followers would have been a band of robbers living on the country. But David prevented that, and made them as useful as was possible. His headquarters were at the cave of Adullam, or what is now called Engedi. While here, the Philistines came on a foraging expedition as far as Bethlehem, and with so large a force that David and his few followers were shut up in their fortress—for how long we do not know—probably for some days. It was very dull and wearisome business, imprisoned in a rocky defile and unable to do anything, while the Philistines were stealing the harvests that grew on the very spot where he had spent his boyhood.

It was then that what has always seemed to me a very touching and beautiful trait of David's character showed itself, and that is—*a feeling of homesickness*. Now, there is very little respect to be had for a person who is not capable of homesickness. To give up to it may be weak, but to be incapable of it is a bad sign. But in David it took a very poetic form. Close by was the home where he was born. There, in Bethlehem, he had passed the dreamy years of his childhood and youth amid the love of his parents and brothers, whom he now had with him; there he fed his sheep and sang to his harp; and there, morning and evening, he gathered with others about the well—the meeting-place of his companions—loved with all the passionate energy of his nature, and still loved in spite of the troublous times that had come upon him. As David broods over these memories, he longs with a yearning, homesick feeling for Bethlehem and its well. And, like a poet as he was, he conceives that if he could but drink of its water, it would relieve this feverish unrest and longing for the past. It was a very natural feeling. You are too young to know what it means; but we who are older think of these little things in a strange, yearning way. It is the little things of childhood that we long for—to lie under the roof on which we heard the rain patter years and years ago; to gather fruit in the old orchard; to fish in the same streams; to sit on the same rock, or under the same elm or maple, and see the sun go down behind the same old hills; to drink from the same spring that refreshed us in summer days that will not come again—*you* are too young for this, but we who are older know well how David felt. He was not a man to hide his feelings, and so he uttered his longing for the water of the well by the gate of Bethlehem. His words are overheard; and three of these terrible followers of his—fierce as lions and fleet as deer—took their swords and fought their way through the Philistines, slaying we know not how many, and brought back some of the water. It was enough for *them* that David wanted it.

Now, some people would say that it was very foolish and sentimental of David to be indulging in such a whim, and still more foolish in these men to gratify it at the risk of their lives; but I think there is a better way of looking at it. If David had *required* them to procure the water at the risk of their lives, it would have been very wrong; but the whole thing was unknown to him till the water was brought. I prefer to regard it as an act of splendid heroism, prompted by chivalric devotion, and I will not stop to consider whether or not it was sensible and prudent. And I want to say to you that whenever you see or hear of an action that has these qualities of heroism and generosity and devotion, it is well to admire and praise it, whether it will bear the test of cold reason or not. I hope your hearts will never get to be so dry and hard that they will not beat responsive to brave and noble deeds, even if they are not exactly prudent.

But David took even a higher view of this brave and tender act of his lion-faced, deer-footed followers. It awoke his religious feelings; for our sense of what is noble and generous and brave lies very close to our religious sensibilities. The whole event passes, in David's mind, into the field of religion; and so what does he do? Drink the water, and praise his three mighty warriors, and bid them never again run such risks to gratify his chance wishes? No. David looks a great deal further into the matter than this. The act seemed to him to have a religious character; its devotion was so complete and unselfish that it became sacred. He felt what I have just said—that a brave and devoted act that incurs danger is almost if not quite a religious act. And so he treats it in a religious way. He is anxious to separate it from himself, although done for him, and get it into a service done for God; and he may have thought that he had himself been a little selfish. To his mind it would have been a mean and low repayment to these men to drink their water with loud praises of their valor. They had done a Godlike deed, and so he will transfer it to God, and make it an act as between them and God. I do not know that those lion-faced, deer-footed warriors understood or appreciated his treatment of their act; but David himself very well knew what he was about, and you can see that he acted in a very high and true way. He will not drink the water, but pours it out unto the Lord, and lets it sink into the ground unused, and, because unused, a sort of sacrifice and offering to God. Water got with such valor and risk was not for man, but for God. Much less was it right to use it to gratify a dreamy whim that had in it perhaps just a touch of selfishness. The bravery and danger had made the water sacred, and so he will make a sacred use of it.

If any one thinks that David was carried away by sentimentality, or that he was overscrupulous, one has only to recall how, when *actually* in want, he took the consecrated bread from the Tabernacle at Nob, and ate it and gave it to his followers. His strong common-sense told him that even consecrated bread was not too good for hungry men; but that same fine common-sense told him that water procured at the risk of life, when not actually wanted, had become sacred, and had better be turned into a sort of prayer and offering to God than wantonly drunk.

And now, having the story well in mind, I will close by drawing out from it one or two lessons that seem to me very practical.

Suppose we were to ask, Who acted in the noblest way—the three strong men who got the water, or David, who made a sacrifice or libation of it? It does not take us long to answer. The real greatness of the whole affair was with the three men, though David put a beautiful meaning upon it, and exalted it to its true place. Their act was very brave and lofty; but David crowned it with its highest grace by carrying it on into religion—that is, by setting it before God.

I see a great many people who are living worthy lives, doing a great many kind acts and rendering beautiful services, but do not take God into their thoughts, nor render their services as unto Him. I think everybody must see that this act of these lion-faced men was more complete when David took it before God than as rendered for himself. Why, it might take long to tell; but, briefly, it was because the nameless grace of religion has been added to it, and because it was connected with that great, dear Name that hallows everything brought under it.

Many of you have brought here offerings of flowers, sweet and fit for this day and place and purpose. Some may have brought them simply with the thought of helping out the occasion, or to please your teacher, or because it is beautiful in itself to heap up beauty in this large way; but if, as you worked here yesterday, or brought your flowers to-day, your thoughts silently rose to God, saying, "These are for *Thy* altars—this glory of tint and perfume is not for us, but for *Thee*"—then, I think, every poet, every person of fine feeling, every true thinker, would say that the latter is more beautiful than the former. I hate to see a life that does not take hold of God; I hate to see fine acts and brave lives and noble dispositions and generous emotions that do not reach up into a sense of God; I hate to see persons—and I see a great many such nowadays—striving after beautiful lives and true sentiments and large thoughts without ever a word of prayer, or thought of God, or anything to show they love and venerate Christ. I hate to see it, both because they might rise so much higher and because at last it fails; for God must enter into every thought and sentiment and purpose in order to make it genuine, and truly beautiful, and altogether right. That God may be in your thoughts; that you may learn to confess Him in all your ways, to serve and fear and know and love him—this is the wish with which I greet you to-day, and the prayer that I offer in your behalf.

I found, the other day, some lines by Faber—a Catholic poet—so beautifully giving this last thought of our sermon that I will read them to you:

"Oh God! who wert my childhood's love,
  My boyhood's pure delight,
A presence felt the livelong day,
  A welcome fear at night,

"I know not what I thought of Thee;
  What picture I had made
Of that Eternal Majesty
  To whom my childhood prayed.

"With age Thou grewest more divine,
  More glorious than before;
I feared Thee with a deeper fear,
  Because I loved Thee more.

"Thou broadenest out with every year
  Each breath of life to meet.
I scarce can think Thou art the same,
  Thou art so much more sweet.

"Father! what hast Thou grown to now?
  A joy all joys above,
Something more sacred than a fear,
  More tender than a love.

"With gentle swiftness lead me on,
  Dear God! to see Thy face;
And meanwhile in my narrow heart,
  Oh, make Thyself more space."

THE HISTORY OF SOLOMON

After David, reigned Solomon his son, which was in the beginning a good man and walked in the ways and laws of God. And all the kings about him made peace with him and was king confirmed, obeyed and peaceable in his possession, and according to his father's commandment did justice. First on Joab that had been prince of his father's host, because he slew two good men by treason and guile, that was Abner the son of Ner, and Amasa the son of Ithra. And Joab was afeard and dreaded Solomon, and fled into the Tabernacle of our Lord and held the end of the altar. And Solomon sent Benaiah and slew him there, and after buried him in his house in desert. And after this on a night as he lay in his bed after he had sacrificed to our Lord in Gibeon, our Lord appeared to him in his sleep saying to him: Ask and demand what thou wilt that I may give to thee. And Solomon said: Lord, thou hast done to my father great mercy; because he walked in thy ways in truth, justice, and a rightful heart, thou hast always kept for him thy great mercy, and hast given to him a son sitting upon this throne as it is this day. And now Lord thou hast made me thy servant to reign for my father David. I am a little child and know not my going out and entering in, and I thy servant am set in the middle of the people that thou hast chosen which be infinite, and may not be numbered for multitude; therefore Lord give to me thy servant a heart docile and taught in wisdom that may judge thy people, and discern between good and evil. Who may judge this people, thy people that be so many? This request and demand pleased much unto God that Solomon had asked such a thing. And God said to Solomon: Because thou hast required and asked this and hast not asked long life, ne riches, ne the souls of thine enemies, but hast asked sapience and wisdom to discern doom and judgment, I have given to thee after thy desire and request, and I have given to thee a wise heart and understanding insomuch that there was never none such tofore, ne never after shall be. And also those things that thou hast not asked I have given also to thee, that is to say riches and glory, that no man shall be like to thee among all the kings that shall be after thy days. If thou walk in my ways and keep my precepts and observe my commandments as thy father walked, I shall make thy days long. After this Solomon awoke and came to Jerusalem, and stood tofore the Ark of our Lord and offered sacrifices and victims unto our Lord, and made a great feast unto all his servants and household. Then came tofore him two women, of which that one said: I beseech thee my lord hear me; this woman and I dwelled together in one house, and I was delivered of a child in my cubicle [sleeping room], and the third day after she bare a child, and was also delivered, and we were together and none other in the house but we twain, and it was so that this woman's son was dead in the night; for she sleeping, overlaid and oppressed him, and she arose in the darkest of the night privily, and took my son from the side of me thy servant and laid him by her, and her son that was dead she laid by me. When I arose in the morning for to give milk to my son it appeared dead, whom I took beholding him diligently in the clear light, understood well anon that it was not my son that I had borne. The other woman answered and said: It was not so as thou sayest, but my son liveth and thine is dead. And contrary that other said: Thou liest: my son liveth and thine is dead. Thus in this wise they strove tofore the king. Then the king said: This woman saith my son liveth and thine is dead, and this answereth Nay, but thy son is dead, and mine liveth. Then the king said: Bring to me here a sword. When they had brought forth a sword the king said: Divide ye, said he, the living child in two parts, and give that one half to that one, and that other half to that other. Then said the woman that was mother of the living child to the king, for all her members and bowels were moved upon her son: I beseech and pray thee, my lord, give to her the child alive, and slay him not, and contrary said that other woman: Let it not be given to me ne to thee, but let it be divided. The king then answered and said: Give the living child to this woman, and let it not be slain; this is verily the mother. All Israel heard how wisely the king had given this sentence and dreaded him, seeing that the wisdom of God was in him in deeming of rightful dooms.

After this Solomon sent his messengers to divers kings for cedar trees and for workmen, for to make and build a temple unto our Lord. Solomon was rich and glorious, and all the realms from the river of the ends of the Philistines unto the end of Egypt were accorded with him, and offered to him gifts and to serve him all the days of his life. Solomon had daily for the meat of his household thirty measures, named chores, of corn, and sixty of meal, ten fat oxen, and twenty oxen of pasture and an hundred wethers, without venison that was taken, as harts, goats, bubals, and other flying fowls and birds. He obtained all the region that was from Tiphsa unto Azza, and had peace with all the kings of all the realms that were in every part round about him. In that time Israel and Judah dwelled without fear and dread, every each under his vine and fig tree from Dan unto Beersheba.

Solomon had forty thousand racks for the horses of his carts, chariots and cars, and twelve thousand for horses to ride on, by which prefects brought necessary things for the table of King Solomon, with great diligence in their time. God gave to Solomon much wisdom and prudence in his heart, like to the gravel that is in the sea-side, and the sapience and wisdom of Solomon passed and went tofore the sapience of all them of the Orient and of Egypt, and he was the wisest of all men, and so he was named. He spake three thousand parables, and five thousand songs, and disputed upon all manner trees and virtue of them, from the cedar that is in Lebanon unto the hissop that groweth on the wall, and discerned the properties of beasts, fowls, reptiles and fishes, and there came people from all regions of the world for to hear the wisdom of Solomon,

And Solomon sent letters to Hiram, king of Tyre, for to have his men to cut cedar trees with his servants, and he would yield to them their hire and meed, and let him wit how that he would build and edify a temple to our Lord. And Hiram sent to him that he should have all that he desired, and sent to him cedar trees and other wood. And Solomon sent to him corn in great number, and Solomon and Hiram confederated them together in love and friendship. Solomon chose out workmen of all Israel the number of thirty thousand men of whom he sent to Lebanon ten thousand every month, and when ten thousand went the others came home, and so two months were they at home, and Adonias was overseer and commander on them. Solomon had seventy thousand men that did nothing but bear stone and mortar and other things to the edifying of the temple, and were bearers of burdens only, and he had eighty thousand of hewers of stone and masons in the mountain, without the prefects and masters, which were three thousand three hundred that did nothing but command and oversee them that wrought. Solomon commanded the workmen to make square stones, great and precious, for to lay in the foundament, which the masons of Israel and masons of Hiram hewed, and the carpenters made ready the timber.

Then began Solomon the temple to our Lord, in the fourth year of his reign he began to build the temple. The house that he builded had seventy cubits in length, and twenty cubits in breadth, and thirty in height, and the porch tofore the temple was twenty cubits long after the measure of the breadth of the temple, and had ten cubits of breadth tofore the face of the temple, and for to write the curiosity and work of the temple, and the necessaries, the tables and cost that was done in gold, silver and latten, it passeth my cunning to express and English them. Ye that be clerks may see it in the Second Book of Kings and the Second Book of Paralipomenon. It is wonder to hear the costs and expenses that was made in that temple, but I pass over. It was on making seven years, and his palace was thirteen years ere it was finished. He made in the temple an altar of pure gold, and a table to set on the loaves of proposition of gold, five candlesticks of gold on the right side and five on the left side, and many other things, and took all the vessels of gold and silver that his father David had sanctified and hallowed, and brought them into the treasury of the house of our Lord. After this he assembled all the noblest and greatest of birth of them of Israel, with the princes of the tribes and dukes of the families, for to bring the Ark of God from the city of David, Sion, into the temple. And the priests and Levites took the Ark and bare it and all the vessels of the sanctuary that were in the tabernacle. King Solomon, with all the multitude of the children that were there, went tofore the Ark and offered sheep and oxen without estimation and number.

And the priests set the Ark in the house of our Lord in the oracle of the temple, in sancta sanctorum, under the wings of cherubim. In the ark was nothing but the two tables of Moses of stone which Moses had put in. And then Solomon blessed our Lord tofore all the people, and thanked him that he had suffered him to make an house unto his name, and besought our Lord that he whosomever prayed our Lord for any petition in that temple, that he of his mercy would hear him and be merciful to him. And our Lord appeared to him when the edifice was accomplished perfectly, and said to Solomon: I have heard thy prayer and thine oration that thou hast prayed tofore me. I have sanctified and hallowed this house that thou hast edified for to put my name therein for evermore, and my eyes and heart shall be thereon always. And if thou walk before me like as thy father walked in the simplicity of heart and in equity, and wilt do all that I have commanded thee, and keep my judgments and laws, I shall set the throne of thy reign upon Israel evermore, like as I have said to thy father David, saying: There shall not be taken away a man of thy generation from the reign and seat of Israel. If ye avert and turn from me, ye and your sons, not following ne keeping my commandments and ceremonies that I have showed tofore you, but go and worship strange gods, and honor them, I shall cast away Israel from the face of the earth that I have given to them, and the temple that I have hallowed to my name, I shall cast it away from my sight. And it shall be a fable and proverb, and thy house an example shall be to all people; every man that shall go thereby shall be abashed and astonied, and shall say: Why hath God done thus to this land and to thy house? And they shall answer: For they have forsaken their Lord God that brought them out of the land of Egypt, and have followed strange gods, and them adored and worshipped, and therefore God hath brought on them all this evil: here may every man take ensample how perilous and dreadful it is to break the commandment of God.

Twenty years after that Solomon had edified the temple of God and his house, and finished it perfectly, Hiram the king of Tyre went for to see towns that Solomon had given to him, and they pleased him not. Hiram had sent to King Solomon an hundred and twenty besants of gold, which he had spent on the temple and his house, and on the wall of Jerusalem and other towns and places that he had made. Solomon was rich and glorious that the fame ran, of his sapience and wisdom and of his building and dispense in his house, through the world, insomuch that the queen of Sheba came from far countries to see him and to tempt him in demands and questions. And she came into Jerusalem with much people and riches, with camels charged with aromatics and gold infinite. And she came and spake to King Solomon all that ever she had in her heart. And Solomon taught her in all that ever she purposed tofore him. She could say nothing but that the king answered to her, there was nothing hid from him. The queen of Sheba then seeing all the wisdom of Solomon, the house that he had builded, and the meat and service of his table, the habitacles of his servants, the order of the ministers, their clothing and array, his butlers and officers, and the sacrifices that he offered in the house of our Lord, when she saw all these things, she had no spirit to answer, but she said to King Solomon: The word is true that I heard in my land, of thy words and thy wisdom, and I believed not them that told it to me, unto the time that I myself came and have seen it with mine eyes, and I have now well seen and proved that the half was not told to me. Thy sapience is more, and thy works also, than the tidings that I heard. Blessed be thy servants, and blessed be these that stand always tofore thee and hear thy sapience and wisdom, and thy Lord God be blessed whom thou hast pleased, and hath set thee upon the throne of Israel, for so much as God of Israel loveth thee and hath ordained thee a king for to do righteousness and justice. She gave then to the king an hundred and twenty besants of gold, many aromatics, and gems precious. There were never seen tofore so many aromatics ne so sweet odors smelling as the queen of Sheba gave to King Solomon.

King Solomon gave to the queen of Sheba all that ever she desired and demanded of him, and after returned into her country and land. The weight of pure gold that was offered every year to Solomon was six hundred and sixty-six talents of gold, except that that the merchants offered, and all they that sold, and all the kings of Arabia and dukes of that land. Solomon made two hundred shields of the purest gold and set them in the house of Lebanon; he made him also a throne of ivory which was great and was clad with gold, which had six grees or steps, which was richly wrought with two lions of gold holding the seat above, and twelve small lions standing upon the steps, on every each twain, here and there. There was never such a work in no realm. And all the vessels that King Solomon drank of were of gold, and the ceiling of the house of Lebanon in which his shields of gold were in was of the most pure gold. Silver was of no price in the days of King Solomon, for the navy of the king, with the navy of Hiram, went in three years once into Tarsis and brought them thence gold and silver, teeth of elephants and great riches. The King Solomon was magnified above all the kings of the world in riches and wisdom, and all the world desired to see the cheer and visage of Solomon, and to hear his wisdom that God had given to him. Every man brought to him gifts, vessels of gold and silver, clothes and armor for war, aromatics, horses and mules every year. Solomon gathered together chariots and horsemen; he had a thousand four hundred chariots and cars, and twelve thousand horsemen, and were lodged in small cities and towns about Jerusalem by the king. There was as great abundance and plenty of gold and silver in those days in Jerusalem as stones or sycamores that grow in the field, and horses were brought to him from Egypt and Chao. What shall I all day write of the riches, glory and magnificence of King Solomon? It was so great that it cannot be expressed, for there was never none like to him, ne never shall none come after him like unto him. He made the book of the parables containing thirty-one chapters, the book of the Canticles, the book of Ecclesiastes, containing twelve chapters, and the book of Sapience containing nineteen chapters. This King Solomon loved overmuch women, and specially strange women of other sects; as King Pharaoh's daughters and many other of the gentiles. He had seven hundred wives which were as queens, and three hundred concubines, and these women turned his heart. For when he was old he so doted and loved them that they made him honor their strange gods, and worshipped Ashtareth, Chemosh and Moloch, idols of Zidonia, of Moabites, and Ammonites, and made to them Tabernacles for to please his wives and concubines, wherefore God was wroth with him, and said to him: Because thou hast not observed my precepts and my commandments that I commanded thee, I shall cut thy kingdom and divide it and give it to thy servant but not in thy day, I shall not do it for love that I had to David thy father; but from the hand of thy son I shall cut it but not all,

I shall reserve to him one tribe for David's love, and Jerusalem that I have chosen. And after this divers kings became adversaries to Solomon, and was never in peace after.

It is said, but I find it not in the Bible, that Solomon repented him much of this sin of idolatry and did much penance therefor, for he let him be drawn through Jerusalem and beat himself with rods and scourges, that the blood flowed in the sight of all the people. He reigned upon all Israel in Jerusalem forty years, and died and was buried with his fathers in the city of David, and Rehoboam his son reigned after him.

THE HISTORY OF REHOBOAM

After Solomon, reigned his son Rehoboam. He came to Sichem and thither came all the people for to ordain him king. Jeroboam and all the multitude of Israel spake to Rehoboam, and said: Thy father set on us an hard yoke and great impositions, now thou hast not so much need, therefore less it and minish it, and ease us of the great and hard burden and we shall serve thee. Rehoboam answered and said: Go ye and come again the third day and ye shall have an answer. When the people was departed, Rehoboam made a counsel of the seniors and old men that had assisted his father Solomon whiles he lived, and said to them: What say ye? and counsel me that I may answer to the people, which said to Rohoboam: If thou wilt obey and agree to this people, and agree to their petition, and speak fair and friendly to them, they shall serve thee always. But Rehoboam forsook the counsel of the old men, and called the young men that were of his age, and asked of them counsel. And the young men that had been nourished with him bade him say to the people in this wise: Is not my finger greater than the back of my father? If my father hath laid on you a heavy burden, I shall add and put more to your burden; my father beat you with scourges, and I shall beat you with scorpions. The third day after, Jeroboam and all the people came to Rehoboam to have their answer, and Rehoboam left the counsel of the old men, and said to them like as the young men had counselled him. And anon the people of Israel forsook Rehoboam, and of twelve tribes, there abode with him no more but the tribe of Judah and Benjamin. And the other ten tribes departed and made Jeroboam their king, and never returned unto the house of David after unto this day. And thus for sin of Solomon, and because Rehoboam would not do after the counsel of the old men, but was counselled by young men, the ten tribes of Israel forsook him, and departed from Jerusalem, and served Jeroboam, and ordained him king upon Israel. Anon after this, Jeroboam fell to idolatry and great division was ever after between the kings of Judah and the kings of Israel. And so reigned divers kings each after other in Jerusalem after Rehoboam, and in Israel after Jeroboam. And here I leave all the history and make an end of the book of Kings for this time, etc. For ye that list to know how every king reigned after other, ye may find it in the first chapter of Saint Matthew which is read on Christmas day in the morning before Te Deum, which is the genealogy of our Lady.

A LITTLE MAID

BY THEODORE T. MUNGER

[From "Lamps and Paths," by courtesy of Houghton, Mifflin & Co.]

In old days we read of angels who came and took men by the hand, and led them away from the city of Destruction. We see no white-robed angels now; yet men are led away from threatening destruction: a hand is put into theirs, and they are gently guided toward a bright and calm land, so that they look no more backward; and the hand may be that of a little child.— GEORGE ELIOT

As aromatic plants bestow
No spicy fragrance while they grow,
But crushed, or trodden to the ground,
Diffuse their balmy sweets around.

—GOLDSMITH: *The Captivity*

"*Now Naaman, captain of the host of the king of Syria, was a great man with his master, and honorable, because by him the Lord had given deliverance unto Syria: he was also a mighty man in valor, but he was a leper. And the Syrians had gone out by companies, and had brought away captive out of the land of Israel a little maid; and she waited on Naaman's wife. And she said unto her mistress. Would God my lord were with the prophet that is in Samaria! for he would recover him of his leprosy.*"—2 KINGS v. 1-3

I think upon the whole that old stories are better than new ones; I mean, stories of old times. It is perhaps because only the very best are remembered while the poorer ones are forgotten, so that those which have come down to us through past ages are the choice ones selected from a great number that pleased people for a while, but not well nor long enough to get fixed in their minds.

Of all old stories, I hardly know a better one than this of Naaman and the little maid from Samaria. It is full of human nature; that is, it shows that people acted and felt three thousand years ago just as they do now: they were kind and sympathetic, and proud and grateful and covetous and deceitful, just as people are nowadays. And the story has a fine romantic setting; that is, its incidents take hold of our fancy and charm us;—a little girl stolen in war and carried to a foreign country and put into the house of a great general, who falls very ill and is cured in a wonderful way, and so on. I think it will please us all to hear it over again.

Syria and Israel stood to each other very much like Germany and Switzerland. One was a great, rich country, with fine rivers like the Rhine and Danube, and a capital city so beautiful that it was called "the eye of the East"; while Israel was a small country, full of mountains, and with only one small river that ran nearly dry in summer. To tell the truth, Syria looked down on Israel, and—what is worse—often made war on it. In those days war was even more cruel and senseless than it is now; for it was not confined to the armies that fought and captured one another, but extended to women and children, who were often seized, carried away from their homes into the country of the enemy, and made slaves. It is bad and senseless enough for men to stand up and stab one another as they used to in old times, or shoot one another as they do now; but to carry a mother away from her children, or take a little girl away from her home and playmates and make a slave of her, is something worse. But it was often done in those ancient days, as you will learn when you read history, and the story of the siege of Troy, which sprang out of stealing a beautiful woman.

There were frequent wars between Syria and Israel. Israel had once conquered Syria, and Syria had broken away, and so it went on back and forth, year after year. When our story begins, Naaman, a great general, had delivered his country from Israel, and brought home with him a little Hebrew girl, who was so beautiful and sweet in her ways that he gave her to his wife on his return from the war. A strange present, you say, but it proved a very valuable one. It seems to us very cruel. One would think that if Naaman and his wife loved this little girl—and I am sure they did—they would have sent her back to her home, for she must have had a heartbreaking time of it at first; but people were not kind in that way in those days. Yes, I am sure they loved her and were kind to her, for the simple reason that she evidently loved them; and I am also sure that the reason they loved her was that they could not help it, as we shall see further on.

Not long after the war, Naaman was attacked with a disease so dreadful and repulsive that I cannot describe it to you. Let us be thankful that leprosy is unknown here. It is not only incurable, but as it goes on it becomes so terrible that one cannot stay at home with his family, but must go out and live alone, or with other lepers, and wait for death, which often does not happen for years. It was a sad time for the great Naaman when he discovered that it had seized him. He felt well and strong, but the fearful signs made it sure. It was a sadder time when he told his wife; for both knew that the day would soon come when they could no longer stay together at home, and that he must leave beautiful Damascus, and give up his place in the army, and go off into the mountains and live alone, or with others like himself. The saddest feature of all was that there was no hope: all this was sure to take place. If you have ever been in a house where some one is very ill and likely to die, or some terrible accident has occurred, you have felt what a gloom overhangs it, and have been glad to escape from it and get out under the open sky. But our little Hebrew girl could not escape. She must stay through it all, and wait on Naaman's wife, and see her weep and Naaman's strong face grow sadder every day. Now I think we shall begin to see what a rare, noble, sweet child this was that we are talking about. What a pity that we do not know her name—for she is a nameless child! I would like to call her Anna if I had any right to leave off the *H* that the Hebrews put before and after this beautiful name. And I should not change it by turning the *a* at the close into *ie*, as so many young people—and older ones, too, who ought to know better—are in the habit of doing; for I never could understand why girls with so noble names as Anna and Mary and Helen and Margaret and Caroline should change them into the weak and silly forms that we hear every day. This change, which usually shortens the name and ends it with an *ie*, is called a *diminutive*, which, according to Worcester, means "a thing little of its kind," and so may well enough be used in the nursery; but that grown women should use it seems to me foolish and even ignoble, and I often fear it may indicate a lack of fine sentiment. We do not know the name of our little maiden, but we can safely imagine her appearance for two reasons: we know her circumstances and her character. Is it not quite sure that when Naaman selected from his captives a little girl to wait on his wife, he would take the most beautiful one? When we make presents to those we love, we always get the best we can. Now we can go a step further, and ask what made her beautiful *in such a way* that Naaman thought she would please his wife. It must have been her sweet and amiable expression; and that came from her character, for nothing else can make beauty of this sort. And so we picture her with black, wavy hair and soft, dark eyes, with red cheeks glowing through an olive-colored skin, lips like a pomegranate, a sweet, patient, loving expression, and a voice "gentle and low" and full of sympathy and readiness. I am very sure about her voice and expression, because I know her character. I never have seen any one with a loving and helpful spirit who had not a gentle voice and a sweet expression. I think she must have been about twelve years old; for if she had been younger she would not have known all about Elisha, and if older she would not have been called "a *little* maid."

When the trouble came upon Naaman's family, she felt it grievously, and was more attentive and gentle in her services than ever. Just here she showed the beauty of her character. She had been cruelly wronged—stolen away from her country and home, and made a slave without hope of ever seeing them again—and so might naturally feel revengeful, and say that Naaman's leprosy was a punishment for the wrong he had done her. But instead she pitied him, and in her sympathy with his sufferings forgot her own. So, as she brooded on the trouble, she happened to remember one day that Elisha had cured people who were very ill, and done many wonderful things, and she said to her mistress, "Would God my lord were with the prophet that is in Samaria! for he would recover him of his leprosy." Probably Naaman's wife questioned her closely about Elisha, and got at all she knew about him, and so heard about the child that fell sick among the reapers, and the poor widow whose two sons were to be sold as slaves, and the mantle of Elijah, that Elisha had caught upon the banks of the Jordan, with which he smote the waters. At any rate, she heard enough to awaken some hope, and so told her husband what our little maid had said. When people are hopelessly ill, they are willing to try anything; a drowning man will catch at a straw, and Naaman caught at this little straw of hope that the wind of war had blown across his path. He thought it over and said to himself, "It is my only chance; no one here can do anything for me. I will go down to Samaria and find Elisha. I have often heard that the prophets there did wonderful things; if what the little maid says of the boy among the reapers is true, perhaps Elisha can cure me." And so he went; but it was very humiliating. He thought of Israel and the little city of Samaria and the Jordan in a scornful way, comparing them with his splendid Damascus, and its green, beautiful plain, thirty miles wide, and the great river Abana, that gushed from the side of the mountain, and flowed through and all about the city, making the whole country one vast garden. He despised, too, the people of Israel. They were rude and poor and ignorant, while his own people were rich and cultivated. Perhaps he had borne himself proudly when he was at war there; and now to go back and ask favors—to ask for himself what he could not get at home—was humiliating indeed. But he made the best of it; and to cover his pride and make it seem as though he were not asking favors, he took with him an immense amount of silver and gold, and ten suits of raiment—perhaps of linen *damask*, that was first made in Damascus.

I shall not follow the story further, except to say that because Naaman went in such a proud spirit, Elisha used every means to make him humble. He seemed to be anxious to send Naaman home, not only a well, but a better man, and to teach him that there were other things to be thought of than great rivers, and fine cities, and temples of Rimmon. Especially he wanted to teach him that the one, true God could make a small, rough nation greater and stronger than one that worshipped idols. Naaman went home cured of his leprosy, with some earth to make an altar of, and all his gold and silver and fine garments, except what the foolish Gehazi got from him by lying. How Naaman proposed to act when he should get home and be forced to go with the king into the temple of Rimmon, you will find discussed in the second chapter of the second part of "School Days at Rugby." My opinion is that Elisha told him he must settle that matter with his own conscience; but I can imagine that when he had worshipped God before the altar built of the earth brought from the Jordan, and then went into the temple of Rimmon and did what the king did, his conscience must have troubled him.

But I care a great deal more for our little maid than for Naaman. I wonder what became of her. If Naaman did what he ought, he sent her back to her home, and gave her all the gold and silver he had offered to Elisha. I am quite inclined to believe this for several reasons. Naaman was a *reasonable* man. When he was told to "go and wash himself seven times in Jordan," he was surprised and angry, because it was so different from what he had expected, and because he thought it was an insult to his own great rivers. But when his servants reminded him that it was just as easy to do a little thing as a great thing, he saw the wisdom of it, and let good sense triumph over pride. He was also a *generous* man, as the gifts he offered to Elisha show. And he was *conscientious*, or he would not have asked Elisha about bowing down in the temple of Rimmon as a part of his duty to the king. All through he showed himself *grateful*. Yes; I think he went back to Syria not only with "the flesh of a little child," but with a child's heart. And because he was reasonable and generous and conscientious and grateful, he did not forget the little maid who was at the bottom of the whole affair. He owed quite as much to her as to Elisha; for people who start good enterprises deserve more praise and reward than those who carry them out. So, when he reached home and met his wife and children—why, it was almost like coming back from the dead!—his first thought must have been of the little maid. We can imagine the great Naaman taking her in his arms with tears, and saying, "What can I do for you, my little maid? Tell me what you most want, and I will give it to you, even if it is the half of my possessions." We know that Eastern princes often said such things when their fancy or their gratitude was deeply stirred; they gave full course to all their feelings, good and bad. Perhaps she had become fond of Naaman's wife, and would like to stay with her. Perhaps they told her they would adopt her, and clothe her with rich damask and jewels of gold and silver. But I doubt if she was a child who cared more for such things than for her parents and her home.

And as she heard the story of Naaman's cure, and of Elisha and the Jordan, her mind went back to her native land and to her home, and a great longing filled her heart to see it again, and to live the old life with her parents and brothers and sisters. The Jews do not easily forget their country nor their families; and this little maid was a true Jewess. It might be a fine thing to live in a palace and wear jewels, but she would rather go home, and tend the sheep and goats, and pick the grapes, and go to the fountain for water. Perhaps she had lived on the slope of Hermon, where the dew fell heavily every night, and the brooks ran full all summer; for Naaman's march home led near it.

We found her in Damascus a slave; but we will leave her at home among the vines and flowers and kids, with father and mother and mates, for she was a child who lived in her affections rather than in her ambitions.

The chief thing she teaches us is the beauty and blessedness of returning good for evil. Long before Christ's day she was Christ's own child; for she loved her enemies, and prayed for those who had persecuted her.

HERE FOLLOWETH THE HISTORY OF JOB

Read on the first Sunday of September

There was a man in the land of Uz named Job, and this man was simple, rightful and dreading God, and going from all evil. He had seven sons and three daughters, and his possession was seven thousand sheep, three thousand camels, five hundred yoke of oxen, five hundred asses, and his family and household passing much and great. He was a great man and rich among all the men of the orient. And his sons went daily each to other house making great feasts, ever each one as his day came, and they sent for their three sisters for to eat and drink with them. When they had thus feasted each other, Job sent to them and blessed and sanctified them, and rising every day early, he offered sacrifices for them all, saying: Lest my children sin and bless not God in their hearts. And thus did Job every day.

On a day when the sons of God were tofore our Lord, Satan came and was among them, to whom our Lord said: Whence comest thou? Which answered, I have gone round about the earth and through walked it. Our Lord said to him: Hast thou not considered my servant Job, that there is none like unto him in the earth, a man simple, rightful, dreading God, and going from evil? To whom Satan answered: Doth Job dread God idly? If so were that thou overthrewest him, his house and all his substance round about, he should soon forsake thee. Thou hast blest the work of his hands, and his possession is increased much in the earth, but stretch out thy hand a little, and touch all that he hath in possession, and he shall soon grudge and not bless thee. Then said our Lord to Satan: Lo! all that which he owneth and hath in possession, I will it be in thy hand and power, but on his person ne body set not thy hand. Satan departed and went from the face of our Lord. On a day as his sons and daughters ate, and drank wine, in the house of the oldest brother, there came a messenger to Job which said: The oxen eared in the plough and the ass pastured in the pasture by them, and the men of Sabea ran on them, and smote thy servants, and slew them with sword, and I only escaped for to come and to show it to thee. And whiles he spake came another and said: The fire of God fell down from heaven and hath burned thy sheep and servants and consumed them, and I only escaped for to come and show it to thee. And yet whiles he spake came another and said: The

Chaldees made three hosts and have enveigled thy camels and taken them, and have slain thy servants with sword, and I only escaped for to bring thee word. And yet he speaking another entered in and said: Thy sons and daughters, drinking wine in the house of thy first begotten son, suddenly came a vehement wind from the region of desert and smote the four corners of the house, which falling oppressed thy children, and they be all dead, and I only fled for to tell it to thee. Then Job arose, and cut his coat, and did do shave his head, and falling down to the ground, worshipped and adored God, saying: I am come out naked from the womb of my mother and naked shall return again thereto. Our Lord hath given and our Lord hath taken away, as it hath pleased our Lord, so it is done, the name of our Lord be blessed. In all these things Job sinned not with his lips, ne spake nothing follily against our Lord, but took it all patiently.

After this it was so that on a certain day when the children of God stood tofore our Lord, Satan came and stood among them, and God said to him: Whence comest thou? To whom Satan answered: I have gone round the earth, and walked through it. And God said to Satan, Hast thou not considered my servant Job that there is no man like him in the earth, a man simple, rightful, dreading God, and going from evil, and yet retaining his innocency? Thou hast moved me against him that I should put him to affliction without cause. To whom Satan said: Skin for skin, and all that ever a man hath he shall give for his soul. Nevertheless, stretch thine hand and touch his mouth and his flesh, and thou shalt see that he shall not bless thee. Then said God to Satan: I will well that his body be in thine hand, but save his soul and his life. Then Satan departed from the face of our Lord and smote Job with the worst blotches and blains from the plant of his foot, unto the top of his head, which was made like a lazar [leper] and was cast out and sat on the dunghill. Then came his wife to him and said: Yet thou abidest in thy simpleness, forsake thy God and bless him no more, and go die. Then Job said to her: Thou hast spoken like a foolish woman; if we have received and taken good things of the hand of our Lord, why shall we not sustain and suffer evil things? In all these things Job sinned not with his lips. Then three men that were friends of Job, hearing what harm was happed and come to Job, came ever each one from his place to him, that one was named Eliphas the Temanite, another Bildad the Shuhite, and the third, Zophar Naamathite. And when they saw him from far they knew him not, and crying they wept. They came for to comfort him, and when they considered his misery they tare their clothes and cast dust on their heads, and sat by him seven days and seven nights, and no man spake to him a word, seeing his sorrow. Then after that Job and they talked and spake together of his sorrow and misery, of which S. Gregory hath made a great book called: The morals of S. Gregory, which is a noble book and a great work.

But I pass over all the matters and return unto the end, how God restored Job again to prosperity. It was so that when these three friends of Job had been long with Job, and had said many things each of them to Job, and Job again to them, our Lord was wroth with these three men and said to them: Ye have not spoken rightfully, as my servant Job hath spoken. Take ye therefore seven bulls and seven wethers and go to my servant Job and offer ye sacrifice for you. Job my servant shall pray for you. I shall receive his prayer and shall take his visage. They went forth and did as our Lord commanded them. And our Lord beheld the visage of Job, and saw his penance when he prayed for his friends. And our Lord added to Job double of all that Job had possessed. All his brethren came to him, and all his sisters, and all they that tofore had known him, and ate with him in his house, and moved their heads upon him, and comforted him upon all the evil that God had sent to him. And each of them gave him a sheep and a gold ring for his ears. Our Lord blessed more Job in his last days than he did in the beginning. And he had then after fourteen thousand sheep, six thousand camels, one thousand yoke of oxen, one thousand asses. And he had seven sons and three daughters. And the first daughter's name was Jemima, the second Kezia, and the third Keren-happuch. There was nowhere found in the world so fair women as were the daughters of Job. Their father Job gave to them heritage among their brethren, and thus Job by his patience gat so much love of God, that he was restored double of all his losses. And Job lived after, one hundred and forty years, and saw his sons and the sons of his sons unto the fourth generation, and died an old man, and full of days.

THE DESTRUCTION OF SENNACHERIB

The Assyrian came down like the wolf on the fold,
And his cohorts were gleaming in purple and gold,
And the sheen of their spears was like stars on the sea,
When the blue wave rolls nightly on deep Galilee.

Like the leaves of the forest when summer is green,
That host with their banners at sunset were seen;
Like the leaves of the forest when autumn hath blown,
That host on the morrow lay wither'd and strown.

For the Angel of Death spread his wings on the blast,
And breathed in the face of the foe as he pass'd;
And the eyes of the sleepers wax'd deadly and chill,
And their hearts but once heaved, and forever grew still.

And there lay the steed with his nostril all wide,
But through it there roll'd not the breath of his pride:
And the foam of his gasping lay white on the turf,
And cold as the spray of the rock-beating surf.

And there lay the rider, distorted and pale,
With the dew on his brow, and the rust on his mail;
And the tents were all silent, the banners alone,
The lances unlifted, the trumpet unblown.

And the widows of Ashur are loud in their wail,
And the idols are broke in the temple of Baal,
And the might of the Gentile, unsmote by the sword,
Hath melted like snow in the glance of the Lord!

—*Lord Byron*

HERE FOLLOWETH THE HISTORY OF TOBIT

Which is read the third Sunday of September

Tobit of the tribe and of the city of Nephthali, which is in the overparts of Galilee upon Aser, after the way that leadeth men westward, having on his left side the city of Sepheth, was taken in the days of Salmanazar, King of the Assyrians, and put in captivity, yet he forsook not the way of truth, but all that he had or could get he departed daily with his brethren of his kindred which were prisoners with him. And howbeit that he was youngest in all the tribe of Nephthali yet did he nothing childishly. Also when all other went unto the golden calves that Jeroboam, King of Israel, had made, this Tobit only fled the fellowship of them all, and went to Jerusalem into the temple of our Lord. And there he adored and worshipped the Lord God of Israel, offering truly his first fruits and tithes insomuch that in the third year he ministered unto proselytes and strangers all the tithe. Such things and other like to these he observed while he was a child, and when he came to age and was a man he took a wife named Anna, of his tribe, and begat on her a son, naming after his own name Tobias, whom from his childhood he taught to dread God and abstain him from all sin. Then after when he was brought by captiviy with his wife and his son into the city of Nineveh with all his tribe, and when all ate of the meats of the Gentiles and Paynims, this Tobit kept his soul clean and was never defouled in the meats of them. And because he remembered our Lord in all his heart, God gave him grace to be in the favor of Salmanazar the king which gave to him power to go where he would. Having liberty to do what he would, he went then to all them in captivity and gave to them warnings of health. When he came on a time in Rages, city of the Jews, he had such gifts as he had been honored with of the king, ten besants of silver. And when he saw one Gabael being needy which was of his tribe, he lent him the said weight of silver upon his obligation. Long time after this when Salmanazar the king was dead, Sennacherib his son reigned for him, and hated, and loved not, the children of Israel. And Tobit went unto all his kindred and comforted them, and divided to every each of them as he might of his faculties and goods.

He fed the hungry and gave to the naked clothes, and diligently he buried the dead men and them that were slain. After this when Sennacherib returned, fleeing the plague from the Jewry, that God had sent him for his blasphemy, and he, being wroth, slew many of the children of Israel, and Tobit always buried the bodies of them, which was told to the king, which commanded to slay him, and took away all his substance. Tobit then with his wife and his son hid him and fled away all naked, for many loved him well. After this, forty-five days, the sons of the king slew the king, and then returned Tobit unto his house, and all his faculties and goods were restored to him again. After this on a high festival day of our Lord when that Tobit had a good dinner in his house, he said to his son: Go and fetch to us some of our tribe dreading God, that they may come and eat with us. And he went forth and anon he returned telling to his father that one of the children of Israel was slain and lay dead in the street. And anon he leapt out of his house, leaving his meat, and fasting came to the, body, took it and bare it in to his house privily, that he might secretly bury it when the sun went down. And when he had hid the corpse, he ate his meat with wailing and dread, remembering that word that our Lord said by Amos the prophet: The day of your feast shall be turned into lamentation and wailing. And when the sun was gone down he went and buried him. All his neighbors reproved and chid him, saying for this cause they were commanded to be slain, and unnethe [hardly] thou escapedst the commandment of death, and yet thou buriest dead men. But Tobit, more dreading God than the king, took up the bodies of dead men and hid them in his house, and at midnight he buried them.

It happed on a day after this that when he was weary of burying dead men, he came home and laid him down by a wall and slept. And he became blind. This temptation suffered God to fall to him, that it should be an example to them that shall come after him of his patience, like as it was of holy Job. For from his infancy he dreaded ever God and kept his precepts and was not grudging against God for his blindness, but he abode immovable in the dread of God, giving and rendering thankings to God all the days of his life. For like as Job was assailed so was Tobit assailed of his kinsmen, scorning him and saying to him: Where is now thy hope and reward for which thou gavest thy alms and madest sepulchres? Tobit blamed them for such words, saying to them: In no wise say ye not so, for we be the sons of holy men, and we abide that life that God shall give to them that never shall change their faith from him. Anna his wife went daily to the work of weaving, and got by the labor of her hands their livelihood as much as she might. Whereof on a day she gat a kid and brought it home. When Tobit heard the voice of the kid bleating, he said: See that it be not stolen, yield it again to the owner, for it is not lawful for us to eat ne touch anything that is stolen. To that his wife all angry answered: Now manifestly and openly is thine hope made vain, and thy alms lost. And thus with such and like words she chid him. Then Tobit began to sigh and began to pray our Lord with tears saying: O Lord, thou art rightful, and all thy dooms be true, and all thy ways be mercy, truth, and righteousness. And now, Lord, remember me, and take now no vengeance of my sins, ne remember not my trespasses, ne the sins of my fathers. For'we have not obeyed thy commandments, therefore we be betaken in to direption, captivity, death, fables, and into reproof and shame to all nations in which thou hast dispersed us. And now, Lord, great be thy judgments, for we have not done according to thy precepts, ne have not walked well tofore thee. And now, Lord, do to me after thy will, and command my spirit to be received in peace, it is more expedient to me to die than to live.

The same day it happed that Sara, daughter of Raguel in the city of Medes, that she was rebuked and heard reproof of one of the handmaidens of her father. For she had been given to seven men, and a devil named Asmodeus slew them as soon as they would have gone to her; therefore the maid reproved her saying: We shall never see son ne daughter of thee on the earth, thou slayer of thy husbands. Wilt thou slay me as thou hast slain seven men? With this voice and rebuke she went up in the upperest cubicle of the house. And three days and three nights she ate not, ne drank not, but was continually in prayers beseeching God for to deliver her from this reproof and shame. And on the third day, when she had accomplished her prayer, blessing our Lord she said: Blessed be thy name, God of our fathers, for when thou art wroth thou shalt do mercy and in a time of tribulation thou forgivest sins to them that call to thee. Unto thee, Lord, I convert my visage, and unto thee I address mine eyes. I ask and require thee that thou assoil me from the bond of the reproof and shame, or certainly upon the earth keep me. Thou knowest well, Lord, that I never desired man, but I have kept clean my soul. I never meddled me with players, ne never had part of them that walk in lightness. I consented for to take an husband with thy dread. Or I was unworthy to them or haply they were unworthy to me, or haply thou hast conserved and kept me for some other man. Thy counsel is not in man's power. This knoweth every man that worshippeth thee, for the life of him if it be in probation shall be crowned, and if it be in tribulation it shall be delivered, and if it be in correction, it shall be lawful to come to mercy. Thou hast none delectation in our perdition, for after tempest thou makest tranquillity, and after weeping and shedding of tears thou bringest in exultation and joy. Thy name, God of Israel, be blessed, world without end.

In that same time were the prayers of them both heard in the sight of the glory of the high God. And the holy angel of God, Raphael, was sent to heal them both. Of whom in one time were the prayers recited in the sight of our Lord God. Then when Tobit supposed his prayers to be heard that he might die, he called to him his son Tobias, and said to him: Hear, my son, the words of my mouth, and set them in thy heart as a fundament. When God shall take away my soul, bury my body, and thou shalt worship thy mother all the days of her life, thou owest to remember what and how many perils she hath suffered for thee in her womb. When she shall have accomplished the time of her life, bury her by me. All the days of thy life have God in thy mind, and beware that thou never consent to sin, ne to disobey ne break the commandments of God. Of thy substance do alms, and turn never thy face from any poor man, so do that God turn not his face from thee. As much as thou mayst, be merciful, if thou have much good give abundantly, if thou have but little, yet study to give and to depart thereof gladly, for thou makest to thee thereof good treasure and meed in the day of necessity, for alms delivereth a man from all sin and from death, and suffereth not his soul to go in to darkness. Alms is a great sikerness [surety] tofore the high God unto all them that do it. Beware, my son, keep thee from all uncleanness, and suffer not thyself to know that sin; and suffer never pride to have domination in thy wit, ne in thy word, that sin was the beginning of all perdition. Whosomever work to thee any thing, anon yield to him his meed and hire, let never the hire of thy servant ne meed of thy mercenary remain in no wise with thee. That thou hatest to be done to thee of other, see that thou never do to an other. Eat thy bread with the hungry and needy, and cover the naked with thy clothes. Ordain thy bread and wine upon the sepulture of a righteous man, but eat it not ne drink it with sinners. Ask and demand counsel of a wise man. Always and in every time bless God and desire of him that he address thy ways, and let all thy counsels abide in him. I tell to thee, my son, that when thou wert a little child I lent to Gabael ten besants of silver, dwelling in Rages the city of Medes, upon an obligation, which I have by me. And therefore spere [search] and ask how thou mayst go to him, and thou shalt receive of him the said weight of silver and restore to him his obligation. Dread thou not, my son; though we lead a poor life, we shall have much good if we dread God and go from sin and do well. Then young Tobias answered to his father: All that thou hast commanded me I shall do, father; but how I shall get this money I wot never; he knoweth not me, ne I know not him; what token shall I give him? And also I know not the way thither. Then his father answered to him and said: I have his obligation by me, which when thou shewest him, anon he shall pay thee. But go now first and seek for thee some true man, that for his hire shall go with thee whiles I live, that thou mayst receive it.

Then Tobias went forth and found a fair young man girt up and ready for to walk, and not knowing that it was the angel of God, saluted him and said: From whence have we thee, good young man? And he answered: Of the children of Israel. And Tobias said to him: Knowest thou the way that leadeth one into the region of Medes? To whom he answered: I know it well, and all the journeys I have oft walked and have dwelled with Gabael our brother which dwelled in Rages the city of Medes, which standeth in the hill of Ecbathanis. To whom Tobias said: I pray thee tary here a while till I have told this to my father. Then Tobias went in to his father and told to him all these things, whereon his father marvelled and prayed him that he should bring him in. Then the angel came in and saluted the old Tobit and said: Joy be to thee always. And Tobit said: What joy shall be to me that sit in darkness, and see not the light of heaven. To whom the youngling said: Be of strong belief; it shall not be long but of God thou shalt be cured and healed. Then said Tobit to him: Mayst thou lead my son unto Gabael in Rages city of Medes, and when thou comest again I shall restore to thee thy meed. And the angel said: I shall lead him thither and bring him again to thee. To whom Tobit said: I pray thee to tell me of what house or of what kindred art thou. To whom Raphael the angel said: Thou needest not to ask the kindred of him that shall go with thy son, but lest haply I should not deliver him to thee again: I am Azarias son of great Ananias. Tobit answered: Thou art of a great kindred, but I pray thee be not wroth, though I would know thy kindred. The angel said to him: I shall safely lead thy son thither, and safely bring him and render him to thee again. Tobit then answered saying: Well mote ye walk, and our Lord be in your journey, and his angel fellowship with you. Then, when all was ready that they should have with them by the way, young Tobias took leave of his father and mother, and bade them farewell. When they should depart the mother began to weep and say: Thou has taken away and sent from us the staff of our old age, would God that thilke [that] money had never been for which thou hast sent him, our poverty sufficeth enough to us that we might have seen our son. Tobit said to her: Weep not, our son shall come safely again and thine eyes shall see him. I believe that the good angel of God hath fellowship with him, and shall dispose all things that shall be needful to him, and that he shall return again to us with joy. With this the mother ceased of her weeping and was still.

Then young Tobias went forth and an hound followed him. And the first mansion [stay] that they made was by the river of Tigris, and Tobias went out for to wash his feet, and there came a great fish for to devour him, whom Tobias fearing cried out with a great voice: Lord, he cometh on me, and the angel said to him: Take him by the fin and draw him to thee. And so he did and drew him out of the water to the dry land. Then said the angel to him: Open the fish and take to thee the heart, the gall, and the milt, and keep them by thee; they be profitable and necessary for medicines. And when he had done so he roasted of the fish, and took it with them for to eat by the way, and the remnant they salted, that it might suffice them till they came into the city of Rages. Then Tobias demanded of the angel and said: I pray thee, Azarias, brother, to tell me whereto these be good that thou hast bidden me keep. And the angel answered and said: If thou take a little of his heart and put it on the coals, the smoke and fume thereof driveth away all manner kind of devils, be it from man or from woman, in such wise that he shall no more come to them. And Tobias said: Where wilt thou that we shall abide? And he answered and said: Hereby is a man named Raguel, a man nigh to thy kindred and tribe, and he hath a daughter named Sara, he hath neither son ne daughter more than her. Thou shalt owe all his substance, for thee behoveth to take her to thy wife. Then Toby answered and said: I have heard say that she hath been given to seven men, and they be dead, and I have heard that a devil slayeth them. I dread therefore that it might hap so to me, and I that am an only son to my father and mother, I should depose their old age with heaviness and sorrow to hell. Then Raphael the angel said to him: Hear me, and I shall show thee wherewith thou mayst prevail against that devil; these that took their wedlock in such wise that they exclude God from them and their mind, the devil hath power upon them. Thou therefore when thou shalt take a wife, and enterest into her cubicle, be thou continent by the space of three days from her, and thou shalt do nothing but be in prayers with her: and that same night put the heart of the fish on the fire, and that shall put away the devil, and after the third night thou shalt take the virgin with dread of God, that thou mayst follow the blessing of Abraham in his seed. Then they went and entered into Raguel's house, and Raguel received them joyously, and Raguel, beholding well Tobias, said to Anna his wife: How like is this young man unto my cousin! And when he had so said he asked them: Whence be ye, young men my brethren? And they said: Of the tribe of Nephthalim, of the captivity of Nineveh. Raguel said to them: Know ye Tobit my brother? Which said: We know him well. When Raguel had spoken much good of him, the angel said to Raguel: Tobit of whom thou demandest is father of this young man. And then went Raguel, and with weeping eyes kissed him, and weeping upon his neck said: The blessing of God be to thee, my son, for thou art son of a blessed and good man. And Anna his wife and Sara his daughter wept also.

And after they had spoken, Raguel commanded to slay a wether, and make ready a feast. When he then should bid them sit down to dinner, Tobias said: I shall not eat here this day ne drink but if thou first grant to me my petition, and promise to me to give me Sara thy daughter. Which when Raguel heard he was astonied and abashed, knowing what had fallen to seven men that tofore had wedded her, and dreaded lest it might happen to this young man in likewise. And when he held his peace and would give him none answer the angel said to him: Be not afeard to give thy daughter to this man dreading God, for to him thy daughter is ordained to be his wife, therefore none other may have her. Then said Raguel: I doubt not God hath admitted my prayers and tears in his sight, and I believe that therefore he hath made you to come to me that these may be joined in one kindred after the law of Moses, and now have no doubt but I shall give her to thee. And he taking the right hand of his daughter delivered it to Tobias saying: God of Abraham, God of Isaac, and God of Jacob be with you, and he conjoin you together and fulfil his blessing in you. And took a charter and wrote the conscription of the wedlock. And after this they ate, blessing our Lord God. Raguel called to him Anna his wife and bade her to make ready another cubicle. And she brought Sara her daughter therein, and she wept, to whom her mother said: Be thou strong of heart, my daughter, our Lord of heaven give to thee joy for the heaviness that thou hast suffered. After they had supped, they led the young man to her. Tobias remembered the words of the angel, and took out of his bag part of the heart of the fish, and laid it on burning coals. Then Raphael the angel took the devil and bound him in the upperest desert of Egypt. Then Tobias exhorted the virgin and said to her: Arise, Sara, and let us pray to God this day, and to-morrow, and after to-morrow, for these three nights we be joined to God. And after the third night we shall be in our wedlock. We be soothly the children of saints, and we may not so join together as people do that know not God. Then they both arising prayed together instantly that health might be given to them. Tobias said: Lord God of our fathers, heaven and earth, sea, wells, and floods, and all creatures that be in them, bless thee. Thou madest Adam of the slime of the earth, and gavest to him for an help Eve, and now, Lord, thou knowest that I take my sister to wife, only for the love of posterity, in which thy name be blessed world without end. Then said Sara: Have mercy on us, Lord, have mercy, and let us wax old both together in health. And after this the cocks began to crow, at which time Raguel commanded his servants to come to him, and they together went for to make and delve a sepulchre. He said: Lest haply it happen to him as it hath happed to the seven men that wedded her. When they had made ready the foss and pit, Raguel returned to his wife and said to her: Send one of thy handmaidens, and let her see if he be dead, that he may be buried ere it be light day. And she sent forth one of her servants, which entered into the cubicle and found them both safe and whole, and sleeping together, and she returned and brought good tidings. And Raguel and Anna blessed our Lord God and said: We bless thee, Lord

God of Israel, that it hath not happed to us as we supposed; thou hast done to us thy mercy, and thou hast excluded from us our enemy pursuing us, thou hast done mercy on two only children. Make them, Lord, to bless thee to full, and to offer to thee sacrifice of praising and of their health, that the university of peoples may know that thou art God only in the universal earth.

Anon then Raguel commanded his servants to fill again the pit that they had made ere it waxed light, and bade his wife to ordain a feast, and make all ready that were necessary to meat. He did do slay two fat kine and four wethers, and to ordain meat for all his neighbors and friends, and Raguel desired and adjured Tobias that he should abide with him two weeks. Of all that ever Raguel had in possession of goods he gave half part to Tobias, and made to him a writing that the other half part he should have after the death of him and his wife. Then Tobias called the angel to him, which he trowed had been a man, and said to him: Azarias, brother, I pray thee to take heed to my words; if I make myself servant to thee I shall not be worthy to satisfy thy providence. Nevertheless I pray thee to take to thee the beasts and servants and go to Gabael in Rages the city of Medes, and render to him his obligation, and receive of them the money and pray him to come to my wedding. Thou knowest thyself that my father numbereth the days of my being out, and if I tarry more his soul shall be heavy, and certainly thou seest how Raguel hath adjured me, whose desire I may not despise. Then Raphael, taking four of the servants of Raguel and two camels, went to Rages the city of Medes, and there finding Gabael, gave to him his obligation and received all the money, and told to him of Tobias, son of Tobit, all that was done, and made him come with him to the wedding. When then he entered the house of Raguel, he found Tobias sitting at meat, and came to him and kissed him, and Gabael wept and blessed God saying: God of Israel bless thee, for thou art son of the best man and just, dreading God and doing alms, and the blessing be said upon thy wife and your parents, and that you may see the sons of your sons unto the third and fourth generation, and your seed be blessed of the God of Israel, which reigneth in secula seculorum [forever]. And when all had said Amen, they went to the feast. And with the dread of God they exercised the feast of their weddings. Whiles that Tobias tarried because of his marriage, his father Tobit began to be heavy saying: Trowest thou wherefore my son tarrieth and why he is holden there? Trowest thou that Gabael be dead, and no man is there that shall give him his money?

He began to be sorry and heavy greatly, both he and Anna his wife with him, and began both to weep because at the day set he came not home. His mother therefore wept with unmeasurable tears, and said: Alas, my son, wherefore sent we thee to go this pilgrimage? The light of our eyes, the staff of our age, the solace of our life, the hope of our posterity, all these only having in thee, we ought not to have let thee go from us. To whom Tobit said: Be still and trouble thee not, our son is safe enough, the man is true and faithful enough with whom we sent him. She might in no wise be comforted, but every day she went and looked and espied the way that he should come if she might see him come from far. Then Raguel said to Tobias his son-in-law: Abide here with me, and I shall send messengers of thy health and welfare to Tobit thy father. To whom Tobias said: I know well that my father and my mother accompt the days, and the spirit is in great pain within them. Raguel prayed him with many words, but Tobias would in no wise grant him. Then he delivered to him Sara his daughter, and half part of all his substance in servants, men and women, in beasts, camels, in kine and much money. And safe and joyful he let him depart from him, saying: The angel of God that is holy be in your journey, and bring you home whole and sound, and that ye may find all things well and rightful about your father and mother, and that mine eyes may see your sons ere I die. And the father and mother taking their daughter kissed her and let her depart, warning her to worship her husband's father and mother, love her husband, to rule well the meiny [retinue], to govern the house and to keep herself irreprehensible, that is to say, without reproof.

When they thus returned and departed, they came to Charram, which is the half way to Nineveh, the thirteenth day. Then said the angel to Tobias: Tobias, brother, thou knowest how thou hast left thy father, if it please thee we will go tofore and let thy family come softly after, with thy wife and with thy beasts. This pleased well to Tobias; and then said Raphael to Tobias: Take with thee of the gall of the fish, it shall be necessary. Tobias took of the gall and went forth tofore. Anna his mother sat every day by the way in the top of the hill, from whence she might see him come from far, and whilst she sat there and looked after his coming, she saw afar and knew her son coming, and running home she told to her husband saying: Lo! thy son cometh. Raphael then said to young Tobias: Anon as thou enterest in to the house adore thy Lord God, and giving to him thankings, go to thy father and kiss him. And anon then anoint his eyes with the gall of the fish that thou bearest with thee, thou shalt well know that his eyes shall be opened, and thy father shall see the light of heaven and shall joy in thy sight. Then ran the dog that followed him and had been with him in the way, and came home as a messenger, fawning and making joy with his tail. And the blind father arose and began offending his feet to run to meet his son, giving to him his hand, and so taking, kissed him with his wife, and began to weep for joy. When then they had worshipped God and thanked him, they sat down together. Then Tobias taking the gall of the fish anointed his father's eyes, and abode as it had been half an hour, and the slime of his eyes began to fall away like as it had been the white of an egg, which Tobias took and drew from his father's eyes, and anon he received sight. And they glorified God, that is to wit he and his wife and all they that knew him.

Then said Tobit the father: I bless thee, Lord God of Israel, for thou hast chastised me, and thou hast saved me, and, lo! I see Tobias my son. After these seven days Sara the wife of his son came and entered in with all the family, and the beasts whole and sound, camels and much money of his wife's, and also the money that he had received of Gabael. And he told to his father and mother all the benefits of God that was done to him by the man that led him. Then came Achiacharus and Nasbas, cousins of Tobias, joying and thanking God of all the goods that God had showed to him. And seven days they ate together making feast, and were glad with great joy. Then old Tobit call his son Tobias to him, and said: What may we give to this holy man that cometh with thee? Then Tobias answering said to his father: Father, what meed may we give to him, or what may be worthy to him for his benefits? He led me out and hath brought me whole again, he received the money of Gabael; he did me have my wife and he put away the devil from her; he hath made joy to my parents, and saved myself from devouring of the fish, and hath made thee see the light of heaven, and by him we be replenished with all goods; what may we then worthily give to him? Wherefore I pray thee, father, that thou pray him if he vouchsafe to take the half of all that I have. Then the father and the son calling him took him apart and began to pray him that he would vouchsafe to take half the part of all the goods that they had brought. Then said he to them privily: Bless ye God of heaven and before all living people knowledge ye him, for he hath done to you his mercy. Forsooth to hide the sacrament of the king it is good, but for to show the works of God and to knowledge them it is worshipful. Oration and prayer is good, with fasting and alms, and more than to set up treasures of gold. For alms delivereth from death, and it is she that purgeth sins and maketh a man to find everlasting life. Who that do sin and wickedness they be enemies of his soul. I show to you therefore the truth and I shall not hide from you the secret word. When thou prayedst with tears and didst bury the dead men and leftest thy dinner and hiddest dead men by the day in thine house, and in the night thou buriedst them, I offered thy prayer unto God. And forasmuch as thou wert accepted tofore God, it was necessary, thou being tempted, that he should prove thee. And now hath our Lord sent me for to cure thee, and Sara the wife of thy son I have delivered from the devil. I am soothly Raphael the angel, one of the seven which stand tofore our Lord God. When they heard this they were troubled, and trembling fell down on their faces upon the ground. The angel said to them: Peace be to you, dread you not. Forsooth I was with you by the will of God, him alway bless ye and sing ye to him, I was seen of you to eat and drink, but I use meat and drink invisible, which of men may not be seen. It is now therefore time that I return to him which sent me. Ye alway bless God and tell ye all his marvels. And when he had said this he was taken away from the sight of them, and after that they might no more see him. Then they fell down flat on their faces by the space of three hours and blessed God, and arising up they told all the marvels of him.

Then the older Tobit opening his mouth blessed our Lord and said: Great art thou, Lord, evermore, and thy reign is in to all worlds, for thou scourgest and savest, thou leadest to hell and bringest again, and there is none that may flee thy hand. Knowledge and confess you to the Lord, ye children of Israel, and in the sight of Gentiles praise ye him. Therefore he hath disperpled [scattered] you among Gentiles that know him not, that ye tell his marvels, and make them to be known. For there is none other God Almighty but he; he hath chastised us for our wickedness and he shall save us for his mercy. Take heed and see therefore what he hath done to us, and with fear and dread, knowledge ye to him, and exalt him king of all worlds in your works. I soothly in the land of my captivity shall knowledge to him, for he hath showed his majesty into the sinful people. Confess ye therefore sinners, and do ye justice tofore our Lord by believing that he shall do to you his mercy, aye soothly, and my soul shall be glad in him. All ye chosen of God, bless ye him and make ye days of gladness and knowledge ye to him. Jerusalem city of God, our Lord hath chastised thee in the works of his hands, confess thou to our Lord in his good things and bless thou the God of worlds that he may re-edify in thee his tabernacle, and that he may call again to thee all prisoners and them that be in captivity and that thou joy in omnia secula seculorum. Thou shalt shine with a bright light, and all the ends of the earth shall worship thee. Nations shall come to thee from far, and bringing gifts shall worship in thee our Lord, and shall have thy land into sanctification. They shall call in thee a great name, they shall be cursed that shall despise thee, and they all shall be condemned that blaspheme thee. Blessed be they that edify thee, thou shalt be joyful in thy sons, for all shall be blessed, and shall be gathered together unto our Lord. Blessed be they that love thee and that joy upon thy peace. My soul, bless thou our Lord, for he hath delivered Jerusalem his city. I shall be blessed if there be left of my seed for to see the clearness of Jerusalem. The gates of Jerusalem shall be edified of sapphire and emerald, and all the circuit of his walls of precious stone; all the streets thereof shall be paved with white stone and clean; and Alleluia shall be sung by the ways thereof. Blessed be the Lord that hath exalted it that it may be his kingdom in secula seculorum, Amen.

And thus Tobit finished these words. And Tobit lived after he had received his sight forty-two years, and saw the sons of his nephews, that is, the sons of the sons of his son young Tobias. And when he had lived one hundred and two years he died, and was honorably buried in the city of Nineveh.

He was fifty-six years old when he lost his sight, and when he was sixty years old he received his sight again. The residue of his life was in joy, and with good profit of the dread of God he departed in peace. In the hour of his death he called to him Tobias his son, and seven of his young sons, his nephews, and said to them: The destruction of Nineveh is nigh, the word of God shall not pass, and our brethren that be disperpled [scattered] from the land of Israel shall return thither again. All the land thereof shall be fulfilled with desert, and the house that is burnt therein shall be re-edified, and thither shall return all people dreading God. And Gentiles shall leave their idols and shall come in Jerusalem and shall dwell, therein, and all the kings of the earth shall joy in her, worshipping the king of Israel. Hear ye therefore, my sons, me your father, serve ye God in truth and seek ye that ye do that may be pleasing to him, and command ye to your sons that they do righteousness and alms, that they may remember God and bless him in all time in truth and in all their virtue. Now therefore, my sons, hear me and dwell ye no longer here, but whensoever your mother shall die, bury her by me and from then forthon dress ye your steps that ye go hence, I see well that wickedness shall make an end of it. It was so then after the death of his mother, Tobias went from Nineveh with his wife and his sons, and the sons of his sons, and returned unto his wife's father and mother, whom they found in good health and good age, and took the cure and charge of them, and were with them unto their death, and closed their eyes. And Tobias received all the heritage of the house of Raguel and saw the sons of his sons unto the fifth generation. And when he had complished ninety-nine years he died in the dread of God, and with joy they buried him. All his cognation [kindred] and all his generation [offspring] abode in good life and in holy conversation, and in such wise as they were acceptable as well to God as to men, and to all dwelling on the earth.

HERE BEGINNETH THE STORY OF JUDITH

Which is read the last Sunday of October

Arpaxhad, king of the Medes, subdued into his empire many peoples and edified a mighty city, which he named Ecbatane, and made it with stones squared, and polished them. The walls thereof were of height seventy cubits, and of breadth thirty cubits, and the towers thereof were an hundred cubits high. And he glorified himself as he that was mighty in puissance and in the glory of his host and of his chariots. Nebuchadnezzar then in the twelfth year of his reign, which was king of the Assyrians, and reigned in the city of Nineveh, fought against Arphaxad and took him in the field, whereof Nebuchadnezzar was exalted and enhanced himself, and sent unto all regions about and unto Jerusalem till the Mounts of Ethiopia, for to obey and hold of him. Which all gainsaid him with one will, and without worship sent home his messengers void, and set nought by him. Then Nebuchadnezzar, having them at great indignation, swore by his reign and by his throne that he would avenge him on them all, and thereupon called all his dukes, princes, and men of war, and held a counsel in which was decreed that he should subdue all the world unto his empire. And thereupon he ordained Holofernes prince of his knighthood, and bade him go forth, and in especial against them that had despised his empire; and bade him spare no realm ne town but subdue all to him. Then Holofernes assembled dukes and masters of the strength of Nebuchadnezzar, and numbered one hundred and twenty thousand footmen, and horsemen shooters twelve thousand. And tofore them he commanded to go a multitude of innumerable camels laden with such things as were needful to the host, as victual, gold and silver, much that was taken out of the treasury of the kings. And so went to many realms which he subdued; and occupied a great part of the orient till he came approaching the land of Israel. And when the children of Israel heard thereof they dreaded sore lest he should come among them into Jerusalem and destroy the temple, for Nebuchadnezzar had commanded that he should extinct all the gods of the earth, and that no god should be named ne worshipped but he himself, of all the nations that Holofernes should subdue.

Eliachim, then priest in Israel, wrote unto all them in the mountains that they should keep the strait ways of the mountains, and so the children of Israel did as the priest had ordained. Then Eliachim, the priest, went about all Israel and said to them: Know ye that God hath heard your prayers, if ye abide and continue in your prayers and fastings in the sight of God. Remember ye of Moses, the servant of God, which overthrew Amalek trusting in his strength, and in his power, in his host, in his helmets, in his chariots, and in his horsemen; not fighting with iron, but with praying of holy prayers. In like wise shall it be with all the enemies of Israel if ye persevere in this work that ye have begun. With this exhortation they continued praying God. They persevered in the sight of God, and also they that offered to our Lord were clad with sackcloth, and had ashes on their heads, and with all their heart they prayed God to visit his people Israel. It was told to Holofernes prince of the knighthood of the Assyrians that the children of Israel made them ready to resist him, and had closed the ways of the mountains, and he was burned in overmuch fury in great ire. He called all the princes of Moab and dukes of Ammon and said to them: Say ye to me, what people is this that besiege the mountains, or what or how many cities have they? And what is their virtue, and what multitude is of them? Or who is king of their knighthood? Then Achior, duke of all of them of Ammon, answering said: If thou deignest to hear me I shall tell thee truth of this people that dwelleth in the mountains, and there shall not issue out of my mouth one false word. This people dwelled first in Mesopotamia, and was of the progeny of the Chaldees, but would not dwell there for they would not follow the gods of their fathers that were in the land of Chaldees, and going and leaving the ceremonies of their fathers, which was in the multitude of many gods, they honored one, God of heaven, which commanded them to go thence that they should dwell in Canaan. Then after was there much hunger, that they descended into Egypt, and there abode four hundred years, and multiplied that they might not be numbered. When the king of Egypt grieved them in his buildings, bearing clay tiles, and subdued them, they cried to their Lord, and he smote the land of Egypt with divers plagues. When they of Egypt had cast them out from them, the plagues ceased from them and then they would have taken them again and would have called them to their service, and they fleeing, their God opened the sea to them that they went through dry-foot, in which the innumerable host of the Egyptians pursuing them were drowned, that there was not one of them saved for to tell to them that came after them. They passed thus the Red Sea, and he fed them with manna forty years, and made bitter waters sweet, and gave them water out of a stone. And wheresoever this people entered without bow or arrow, shield or sword, their God fought for them, and there is no man may prevail against this people but when they departed from the culture and honor of their God. And as oft as they have departed from their God and worshipped other strange gods, so oft have they been overcome with their enemies. And when they repent and come to the knowledge of their sin, and cry their God mercy, they be restored again, and their God giveth to them virtue to resist their enemies. They have overthrown Cananeum the king, Jebusee, Pheresee, Eneum, Etheum and Amoreum, and all the mighty men in Esebon, and have taken their lands and cities and possess them, and shall, as long as they please their God. Their God hateth wickedness, for tofore this time when they went from the laws that their God gave to them, he suffered them to be taken of many nations into captivity, and were disperpled. And now late they be come again and possess Jerusalem wherein is sancta sanctorum, and be come over these mountains whereas some of them dwell. Now therefore, my lord, see and search if there be any wickedness of them in the sight of their God, and then let us go to them, for their God shall give them into thy hands and they shall be subdued under the yoke of thy power.

And when Achior had said thus, all the great men about Holofernes were angry and had thought for to have slain him, saying each to other: Who is this that may make the children of Israel resist the king Nebuchadnezzar and his army and host? Men cowards and without might and without any wisdom of war. Therefore that Achior may know that he saith not true, let us ascend the mountains, and when the mighty men of them be taken let him be slain with them, that all men may know that Nebuchadnezzar is god of the earth, and that there is none other but he. Then when they ceased to speak, Holofernes having indignation said to Achior: Because thou hast prophesied to us of the children of Israel saying, that their God defend them, I shall show to thee that there is no god but Nebuchadnezzar, for whom we have overcome them all and slain them as one man, then shalt thou die with them by the sword of the Assyrians, and all Israel shall be put into ruin and perdition, and then shall be known that Nebuchadnezzar is lord of all the earth, and the sword of my knighthood shall pass through thy sides. And thou shalt depart hence and go to them, and shalt not die unto the time that I have them and thee. And when I have slain them with my sword thou shalt in like wise be slain with like vengeance. After this Holofernes commanded his servants to take Achior, and lead him to Bethulia and to put him in the hands of them of Israel. And so they took Achior and ascended the mountains, against whom came out men of war. Then the servants of Holofernes turned aside and bound Achior to a tree hands and feet with cords, and left him and so returned to their lord. Then the sons of Israel coming down from Bethulia loosed and unbound him, and brought him to Bethulia, and he being set amid the people was demanded what he was, and why he was so sore there bounden. And he told to them all the matter like as it is aforesaid, and how Holofernes had commanded him to be delivered unto them of Israel. Then all the people fell down on to their faces worshipping God, and with great lamentation and weeping, with one will made their prayers unto our Lord God of heaven, and that he would behold the pride of them, and to the meekness of them of Israel, and to take heed to the faces of his hallows and show to them his grace and not forsake them, and prayed God to have mercy on them and defend them from their enemies. And on that other side, Holofernes commanded his hosts to go up and assail Bethulia, and so went up, of footmen one hundred and twenty thousand, and twelve thousand horsemen, and besieged the town, and took their water from them, insomuch that they that were in the town were in great penury of water, for in all the town was not water enough for one day, and such as they had was given to the people by measure. Then all the people young and old came to Ozias which was their prince, with Charmis and Gothoniel, all with one voice crying: God the Lord deem between us and thee, for thou hast done to us evil what thou spakest not peaceably with Assyrians, for now we shall be delivered into the hands of them. It is better for us to live in captivity under Holofernes and live, than to die here for thirst, and see our wives and children die before our eyes. And when they had made this piteous crying and yelling, they went all to their church, and there a long while prayed and cried unto God knowledging their sins and wickedness, meekly beseeching him to show his grace and pity on them. Then at last Ozias arose up, and said to the people: Let us abide yet five days, and if God send us no rescue ne help us not in that time that we may give glory to his name, else we shall do as ye have said. And when that Judith heard thereof, which was a widow and a blessed woman, and was left widow three years and six months.

After that Manasses her husband died, anon she went into the overest part of her house in which she made a privy bed, which she and her servants closed, and having on her body a hair [hair cloth], had fasted all the days of her life save Sabbaths and new moons, and the feasts of the house of Israel. She was a fair woman and her husband had left her much riches, with plentiful meiny, and possessions of droves of oxen and flocks of sheep, and she was a famous woman and dreaded God greatly. And when she had heard that Ozias had said, that the fifth day the city should be given over if God helped them not, she sent for the priests Chambris and Charmis and said to them: What is this word in which Ozias hath consented that the city should be delivered to the Assyrians if within five days there come no help to us? And who be ye that tempt the Lord God? This word is not to stir God to mercy but rather to arouse wrath and woodness. Ye have set a time of mercy doing by God, and in your doom ye have ordained a day to him. O good Lord, how patient is he, let us ask him for forgiveness with weeping tears; he shall not threaten as a man, ne inflame in wrath as a son of a man, therefore meek we our souls to him and in a contrite spirit and meeked, serve we to him, and say we weeping to God, that after his will he show to us his mercy, and as our heart is troubled in the pride of them, so also of our humbleness and meekness let us be joyful. For we have not followed the sin of our fathers that forsook their God and worshipped strange gods, wherefore they were given and be taken into hideous and great vengeance, into sword, ravin, and into confusion to their enemies; we forsooth know no other god but him. Abide we meekly the comfort of him, and he shall keep us from our enemies and he shall make all gentiles that arise against him, and shall make them without worship the Lord our God. And now ye brethren, ye that be priests, on whom hangeth the life of the people of God, pray ye unto Almighty God that he make me steadfast in the purpose that I have proposed. Ye shall stand at the gate and I shall go out with my handmaid. And pray ye the Lord that he steadfast make my soul, and do ye nothing till I come again.

And then Judith went into her oratory, and arrayed her with her precious clothing and adornments, and took unto her handmaid certain victuals such as she might lawfully eat, and when she had made her prayers unto God she departed in her most noble array toward the gate, whereas Ozias and the priests abode her, and when they saw her they marvelled of her beauty. Notwithstanding they let her go, saying: God of our fathers give thee grace and strengthen all the counsel of thine heart with his virtue and glory to Jerusalem, and be thy name in the number of saints and of righteous men. And they all that were there said: Amen, and, fiat! fiat! [let it be done]. Then she praising god passed through the gate, and her handmaid with her. And when she came down the hill, about the springing of the day, anon the spies of the Assyrians took her saying: Whence comest thou, or whither goest thou? The which answered: I am a daughter of the Hebrews and flee from them, knowing that they shall be taken by you, and come to Holofernes for to tell him their privities, and I shall show him by what entry he may win them, in such wise as one man of his host shall not perish. And the men that heard these words beheld her visage and wondered of her beauty, saying to her: Thou hast saved thy life because thou hast founden such counsel, come therefore to our Lord, for when thou shalt stand in his sight he shall accept thee. And they led her to the tabernacle of Holofernes. And when she came before him anon Holofernes was caught by his eyes, and his tyrant knights said to him: Who despised the people of Jews that have so fair women, that not for them of right we ought to fight against them? And so Judith seeing Holofernes sitting in his canape that was of purple, of gold, smaragdos and precious stones within woven, and when she had seen his face she honored him, falling down herself unto the earth. And the servants of Holofernes took her up, he so commanding. Then Holofernes said to her: Be thou not afeard ne dread thee not. I never grieved ne noyed man that would serve Nebuchadnezzar. Thy people soothly, if they had not despised me, I had not raised my people ne strength against them. Now tell to me the cause why thou wentest from them, and that it hath pleased thee to come to us. And Judith said: Take the words of thine handmaid, and if thou follow them, a perfect thing God shall do with thee. Forsooth Nebuchadnezzar is the living king of the earth, and thou hast his power for to chastise all people, for men only serve not him, but also the beasts of the field obey to him, his might is known over all. And the children of Israel shall be yielded to thee, for their God is angry with them for their wickedness. They be enfamined and lack bread and water, they be constrained to eat their horse and beasts, and to take such holy things as be forbidden in their law, as wheat, wine, and oil, all these things God hath showed to me. And they purpose to waste such things as they ought not touch, and therefore and for their sins they shall be put in the hands of their enemies, and our Lord hath showed me these things to tell thee. And I thine handmaid shall worship God, and shall go out and pray him, and come in and tell thee what he shall say to me, in such wise that I shall bring thee through the middle of Jerusalem, and thou shalt have all the people of Israel under thee, as the sheep be under the shepherd, insomuch there shall not an hound burk against thee. And because these things be said to me by the providence of God, and that God is wroth with them, I am sent to tell thee these things.

Forsooth, all these words pleased much to Holofernes, and to his people, and they marvelled of the wisdom of her. And one said to another. There is not such a woman upon earth in sight, in fairness, and in wit of words. And Holofernes said to her: God hath done well that he hath sent thee hither for to let me have knowledge, and if thy God do to me these things he shall be my God, and thou and thy name shall be great in the house of Nebuchadnezzar. Then commanded Holofernes her to go in where his treasure lay, and to abide there, and to give to her meat from his feast, to whom she said that she might not eat of his meat, but that she had brought meat with her for to eat. Then Holofernes said: When that meat faileth what shall we give to thee to eat? And Judith said that she should not spend all till God shall do in my hands those things that I have thought. And the servants led her into his tabernacle, and she desired that she might go out in the night and before day to pray, and come in again. And the lord commanded his cubiculers that she should go and come at her pleasure three days during. And she went out into the valley of Bethulia and baptized her in the water of the well. And she stretched her hands up to the God of Israel, praying the good Lord that he would govern her way for to deliver his people; and thus she did unto the fourth day. Then Holofernes made a great feast, and sent a man of his, named Bagoas, for to entreat Judith to come eat and drink with him. And Judith said: What am I that should gainsay my lord's desire. I am at his commandment, whatsomever he will that I do, I shall do, and please him all the days of my life. And she rose and adorned herself with her rich and precious clothes, and went in and stood before Holofernes, and Holofernes' heart was pierced with her beauty, and he said to her: Sit down and drink in joy, for thou hast found grace before me. Judith said: I shall drink my lord, for my life is magnified this day before all the days of my life. And she ate and drank such as her handmaid had ordained for her. And Holofernes was merry and drank so much wine that he never drank so much in one day in all his life, and was drunken. And at even, when it was night, Holofernes went into his bed, and Bagoas brought Judith in to his chamber and closed the door. And when Judith was alone in the chamber, and Holofernes lay and slept in overmuch drunkenness, Judith said to her handmaid that she should stand without forth before the door of the privy chamber and wait about, and Judith stood before the bed praying with tears and with moving of her lips secretly, saying: O Lord God of Israel, conform me in this hour to the works of my hands, that thou raise up the city of Jerusalem as thou hast promised, and that I may perform this that I have thought to do. And when she had thus said, she went to the pillar that was at his bed's head, and took his sword and loosed it, and when she had drawn it out, she took his hair in her hand and said: Confirm me God of Israel in this hour, and smote twice in the neck and cut off his head, and left the body lie still, and took the head and wrapped it in the canape and delivered it to her maid, and bade her to put it in her scrip, and they two went out after their usage to pray. And they passed the tents, and going about the valley came to the gate of the city, and Judith said to the keepers of the walls: Open the gates, for God is with us that hath done great virtue in Israel. And anon when they heard her call, they called the priests of the city, and they came running for they had supposed no more to have seen her, and lighting lights all went about her.

She then entered in and stood up in a high place and commanded silence, and said: Praise ye the Lord God that forsaketh not men hoping in him; and in me his handwoman, hath fulfilled his mercy that he promised to the house of Israel, and hath slain in my hand the enemy of his people this night. And then she brought forth the head of Holofernes and showed it to them, saying: Lo! here the head of Holofernes, prince of the chivalry of Assyrians, and lo! the canape of him in which he lay in his drunkenhood, where our Lord hath smitten him by the hand of a woman. Forsooth God liveth, for his angel kept me hence going, there abiding, and from thence hither returning, and the Lord hath not suffered me, his handwoman, to be defouled, but without pollution of sin hath called me again to you joying in his victory, in my escaping and in your deliverance. Knowledge ye him all for good, for his mercy is everlasting, world without end. And all they, honoring our Lord, said to her: The Lord bless thee in his virtue, for by thee he hath brought our enemies to naught. Then Ozias, the prince of the people, said to her: Blessed be thou of the high God before all women upon earth, and blessed be the Lord that made heaven and earth, that hath addressed thee in the wounds of the head of the prince of our enemies. After this Judith bade that the head should be hanged up on the walls, and at the sun rising every man in his arms issue out upon your enemies, and when their spies shall see you, they shall run into the tent of their prince, to raise him and to make him ready to fight, and when his lords shall see him dead, they shall be smitten with so great dread and fear that they shall flee, whom ye then shall pursue, and God shall bring them and tread them under your feet. Then Achior seeing the virtue of the God of Israel, left his old heathen's customs and believed in God, and put himself to the people of Israel, and all the succession of his kindred unto this day. Then at the springing of the day they hung the head of Holofernes on the walls, and every man took his arms and went out with great noise, which thing seeing, the spies ran together to the tabernacle of Holofernes, and came making noise for to make him to arise, and that he should awake, but no man was so hardy to knock or enter into his privy chamber. But when the dukes and leaders of thousands came, and other, they said to the privy chamberlains: Go and awake your lord, for the mice be gone out of their caves and be ready to call us to battle. Then Bagoas went into his privy chamber and stood before the curtain, and clapped his hands together. And when he perceived no moving of him, he drew the curtain and seeing the dead body of Holofernes, without head, lying in his blood, cried with great voice, weeping and rending his clothes, and went in to the tabernacle of Judith and found her not, and started out to the people and said: A woman of the Hebrews hath made confusion in the house of Nebuchadnezzar, she hath slain Holofernes, and he is dead, and she hath his head with her.

And when the princes and captains of the Assyrians heard this, anon they rent their clothes, and intolerable dread fell on them, and were sore troubled in their wits and made a horrible cry in their tents. And when all the host had heard how Holofernes was beheaded, counsel and mind flew from them, and with great trembling for succor began to flee, in such wise that none would speak with other, but with their heads bowed down fled for to escape from the Hebrews, whom they saw armed coming upon them, and departed fleeing by fields and ways of hills and valleys. And the sons of Israel, seeing them fleeing, following them, crying with trumps and shouting after them, and slew and smote down all them that they overtook. And Ozias sent forth unto all the cities and regions of Israel, and they sent after all the young men and valiant to pursue them by sword, and so they did unto the uttermost coasts of Israel. The other men soothly, that were in Bethulia, went in to the tents of the Assyrians, and took all the prey that the Assyrians had left, and when the men had pursued them were returned, they took all their beasts and all the movable goods and things that they had left, so much that every man from the most to the least were made rich by the prey that they took. Then Joachim the high bishop of Jerusalem came unto Bethulia, with all the priests, for to see Judith, and when she came tofore them all, they blessed her with one voice, saying: Thou glory of Jerusalem, thou gladness of Israel, thou the worship doing of our people, thou didst manly, and thy heart is comforted because thou lovedst chastity and knewest no man after the death of thy husband, and therefore the hand of God hath comforted thee. And therefore thou shalt be blessed world without end, and all the people said: Fiat! fiat! be it done, be it done. Certainly the spoils of the Assyrians were unnethe gathered and assembled together in thirty days, of the people of Israel, but all the proper riches that were appertaining to Holofernes and could be found that had been his, they were given to Judith as well gold, silver, gems, clothes, as all other appurtenances to household; and all was delivered to her of the people, and the folks, with women and maidens, joyed in organs and harps. Then Judith sang this song unto God saying: Begin ye in timbrels, sing ye to the Lord in cymbals, mannerly sing to him a new psalm. Fully joy ye, and inwardly call ye his name, and so forth. And for this great miracle and victory all the people came to Jerusalem for to give laud, honor, and worship unto our Lord God. And after they were purified they offered sacrifices, vows, and behests unto God, and the joy of this victory was solemnized during three months, and after that, each went home again into his own city and house, and Judith returned into Bethulia, and was made more great and clear to all men of the land of Israel. She was joined to the virtue of chastity, so that she knew no man all the days of her life after the death of Manasses, her husband, and dwelled in the house of her husband an hundred and five years, and she left her demoiselle free. After this she died and is buried in Bethulia and all the people bewailed her seven days. During her life after this journey was no trouble among the Jews, and the day of this victory of the Hebrews was accepted for a feastful day, and hallowed of the Jews and numbered among their feasts unto this day.

THE VISION OF BELSHAZZAR

The King was on his throne,
  The Satraps throng'd the hall;
A thousand bright lamps shone
  O'er that high festival.
A thousand cups of gold,
  In Judah deem'd divine—
Jehovah's vessels hold
  The godless Heathen's wine.

In that same hour and hall
  The fingers of a Hand
Came forth against the wall,
  And wrote as if on sand:
The fingers of a man;—
  A solitary hand
Along the letters ran,
  And traced them like a wand.

The monarch saw, and shook,
  And bade no more rejoice;
All bloodless wax'd his look,
  And tremulous his voice:—
"Let the men of lore appear,
  The wisest of the earth,
And expound the words of fear,
  Which mar our royal mirth."

Chaldea's seers are good,
  But here they have no skill;
And the unknown letters stood
  Untold and awful still.
And Babel's men of age
  Are wise and deep in lore;
But now they were not sage,
  They saw—but knew no more.

A Captive in the land,
  A stranger and a youth,
He heard the king's command,
  He saw that writing's truth;
The lamps around were bright,
  The prophecy in view;
He read it on that night, —
  The morrow proved it true!

"Belshazzar's grave is made,
  His kingdom pass'd away,
He, in the balance weigh'd,
  Is light and worthless clay;
The shroud, his robe of state;
  His canopy, the stone:
The Mede is at his gate!
  The Persian on his throne!"

—Lord Byron

A CHRISTMAS CAROL

As Joseph was a-walking,
  He heard an angel sing,
"This night shall be the birth-time
  Of Christ, the heavenly king.

"He neither shall be born
  In housen nor in hall,
Nor in the place of paradise,
  But in an ox's stall.

"He neither shall be clothed
  In purple nor in pall,
But in the fair white linen
  That usen babies all.

"He neither shall be rocked
  In silver nor in gold,
But in a wooden manger
  That resteth on the mould."

As Joseph was a-walking,
  There did an angel sing,
And Mary's child at midnight
  Was born to be our king.

Then be ye glad, good people,
  This night of all the year,
And light ye up your candles,
  For his star it shineth clear.

ON THE MORNING OF CHRIST'S NATIVITY

This is the month, and this the happy morn
Wherein the Son of heav'n's eternal king
Of wedded Maid, and Virgin Mother born,
Our great redemption from above did bring;
For so the holy sages once did sing,
That He our deadly forfeit should release,
And with His Father work us a perpetual peace.

That glorious Form, that Light unsufferable,
And that far-beaming blaze of Majesty
Wherewith He wont at Heav'n's high council-table
To sit the midst of Trinal Unity,
He laid aside; and here with us to be,
Forsook the courts of everlasting day,
And chose with us a darksome house of mortal clay.

Say, heav'nly Muse, shall not thy sacred vein
Afford a present to the Infant God?
Hast thou no verse, no hymn, or solemn strain,
To welcome Him to this His new abode,
Now while the heav'n by the sun's team untrod,
Hath took no print of the approaching light,
And all the spangled host keep watch in squadrons bright?

See how from far, upon the eastern road
The star-led wizards haste with odors sweet:
O run, prevent them with thy humble ode,
And lay it lowly at His blessèd feet;
Have thou the honor first thy Lord to greet,
And join thy voice unto the angel quire,
From out His secret altar touch'd with hallow'd fire.

THE HYMN

It was the winter wild
While the heav'n-born Child
All meanly wrapt in the rude manger lies;
Nature in awe to Him
Had doff'd her gaudy trim,
With her great Master so to sympathize:
It was no season then for her
To wanton with the sun, her lusty paramour.

Only with speeches fair
She woos the gentle air
To hide her guilty front with innocent snow,
And on her naked shame,
Pollute with sinful blame,
The saintly veil of maiden white to throw,
Confounded that her Maker's eyes
Should look so near upon her foul deformities.

But He, her fears to cease,
Sent down the meek-ey'd Peace;
She crown'd with olive-green, came softly sliding
Down through the turning sphere,
His ready harbinger,
With turtle wing the amorous clouds dividing;
And waving wide her myrtle wand,
She strikes a universal peace through sea and land.

No war, or battle's sound
Was heard the world around:
The idle spear and shield were high up hung,
The hooked chariot stood
Unstain'd with hostile blood,
The trumpet spake not to the armed throng,
And kings sat still with awful eye,
As if they surely knew their sov'reign Lord was by.

But peaceful was the night,
Wherein the Prince of Light
His reign of peace upon the earth began:
The winds, with wonder whist,
Smoothly the waters kist,
Whispering new joys to the mild ocean,

Who now hath quite forgot to rave,
While birds of calm sit brooding on the charmed wave.

The stars with deep amaze,
Stand fix'd in steadfast gaze,
Bending one way their precious influence,
And will not take their flight,
For all the morning light,
Or Lucifer that often warn'd them thence;
But in their glimmering orbs did glow,
Until their Lord Himself bespake, and bid them go,

And though the shady gloom
Had given day her room,
The sun himself withheld his wonted speed,
And hid his head for shame,
As his inferior flame
The new-enlighten'd world no more should need;
He saw a greater Sun appear
Than his bright throne, or burning axle-tree, could bear.

The shepherds on the lawn,
Or ere the point of dawn,
Sate simply chatting in a rustic row;
Full little thought they then
That the mighty Pan
Was kindly come to live with them below;
Perhaps their loves, or else their sheep,
Was all that did their silly thoughts so busy keep.

When such music sweet
Their hearts and ears did greet,
As never was by mortal finger strook,
Divinely warbled voice
Answering the stringèd noise,
As all their souls in blissful rapture took:
The air, such pleasure loth to lose,
With thousand echoes still prolongs each heavenly close.

Nature that heard such sound,
Beneath the hollow round
Of Cynthia's seat, the airy region thrilling,
Now was almost won
To think her part was done,

And that her reign had here its last fulfilling;
She knew such harmony alone
Could hold all heav'n and earth in happier union.

At last surrounds their sight
A globe of circular light,
That with long beams the shamefac'd night array'd;
The helmèd Cherubim,
And sworded Seraphim,
Are seen in glittering ranks with wings display'd,
Harping in loud and solemn quire,
With unexpressive notes to Heaven's new-born Heir.

Such music (as 'tis said)
Before was never made,
But when of old the Sons of Morning sung,
While the Creator great
His constellations set,
And the well-balanc'd world on hinges hung,
And cast the dark foundations deep,
And bid the welt'ring waves their oozy channel keep.

Ring out, ye crystal spheres,
Once bless our human ears,
If ye have power to touch our senses so;
And let your silver chime
Move in melodious time,
And let the bass of Heav'n's deep organ blow;
And with your ninefold harmony
Make up full consort to th' angelic symphony.

For if such holy song
Inwrap our fancy long,
Time will run back, and fetch the age of gold,
And speckled Vanity
Will sicken soon and die,
And leprous Sin will melt from earthly mould
And Hell itself will pass away,
And leave her dolorous mansions to the peering day.

Yea, Truth and Justice then
Will down return to men,
Orb'd in a rainbow; and, like glories wearing,
Mercy will set between,

Throned in celestial sheen,
With radiant feet the tissued clouds down steering:
And Heav'n, as at some festival,
Will open wide the gates of her high palace hall.

But wisest Fate says, No.
This must not yet be so,
The Babe yet lies in smiling infancy,
That on the bitter cross
Must redeem our loss;
So both himself and us to glorify;
Yet first to those ychain'd in sleep,
The wakeful trump of doom must thunder through the deep,

With such a horrid clang
As on Mount Sinai rang,
While the red fire and smouldering clouds out-brake:
The aged Earth aghast,
With terror of that blast,
Shall from the surface to the centre shake;
When at the world's last sessiòn,
The dreadful Judge in middle air shall spread his throne.

And then at last our bliss
Full and perfect is,
But now begins; for from this happy day
The old Dragon under ground
In straiter limits bound,
Not half so far casts his usurped sway,
And wroth to see his kingdom fail,
Swinges the scaly horror of his folded tail.

The oracles are dumb,
No voice or hideous hum
Runs thro' the arched roof in words deceiving.
Apollo from his shrine
Can no more divine,
With hollow shriek the steep of Delphos leaving.
No nightly trance or breathèd spell
Inspires the pale-ey'd priest from the prophetic cell.

The lonely mountains o'er,
And the resounding shore,
A voice of weeping heard, and loud lament;

From haunted spring and dale
Edg'd with poplar pale,
The parting Genius is with sighing sent;
With flow'r-inwoven tresses torn
The Nymphs in twilight shade of tangled thickets mourn.

In consecrated earth,
And on the holy hearth,
The Lars, and Lemures moan with midnight plaint;
In urns, and altars round,
A drear and dying sound
Affrights the Flamens at their service quaint;
And the chill marble seems to sweat,
While each peculiar Power forgoes his wonted seat.

Peor and Baälim
Forsake their temples dim,
With that twice-batter'd god of Palestine;
And moonèd Ashtaroth,
Heaven's queen and mother both,
Now sits not girt with tapers' holy shine;
The Lybic Hammon shrinks his horn.
In vain the Tyrian maids their wounded Thammuz mourn.

And sullen Moloch fled,
Hath left in shadows dread
His burning idol all of blackest hue;
In vain with cymbals' ring
They call the grisly king,
In dismal dance about the furnace blue:
The brutish gods of Nile as fast,
Isis and Orus, and the dog Anubis haste.

Nor is Osiris seen
In Memphian grove or green,
Trampling the unshow'r'd grass with lowings loud:
Nor can he be at rest
Within his sacred chest,
Naught but profoundest hell can be his shroud;
In vain with timbrell'd anthems dark
The sable-stolèd sorcerers bear his worship'd ark.

He feels from Juda's land
The dreaded infant's hand,

The rays of Bethlehem blind his dusky eyn;
Not all the gods beside,
Longer dare abide,
Not Typhon huge ending in snaky twine:
Our Babe, to show his Godhead true,
Can in his swaddling bands control the damnèd crew.

So, when the sun in bed
Curtain'd with cloudy red
Pillows his chin upon an orient wave,
The flocking shadows pale
Troop to the infernal jail,
Each fetter'd ghost slips to his several grave;
And the yellow-skirted fays
Fly after the night-steeds, leaving their moon-loved maze.

But see, the Virgin blest
Hath laid her Babe to rest;
Time is, our tedious song should here have ending:
Heaven's youngest-teemèd star
Hath fix'd her polish'd car,
Her sleeping Lord with handmaid lamp attending:
And all about the courtly stable
Bright-harness'd angels sit in order serviceable.

—J. Milton

THE BURNING BABE

As I in hoary winter's night stood shivering in the snow,
Surprised I was with sudden heat, which made my heart to glow;
And lifting up a fearful eye to view what fire was near,
A pretty babe, all burning bright, did in the air appear;
Who, scorchèd with excessive heat, such floods of tears did shed,
As though his floods should quench his flames which with his
    tears were fed:—
"Alas!" quoth He, "but newly born, in fiery heats I fry,
Yet none approach to warm their hearts or feel my fire but I!
My faultless breast the furnace is, the fuel wounding thorns;
Love is the fire, and sighs the smoke, the ashes shame and scorns;
The fuel Justice layeth on, and Mercy blows the coals,
The metal in this furnace wrought are men's defilèd souls,
For which, as now on fire I am, to work them to their good,
So will I melt into a bath to wash them in my blood."—
With this He vanish'd out of sight, and swiftly shrunk away;
And straight I called unto mind that it was Christmasday.

    —R. Southwell

A CRADLE SONG

Hush! my dear, lie still and slumber;
Holy angels guard thy bed!
Heavenly blessings without number
Gently falling on thy head.

Sleep, my babe; thy food and raiment,
House and home, thy friends provide,
All without thy care or payment
All thy wants are well supplied.

How much better thou'rt attended
Than the Son of God could be,
When from heaven He descended,
And became a child like thee!

Soft and easy is thy cradle;
Coarse and hard thy Saviour lay:
When his birthplace was a stable,
And his softest bed was hay.

See the kindly shepherds round him,
Telling wonders from the sky!
Where they sought him, there they found him,
With his Virgin-Mother by.

See the lovely babe a-dressing:
Lovely infant, how he smiled!
When he wept, the mother's blessing
Soothed and hush'd the holy child.

Lo, he slumbers in his manger,
Where the hornèd oxen fed;
—Peace, my darling! here's no danger!
Here's no ox a-near thy bed!

—May'st thou live to know and fear him,
Trust and love him all thy days:

Then go dwell forever near him;
See his face, and sing his praise.

I could give thee thousand kisses,
Hoping what I most desire:
Not a mother's fondest wishes
Can to greater joys aspire.

—*I. Watts*

EASTER

I got me flowers to straw Thy way,
I got me boughs off many a tree;
But Thou wast up by break of day,
And brought'st Thy sweets along with Thee.

The sun arising in the East,
Though he give light, and th' East perfume,
If they should offer to contest
With Thy arising, they presume.

Can there be any day but this,
Though many suns to shine endeavor?
We count three hundred, but we miss:
There is but one, and that one ever.

—*George Herbert*

THE LIFE OF ST. PETER THE APOSTLE

St. Peter the apostle among all other, and above all other, was of most fervent and burning love, for he would have known the traitor that should betray our Lord Jesu Christ, as St. Austin saith: If he had known him he would have torn him with his teeth, and therefore our Lord would not name him to him, for as Chrysostom, saith: If he had named him, Peter had arisen and all to-torn him. Peter went upon the sea; he was chosen of God to be at his transfiguration, and raised a maid from death to life; he found the stater or piece of money in the fish's mouth; he received of our Lord the keys of the kingdom of heaven; he took the charge to feed the sheep of Jesu Christ. He converted at a Whitsuntide three thousand men, he healed Claude with John, and then converted five thousand men; he said to Ananias and Saphira their death before; he healed Æneas of the palsy; he raised Tabitha; he baptized Cornelia; with the shadow of his body he healed sick men; he was put in prison by Herod, but by the angel of our Lord he was delivered. What his meat was and his clothing, the book of St. Clement witnesseth, for he said: Bread only with olives, and seldom with worts, is mine usage, and I have such clothing as thou seest, a coat and a mantle, and when I have that, I demand no more. It is said for certain that he bare always a sudary in his bosom, with which he wiped the tears that ran from his eyes; for when he remembered the sweet presence of our Lord, for the great love that he had to him he might not forbear weeping. And also when he remembered that he had renied him, he wept abundantly great plenty of tears, in such wise that he was so accustomed to weep that his face was burned with tears as it seemed, like as Clement saith. And saith also that in the night when he heard the cock crow he would weep customably. And after that it is read in Historia Ecclesiastica that, when St. Peter's wife was led to her passion, he had great joy and called her by her proper name, and said to her: My wife, remember thee of our Lord.

On a time when St. Peter had sent two of his disciples for to preach the faith of Jesu Christ, and when they had gone twenty days' journey, one of them died, and that other then returned to St. Peter and told him what had happened, some say that it was St. Marcial that so died, and some say it was St. Maternus, and others say that it was St. Frank. Then St. Peter gave to him his staff and commanded that he should return to his fellow, and lay it upon him, which he so did, then he which had been forty days dead, anon arose all living.

That time Simon the enchanter was in Jerusalem, and he said he was first truth, and affirmed that who that would believe in him he would make them perpetual. And he also said that nothing to him was impossible. It is read in the book of St. Clement that he said that he should be worshipped of all men as God, and that he might do all that he would. And he said yet more: When my mother Rachel commanded me that I should go reap corn in the field, and saw the sickle ready to reap with, I commanded the sickle to reap by itself alone, and it reaped ten times more than any other. And yet he added hereto more, after Jerome, and said: I am the Word of God, I am the Holy Ghost, I am Almighty, I am all that is of God. He made serpents of brass to move, and made the images of iron and of stone to laugh, and dogs to sing, and as St. Linus saith, he would dispute with St. Peter and show, at a day assigned, that he was God. And Peter came to the place where the strife should be, and said to them that were there: Peace to you brethren that love truth. To whom Simon said: We have none need of thy peace, for if peace and concord were made, we should not profit to find the truth, for thieves have peace among them. And therefore desire no peace but battle, for when two men fight and one is overcome then is it peace. Then said Peter: Why dreadest thou to hear of peace? Of sins grow battles, where is no sin there is peace; in disputing is truth found, and in works righteousness. Then said Simon: It is not as thou sayest, but I shall show to thee the power of my dignity, that anon thou shalt adore me; I am first truth, and may flee by the air; I can make new trees and turn stones into bread; endure in the fire without hurting; and all that I will I may do. St. Peter disputed against all these, and disclosed all his malefices. Then Simon Magus, seeing that he might not resist Peter, cast all his books into the sea, lest St. Peter should prove him a magician, by his books, and went to Rome where he was had and reputed as a god. And when Peter knew that, he followed and came to Rome. The fourth year of Claudius the emperor, Peter came to Rome, and sat there twenty-five years, and ordained two bishops as his helpers, Linus and Cletus, one within the walls, and that other without. He entended much to preaching of the Word of God, by which he converted much people to the faith of Christ, and healed many sick men, and in his preaching always he praised and preferred chastity. He converted four concubines, of Agrippa the provost, so that they would no more come to him, wherefore the provost sought occasion against Peter.

After this, our Lord appeared to St. Peter, saying to him: Simon Magus and Nero purpose against thee, dread thee not, for I am with thee, and shall give to thee the solace of my servant Paul, which to-morn shall come in to Rome. Then Peter, knowing that he should not long abide here, assembled all his brethren, and took Clement by the hand and ordained him a bishop, and made him to sit in his own seat. After this, as our Lord had said tofore, Paul came to Rome, and with Peter began to preach the faith of Christ.

Simon Magus was so much beloved of Nero that he weened that he had been the keeper of his life, of his health, and of all the city. On a day, as Leo the pope saith, as he stood tofore Nero, suddenly his visage changed, now old and now young, which, when Nero saw, he supposed that he had been the son of God. Then said Simon Magus to Nero: Because that thou shalt know me to be the very son of God, command my head to be smitten off and I shall arise again the third day. Then Nero commanded to his brother to smite off his head, and when he supposed to have beheaded Simon, he beheaded a ram. Simon, by his art magic went away unhurt, and gathered together the members of the ram, and hid him three days. The blood of the ram abode and congealed. The third day he came and showed him to Nero, saying: Command my blood to be washed away, for lo I am he that was beheaded, and as I promised I have risen again the third day. Whom Nero seeing, was abashed and trowed verily that he had been the son of God. All this saith Leo. Sometime also, when he was with Nero secretly within his conclave, the devil in his likeness spake without to the people. Then the Romans had him in such worship that they made to him an image, and wrote above, this title: To Simon the holy God. Peter and Paul entered to Nero and discovered all the enchantments and malefices of Simon Magus, and Peter added thereto, seeing that like as in Christ be two substances that is of God and man, so are in this magician two substances, that is of man and of the devil. Then said Simon Magus, as St. Marcelle and Leo witness, lest I should suffer any longer this enemy, I shall command my angels that they shall avenge me on him. To whom Peter said: I dread nothing thine angels, but they dread me. Nero said: Dreadest thou not Simon, that by certain things affirmeth his godhead? To whom Peter said: If dignity or godhead be in him let him tell now what I think or what I do, which thought I shall first tell to thee, that he shall not mow lie what I think. To whom Nero said: Come hither and say what thou thinkest. Then Peter went to him and said to him secretly: Command some man to bring to me a barley-loaf, and deliver it to me privily. When it was taken to him, he blessed it, and hid it under his sleeve, and then said he: Now Simon say what I think, and have said and done. Simon answered: Let Peter say what I think. Peter answered: What Simon thinketh that I know, I shall do it when he hath thought. Then Simon having indignation, cried aloud: I command that dogs come and devour him. And suddenly there appeared great dogs and made an assault against

Peter. He gave to them of the bread that he had blessed, and suddenly he made them to flee. Then said Peter to Nero: Lo! I have showed you what he thought against me, not in words but in deeds, for where he promised angels to come against me he brought dogs, thereby he showeth that he hath none angels but dogs. Then said Simon: Hear ye, Peter and Paul; if I may not grieve you here, ye shall come where me it shall behove to judge you. I shall spare you here. Hæc Leo. Then Simon Magus, as Hegesippus and Linus say, elate in pride avaunted him that he can raise dead men to life. And it happed that there was a young man dead, and then Nero let call Peter and Simon, and all gave sentence by the will of Simon that he should be slain that might not arise the dead man to life. Simon then, as he made his incantations upon the dead body, he was seen move his head of them that stood by; then all they cried for to stone Peter. Peter unnethe getting silence said: If the dead body live, let him arise, walk and speak, else know ye that it is a fantasy that the head of the dead man moveth. Let Simon be taken from the bed. And the body abode immovable. Peter standing afar making his prayer cried to the dead body, saying: Young man, arise in the name of Jesu Christ of Nazareth crucified, and anon, he arose living, and walked. Then, when the people would have stoned Simon Magus, Peter said: He is in pain enough, knowing him to be overcome in his heart; our master hath taught us for to do good for evil. Then said Simon to Peter and Paul: Yet is it not come to you that ye desire, for ye be not worthy to have martyrdom, the which answered: That is, that we desire to have, to thee shall never be well, for thou liest all that thou sayest.

Then as Marcel saith: Simon went to the house of Marcel and bound there a great black dog at the door of the house, and said: Now I shall see if Peter, which is accustomed to come hither, shall come, and if he come this dog shall strangle him. And a little after that, Peter and Paul went thither, and anon Peter made the sign of the cross and unbound the hound, and the hound was as tame and meek as a lamb, and pursued none but Simon, and went to him and took and cast him to the ground under him, and would have strangled him. And then ran Peter to him and cried upon the hound that he should not do him any harm. And anon the hound left and touched not his body, but he all torent and tare his gown in such wise that he was almost naked. Then all the people, and especially children, ran with the hound upon him and hunted and chased him out of the town as he had been a wolf. Then for the reproof and shame he durst not come in to the town of all a whole year after. Then Marcel that was disciple of Simon Magus, seeing these great miracles, came to Peter, and was from then forthon his disciple.

And after, at the end of the year, Simon returned and was received again into the amity of Nero. And then, as Leo saith, this Simon Magus assembled the people and showed to them how he had been angered of the Galileans, and therefore he said that he would leave the city which he was wont to defend and keep, and set a day in which he would ascend into heaven, for he deigned no more to dwell in the earth. Then on the day that he had stablished, like as he had said, he went up to an high tower, which was on the capitol, and there being crowned with laurel, threw himself out from place to place, and began to fly in the air. Then said St. Paul to St. Peter: It appertaineth to me to pray, and to thee for to command. Then said Nero: This man is very God, and ye be two traitors. Then said St. Peter to St. Paul: Paul, brother, lift up thine head and see how Simon flyeth. Then St. Paul said to St. Peter when he saw him fly so high: Peter, why tarriest thou? perform that thou hast begun, God now calleth us. Then said Peter: I charge and conjure you angels of Sathanas, which bear him in the air, by the name of our Lord Jesu Christ, that ye bear ne sustain him no more, but let him fall to the earth. And anon they let him fall to the ground and brake his neck and head, and he died there forthwith. And when Nero heard say that Simon was dead, and that he had lost such a man, he was sorrowful, and said to the apostles: Ye have done this in despite of me, and therefore I shall destroy you by right evil example. Hæc Leo. Then he delivered them to Paulin, which was a much noble man, and Paulin delivered them to Mamertin under the keeping of two knights, Processe and Martinian, whom St. Peter converted to the faith. And they then opened the prison and let them all go out that would go, wherefore, after the passion of the apostles, Paulin, when he knew that they were Christian, beheaded both Processe and Martinian.

The brethren then, when the prison was opened, prayed Peter to go thence, and he would not, but at the last he being overcome by their prayers went away. And when he came to the gate, as, Leo witnesseth, which is called Sancta Maria ad passus, he met Jesu Christ coming against him, and Peter said to him: Lord, whither goest thou? And he said to him: I go to Rome for to be crucified again, and Peter demanded him: Lord, shalt thou be crucified again? And he said: Yea, and Peter said then: Lord, I shall return again then for to be crucified with thee. This said, our Lord ascended into heaven, Peter beholding it, which wept sore. And when Peter understood that our Lord had said to him of his passion, he returned, and when he came to his brethren, he told to them what our Lord had said. And anon he was taken of the ministers of Nero and was delivered to the provost Agrippa, then was his face as clear as the sun, as it is said. Then Agrippa said to him: Thou art he that glorifiest in the people, and in women, that thou departest from the bed of their husbands. Whom the apostle blamed, and said to him that he glorified in the cross of the Lord Jesu Christ. Then Peter was commanded to be crucified as a stranger, and because that Paul was a citizen of Rome it was commanded that his head should be smitten off. And of this sentence given against them, St. Dionysius in an epistle to Timothy saith in this wise: O my brother Timothy, if thou hadst seen the agonies of the end of them thou shouldst have failed for heaviness and sorrow. Who should not weep that hour when the commandment of the sentence was given against them, that Peter should be crucified and Paul be beheaded? Thou shouldst then have seen the turbes of the Jews and of the paynims that smote them and spit in their visages. And when the horrible time came of their end that they were departed that one from that other, they bound the pillars of the world, but that was not without wailing and weeping of the brethren. Then said St. Paul to St. Peter: Peace be with thee that are foundement of the church and pastor of the sheep and lambs of our Lord. Peter then said to Paul: Go thou in peace, preacher of good manners, mediator, leader, and solace of rightful people. And when they were withdrawn far from other I followed my master. They were not both slain in one street. This saith St. Dionysius, and as Leo the pope and Marcel witness, when Peter came to the cross, he said: When my Lord descended from heaven to the earth he was put on the cross right up, but me whom it pleaseth him to call from the earth to heaven, my cross shall show my head to the earth and address my feet to heaven, for I am not worthy to be put on the cross like as my Lord was, therefore turn my cross and crucify me my head downward. Then they turned the cross, and fastened his feet upward and the head downward. Then the people were angry against Nero and the provost, and would have slain them because they made St. Peter so to die; but he required them that they should not let his passion, and as Leo witnesseth, our Lord opened the eyes of them that were there, and wept so that, they saw the angels with crowns of roses and of lilies standing by Peter that was on the cross with the angels.

And then Peter received a book of our Lord, wherein he learned the words that he said. Then as Hegesippus saith: Peter said thus: Lord, I have desired much to follow thee, but to be crucified upright I have not usurped, thou art always rightful, high and sovereign, and we be sons of the first man which have the head inclined to the earth, of whom the fall signifieth the form of the generation human. Also we be born that we be seen inclined to the earth by effect, and the condition is changed for the world weeneth that such thing is good, which is evil and bad. Lord, thou art all things to me, and nothing is to me but thou only, I yield to thee thankings with all the spirit of which I live, by which I understand, and by whom I call thee. And when St. Peter saw that the good Christian men saw his glory, in yielding thankings to God and commending good people to him, he rendered up his spirit. Then Marcel and Apuleius his brother, that were his disciples, took off the body from the cross when he was dead, and anointed it with much precious ointment, and buried him honorably. Isidore saith in the book of the nativity and death of saints thus: Peter, after that he had governed Antioch, he founded a church under Claudius the emperor, he went to Rome against Simon Magus, there he preached the gospel twenty-five years and held the bishopric, and thirty-six years after the passion of our Lord he was crucified by Nero turned the head downward, for he would be so crucified: Hæc Isidorus.

That same day Peter and Paul appeared to St. Dionysius, as he saith in his foresaid epistle in these words: Understand the miracle and see the prodigy, my brother Timothy, of the day of the martyrdom of them, for I was ready in the time of departing of them. After their death I saw them together, hand in hand, entering the gates of the city, and clad with clothes of light, and arrayed with crowns of clearness and light. Hæc Dionysius.

Nero was not unpunished for their death and other great sins and tyrannies that he committed, for he slew himself with his own hand, which tyrannies were overlong to tell, but shortly I shall rehearse here some. He slew his master Seneca because he was afraid of him when he went to school. Also Nero slew his mother. Then for his pleasure he set Rome afire, which burned seven days and seven nights, and was in a high tower and enjoyed him to see so great a flame of fire, and sang merrily. He slew the senators of Rome to see what sorrow and lamentation their wives would make. He fished with nets of gold thread, and the garment that he had worn one day he would never wear it ne see it after. Then the Romans seeing his woodness [madness], assailed him and pursued him unto without the city, and when he saw he might not escape them, he took a stake and sharped it with his teeth, and therewith stuck himself through the body and so slew himself. In another place it is read that he was devoured of wolves. Then the Romans returned and found the frog, and threw it out of the city and there burned it.

In the time of St. Cornelius the pope, Greeks stole away the bodies of the apostles Peter and Paul, but the devils that were in the idols were constrained by the divine virtue of God, and cried and said: Ye men of Rome, succor hastily your gods which be stolen from you; for which thing the good Christian people understood that they were the bodies of Peter and Paul. And the Paynims had supposed that it had been their gods. Then assembled great number of Christian men and of Paynims also, and pursued so long the Greeks that they doubted to have been slain, and threw the bodies in a pit at the catacombs, but afterward they were drawn out by Christian men. St. Gregory saith that the great force of thunder and lightning that came from heaven made them so afraid that they departed each from other, and so left the bodies of the apostles at the catacombs in a pit, but they doubted which bones were Peter's and which Paul's, wherefore the good Christian men put them to prayers and fastings, and it was answered them from heaven that the great bones longed to the preacher, and the less to the fisher, and so were departed, and the bones were put in the church of him that it was dedicate of. And others say that Silvester the pope would hallow the churches and took all the bones together, and departed them by weight, great and small, and put that one-half in one church, and that other half in that other.

And St. Gregory recounteth in his dialogues that, in the church of St. Peter, where his bones rest, was a man of great holiness and of meekness named Gentian, and there came a maid into the church which was cripple, and drew her body and legs after her with her hands, and when she had long required and prayed St. Peter for health, he appeared to her in a vision, and said to her: Go to Gentian, my servant, and he shall restore thy health. Then began she to creep here and there through the church, and inquired who was Gentian, and suddenly it happed that he came to her that him sought, and she said to him: The holy apostle St. Peter sent me to thee that thou shouldest make me whole and deliver me from my disease, and he answered: If thou be sent to me from him, arise thou anon and go on thy feet. And he took her by the hand and anon she was all whole, in such wise as she felt nothing of her grief nor malady, and then she thanked God and St. Peter.

And in the same book St. Gregory saith when that a holy priest was come to the end of his life, he began to cry in great gladness: Ye be welcome, my lords, ye be welcome that ye vouchsafe to come to so little and poor a servant, and he said: I shall come and thank you. Then they that stood by demanded who they were that he spake to, and he said to them wondering: Have ye not seen the blessed apostles Peter and Paul? and as he cried again, his blessed soul departed from the flesh.

Some have doubt whether Peter and Paul suffered death in one day, for some say it was the same one day, but one a year after the other. And Jerome and all the Saints that treat of this matter accord that it was on one day and one year, and so is it contained in an epistle of Denis, and Leo the pope saith the same in a sermon, saying: We suppose but that it was not done without cause that they suffered in one day and in one place the sentence of the tyrant, and they suffered death in one time, to the end that they should go together to Jesu Christ, and both under one persecutor to the end that equal cruelty should strain that one and that other. The day for their merit, the place for their glory, and the persecution overcome by virtue.

Though they suffered both death in one day and in one hour, yet it was not in one place but in diverse within Rome, and hereof saith a versifier in this wise: Ense coronatus Paulus, cruce Petrus, eodem—Sub duce, luce, loco, dux Nero, Roma locus. That is to say, Paul crowned with the sword, and Peter had the cross reversed, the place was the city of Rome. And howbeit that they suffered death in one day, yet St. Gregory ordained that that day specially should be the solemnity of St. Peter, and the next day commemoration of St. Paul, for the church of St. Peter was hallowed that same day, and also forasmuch as he was more in dignity, and first in conversion, and held the principality at Rome.

THE LIFE OF ST. PAUL THE APOSTLE

St. Paul the apostle, after his conversion, suffered many persecutions, the which the blessed Hilary rehearseth shortly, saying: Paul the Apostle was beaten with rods at Philippi, he was put in prison, and by the feet fast set in stocks, he was stoned in Lystra. In Iconia and Thessalonica he was pursued of wicked people. In Ephesus he was delivered to wild beasts. In Damascus he was let by a lepe down of the wall. In Jerusalem he was arrested, beaten, bound, and awaited to be slain. In Cæsarea he was inclosed and defamed. Sailing toward Italy he was in peril of death, and from thence he came to Rome and was judged under Nero, and there finished his life. This saith St. Hilary: Paul took upon him to be apostle among the Gentiles. In Lystra was a contract which he lost and redressed. A young man that fell out of a window and died, he raised to life, and did many other miracles. At the Isle of Melita a serpent bit his hand, and hurted him not, and he threw it into the fire. It is said that all they that came of the progeny and lineage of that man that then harbored Paul may in no wise be hurt of no venemous beasts, wherefore when their children be born they put serpents in their cradles for to prove if they be verily their children or no. In some place it is said that Paul is less than Peter, otherwhile more, and sometimes equal and like, for in dignity he is less, in preaching greater, and in holiness they be equal. Haymo saith that Paul, from the cock-crow until the hour of five, he labored with his hands, and after entended to preaching, and that endured almost to night, the residue of the time was for to eat, sleep, and for prayer, which was necessary. He came to Rome when Nero was not fully confirmed in the empire, and Nero hearing that there was disputing and questions made between Paul and the Jews, he, recking not much thereof, suffered Paul to go where he would, and preach freely. Jeronimus saith in his book, De viris illustribus, that the thirty-sixth year after the Passion of our Lord, the second year of Nero, St. Paul was sent to Rome bound, and two years he was in free keeping and disputed against the Jews, and after, he was let go by Nero, and preached the gospel in the west parts. And the fourteenth year of Nero, the same year and day that Peter was crucified, his head was smitten off. Hæc Jeronimus. The wisdom and religion of him was published over all, and was reputed marvellous. He gat to him many friends in the emperor's house and converted them to the faith of Christ, and some of his writings were recited and read tofore the emperor, and of all men marvellously commended, and the senate understood of him by things of authority.

It happed on a day that Paul preached about evensong time in a loft, a young man named Patroclus, butler of Nero, and with him well-beloved, went for to see the multitude of people, and the better for to hear Paul he went up into a window, and there sleeping, fell down and died, which when Nero heard he was much sorry and heavy therefor, and anon ordered another in his office. Paul knowing hereof by the Holy Ghost, said to them standing by him that they should go and bring to him Patroclus, which was dead, and that the emperor loved so much. Whom when he was brought, he raised to life and sent him with his fellows to the emperor, whom the emperor knew for dead, and, while he made lamentation for him, it was told to the emperor that Patroclus was come to the gate. And when he heard that Patroclus was alive he much marvelled, and commanded that he should come in. To whom Nero said: Patroclus, livest thou? And he said: Yea, emperor, I live; and Nero said: Who hath made thee to live again? And he said: The Lord Jesu Christ, king of all worlds. Then Nero being wroth said: Then shall he reign ever and resolve all the royaumes of the world? To whom Patroclus said: Yea, certainly, emperor; then Nero gave to him a buffet, saying: Therefore thou servest him, and he said: Yea, verily, I serve him that hath raised me from death to life. Then five of the ministers of Nero, that assisted him, said to him: O emperor, why smitest thou this young man, truly and wisely answering to thee? Trust verily we serve that same King Almighty. And when Nero heard that he put them in prison, for strongly to torment them, whom he much had loved. Then he made to inquire and to take all Christian men, and without examination made them to be tormented with overgreat torments. Then was Paul among others bound and brought tofore Nero, to whom Nero said: O thou man, servant of the great King, bound tofore me, why withdrawest thou my knights and drawest them to thee? To whom Paul said: Not only from thy corner I have gathered knights, but also I gather from the universal world to my Lord, to whom our king giveth such gifts that never shall fail, and granteth that they shall be excluded from all indigence and need; and if thou wilt be to him subject, thou shalt be safe, for he is of so great power that he shall come and judge all the world, and destroy the figure thereof by fire. And when Nero heard that he should destroy the figure of the world by fire, he commanded that all the Christian men should be burned by fire, and Paul to be beheaded, as he that is guilty against his majesty. And so great a multitude of Christian people were slain then, that the people of Rome brake up his palace and cried and moved sedition against him, saying: Cæsar, amend thy manners and attemper thy commandments, for these be our people that thou destroyest, and defend the empire of Rome. The emperor then dreading the noise of the people, changed his decree and edict that no man should touch ne hurt no Christian man till the emperor had otherwise ordained, wherefore Paul was brought again tofore Nero, whom as soon as Nero saw, he cried and said: Take away this wicked man and behead him, and suffer him no longer to live upon the earth. To whom Paul said: Nero, I shall suffer a little while, but I shall live eternally with my Lord Jesu Christ. Nero said: Smite off his head, that he may understand me stronger than his king, that when he is overcome we may see whether he may live after. To whom Paul said: To the end that thou know me to live everlastingly, when my head shall be smitten off, I shall appear to thee living, and then thou mayst know that Christ is God of life and of death. And when he had said this he was led to the place of his martyrdom, and as he was led, the three knights that led him said to him: Tell to us, Paul, who is he your king that ye love so much that for his love ye had liefer die than live, and what reward shall ye have therefor? Then Paul preached to them of the kingdom of heaven and of the pain of hell, in such wise that he converted them to the faith, and they prayed him to go freely whither he would. God forbid, brethren, said he, that I should flee, I am not fugitive, but the lawful knight of Christ. I know well that from this transitory life I shall go to everlasting life. As soon as I shall be beheaded, true men shall take away my body; mark ye well the place, and come thither to-morrow, and ye shall find by my sepulchre two men, Luke and Titus, praying. To whom when ye shall tell for what cause I have sent you to them, they shall baptize you and make you heirs of the kingdom of heaven.

And whiles they thus spake together, Nero sent two knights to look if he were slain and beheaded or no, and when thus St. Paul would have converted them, they said: When thou art dead and risest again, then we shall believe, now come forth and receive that thou hast deserved. And as he was led to the place of his passion in the gate of Hostence, a noble woman named Plautilla, a disciple of Paul, who after another name was called Lemobia, for haply she had two names, met there with Paul, which weeping, commended her to his prayers. To whom Paul said: Farewell, Plautilla, daughter of everlasting health, lend to me thy veil or keverchief with which thou coverest thy head, that I may bind mine eyes therewith, and afterward I shall restore it to thee again. And when she had delivered it to him, the butchers scorned her, saying: Why hast thou delivered to this enchanter so precious a cloth for to lose it? Then, when he came to the place of his passion, he turned him toward the east, holding his hands up to heaven right long, with tears praying in his own language and thanking our Lord; and after that bade his brethren farewell, and bound his eyes himself with the keverchief of Plautilla, and kneeling down on both knees, stretched forth his neck, and so was beheaded. And as soon as the head was from the body, it said: Jesus Christus! which had been to him so sweet in his life. It is said that he named Jesus or Christus, or both, fifty times. From his wound sprang out milk into the clothes of the knight, and afterward flowed out blood. In the air was a great shining light, and from the body came a much sweet odor.

Dionysius, in an epistle to Timothy, saith of the death of Paul thus: In that hour full of heaviness, my well-beloved brother, the butcher, saying: Paul, make ready thy neck; then blessed Paul looked up into heaven marking his forehead and his breast with the sign of the cross, and then said anon: My Lord Jesus Christ, into thy hands I commend my spirit, etc. And then without heaviness and compulsion he stretched forth his neck and received the crown of martyrdom, the butcher so smiting off his head. The blessed martyr Paul took the keverchief, and unbound his eyes, and gathered up his own blood, and put it therein and delivered to the woman, Then the butcher returned, and Plautilla met him and demanded him, saying: Where hast thou left my master? The knight answered: He lieth without the town with one of his fellows, and his visage is covered with thy keverchief, and she answered and said: I have now seen Peter and Paul enter into the city clad with right noble vestments, and also they had right fair crowns upon their heads, more clear and more shining than the sun, and hath brought again my keverchief all bloody which he hath delivered me. For which thing and work many believed in our Lord and were baptized. And this is that St. Dionysius saith. And when Nero heard say this thing he doubted him, and began to speak of all these things with his philosophers and with his friends; and as they spake together of this matter, Paul came in, and the gates shut, and stood tofore Cæsar and said: Cæsar, here is tofore thee Paul the knight of the king perdurable, and not vanquished. Now believe then certainly that I am not dead but alive, but thou, caitiff, thou shalt die of an evil death, because thou hast slain the servants of God. And when he had said thus he vanished away. And Nero, what for dread and what for anger, he was nigh out of his wit, and wist not what to do. Then by the counsel of his friends he unbound Patroclus and Barnabas and let them go where they would.

And the other knights, Longinus, master of the knights, and Accestus, came on the morn to the sepulchre of Paul, and there they found two men praying, that were Luke and Titus, and between them was Paul. And when

Luke and Titus saw them they were abashed and began to flee, and anon Paul vanished away, and the knights cried after them and said: We come not to grieve you, but know ye for truth that we come for to be baptized of you, like as Paul hath said whom we saw now praying with you. When they heard that they returned and baptized them with great joy. The head of St. Paul was cast in a valley, and for the multitude of other heads of men that were slain and thrown there, it could not be known which it was.

THE LIFE OF ST. CHRISTOPHER

Christopher tofore his baptism was named Reprobus, but afterward he was named Christopher, which is as much to say as bearing Christ. Christopher was of the lineage of the Canaanites, and he was of a right great stature, and had a terrible and fearful cheer and countenance. And he was twelve cubits of length, and as it is read in some histories that, when he served and dwelled with the king of Canaan, it came in his mind that he would seek the greatest prince that was in the world, and him would he serve and obey. And so far he went that he came to a right great king, of whom the renomee generally was that he was the greatest of the world. And when the king saw him, he received him into his service, and made him to dwell in his court. Upon a time a minstrel sang tofore him a song in which he named oft the devil, and the king, which was a Christian man, when he heard him name the devil, made anon the sign of the cross in his visage. And when Christopher saw that, he had great marvel what sign it was, and wherefore the king made it, and he demanded of him. And because the king would not say, he said: If thou tell me not, I shall no longer dwell with thee, and then the king told to him, saying: Alway when I hear the devil named, I fear that he should have power over me, and I garnish me with this sign that he grieve not ne annoy me. Then Christopher said to him: Doubtest thou the devil that he hurt thee not? Then is the devil more mighty and greater than thou art. I am then deceived of my hope and purpose, for I had supposed I had found the most mighty and the most greatest Lord of the world, but I commend thee to God, for I will go seek him for to be my Lord, and I his servant. And then departed from this king, and hasted him for to seek the devil.

And as he went by a great desert, he saw a great company of knights, of which a knight cruel and horrible came to him and demanded whither he went, and Christopher answered to him and said: I go seek the devil for to be my master. And he said: I am he that thou seekest. And then Christopher was glad, and bound him to be his servant perpetual, and took him for his master and Lord. And as they went together by a common way, they found there a cross, erect and standing. And anon as the devil saw the cross he was afeard and fled, and left the right way, and brought Christopher about by a sharp desert. And after, when they were past the cross, he brought him to the highway that they had left. And when Christopher saw that, he marvelled, and demanded whereof he doubted, and had left the high and fair way, and had gone so far about by so aspre a desert. And the devil would not tell him in no wise. Then Christopher said to him: If thou wilt not tell me, I shall anon depart from thee, and shall serve thee no more. Wherefor the devil was constrained to tell him, and said: There was a man called Christ which was hanged on the cross, and when I see his sign I am sore afraid, and flee from it wheresoever I see it. To whom Christopher said: Then he is greater, and more mightier than thou, when thou art afraid of his sign, and I see well that I have labored in vain, when I have not founden the greatest Lord of the world. And I will serve thee no longer, go thy way then, for I will go seek Christ. And when he had long sought and demanded where he should find Christ, at last he came into a great desert, to an hermit that dwelt there, and this hermit preached to him of Jesu Christ and informed him in the faith diligently, and said to him: This king whom thou desirest to serve, requireth the service that thou must oft fast. And Christopher said to him: Require of me some other thing, and I shall do it, for that which thou requirest I may not do. And the hermit said: Thou must then wake and make many prayers. And Christopher said to him: I wot not what it is; I may do no such thing. And then the hermit said to him: Knowest thou such a river, in which many be perished and lost? To whom Christopher said: I know it well. Then said the hermit: Because thou art noble and high of stature and strong in thy members, thou shalt be resident by that river, and thou shalt bear over all them that shall pass there, which shall be a thing right convenable to our Lord Jesu Christ whom thou desirest to serve, and I hope he shall show himself to thee. Then said Christopher: Certes, this service may I well do, and I promise to him for to do it. Then went Christopher to this river, and made there his habitacle for him, and bare a great pole in his hand instead of a staff, by which he sustained him in the water, and bare over all manner of people without ceasing. And there he abode, thus doing, many days. And in a time, as he slept in his lodge, he heard the voice of a child which called him and said: Christopher, come out and bear me over. Then he awoke and went out, but he found no man. And when he was again in his house, he heard the same voice and he ran Out and found nobody. The third time he was called and came thither, and found a child beside the rivage of the river, which prayed him goodly to bear him over the water. And then Christopher lift up the child on his shoulders, and took his staff, and entered into the river for to pass. And the water of the river arose and swelled more and more: and the child was heavy as lead, and alway as he went further the water increased and grew more, and the child more and more waxed heavy, insomuch that Christopher had great anguish and was afeard to be drowned. And when he was escaped with great pain, and passed the water, and set the child aground, he said to the child: Child, thou hast put me in great peril; thou weighest almost as I had all the world upon me, I might bear no greater burden. And the child answered: Christopher, marvel thee nothing, for thou hast not only borne all the world upon thee, but thou hast borne him that created and made all the world, upon thy shoulders. I am Jesu Christ the king, to whom thou servest in this work. And because that thou know that I say to be the truth, set thy staff in the earth by thy house, and thou shalt see to-morn that it shall bear flowers and fruit, and anon he vanished from his eyes. And then Christopher set his staff in the earth, and when he arose on the morn, he found his staff like a palmier bearing flowers, leaves and dates.

And then Christopher went into the city of Lycia, and understood not their language. Then he prayed our Lord that he might understand them, and so he did. And as he was in this prayer, the judges supposed that he had been a fool, and left him there. And then when Christopher understood the language, he covered his visage and went to the place where they martyred Christian men, and comforted them in our Lord. And then the judges smote him in the face, and Christopher said to them: If I were not Christian I should avenge mine injury. And then Christopher pitched his rod in the earth, and prayed to our Lord that for to convert the people it might bear flowers and fruit, and anon it did so. And then he converted eight thousand men. And then the king sent two knights for to fetch him to the king, and they found him praying, and durst not tell to him so. And anon after, the king sent as many more, and they anon set them down for to pray with him. And when Christopher arose, he said to them: What seek ye? And when they saw him in the visage they said to him: The king hath sent us, that we should lead thee bound unto him. And Christopher said to them: If I would, ye should not lead me to him, bound ne unbound. And they said to him: If thou wilt go thy way, go quit, where thou wilt. And we shall say to the king that we have not found thee. It shall not be so, said he, but I shall go with you. And then he converted them in the faith, and commanded them that they should bind his hands behind his back, and lead him so bound to the king. And when the king saw him he was afeard and fell down off the seat, and his servants lifted him up and releved him again. And then the king inquired his name and his country; and Christopher said to him: Tofore or I was baptized I was named Reprobus, and after, I am Christopher; tofore baptism, a Canaanite, now, a Christian man. To whom the king said: Thou hast a foolish name, that is to wit of Christ crucified, which could not help himself, ne may not profit to thee. How therefore, thou cursed Canaanite, why wilt thou not do sacrifice to our gods? To whom Christopher said: Thou art rightfully called Dagnus, for thou art the death of the world, and fellow of the devil, and thy gods be made with the hands of men. And the king said to him: Thou wert nourished among wild beasts, and therefore thou mayst not say but wild language, and words unknown to men. And if thou wilt now do sacrifice to the gods I shall give to thee great gifts and great honors, and if not, I shall destroy thee and consume thee by great pains and torments. But, for all this, he would in no wise do sacrifice, wherefore he was sent in to prison, and the king did do behead the other knights that he had sent for him, whom he had converted.

After this Christopher was brought tofore the king, and the king commanded that he should be beaten with rods of iron, and that there should be set upon his head a cross of iron red hot and burning, and then after, he did do make a siege or a stool of iron, and made Christopher to be bounden thereon, and after, to set fire under it, and cast therein pitch. But the siege or settle melted like wax, and Christopher issued out without any harm or hurt. And when the king saw that, he commanded that he should be bound to a strong stake, and that he should be through-shotten with arrows with forty knights archers. But none of the knights might attain him, for the arrows hung in the air about, nigh him, without touching. Then the king weened that he had been through-shotten with the arrows of the knights, and addressed him for to go to him. And one of the arrows returned suddenly from the air and smote him in the eye, and blinded him. To whom Christopher said: Tyrant, I shall die to-morn, make a little clay, with my blood tempered, and anoint therewith thine eye, and thou shalt receive health. Then by the commandment of the king he was led for to be beheaded, and then, there made he his orison, and his head was smitten off, and so suffered martyrdom. And the king then took a little of his blood and laid it on his eye, and said: In the name of God and of St. Christopher! and was anon healed. Then the king believed in God, and gave commandment that if any person blamed God or St. Christopher, he should anon be slain with the sword.

Ambrose saith in his preface thus, of this holy martyr: Lord, thou hast given to Christopher so great plenty of virtues, and such grace of doctrine, that he called from the error of Paynims forty-eight thousand men, to the honor of Christian faith, by his shining miracles. And with this, he being strained and bounden in a seat of iron, and great fire put under, doubted nothing the heat. And all a whole day during, stood bounden to a stake, yet might not be through-pierced with arrows of all the knights. And with that, one of the arrows smote out the eye of the tyrant, to whom the blood of the holy martyr re-established his sight, and enlumined him in taking away the blindness of his body, and gat of the Christian mind and pardon, and he also gat of thee by prayer power to put away sickness and sores from them that remember his passion and figure. Then let us pray to St. Christopher that he pray for us, etc.

THE SEVEN SLEEPERS

The seven sleepers were born in the city of Ephesus. And when Decius the emperor came into Ephesus for the persecution of Christian men, he commanded to edify the temples in the middle of the city, so that all should come with him to do sacrifice to the idols, and did do seek all the Christian people, and bind them for to make them to do sacrifice, or else to put them to death; in such wise that every man was afeard of the pains that he promised, that the friend forsook his friend, and the son renied his father, and the father the son. And then in this city were founden seven Christian men, that is to wit, Maximian, Malchus, Marcianus, Denis, John, Serapion, and Constantine. And when they saw this, they had much sorrow, and because they were the first in the palace that despised the sacrifices, they hid them in their houses, and were in fastings and in prayers. And then they were accused tofore Decius, and came thither, and were found very Christian men. Then was given to them space for to repent them, unto the coming again of Decius. And in the meanwhile they dispended their patrimony in alms to the poor people; and assembled them together, and took counsel, and went to the mount of Celion, and there ordained to be more secretly, and there hid them long time. And one of them administered and served them always. And when he went into the city, he clothed him in the habit of a beggar.

When Decius was come again, he commanded that they should be fetched, and then Malchus, which was their servant and ministered to them meat and drink, returned in great dread to his fellows, and told and showed to them the great fury and woodness of them, and then were they sore afraid. And Malchus set tofore them the loaves of bread that he had brought, so that they were comforted of the meat, and were more strong for to suffer torments. And when they had taken their refection and sat in weeping and wailings, suddenly, as God would, they slept, and when it came on the morn they were sought and could not be found. Wherefore Decius was sorrowful because he had lost such young men. And then they were accused that they were hid in the mount of Celion, and had given their goods to poor men, and yet abode in their purpose. And then commanded Decius that their kindred should come to him, and menaced them to the death if they said not of them all that they knew. And they accused them, and complained that they had dispended all their riches. Then Decius thought what he should do with them, and, as our Lord would, he inclosed the mouth of the cave wherein they were with stones, to the end that they should die therein for hunger and fault of meat. Then the ministers and two Christian men, Theodorus and Rufinus, wrote their martyrdom and laid it subtlely among the stones. And when Decius was dead, and all that generation, three hundred and sixty-two years after, and the thirtieth year of Theodosius the emperor, when the heresy was of them that denied the resurrection of dead bodies, and began to grow; Theodosius, then the most Christian emperor, being sorrowful that the faith of our Lord was so felonously demened, for anger and heaviness he clad him in hair and wept every day in a secret place, and led a full holy life, which God, merciful and piteous, seeing, would comfort them that were sorrowful and weeping, and give to them esperance and hope of the resurrection of dead men, and opened the precious treasure of his pity, and raised the foresaid martyrs in this manner following.

He put in the will of a burgess of Ephesus that he would make in that mountain, which was desert and aspre, a stable for his pasturers and herdmen. And it happed that of adventure the masons, that made the said stable, opened this cave. And then these holy saints, that were within, awoke and were raised and intersalued each other, and had supposed verily that they had slept but one night only, and remembered of the heaviness that they had the day tofore. And then Malchus, which ministered to them, said what Decius had ordained of them, for he said: We have been sought, like as I said to you yesterday, for to do sacrifice to the idols, that is it that the emperor desireth of us. And then Maximian answered: God our Lord knoweth that we shall never sacrifice, and comforted his fellows. He commanded to Malchus to go and buy bread in the city, and bade him bring more that he did yesterday, and also to inquire and demand what the emperor had commanded to do. And then Malchus took five shillings, and issued out of the cave, and when he saw the masons and the stones tofore the cave, he began to bless him, and was much amarvelled. But he thought little on the stones, for he thought on other things. Then came he all doubtful to the gates of the city, and was all amarvelled. For he saw the sign of the cross about the gate, and then, without tarrying, he went to that other gate of the city, and found there also the sign of the cross thereon, and then he had great marvel, for upon every gate he saw set up the sign of the cross; and therewith the city was garnished. And then he blessed him and returned to the first gate, and weened he had dreamed; and after he advised and comforted himself and covered his visage and entered into the city. And when he came to the sellers of bread, and heard the men speak of God, yet then was he more abashed, and said: What is this, that no man yesterday durst name Jesu Christ, and now every man confesseth him to be Christian? I trow this is not the city of Ephesus, for it is all otherwise builded. It is some other city, I wot not what.

And when he demanded and heard verily that it was Ephesus, he supposed that he had erred, and thought verily to go again to his fellows, and then went to them that sold bread. And when he showed his money the sellers marvelled, and said that one to that other, that this young man had found some old treasure. And when Malchus saw them talk together, he doubted not that they would lead him to the emperor, and was sore afeard, and prayed them to let him go, and keep both money and bread, but they held him, and said to him: Of whence art thou? For thou hast found treasure of old emperors, show it to us, and we shall be fellows with thee and keep it secret. And Malchus was so afeard that he wist not what to say to them for dread. And when they saw that he spake not they put a cord about his neck, and drew him through the city unto the middle thereof. And tidings were had all about in the city that a young man had found ancient treasure, in such wise that all they of the city assembled about him, and he confessed there that he had found no treasure. And he beheld them all, but he could know no man there of his kindred ne lineage, which he had verily supposed that they had lived, but found none, wherefore he stood as he had been from himself, in the middle of the city. And when St. Martin the bishop, and Antipater the consul, which were new come into this city, heard of this thing they sent for him, that they should bring him wisely to them, and his money with him. And when he was brought to the church he weened well he should have been led to the Emperor Decius. And then the bishop and the consul marvelled of the money, and they demanded him where he had found this treasure unknown. And he answered that he had nothing founden, but it was come to him of his kindred and patrimony, and they demanded of him of what city he was. I wot well that I am of this city, if this be the city of Ephesus. And the judge said to him: Let thy kindred come and witness for thee. And he named them, but none knew them. And they said that he feigned, for to escape from them in some manner. And then said the judge: How may we believe thee that this money is come to thee of thy friends, when it appeareth in the scripture that it is more than three hundred and seventy-two years sith it was made and forged, and is of the first days of Decius the emperor, and it resembleth nothing to our money; and how may it come from thy lineage so long since, and thou art young, and wouldst deceive the wise and ancient men of this city of Ephesus? And therefore I command that thou be demened after the law till thou hast confessed where thou hast found this money. Then Malchus kneeled down tofore them and said: For God's sake, lords, say ye to me that I shall demand you, and I shall tell to you all that I have in my heart. Decius the emperor that was in this city, where is he? And the bishop said to him there is no such at this day in the world that is named Decius, he was emperor many years since. And Malchus said: Sire, hereof I am greatly abashed and no man believeth me, for I wot well that we fled for fear of Decius the emperor, and I saw him, that yesterday he entered into this city, if this be the city of Ephesus. Then the bishop thought in himself, and said to the judge that, this is a vision that our Lord will have showed by this young man. Then said the young man: Follow ye me, and I shall show to you my fellows which be in the mount of Celion, and believe ye them. This know I well, that we fled from the face of the Emperor Decius. And then they went with him, and a great multitude of the people of the city with them. And Malchus entered first into the cave to his fellows, and the bishop next after him. And there found they among the stones the letters sealed with two seals of silver. And then the bishop called them that were come thither, and read them tofore them all, so that they that heard it were all abashed and amarvelled. And they saw the saints sitting in the cave, and their visages like unto roses flowering, and they, kneeling down, glorified God. And anon the bishop and the judge sent to Theodosius the emperor, praying him that he would come anon for to see the marvels of our Lord that he had late showed. And anon he arose up from the ground, and took off the sack in which he wept, and glorified our Lord. And came from Constantinople to Ephesus, and all they came against him, and ascended in to the mountain with him together, unto the saints in to the cave.

And as soon as the blessed saints of our Lord saw the emperor come, their visages shone like to the sun. And the emperor entered then, and glorified our Lord and embraced them, weeping upon each of them, and said: I see you now like as I should see our Lord raising Lazarus. And then Maximian said to him: Believe us, for forsooth our Lord hath raised us tofore the day of the great resurrection. And to the end that thou believe firmly the resurrection of the dead people, verily we be raised as ye here see, and live. And in like wise as the child is in the womb of his mother without feeling harm or hurt, in the same wise we have been living and sleeping in lying here without feeling of anything. And when they had said all this, they inclined their heads to the earth, and rendered their spirits at the command of our Lord Jesu Christ, and so died. Then the emperor arose, and fell on them, weeping strongly, and embraced them, and kissed them debonairly. And then he commanded to make precious sepulchres of gold and silver, and to bury their bodies therein. And in the same night they appeared to the emperor, and said to him that he should suffer them to lie on the earth like as they had lain tofore till that time that our Lord had raised them, unto the time that they should rise again. Then commanded the emperor that the place should be adorned nobly and richly with precious stones, and all the bishops that would confess the resurrection should be assoiled. It is in doubt of that which is said that they slept three hundred and sixty-two years, for they were raised the year of our Lord four hundred and seventy-eight, and Decius reigned but one year and three months, and that was in the year of our Lord two hundred and seventy, and so they slept but two hundred and eight years.

THE LIFE OF ST. SILVESTER

Silvester was son of one Justa and was learned and taught of a priest named Cyrinus, which did marvellously great alms and made hospitalities. It happed that he received a Christian man into his house named Timothy, who no man would receive for the persecution of tyrants, wherefore the said Timothy suffered death and passion after that year while he preached justly the faith of Jesu Christ. It was so that the prefect Tarquinius supposed that Timothy had had great plenty of riches, which he demanded of Silvester, threatening him to the death but if he delivered them to him. And when he found certainly that Timothy had no great riches, he commanded to St. Silvester to make sacrifice to the idols, and if he did not he would make him suffer divers torments. St. Silvester answered: False, evil man, thou shalt die this night, and shalt have torments that ever shall endure, and thou shalt know, whether thou wilt or not, that he whom we worship is very God. Then St. Silvester was put in prison, and the provost went to dinner. Now it happed that as he ate, a bone of a fish turned in his throat and stuck fast, so that he could neither have it down ne up, and at midnight died like as St. Silvester had said, and then St. Silvester was delivered out of prison. He was so gracious that all Christian men and Paynims loved him, for he was fair like an angel to look on, a fair speaker, whole of body, holy in work, good in counsel, patient and charitable, and firmly established in the faith. He had in writing the names of all the widows and orphans that were poor, and to them he administered their necessity. He had a custom to fast all Fridays and Saturdays. And it was so that Melchiades, the bishop of Rome, died, and all the people chose St. Silvester for to be the high Bishop of Rome, which sore against his will was made pope. He instituted for to be fasted Wednesday, Friday, and Saturday, and the Thursday for to be hallowed as Sunday.

Now it happed that the Emperor Constantine did do slay all the Christian men over all where he could find them, and for this cause St. Silvester fled out of the town with his clerks, and hid him in a mountain. And for the cruelty of Constantine God sent him such a sickness that he became lazar and measel, and by the counsel of his physicians he got three thousand young children for to have cut their throats, for to have their blood in a bath all hot, and thereby he might be healed of his measelry. And when he should ascend into his chariot for to go to the place where he should be bathed, the mothers of the children came crying and braying for sorrow of their children, and when he understood that they were mothers of the children, he had great pity on them and said to his knights and them that were about him: The dignity of the empire of Rome is brought forth of the fountain of pity, the which hath stablished by decree that who that slayeth a child in battle shall have his head smitten off, then should it be great cruelty to us for to do to ours such thing as we defend to strange nations, for so should cruelty surmount us. It is better that we leave cruelty and that pity surmount us, and therefore me seemeth better to save the lives of these innocents, than by their death I should have again my health, of the which we be not yet certain. Ne we may recover nothing for to slay them, for if so were that I should thereby have health, that should be a cruel health that should be bought with the death of so many innocents. Then he commanded to render and deliver again to the mothers their children, and gave to every each of them a good gift, and thus made them return to their houses with great joy, from whence they departed with great sorrow, and he himself returned again in his chariot unto his palace. Now it happed that the night after St. Peter and St. Paul appeared to this Emperor Constantine, saying to him: Because thou hast had horror to shed and spill the blood of innocents, our Lord Jesu Christ hath had pity on thee, and commandeth thee to send unto such a mountain where Silvester is hid with his clerks, and say to him that thou comest for to be baptized of him and thou shalt be healed of thy malady. And when he was awaked he did do call his knights and commanded them to go to that mountain and bring the Pope Silvester to him courteously and fair, for to speak with him. When St. Silvester saw from far the knights come to him, he supposed they sought him for to be martyred, and began to say to his clerks that they should be firm and stable in the faith for to suffer martyrdom. When the knights came to him they said to him much courteously that Constantine sent for him, and prayed him that he would come and speak with him. And forthwith he came, and when they had intersaluted each other, Constantine told to him his vision. And when Silvester demanded of him what men they were that so appeared to him, the emperor wist not ne could not name them. St. Silvester opened a book wherein the images of St. Peter and St. Paul were portrayed, and demanded of him if they were like unto them. Then Constantine anon knew them and said that he had seen them in his sleep. Then St. Silvester preached to him the faith of Jesu Christ, and baptized him; and when he was baptized, a great light descended upon him so that he said that he had seen Jesu Christ, and was healed forthwith of his measelry. And then he ordained seven laws unto holy church, the first was that all the city should worship Jesu Christ as very God, the second thing was that whosoever should say any villany of Jesu Christ he should be punished, the third, whosomever should do villany to Christian men, he should lose half his goods. The fourth, that the Bishop of Rome should be chief of all holy church, like as the emperor is chief of all the world. The fifth, that who that had done or should do trespass and fled to the church, that he should be kept there free from all injury. The sixth, that no man should edify any churches without license of holy church and consent of the bishop. The seventh, that the dime and tenth part of the possessions should be given to the church.

After this the emperor came to St. Peter's church and confessed meekly all his sins tofore all people, and what wrong he had done to Christian men, and made to dig and cast out to make the foundements for the churches, and bare on his shoulders twelve hods or baskets full of earth. When Helen, the mother of Constantine, dwelling in Bethany, heard say that the emperor was become Christian, she sent to him a letter, in which she praised much her son of this that he had renounced the false idols, but she blamed him much that he had renounced the law of the Jews, and worshipped a man crucified. Then Constantine remanded to his mother that she should assemble the greatest masters of the Jews, and he should assemble the greatest masters of the Christian men, to the end that they might dispute and know which was the truest law. Then Helen assembled twelve masters which she brought with her, which were the wisest that they might find in that law, and St. Silvester and his clerks were of that other party. Then the emperor ordained two Paynims, Gentiles, to be their judges, of whom that one was named Crato, and that other Zenophilus, which were proved wise and expert, and they to give the sentence, and be judge of the disputation. Then began one of the masters of the Jews for to maintain and dispute his law, and St. Silvester and his clerks answered to his disputation, and to them all, always concluding them by Scripture. The judges which were true and just, held more of the party of St. Silvester than of the Jews. Then said one of the masters of the Jews named Zambry, I marvel, said he, that ye be so wise and incline you to their words, let us leave all these words and go we to the effect of the deeds. Then he did do come [caused to come] a cruel bull, and said a word in his ear, and anon the bull died. Then the people were all against Silvester. Then said Silvester, believe not thou that he hath named in the ear the name of Jesu Christ, but the name of some devil, know ye verily it is no great strength to slay a bull, for a man, or a lion, or a serpent may well slay him, but it is great virtue to raise him again to life, then if he may not raise him it is by the devil. And if he may raise him again to life, I shall believe that he is dead by the power of God. And when the judges heard this, they said to Zambry, that had slain the bull, that he should raise him again. Then he answered that if Silvester might raise him in the name of Jesus of Galilee his master, then he would believe in him, and thereto bound them all the Jews that were there. And St. Silvester first made his orisons and prayers to our Lord, and sith came to the bull and said to him in his ear: Thou cursed creature that art entered into this bull and hast slain him, go out in the name of Jesu Christ, in whose name I command thee bull, arise thou up and go thou with the other beasts debonairly, and anon the bull arose and went forth softly. Then the queen and the judges, which were Paynims, were converted to the faith.

In this time it happed that there was at Rome a dragon in a pit, which every day slew with his breath more than three hundred men. Then came the bishops of the idols unto the emperor and said unto him: O thou most holy emperor, sith the time that thou hast received Christian faith the dragon which is in yonder foss or pit slayeth every day with his breath more than three hundred men. Then sent the emperor for St. Silvester and asked counsel of him of this matter. St. Silvester answered that by the might of God he promised to make him cease of his hurt and blessure of this people. Then St. Silvester put himself to prayer, and St. Peter appeared to him and said: Go surely to the dragon and the two priests that be with thee take in thy company, and when thou shalt come to him thou shalt say to him in this manner: Our Lord Jesu Christ which was born of the Virgin Mary, crucified, buried and arose, and now sitteth on the right side of the Father, this is he that shall come to deem and judge the living and the dead, I command thee Sathanas that thou abide him in this place till he come. Then thou shalt bind his mouth with a thread, and seal it with thy seal, wherein is the imprint of the cross. Then thou and the two priests shall come to me whole and safe, and such bread as I shall make ready for you ye shall eat. Thus as St. Peter had said, St. Silvester did. And when he came to the pit, he descended down one hundred and fifty steps, bearing with him two lanterns, and found the dragon, and said the words that St. Peter had said to him, and bound his mouth with the thread, and sealed it, and after returned, and as he came upward again he met with two enchanters which followed him for to see if he descended, which were almost dead of the stench of the dragon, whom he brought with him whole and sound, which anon were baptized, with a great multitude of people with them. Thus was the city of Rome delivered from double death, that was from the culture and worshipping of false idols, and from the venom of the dragon. At the last when St. Silvester approached toward his death, he called to him the clergy and admonished them to have charity, and that they should diligently govern their churches, and keep their flock from the wolves. And after the year of the incarnation of our Lord three hundred and twenty, he departed out of this world and slept in our Lord, etc.

OF ST. AUSTIN THAT BROUGHT CHRISTENDOM TO ENGLAND

St. Austin was a holy monk and sent in to England, to preach the faith of our Lord Jesu Christ, by St. Gregory, then being pope of Rome. The which had a great zeal and love unto England, as is rehearsed all along in his legend, how that he saw children of England in the market of Rome for to be sold, which were fair of visage, for which cause he demanded license and obtained to go into England for to convert the people thereof to Christian faith. And he being on the way the pope died and he was chosen pope, and was countermanded and came again to Rome. And after, when he was sacred into the papacy, he remembered the realm of England, and sent St. Austin, as head and chief, and other holy monks and priests with him, to the number of forty persons, unto the realm of England. And as they came toward England they came in the province of Anjou, purposing to have rested all night at a place called Pounte, say a mile from the city and river of Ligerim, but the women scorned and were so noyous to them that they drove them out of the town, and they came unto a fair broad elm, and purposed to have rested there that night, but one of the women which was more cruel than the other purposed to drive them thence, and came so nigh them that they might not rest there that night. And then St. Austin took his staff for to remove from that place, and suddenly his staff sprang out of his hand with a great violence, the space of three furlongs thence, and there sticked fast in the earth. And when St. Austin came to his staff and pulled it out of the earth, incontinent by the might of our Lord, sourded and sprang there a fair well or fountain of clear water which refreshed him well and all his fellowship. And about that well they rested all that night, and they that dwelled thereby saw all that night over that place a great light coming from heaven which covered all that place where these holy men lay. And on the morn St. Austin wrote in the earth with his staff beside the well these words following: Here had Austin, the servant of the servants of God, hospitality, whom St. Gregory the pope hath sent to convert England.

On the morn when the holy men were departed, the dwellers of the coasts thereby which saw the light in the night tofore, came thither and found there a fair well, of the which they marvelled greatly. And when they saw the scripture written in the earth they were greatly abashed because of their unkindness, and repented them full sore of that they had mocked them the day before. And after, they edified there a fair church in the same place in the worship of St. Austin, the which the bishop of Anjou hallowed. And to the hallowing thereof came so great multitude of people that they trod the corn in the fields down all plain, like unto a floor clean swept, for there was no sparing of it. Notwithstanding, at the time of reaping, that ground so trodden bare more corn and better than any other fields beside, not trodden, did. And the high altar of that church standeth over the place where St. Austin wrote with his staff by the well, and yet unto this day may no woman come in to that church. But there was a noble woman that said that she was not guilty in offending St. Austin, and took a taper in her hand and went for to offer it in the said church; but the sentence of Almighty God may not be revoked, for as soon as she entered the church her bowels and sinews began to shrink and she fell down dead in ensample of all other women; whereby we may understand that injury done against a saint displeaseth greatly Almighty God.

And from thence St. Austin and his fellowship came into England and arrived in the isle of Thanet in East Kent, and king Ethelbert reigned that time in Kent, which was a noble man and a mighty. To whom St. Austin sent, showing the intent of his coming from the court of Rome, and said that he had brought to him right joyful and pleasant tidings, and said that if he would obey and do after his preaching that he should have everlasting joy in the bliss of heaven, and should reign with Almighty God in his kingdom. And then King Ethelbert hearing this, commanded that they should abide and tarry in the same isle, and that all things should be ministered to them that were necessary, unto the time that he were otherwise advised. And soon after, the king came to them in the same isle, and he being in the field, St. Austin with his fellowship came and spake with him, having tofore them the sign of the cross, singing by the way the litany, beseeching God devoutly to strengthen them and help. And the king received him and his fellowship, and in the same place St. Austin preached a glorious sermon, and declared to the king the Christian faith openly and the great merit and avail that should come thereof in time coming. And when he had ended his sermon the king said to him: Your promises be full fair that ye bring, but because they be new and have not been heard here before, we may not yet give consent thereto; nevertheless, because ye be come as pilgrims from far countries, we will not be grevious ne hard to you, but we will receive you meekly and minister to you such things as be necessary, neither we will forbid you, but as many as ye can convert to your faith and religion by your preaching ye shall have license to baptize them, and to accompany them to your law. And then the king gave to them a mansion in the city of Dorobernence, which now is called Canterbury. And when they drew nigh the city they came in with a cross of silver, and with procession singing the litany, praying Almighty God of succor and help that he would take away his wrath from the city and to inflame the hearts of the people to receive his doctrine. And then St. Austin and his fellowship began to preach there the word of God, and about there in the province, and such people as were well disposed anon were converted, and followed this holy man. And by the holy conversation and miracles that they did much people were converted and great fame arose in the country. And when it came to the king's ear, anon he came to the presence of St. Austin and desired him to preach again, and then the word of God so inflamed him, that incontinent, as soon as the sermon was ended, the king fell down to the feet of St. Austin and said sorrowfully: Alas! woe is me, that I have erred so long and know not of him that thou speakest of, thy promises be so delectable that I think it all too long till I be christened, wherefore, holy father, I require thee to minister to me the sacrament of baptism. And then St. Austin, seeing the great meekness and obedience of the king that he had to be christened, he took him up with weeping tears and baptized him with all his household and meiny, and informed them diligently in the Christian faith with great joy and gladness. And when all this was done St. Austin, desiring the health of the people of England, went forth on foot to York; and when he came nigh to the city there met him a blind man which said to him: O thou holy Austin, help me that am full needy. To whom St. Austin said: I have no silver, but such as I have I give thee; in the name of Jesu Christ arise and be all whole, and with that word he received his sight and believed in our Lord and was baptized. And upon Christmas day he baptized, in the river named Swale, ten thousand men without women and children, and there was a great multitude of people resorting to the said river, which was so deep that no man might pass over on foot, and yet by miracle of our Lord there was neither man, woman, ne child drowned, but they that were sick were made whole both in body and in soul. And in the same place they builded a church in the worship of God and St. Austin. And when St. Austin had preached the faith to the people and had confirmed them steadfastly therein, he returned again from York, and by the way he met a leper asking help, and when St. Austin had said these words to him: In the name of Jesu Christ be thou cleansed from all thy leprosy, anon all his filth fell away, and a fair new skin appeared on his body so that he seemed all a new man.

Also as St. Austin came into Oxfordshire to a town that is called Compton to preach the word of God, to whom the curate said: Holy father, the lord of this lordship hath been ofttimes warned of me to pay his tithes to

God, and yet he withholdeth them, and therefore I have cursed him, and I find him the more obstinate. To whom St. Austin said: Son, why payest thou not thy tithes to God and to the church? Knowest thou not that the tithes be not thine but belong to God? And then the knight said to him: I know well that I till the ground, wherefore I ought as well to have the tenth sheaf as the ninth, and when St. Austin could not turn the knight's entent, then he departed from him and went to mass. And ere he began he charged that all they that were accursed should go out of the church, and then rose a dead body and went out in to the churchyard with a white cloth on his head, and stood still there till the mass was done. And then St. Austin went to him and demanded him what he was, and he answered and said: I was sometime lord of this town, and because I would not pay my tithes to my curate he accursed me, and so I died and went to hell. And then St. Austin bade bring him to the place where his curate was buried, and then the carrion brought him thither to the grave, and because that all men should know that life and death be in the power of God, St. Austin said: I command thee in the name of God to arise, for we have need of thee, and then he arose anon, and stood before all the people. To whom St. Austin said: Thou knowest well that our Lord is merciful, and I demand thee, brother, if thou knowest this man? and he said: Yea, would God that I had never known him, for he was a withholder of his tithes, and in all his life an, evil doer, thou knowest that our Lord is merciful, and as long as the pains of hell endure let us also be merciful to all Christians. And then St. Austin delivered to the curate a rod, and there the knight kneeling on his knees was assoiled, and then he commanded him to go again to his grave, and there to abide till the day of doom; and he entered anon into his grave and forthwith fell to ashes and powder. And then St. Austin said to the priest: How long hast thou lain here? and he said a hundred and fifty years; and then he asked how it stood with him, and he said: Well, holy father, for I am in everlasting bliss; and then said St. Austin: Wilt thou that I pray to Almighty God that thou abide here with us to confirm the hearts of men in very belief? And then he said: Nay, holy father, for I am in a place of rest; and then said St. Austin: Go in peace, and pray for me and for all holy church, and he then entered again into his grave, and anon the body was turned to earth. Of this sight the lord was sore afeard, and came all quaking to St. Austin and to his curate, and demanded forgiveness of his trespass, and promised to make amends and ever after to pay his tithes and to follow the doctrine of St. Austin.

After this St. Austin entered into Dorsetshire, and came in to a town whereas were wicked people who refused his doctrine and preaching utterly and drove him out of the town, casting on him the tails of thornbacks, or like fishes, wherefore he besought Almighty God to show his judgment on them, and God sent to them a shameful token, for the children that were born after in that place had tails, as it is said, till they had repented them. It is said commonly that this fell at Strood in Kent, but blessed be God at this day is no such deformity. Item in another place there were certain people which would in no wise give faith to his preaching ne his doctrine, but scorned and mocked him, wherefore God took such vengeance that they burned with fire invisible, so that their skin was red as blood, and suffered so great pain that they were constrained to come and ask forgiveness of St. Austin, and then he prayed God for them that they might be acceptable to him and receive baptism and that he would release their pain, and then he christened them and that burning heat was quenched and they were made perfectly whole, and felt never after more thereof. On a time, as St. Austin was in his prayers, our Lord appeared to him, and comforting him with a gentle and familiar speech, said: O thou my good servant and true, be thou comforted and do manly, for I thy Lord God am with thee in all thine affection, and mine ears be open to thy prayers, and for whom thou demandest any petition thou shalt have thy desire, and the gate of everlasting life is open to thee, where thou shalt joy with me without end. And in that same place where our Lord said these words he fixed his staff into the ground, and a well of clear water sourded and sprang up in that same place, the which well is called Cerne, and it is in the country of Dorset, whereas now is builded a fair abbey, and is named Cerne after the well. And the church is builded in the same place whereas our Lord appeared to St. Austin. Also in the same country was a young man that was lame, dumb, and deaf, and by the prayers of St. Austin he was made whole, and then soon after he was dissolute and wanton, and noyed and grieved the people with jangling and talking in the church. And then God sent to him his old infirmity again, because of his misguiding, and at the last he fell to repentance, and asked God forgiveness and St. Austin. And St. Austin prayed for him and he was made whole again the second time, and after that he continued in good and virtuous living to his life's end.

And after this St. Austin, full of virtues, departed out of this world unto our Lord God, and lieth buried at Canterbury in the abbey that he founded there in the worship and rule, whereas our Lord God showeth yet daily many miracles. And the third day before the nativity of our Lady is hallowed the translation of St. Austin. In which night a citizen of Canterbury, being that time at Winchester, saw heaven open over the church of St. Austin, and a burning ladder shining full bright, and angels coming down to the same church. And then him thought that the church had burned of the great light and brightness that came down on the ladder, and marvelled greatly what this should mean, for he knew nothing of the translation of St. Austin; and when he knew the truth, that on that time the body of the glorious saint was translated, he gave laud and thankings to almighty God, and we may verily know by that evident vision that it is an holy and devout place; and as it is said that of old time, ancient holy men that used to come thither would at the entry of it do off their hosen and shoes and durst not presume to go into that holy monastery but barefoot, because so many holy saints be there shrined and buried. And God hath showed so many miracles in that holy place for his blessed saint, St. Austin, that if I should write them here it should occupy a great book.

EDWIN AND PAULINUS

The Conversion of Northumbria

The black-hair'd gaunt Paulinus
 By ruddy Edwin stood:—
"Bow down, O king of Deira,
 Before the blessed Rood!
Cast out thy heathen idols,
 And worship Christ our Lord."
—But Edwin look'd and ponder'd,
 And answer'd not a word.

Again the gaunt Paulinus
 To ruddy Edwin spake:
"God offers life immortal
 For his dear Son's own sake!
Wilt thou not hear his message,
 Who bears the keys and sword?"
—But Edwin look'd and ponder'd,
 And answer'd not a word.

Rose then a sage old warrior;
 Was five-score winters old;
Whose beard from chin to girdle
 Like one long snow-wreath roll'd:—
"At Yule-time in our chamber
 We sit in warmth and light,
While cold and howling round us
 Lies the black land of Night.

"Athwart the room a sparrow
 Darts from the open door:
Within the happy hearth-light
 One red flash—and no more!
We see it come from darkness,
 And into darkness go:—
So is our life, King Edwin!
 Alas, that it is so!

"But if this pale Paulinus
   Have somewhat more to tell;
Some news of Whence and Whither,
   And where the soul will dwell;—
If on that outer darkness
   The sun of hope may shine;—
He makes life worth the living!
   I take his God for mine!"

So spake the wise old warrior;
   And all about him cried:
"Paulinus' God hath conquer'd!
   And he shall be our guide:—
For he makes life worth living
   Who brings this message plain,
When our brief days are over,
   That we shall live again."

   —*Unknown*

THE LIFE OF ST. GEORGE MARTYR

St. George was a knight and born in Cappadocia. On a time he came in to the province of Libya, to a city which is said Silene. And by this city was a stagne or a pond like a sea, wherein was a dragon which envenomed all the country. And on a time the people were assembled for to slay him, and when they saw him they fled. And when he came nigh the city he venomed the people with his breath, and therefore the people of the city gave to him every day two sheep for to feed him, because he should do no harm to the people, and when the sheep failed there was taken a man and a sheep. Then was an ordinance made in the town that there should be taken the children and young people of them of the town by lot, and every each one as it fell, were he gentle or poor, should be delivered when the lot fell on him or her. So it happed that many of them of the town were then delivered, insomuch that the lot fell upon the king's daughter, whereof the king was sorry, and said unto the people: For the love of the gods take gold and silver and all that I have, and let me have my daughter. They said: How sir! ye have made and ordained the law, and our children be now dead, and ye would do the contrary. Your daughter shall be given, or else we shall burn you and your house.

When the king saw he might no more do, he began to weep, and said to his daughter: Now shall I never see thine espousals. Then returned he to the people ami demanded eight days' respite, and they granted it to him. And when the eight days were passed they came to him and said: Thou seest that the city perisheth: Then did the king do array his daughter like as she should be wedded, and embraced her, kissed her and gave her his benediction, and after, led her to the place where the dragon was.

When she was there St. George passed by, and when he saw the lady he demanded the lady what she made there and she said: Go ye your way fair young man, that ye perish not also. Then said he: Tell to me what have and why weep ye, and doubt ye of nothing. When she saw that he would know, she said to him how she was delivered to the dragon. Then said St. George: Fair daughter, doubt ye no thing hereof for I shall help thee in the name of Jesu Christ. She said: For God's sake, good knight, go your way, and abide not with me, for ye may not deliver me. Thus as they spake together the dragon appeared and came running to them, and St. George was upon his horse, and drew out his sword and garnished him with the sign of the cross, and rode hardily against the dragon which came toward him, and smote him with his spear and hurt him sore and threw him to the ground. And after said to the maid: Deliver to me your girdle, and bind it about the neck of the dragon and be not afeard. When she had done so the dragon followed her as it had been a meek beast and debonair. Then she led him into the city, and the people fled by mountains and valleys, and said: Alas! alas! we shall be all dead. Then St. George said to them: Ne doubt ye no thing, without more, believe ye in God, Jesu Christ, and do ye to be baptized and I shall slay the dragon. Then the king was baptized and all his people, and St. George slew the dragon and smote off his head, and commanded that he should be thrown in the fields, and they took four carts with oxen that drew him out of the city.

Then were there well fifteen thousand men baptized, without women and children, and the king did do make a church there of our Lady and of St. George, in the which yet sourdeth a fountain of living water, which healeth sick people that drink thereof. After this the king offered to St. George as much money as there might be numbered, but he refused all and commanded that it should be given to poor people for God's sake; and enjoined the king four things, that is, that he should have charge of the churches, and that he should honor the priests and hear their service diligently, and that he should have pity on the poor people, and after, kissed the king and departed.

Now it happed that in the time of Diocletian and Maximian, which were emperors, was so great persecution of Christian men that within a month were martyred well twenty-two thousand, and therefore they had so great dread that some renied and forsook God and did sacrifice to the idols. When St. George saw this, he left the habit of a knight and sold all that he had, and gave it to the poor, and took the habit of a Christian man, and went into the middle of the Paynims and began to cry: All the gods of the Paynims and Gentiles be devils, my God made the heavens and is very God. Then said the provost to him: Of what presumption cometh this to thee, that thou sayest that our gods be devils? And say to us what thou art and what is thy name. He answered anon and said: I am named George, I am a gentleman, a knight of Cappadocia, and have left all for to serve the God of heaven. Then the provost enforced himself to draw him unto his faith by fair words, and when he might not bring him thereto he did do raise him on a gibbet; and so must beat him with great staves and broches of iron, that his body was all tobroken in pieces. And after he did do take brands of iron and join them to his sides, and his bowels which then appeared he did do frot with salt, and so sent him into prison, but our Lord appeared to him the same night with great light and comforted him much sweetly. And by this great consolation he took to him so good heart that he doubted no torment that they might make him suffer. Then, when Dacian the provost saw that he might not surmount him, he called his enchanter and said to him: I see that these Christian people doubt not our torments. The enchanter bound himself, upon his head to be smitten off, if he overcame not his crafts. Then he did take strong venom and meddled it with wine, and made invocation of the names of his false gods, and gave it to St. George to drink. St. George took it and made the sign of the cross on it, and anon drank it without grieving him any thing. Then the enchanter made it more stronger than it was tofore of venom, and gave it him to drink, and it grieved him nothing. When the enchanter saw that, he kneeled down at the feet of St. George and prayed him that he would make him Christian. And when Dacian knew that he was become Christian he made to smite off his head. And after, on the morn, he made St. George to be set between two wheels, which were full of swords, sharp and cutting on both sides, but anon the wheels were broken and St. George escaped without hurt. And then commanded Dacian that they should put him in a caldron full of molten lead, and when St. George entered therein, by the virtue of our Lord it seemed that he was in a bath well at ease. Then Dacian seeing this began to assuage his ire, and to flatter him by fair words, and said to him: George, the patience of our gods is over great unto thee which hast blasphemed them, and done to them great despite, then fair, and right sweet son, I pray thee that thou return to our law and make sacrifice to the idols, and leave thy folly, and I shall enhance thee to great honor and worship. Then began St. George to smile, and said to him: Wherefore saidst thou not to me thus at the beginning? I am ready to do as thou sayest. Then was Dacian glad and made to cry over all the town that all the people should assemble for to see George make sacrifice which so much had striven there against. Then was the city arrayed and feast kept throughout all the town, and all came to the temple for to see him.

When St. George was on his knees, and they supposed that he would have worshipped the idols, he prayed our Lord God of heaven that he would destroy the temple and the idol in the honor of his name, for to make the people to be converted. And anon the fire descended from heaven and burned the temple, and the idols, and their priests, and sith the earth opened and swallowed all the cinders and ashes that were left. Then Dacian made him to be brought tofore him, and said to him: What be the evil deeds that thou hast done, and also great untruth? Then said to him St. George: Ah, sir, believe it not, but come with me and see how I shall sacrifice. Then said Dacian to him: I see well thy fraud and thy barat, thou wilt make the earth to swallow me, like as thou hast the temple and my gods. Then said St. George: O caitiff, tell me how may thy gods help thee when they may not help themselves! Then was Dacian so angry that he said to his wife: I shall die for anger if I may not surmount and overcome this man. Then said she to him: Evil and cruel tyrant! ne seest thou not the great virtue of the Christian people? I said to thee well that thou shouldst not do to them any harm, for their God fighteth for them, and know thou well that I will become Christian. Then was Dacian much abashed and said to her: Wilt thou be Christian? Then he took her by the hair, and did do beat her cruelly. Then demanded she of St. George: What may I become because I am not christened? Then answered the blessed George: Doubt thee nothing, fair daughter, for thou shalt be baptized in thy blood. Then began she to worship our Lord Jesu Christ, and so she died and went to heaven. On the morn Dacian gave his sentence that St. George should be drawn through all the city, and after, his head should be smitten off. Then made he his prayer to our Lord that all they that desired any boon might get it of our Lord God in his name, and a voice came from heaven which said that it which he had desired was granted; and after he had made his orison his head was smitten off, about the year of our Lord two hundred and eighty-seven. When Dacian went homeward from the place where he was beheaded toward his palace, fire fell down from heaven upon him and burned him and all his servants.

Gregory of Tours telleth that there were some that bare certain relics of St. George, and came into a certain oratory in a hospital, and on the morning when they should depart they could not move the door till they had left there part of their relics. It is also found in the history of Antioch, that when the Christian men went oversea to conquer Jerusalem, that one, a right fair young man, appeared to a priest of the host and counselled him that he should bear with him a little of the relics of St. George, for he was conductor of the battle, and so he did so much that he had some. And when it was so that they had assieged Jerusalem and durst not mount ne go up on the walls for the quarrels and defence of the Saracens, they saw apertly St. George which had white arms with a red cross, that went up tofore them on the walls, and they followed him, and so was Jerusalem taken by his help. And between Jerusalem and port Jaffa, by a town called Ramys, is a chapel of St. George which is now desolate and uncovered, and therein dwell Christian Greeks. And in the said chapel lieth the body of St. George, but not the head. And there lie his father and mother and his uncle, not in the chapel but under the wall of the chapel; and the keepers will not suffer pilgrims to come therein, but if they pay two ducats, and therefore come but few therein, but offer without the chapel at an altar. And there is seven years and seven lents of pardon; and the body of St. George lieth in the middle of the quire or choir of the said chapel, and in his tomb is an hole that a man may put in his hand. And when a Saracen, being mad, is brought thither, and if he put his head in the hole he shall anon be made perfectly whole, and have his wit again.

This blessed and holy martyr St. George is patron of the realm of England and the cry of men of war. In the worship of whom is founded the noble order of the Garter, and also a noble college in the castle of Windsor by kings of England, in which college is the heart of St. George, which Sigismund, the emperor of Almayne, brought and gave for a great and a precious relic to King Harry the Fifth.

THE LIFE OF ST. PATRICK

St. Patrick was born in Britain, which is called England, and was learned at Rome and there flourished in virtues; and after departed out of the parts of Italy, where he had long dwelled, and came home into his country in Wales named Pendyac, and entered into a fair and joyous country called the valley Rosine. To whom the angel of God appeared and said: O Patrick, this see ne bishopric God hath not provided to thee, but unto one not yet born, but shall thirty years hereafter be born, and so he left that country and sailed over into Ireland. And as Higden saith in Polycronicon the fourth book, the twenty-fourth chapter, that St. Patrick's father was named Caprum, which was a priest and a deacon's son which was called Fodum. And St. Patrick's mother was named Conchessa, Martin's sister of France. In his baptism he was named Sucate, and St. Germain called him Magonius, and Celestinus the pope named him Patrick. That is as much to say as father of the citizens.

St. Patrick on a day as he preached a sermon of the patience and sufferance of the passion of our Lord Jesu Christ to the king of the country, he leaned upon his crook or cross, and it happed by adventure that he set the end of the crook, or his staff, upon the king's foot, and pierced his foot with the pike, which was sharp beneath. The king had supposed that St. Patrick had done it wittingly, for to move him the sooner to patience and to the faith of God, but when St. Patrick perceived it he was much abashed, and by his prayers he healed the king. And furthermore he impetred and gat grace of our Lord that no venomous beast might live in all the country, and yet unto this day is no venomous beast in all Ireland.

After it happed on a time that a man of that country stole a sheep, which belonged to his neighbor, whereupon St. Patrick admonested the people that whomsoever had taken it should deliver it again within seven days. When all the people were assembled within the church, and the man which had stolen it made no semblant to render ne deliver again this sheep, then St. Patrick commanded, by the virtue of God, that the sheep should bleat and cry in the belly of him that had eaten it, and so happed it that, in the presence of all the people, the sheep cried and bleated in the belly of him that had stolen it. And the man that was culpable repented him of his trespass, and the others from then forthon kept them from stealing of sheep from any other man.

Also St. Patrick was wont for to worship and do reverence unto all the crosses devoutly that he might see, but on a time tofore the sepulchre of a Paynim stood a fair cross, which he passed and went forth by as he had not seen it, and he was demanded of his fellows why he saw not that cross. And then he prayed to God he said for to know whose it was, and he said he heard a voice under the earth saying: Thou sawest it not because I am a Paynim that am buried here, and am unworthy that the sign of the cross should stand there, wherefore he made the sign of the cross to be taken thence. On a time as St. Patrick preached in Ireland the faith of Jesu Christ, and did but little profit by his predication, for he could not convert the evil, rude and wild people, he prayed to our Lord Jesu Christ that he would show them some sign openly, fearful and ghastful, by which they might be converted and be repentant of their sins. Then, by the commandment of God, St. Patrick made in the earth a great circle with his staff, and anon the earth after the quantity of the circle opened and there appeared a great pit and a deep, and St. Patrick by the revelation of God understood that there was a place of purgatory, in to which whomsoever entered therein he should never have other penance ne feel none other pain, and there was showed to him that many should enter which should never return ne come again. And they that should return should abide but from one morn to another, and no more, and many entered that came not again. As touching this pit or hole which is named St. Patrick's purgatory, some hold opinion that the second Patrick, which was an abbot and no bishop, that God showed to him this place of purgatory; but certainly such a place there is in Ireland wherein many men have been, and yet daily go in and come again, and some have had there marvellous visions and seen grisly and horrible pains, of whom there be books made as of Tundale and others. Then this holy man St. Patrick, the bishop, lived till he was one hundred and twenty-two years old, and was the first that was bishop in Ireland, and died in Aurelius Ambrose's time that was king of Britain. In his time was the Abbot Columba, otherwise named Colinkillus, and St. Bride whom St. Patrick professed and veiled, and she over-lived him forty years. All these three holy saints were buried in Ulster, in the city of Dunence, as it were in a cave with three chambers. Their bodies were found at the first coming of King John, King Harry the second's son, into Ireland. Upon whose tombs these verses following were written: Hic jacent in Duno qui tumulo tumulantur in uno, Brigida, Patricius atque Columba pius, which is for to say in English: In Duno these three be buried all in one sepulchre: Bride, Patrick, and Columba the mild.

Men say that this holy bishop, St. Patrick, did three great things. One is that he drove with his staff all the venomous beasts out of Ireland. The second, that he had grant of our Lord God that none Irish man shall abide the coming of Antichrist. The third wonder is read of his purgatory, which is more referred to the less St. Patrick, the Abbot. And this holy abbot, because he found the people of that land rebel, he went out of Ireland and came in to England in the Abbey of Glastonbury, where he died on a St. Bartholomew's day. He flourished about the year of our Lord eight hundred and fifty.

OF SAINT FRANCIS

HOW HE RECEIVED THE COUNSEL OF ST. CLARE AND OF BROTHER SILVESTER, AND HOW HE PREACHED UNTO THE BIRDS

The humble servant of Christ, St. Francis, a short while after his conversion, having already gathered together many companions and received them into the order, fell into deep thought and much doubting as to what he ought to do: whether to give himself wholly unto prayer, or some time also unto preaching: and on this matter he much desired to learn the will of God. And for that the holy humility that was in him suffered him not to trust over much in himself nor in his own prayers, he thought to search out the will of God through the prayers of others: wherefore he called Brother Masseo, and bespake him thus: "Go unto Sister Clare and tell her on my behalf, that she with certain of her most spiritual companions, should pray devoutly unto God, that it may please Him to show me which of the twain is the better: whether to give myself to preaching or wholly unto prayer. And then go unto Brother Silvester and tell the like to him." This was that Brother Silvester who when he was in the world had seen a cross of gold proceeding from the mouth of St. Francis, the which reached even unto heaven and the arms thereof unto the ends of the world, and this Brother Silvester was of so great devotion and so great sanctity, that whatsoe'er he asked of God was granted him, and oftentimes he spake with God; wherefore St. Francis had a great devotion unto him.

So Brother Masseo departed, and according to the bidding of St. Francis carried his message first unto St. Clare and then unto Brother Silvester. Who, when he had heard thereof, forthwith fell on his knees in prayer, and as he prayed received answer from God, and turned to Brother Masseo, and bespake him thus: "Thus saith the Lord: Say unto Brother Francis that God has not called him to this estate for himself alone, but to the end that he may gain fruit of souls, and that many through him may be saved." With this reply Brother Masseo returned to St. Clare to learn what she had received of God, and she answered that God had sent to her and her companions the same reply as He had given to Brother Silvester. Whereat Brother

Masseo hied him back again to St. Francis; and St. Francis received him with exceeding great love, washing his feet and making ready for him the meal, and after he had eaten, St. Francis called Brother Masseo into the wood; and there kneeled down before him and drew back his hood, stretching out his arms in the shape of a cross, and asked him: "What has my Lord Jesu Christ commanded that I should do?" Replied Brother Masseo: "As unto Brother Silvester, so likewise unto Sister Clare and her sisters, has Christ made answer and revealed: that it is His will that thou go throughout the world to preach, since He hath chosen thee not for thyself alone, but also for the salvation of others." And then St. Francis, when he had heard this answer and known thereby the will of Jesu Christ, rose up with fervor exceeding great, and said: "Let us be going in the name of God"; and he took for his companions Brother Masseo and Brother Agnolo, holy men. And setting forth with fervent zeal of spirit, taking no thought for road or way, they came unto a little town that was called Savurniano, and St. Francis set himself to preach, but first he bade the swallows that were twittering keep silence till such time as he had done the preaching; and the swallows were obedient to his word, and he preached there with such fervor that all the men and women of that town minded through their devotion to come after him and leave the town, but St. Francis suffered them not, saying: "Make not ill haste nor leave your homes; and I will ordain for you what ye should do for the salvation of your souls": and therewith he resolved to found the third Order, for the salvation of all the world.

And so leaving them much comforted and with minds firm set on penitence, he departed thence and came unto a place between Cannaio and Bevagno. And as with great fervor he was going on the way, he lifted up his eyes and beheld some trees hard by the road whereon sat a great company of birds well-nigh without number; whereat St. Francis marvelled, and said to his companions: "Ye shall wait for me here upon the way and I will go to preach unto my little sisters, the birds." And he went unto the field and began to preach unto the birds that were on the ground; and immediately those that were on the trees flew down to him, and they all of them remained still and quiet together, until St. Francis made an end of preaching: and not even then did they depart, until he had given them his blessing. And according to what Brother Masseo afterward related unto Robert Jacques da Massa, St. Francis went among them touching them with his cloak, howbeit none moved from out his place. The sermon that St. Francis preached unto them was after this fashion: "My little sisters, the birds, much bounden are ye unto God, your Creator, and always in every place ought ye to praise Him, for that He hath given you liberty to fly about everywhere, and hath also given you double and triple raiment; moreover, He preserved your seed in the ark of Noah, that your race might not perish out of the world; still more are ye beholden to Him for the element of the air which he had appointed for you; beyond all this, ye sow not, neither do you reap; and God feedeth you, and giveth you the streams and fountains for your drink; the mountains and the valleys for your refuge and the high trees whereon to make your nests; and because ye know not how to spin or sew, God clotheth you, you and your children; wherefore your Creator loveth you much, seeing that He hath bestowed on you so many benefits; and therefore, my little sisters, beware of the sin of ingratitude, and study always to give praises unto God." Whenas St. Francis spake these words to them, those birds began all of them to open their beaks, and stretch their necks, and spread their wings, and reverently bend their heads down to the ground, and by their acts and by their songs to show that the holy Father gave them joy exceeding great. And St. Francis rejoiced with them, and was glad, and marvelled much at so great a company of birds and their most beautiful diversity and their good heed and sweet friendliness, for the which cause he devoutly praised their Creator in them. At the last, having ended the preaching, St. Francis made over them the sign of the cross, and gave them leave to go away; and thereby all the birds with wondrous singing rose up in the air; and then, in the fashion of the cross that St. Francis had made over them, divided themselves into four parts; and the one part flew toward the East, and the other toward the West, and the other toward the South, and the fourth toward the North, and each flight went on its way singing wondrous songs; signifying thereby that even as St. Francis, the standard-bearer of the Cross of Christ, had preached unto them, and made over them the sign of the cross, after the pattern of which they separated themselves unto the four parts of the world: even so the preaching of the Cross of Christ, renewed by St. Francis, would be carried by him and the brothers throughout the world; the which brothers, after the fashion of the birds, possessing nothing of their own in this world, commit their lives wholly unto the providence of God.

HOW ST. FRANCIS CONVERTED THE FIERCE WOLF OF AGOBIO

What time St. Francis abode in the city of Agobio, there appeared in the country of Agobio an exceeding great wolf, terrible and fierce, the which not only devoured animals, but also men, insomuch that all the city folk stood in great fear, sith ofttimes he came near to the city, and all men when they went out arrayed them in arms as it were for the battle, and yet withal they might not avail to defend them against him whensoe'er any chanced on him alone; for fear of this wolf they were come to such a pass that none durst go forth of that place. For the which matter, St. Francis having compassion on the people of that land, wished to go forth unto that wolf, albeit the townsfolk all gave counsel against it: and making the sign of the most holy cross he went forth from that place with his companions, putting all his trust in God. And the others misdoubting to go further, St. Francis took the road to the place where the wolf lay. And lo! in the sight of many of the townsfolk that had come out to see this miracle, the said wolf made at St. Francis with open mouth: and coming up to him, St. Francis made over him the sign of the most holy cross, and called him to him, and bespake him thus: "Come hither, brother wolf: I command thee in the name of Christ that thou do no harm, nor to me nor to any one." O wondrous thing! Whenas St. Francis had made the sign of the cross, right so the terrible wolf shut his jaws and stayed his running: and when he was bid, came gently as a lamb and lay him down at the feet of St. Francis. Thereat St. Francis thus bespake him: "Brother wolf, much harm hast thou wrought in these parts and done grievous ill, spoiling and slaying the creatures of God, without His leave: and not alone hast thou slain and devoured the brute beasts, but hast dared to slay men, made in the image of God; for the which cause thou art deserving of the gibbet as a thief and a most base murderer; and all men cry out and murmur against thee and all this land is thine enemy. But I would fain, brother wolf, make peace between thee and these; so that thou mayest no more offend them, and they may forgive thee all thy past offences, and nor men nor dogs pursue thee any more." At these words the wolf with movements of body, tail, and eyes, and by the bending of his head, gave sign of his assent to what St. Francis said, and of his will to abide therby. Then spake St. Francis again: "Brother wolf, sith it pleaseth thee to make and hold this peace, I promise thee that I will see to it that the folk of this place give thee food alway so long as thou shalt live, so that thou suffer not hunger any more; for that I wot well that through hunger hast thou wrought all this ill. But sith I win for thee this grace, I will, brother wolf, that thou promise me to do none hurt to any more, be he man or beast; dost promise me this?" And the wolf gave clear token by the bowing of his head that he promised. Then quoth St. Francis: "Brother wolf, I will that thou plight me troth for this promise, that I may trust thee full well." And St. Francis stretching forth his hand to take pledge of his troth, the wolf lifted up his right paw before him and laid it gently on the hand of St. Francis, giving thereby such sign of good faith as he was able. Then quoth St. Francis: "Brother wolf, I bid thee in the name of Jesu Christ come now with me, nothing doubting, and let us go stablish this peace in God's name." And the wolf obedient set forth with him, in fashion as a gentle lamb; whereat the townsfolk made mighty marvel, beholding. And straightway the bruit of it was spread through all the city, so that all the people, men-folk and women-folk, great and small, young and old, gat them to the market place for to see the wolf with St. Francis.

And the people being gathered all together, St. Francis rose up to preach, avizing them among other matters how for their sins God suffered such things to be, and pestilences also: and how far more parlous is the flame of hell, the which must vex the damned eternally, than is the fury of the wolf that can but slay the body; how much then should men fear the jaws of hell, when such a multitude stands sore adread of the jaws of one so small a beast? Then turn ye, beloved, unto God, and work out a fit repentance for your sins; and God will set you free from the wolf in this present time, and in time to come from out the fires of hell. And done the preaching, St. Francis said: "Give ear, my brothers: brother wolf, who standeth here before ye, hath promised me and plighted troth to make his peace with you, and to offend no more in any thing; and do ye promise him to give him every day whate'er he needs: and I am made his surety unto you that he will keep this pact of peace right steadfastly." Then promised all the folk with one accord to give him food abidingly. Then quoth St. Francis to the wolf before them all: "And thou, brother wolf, dost thou make promise to keep firm this pact of peace, that thou offend not man nor beast nor any creature?" And the wolf knelt him down and bowed his head: and with gentle movements of his body, tail, and eyes, gave sign as best he could that he would keep their pact entire. Quoth St. Francis: "Brother wolf, I wish that as thou hast pledged me thy faith to this promise without the gate, even so shouldest thou pledge me thy faith to thy promise before all the people, and that thou play me not false for my promise, and the surety that I have given for thee." Then the wolf lifting up his right paw, laid it in the hand of St. Francis. Therewith, this act, and the others set forth above, wrought such great joy and marvel in all the people, both through devotion to the saint, and through the newness of the miracle, and through the peace with the wolf, that all began to lift up their voices unto heaven praising and blessing God, that had sent St. Francis unto them, who by his merits had set them free from the jaws of the cruel beast. And thereafter this same wolf lived two years in Agobio; and went like a tame beast in and out the houses, from door to door, without doing hurt to any or any doing hurt to him, and was courteously nourished by the people; and as he passed thuswise through the country and the houses, never did any dog bark behind him. At length, after a two years' space, brother wolf died of old age: whereat the townsfolk sorely grieved, sith marking him pass so gently through the city, they minded them the better of the virtue and the sanctity of St. Francis.

HOW ST. FRANCIS TAMED THE WILD TURTLE-DOVES

It befell on a day that a certain young man had caught many turtle-doves: and as he was carrying them for sale, St. Francis, who had ever a tender pity for gentle creatures, met him, and looking on those turtle-doves with pitying eyes, said to the youth: "I pray thee give them me, that birds so gentle, unto which the Scripture likeneth chaste and humble and faithful souls, may not fall into the hands of cruel men that would kill them." Forthwith, inspired of God, he gave them all to St. Francis; and he receiving them into his bosom, began to speak tenderly unto them: "O my sisters, simple-minded turtle-doves, innocent and chaste, why have ye let yourselves be caught? Now would I fain deliver you from death and make you nests, that ye may be fruitful and multiply, according to the commandments of your Creator." And St. Francis went and made nests for them all: and they abiding therein, began to lay their eggs and hatch them before the eyes of the brothers: and so tame were they, they dwelt with St. Francis and all the other brothers as though they had been fowls that had always fed from their hands, and never did they go away until St. Francis with his blessing gave them leave to go. And to the young man who had given them to him, St. Francis said: "My little son, thou wilt yet be a brother in this Order and do precious service unto Jesu Christ." And so it came to pass; for the said youth became a brother and lived in the Order in great sanctity.

SONG OF THE EMIGRANTS IN BERMUDA

Where the remote Bermudas ride
In the ocean's bosom unespied,
From a small boat that row'd along
The listening winds received this song:
"What should we do but sing His praise
That led us through the watery maze
Where He the huge sea-monsters wracks
That lift the deep upon their backs,
Unto an isle so long unknown,
And yet far kinder than our own?
He lands us on a grassy stage,
Safe from the storms, and prelate's rage:
He gave us this eternal spring
Which here enamels everything,
And sends the fowls to us in care
On daily visits through the air.
He hangs in shades the orange bright
Like golden lamps in a green night,
And does in the pomegranates close
Jewels more rich than Ormus shows:
He makes the figs our mouths to meet,
And throws the melons at our feet;
But apples plants of such a price,
No tree could ever bear them twice!
With cedars chosen by his hand
From Lebanon he stores the land;
And makes the hollow seas that roar
Proclaim the ambergris on shore.
He cast (of which we rather boast)
The Gospel's pearl upon our coast;
And in these rocks for us did frame
A temple where to sound His name.
O let our voice His praise exalt
Till it arrive at Heaven's vault,

Which then perhaps rebounding may
Echo beyond the Mexique bay!"
—Thus sung they in the English boat
A holy and a cheerful note:
And all the way, to guide their chime,
With falling oars they kept the time.

 —*A. Marvell*

LANDING OF THE PILGRIM FATHERS IN NEW ENGLAND

The breaking waves dash'd high
  On a stern and rock-bound coast,
And the woods against a stormy sky
  Their giant branches toss'd;

And the heavy night hung dark
  The hills and waters o'er,
When a band of exiles moor'd their bark
  On the wild New England shore.

Not as the conqueror comes,
  They, the true-hearted, came;
Not with the roll of the stirring drums,
  And the trumpet that sings of fame;

Not as the flying come,
  In silence and in fear;—
They shook the depths of the desert gloom
  With their hymns of lofty cheer.

Amidst the storm they sang,
  And the stars heard and the sea;
And the sounding aisles of the dim woods rang
  To the anthem of the free!

The ocean eagle soar'd
  From his nest by the white wave's foam;
And the rocking pines of the forest roar'd—
  This was their welcome home!

There were men with hoary hair
  Amidst that pilgrim band;—
Why had *they* come to wither there,
  Away from their childhood's land?

There was woman's fearless eye,
  Lit by her deep love's truth;
There was manhood's brow serenely high,
  And the fiery heart of youth.

What sought they thus afar?—
  Bright jewels of the mine?
The wealth of seas, the spoils of war?—
  They sought a faith's pure shrine!

Ay, call it holy ground,
  The soil where first they trod.
They have left unstain'd what there they found—
  Freedom to worship God.

—*Felicia Browne Hemans*

THE PILGRIM'S PROGRESS

IN THE SIMILITUDE OF A DREAM

As I walked through the wilderness of this world, I lighted on a certain place where was a den, and laid me down in that place to sleep; and as I slept, I dreamed a dream. I dreamed, and behold, I saw a man clothed with rags standing in a certain place, with his face from his own house, a book in his hand, and a great burden upon his back. I looked, and saw him open the book and read therein; and as he read he wept and trembled; and not being able longer to contain, he brake out with a lamentable cry, saying, "What shall I do?"

In this plight, therefore, he went home, and restrained himself as long as he could, that his wife and children should not perceive his distress; but he could not be silent long, because that his trouble increased. Wherefore at length he brake his mind to his wife and children; and thus he began to talk to them: "O my dear wife," said he, "and you the children of my bowels, I, your dear friend, am in myself undone by reason of a burden that lieth hard upon me; moreover, I am certainly informed that this our city will be burned with fire from heaven; in which fearful overthrow, both myself, with thee, my wife, and you, my sweet-babes, shall miserably come to ruin, except (the which yet I see not) some way of escape *can* be found whereby we may be delivered."

At this his relations were sore amazed; not for that they believed that what he said to them was true, but because they thought that some frenzy distemper had got into his head; therefore, it drawing toward night, and they hoping that sleep might settle his brains, with all haste they got him to bed. But the night was as troublesome to him as the day; wherefore, instead of sleeping, he spent it in sighs and tears. So when the morning was come, they would know how he did. He told them, "Worse and worse": he also set to talking to them again; but they began to be hardened. They also thought to drive away his distemper by harsh and surly carriage to him; sometimes they would deride, sometimes they would chide, and sometimes they would quite neglect him. Wherefore he began to retire himself to his chamber to pray for and pity them, and also to condole his own misery; he would also walk solitarily in the fields, sometimes reading and sometimes praying; and thus for some days he spent his time.

Now I saw, upon a time, when he was walking in the fields, that he was, as he was wont, reading in his book, and greatly distressed in his mind; and as he read, he burst out, as he had done before, crying, "What shall I do to be saved?"

I saw also that he looked this way, and that way, as if he would run; yet he stood still, because, as I perceived, he could not tell which way to go. I looked then, and saw a man named Evangelist coming to him, and he asked, "Wherefore dost thou cry?"

He answered, "Sir, I perceive, by the book in my hand, that I am condemned to die, and after that to come to judgment; and I find that I am not willing to do the first, nor able to do the second."

Then said Evangelist, "Why not willing to die, since this life is attended with so many evils?" The man answered, "Because I fear that this burden that is upon my back will sink me lower than the grave and I shall fall into Tophet. And, sir, if I be not fit to go to prison, I am not fit to go to judgment, and from thence to execution; and the thoughts of these things make me cry."

Then said Evangelist, "If this be thy condition, why standest thou still?" He answered, "Because I know not whither to go." Then he gave him a parchment roll, and there was written within, "Flee from the wrath to come."

The man therefore read it and looking upon Evangelist very carefully, said, "Whither must I fly?" Then said Evangelist, pointing with his finger over a very wide field, "Do you see yonder wicket-gate?" The man said, "No." Then said the other, "Do you see yonder shining light?" He said, "I think I do." Then said Evangelist, "Keep that light in your eye, and go up directly thereto, so shalt thou see the gate; at which, when thou knockest, it shall be told thee what thou shalt do." So I saw in my dream that the man began to run. Now he had not run far from his own door when his wife and children, perceiving it, began to cry after him to return; but the man put his fingers in his ears, and ran on, crying, "Life! life! eternal life!" So he looked not behind him; but fled toward the middle of the plain.

The neighbors also came out to see him run; and as he ran some mocked, others threatened, and some cried after him to return; and among those that did so, there were two that resolved to fetch him back by force. The name of the one was Obstinate, and the name of the other Pliable. Now by this time the man was got a good distance from them; but however they were resolved to pursue him, which they did, and in a little time they overtook him. Then said the man, "Neighbors, wherefore are ye come?" They said, "To persuade you to go back with us." But he said, "That can by no means be; you dwell," said he, "in the City of Destruction, the place also where I was born: I see it to be so; and dying there, sooner or later you will sink lower than the grave, into a place that burns with fire and brimstone: be content, good neighbors, and go along with me."

What! said Obstinate, and leave our friends and comforts behind us?

Yes, said Christian, for that was his name, because that all which you forsake is not worthy to be compared with a little of that I am seeking to enjoy; and if you will go along with me, and hold it, you shall fare as I myself; for there, where I go, is enough and to spare. Come away, and prove my words.

Obst. What are the things you seek, since you leave all the world to find them?

Chr. I seek an inheritance incorruptible, undefiled, and that fadeth not away; and it is laid up in heaven, and safe there, to be bestowed at the time appointed, on them that diligently seek it. Read it so, if you will, in my book.

Tush, said Obstinate, away with your book; will you go back with us or no?

No, not I, said the other, because I have laid my hand to the plow.

Obst. Come then, neighbor Pliable, let us turn again, and go home without him; there is a company of these crazy-headed coxcombs, that when they take a fancy by the end, are wiser in their own eyes than seven men that can render a reason.

Pli. Then said Pliable, Don't revile; if what the good Christian says is true, the things he looks after are better than ours; my heart inclines to go with my neighbor.

Obst. What! more fools still? Be ruled by me and go back; who knows whither such a brain-sick fellow will lead you? Go back, go back, and be wise.

Chr. Come with me, neighbor Pliable; there are such things to be had which I spoke of, and many more glories beside. If you believe not me, read here in this book; and for the truth of what is expressed therein, behold, all is confirmed by the blood of him that made it.

Pli. Well, neighbor Obstinate, said Pliable, I begin to come to a point; I intend to go along with this good man, and to cast in my lot with him: but, my good companion, do you know the way to this desired place?

Chr. I am directed by a man, whose name is Evangelist, to speed me to a little gate that is before us, where we shall receive instruction about the way.

Pli. Come then, good neighbor, let us be going.

Then they went both together.

Obst. And I will go back to my place, said Obstinate. I will be no companion of such misled, fantastical fellows.

Now I saw in my dream, that when Obstinate was gone back, Christian and Pliable went talking over the plain, and thus they began their discourse.

Chr. Come, neighbor Pliable, how do you do? I am glad you are persuaded to go along with me. Had even Obstinate himself but felt what I have felt of the powers and terrors of what is yet unseen, he would not thus lightly have given us the back.

Pli. Come, neighbor Christian, since there are none but us two here, tell me now further, what the things are, and how to be enjoyed, whither we are going.

Chr. I can better conceive of them with my mind, than speak of them with my tongue: but yet since you are desirous to know, I will read them in my book.

Pli. And do you think that the words of your book are certainly true?

Chr. Yes, verily; for it was made by him that cannot lie.

Pit. Well said; what things are they?

Chr. There is an endless kingdom to be inhabited, and everlasting life to be given us, that we may inhabit that kingdom forever.

Pli. Well said; and what else?

Chr. There are crowns of glory to be given us; and garments that will make us shine like the sun in the firmament of heaven.

Pli. This is excellent: and what else?

Chr. There shall be no more crying nor sorrow, for he that is owner of the place will wipe all tears from our eyes.

Pli. And what company shall we have there?

Chr. There we shall be with seraphims and cherubims; creatures that will dazzle your eyes to look on them. There also you shall meet with thousands and ten thousands that have gone before us to that holy place; none of them are hurtful, but loving and holy; every one walking in the sight of God, and standing in his presence with acceptance forever. In a word, there we shall see the elders with their golden crowns; there we shall see the holy virgins with their golden harps; there we shall see men that by the world were cut in pieces, burned in flames, eaten of beasts, drowned in the sea for the love they bare to the Lord of the place; all well and clothed with immortality as with a garment.

Pli. The hearing of this is enough to ravish one's heart. But are these things to be enjoyed? How shall we get to be sharers thereof?

Chr. The Lord, the governor of the country, hath recorded that in this book; the substance of which is, If we be truly willing to have it, he will bestow it upon us freely.

Pli. Well, my good companion, glad am I to hear of these things: come on, let us mend our pace.

Chr. I cannot go so fast as I would, by reason of this burden that is on my back.

Now I saw in my dream, that just as they had ended this talk, they drew nigh to a very miry slough that was in the midst of the plain: and they, being heedless, did both fall suddenly into the bog. The name of the slough was Despond. Here, therefore, they wallowed for a time, being grievously bedaubed with dirt; and Christian, because of the burden that was on his back, began to sink in the mire.

Pli. Then said Pliable, Ah, neighbor Christian, where are you now?

Chr. Truly, said Christian, I do not know.

Pli. At this Pliable began to be offended, and angrily said to his fellow, Is this the happiness you have told me all this while of? If we have such ill speed at our first setting out, what may we expect between this and our journey's end? May I get out again with my life, you shall possess the brave country alone for me. And with that he gave a desperate struggle or two, and got out of the mire on that side of the slough which was next to his own house: so away he went, and Christian saw him no more.

Wherefore Christian was left to tumble in the Slough of Despond alone: but still he endeavored to struggle to that side of the slough that was furthest from his own house, and next to the wicket-gate; the which he did, but could not get out because of the burden that was upon his back: but I beheld in my dream, that a man came to him, whose name was Help, and asked him, "What he did there?"

Chr. Sir, said Christian, I was bid to go this way by a man called Evangelist, who directed me also to yonder gate, that I might escape the wrath to come. And as I was going thither I fell in here.

Help. But why did not you look for the steps?

Chr. Fear followed me so hard, that I fled the next way, and fell in.

Help. Then said he, Give me thine hand; so he gave him his hand, and he drew him out, and he set him upon sound ground, and bid him go on his way.

Then I stepped to him that plucked him out, and said, "Sir, wherefore, since over this place is the way from the City of Destruction to yonder gate, is it, that this plat is not mended, that poor travellers might go thither with more security?" And he said unto me, "This miry slough is such a place as cannot be mended: it is the descent whither the scum and filth that attends conviction for sin doth continually run, and therefore it is called the Slough of Despond; for still as the sinner is awakened about his lost condition, there arise in his soul many fears and doubts, and discouraging apprehensions, which all of them get together, and settle in this place: and this is the reason of the badness of this ground.

"It is not the pleasure of the King that this place should remain so bad. His laborers also have, by the direction of his Majesty's surveyors, been for above these sixteen hundred years employed about this patch of ground, if perhaps it might have been mended: yea, and to my knowledge," said he, "here have been swallowed up at least twenty thousand cart-loads, yea, millions, of wholesome instructions, that have at all seasons been brought from all places of the King's dominions—and they that can tell, say, they are the best materials to make good ground of the place—if so be it might have been mended; but it is the Slough of Despond still, and so will be when they have done what they can.

"True, there are, by the direction of the Lawgiver, certain good and substantial steps, placed even through the very midst of this slough; but at such time as this place doth much spew out its filth, as it doth against change of weather, these steps are hardly seen; or if they be, men, through the dizziness of their heads, step beside, and then they are bemired to purpose, notwithstanding the steps be there; but the ground is good when they are once in at the gate."

Now I saw in my dream, that by this time Pliable was got home to his house. So his neighbors came to visit him; and some of them called him wise man for coming back, and some called him fool for hazarding himself with Christian; others again did mock at his cowardliness; saying, "Surely, since you began to venture, I would not have been so base to have given out for a few difficulties:" so Pliable sat sneaking among them. But at last he got more confidence, and then they all turned their tales, and began to deride poor Christian behind his back. And thus much concerning Pliable.

So, in the process of time, Christian got up to the gate. Now, over the gate there was written, "Knock, and it shall be opened unto you."

He knocked, therefore, more than once or twice, saying,

May I now enter here? Will he within
Open to sorry me, though I have been
An undeserving rebel? Then shall I
Not fail to sing his lasting praise on high.

At last there came a grave person to the gate, named Goodwill, who asked who was there, and whence he came, and what he would have.

Chr. Here is a poor burdened sinner. I come from the City of Destruction, but am going to Mount Zion, that I may be delivered from the wrath to come: I would, therefore, sir, since I am informed that by this gate is the way thither, know if you are willing to let me in.

Good. I am willing with all my heart, said he; and with that he opened the gate.

So when Christian was stepping in, the other gave him a pull. Then said Christian, What means that? The other told him, A little distance from this gate there is erected a strong castle, of which Beelzebub is the captain; from thence both he and they that are with him shoot arrows at those who come up to this gate, if haply they may die before they can enter it. Then said Christian, I rejoice and tremble.

Now I saw in my dream, that the highway which Christian was to go was fenced on either side with a wall, and that wall was called Salvation. Up this way therefore did burdened Christian run, but not without great difficulty, because of the load on his back.

He ran thus till he came at a place somewhat ascending; and upon that place stood a cross, and a little below, in the bottom, a sepulchre. So I saw in my dream, that just as Christian came up with the cross, his burden loosed from off his shoulders, and fell from off his back, and began to tumble, and so continued to do till it came to the mouth of the sepulchre, where it fell in, and I saw it no more.

Then was Christian glad and lightsome, and said with a merry heart, "He hath given me rest by his sorrow, and life by his death." Then he stood still awhile to look and wonder; for it was very surprising to him that the sight of the cross should thus ease him of his burden. He looked therefore, and looked again, even till the springs that were in his head sent the waters down his cheeks. Now as he stood looking and weeping, behold, three Shining Ones came to him, and saluted him with "Peace be to thee." So the first said to him, "Thy sins be forgiven thee;" the second stripped him of his rags, and clothed him with change of raiment; the third also set a mark on his forehead, and gave him a roll with a seal upon it, which he bid him look on as he ran, and that he should give it in at the celestial gate; so they went their way.

Then Christian gave three leaps for joy, and went on singing:

Thus far did I come laden with my sin;
Nor could aught ease the grief that I was in,
Till I came hither; what a place is this!
Must here be the beginning of my bliss?
Must here the burden fall from off my back?
Must here the strings that bound it to me crack?
Blest cross! blest sepulchre! blest rather be
The man that there was put to shame for me.

I saw then in my dream, that he went on thus, even until he came at the bottom, where he saw, a little out of the way, three men fast asleep, with fetters upon their heels. The name of the one was Simple, of another Sloth, and of the third Presumption.

Christian then, seeing them lie in this case, went to them, if peradventure he might awake them, and cried, You are like them that sleep on the top of a mast, for the Dead Sea is under you, a gulf that hath no bottom: awake, therefore, and come away; be willing also, and I will help you off with your irons. He also told them, If he that goeth about like a roaring lion, comes by, you will certainly become a prey to his teeth. With that they looked upon him, and began to reply in this sort: Simple said, I see no danger; Sloth said, Yet a little more sleep; and Presumption said, Every tub must stand upon its own bottom.

And so they lay down to sleep again, and Christian went on his way.

Yet was he troubled to think, that men in that danger should so little esteem the kindness of him that so freely offered to help them, both by awakening of them, counselling of them, and proffering to help them off with their irons. And as he was troubled thereabout, he espied two men come tumbling over the wall on the left hand of the narrow way; and they made up apace to him. The name of the one was Formalist, and the name of the other Hypocrisy. So, as I said, they drew up unto him, who thus entered with him into discourse.

Chr. Gentlemen, whence came you, and whither do you go?

Form. and *Hyp.* We were born in the land of Vain-glory, and are going for praise to Mount Zion.

Chr. Why came you not in at the gate which standeth at the beginning of the way? Know ye not that it is written, that "he that cometh not in by the door, but climbeth up some other way, the same is a thief and a robber?"

They said, that to go to the gate for entrance was by all their countrymen counted too far about; and that therefore their usual way was to make a short cut of it, and to climb over the wall as they had done.

Chr. But will it not be counted a trespass against the Lord of the city, whither we are bound, thus to violate his revealed will?

They told him, that as for that, he needed not to trouble his head thereabout: for what they did they had custom for, and could produce, if need were, testimony that would witness it, for more than a thousand years.

But, said Christian, will your practice stand a trial at law?

They told him, that custom, it being of so long standing as above a thousand years, would, doubtless, now be admitted as a thing legal by an impartial judge. And besides, said they, if we get into the way, what matter is it which way we get in? If we are in, we are in: thou art but in the way, who, as we perceive, came in at the gate: and we also are in the way, that came tumbling over the wall: wherein now is thy condition better than ours?

Chr. I walk by the rule of my Master: you walk by the rude working of your fancies. You are counted thieves already by the Lord of the way: therefore I doubt you will not be found true men at the end of the way. You come in by yourselves, without his direction, and shall go out by yourselves, without his mercy.

To this they made him but little answer; only they bid him look to himself. Then I saw that they went on every man in his way, without much conference one with another; save that these two men told Christian, that as to laws and ordinances, they doubted not but that they should as conscientiously do them as he. Therefore, said they, we see not wherein thou differest from us, but by the coat that is on thy back, which was, as we trow, given thee by some of thy neighbors, to hide the shame of thy nakedness.

Chr. By laws and ordinances you will not be saved, since you came not in by the door. And as for this coat that is on my back, it was given me by the Lord of the place whither I go; and that, as you say, to cover my nakedness with. And I take it as a token of his kindness to me; for I had nothing but rags before. And, besides, thus I comfort myself as I go. Surely, think I, when I come to the gate of the city, the Lord thereof will know me for good, since I have his coat on my back; a coat that he gave me freely in the day that he stripped me of my rags. I have, moreover, a mark in my forehead, of which perhaps you have taken no notice, which one of my lord's most intimate associates fixed there in the day that my burden fell off my shoulders. I will tell you, moreover, that I had then given me a roll sealed, to comfort me by reading as I go in the way; I was also bid to give it in at the celestial gate, in token of my certain going in after it; all which things I doubt you want, and want them because you came not in at the gate.

To these things they gave him no answer; only they looked upon each other, and laughed. Then I saw that they went on all, save that Christian kept before, who had no more talk but with himself, and that sometimes sighingly, and sometimes comfortably; also he would be often reading in the roll that one of the Shining Ones gave him, by which he was refreshed.

I beheld, then, that they all went on till they came to the foot of the hill Difficulty, at the bottom of which there was a string. There were also in the same place two other ways besides that which came straight from the gate; one turned to the left hand and the other to the right, at the bottom of the hill; but the narrow way lay right up the hill, and the name of the going up the side of the hill is called Difficulty. Christian now went to the spring; and drank thereof to refresh himself, and then began to go up the hill, saying:

The hill, though high, I covet to ascend;
The difficulty will not me offend;
For I perceive the way to life lies here.
Come, pluck up heart, let's neither faint nor fear.
Better, though *difficult*, the right way to go,
Than wrong, though *easy*, where the end is woe.

The other two also came to the foot of the hill. But when they saw the hill was steep and high, and that there were two other ways to go; and supposing also that these two ways might meet again with that up which Christian went on the other side of the hill; therefore they were resolved to go in those ways. Now the name of one of those ways was Danger, and the name of the other Destruction. So the one took the way which is called Danger, which led him into a great wood; and the other took directly up the way to Destruction, which led him into a wide field, full of dark mountains, where he stumbled and fell, and rose no more.

I looked then after Christian, to see him go up the hill, where I perceived he fell from running to going, and from going to clambering upon his hands and his knees, because of the steepness of the place. Now about midway to the top of the hill was a pleasant arbor, made by the Lord of the hill for the refreshment of weary travellers. Thither, therefore, Christian got, where also he sat down to rest him; then he pulled his roll out of his bosom, and read therein to his comfort; he also now began afresh to take a review of the coat or garment that was given him as he stood by the cross. Thus pleasing himself awhile, he at last fell into a slumber, and thence into a fast sleep, which detained him in that place until it was almost night; and in his sleep his roll fell out of his hand. Now as he was sleeping, there came one to him, and awaked him, saying, "Go to the ant, thou sluggard; consider her ways, and be wise." And with that Christian suddenly started up, and sped him on his way, and went apace till he came to the top of the hill.

Now, when he was got up to the top of the hill, there came two men running to meet him amain; the name of the one was Timorous, and of the other Mistrust: to whom Christian said, Sirs, what's the matter? you run the wrong way. Timorous answered, that they were going to the City of Zion, and had got up that difficult place: but, said he, the further we go the more danger we meet with; wherefore we turned, and are going back again.

Yes, said Mistrust, for just before us lie a couple of lions in the way, whether sleeping or waking we know not, and we could not think, if we came within reach, but they would presently pull us to pieces.

Chr. Then said Christian, you make me afraid; but whither shall I fly to be safe? If I go back to my own country, that is prepared for fire and brimstone, and I shall certainly perish there; if I can get to the Celestial City, I am sure to be in safety there: I must venture. To go back is nothing but death; to go forward is fear of death and life everlasting beyond it. I will yet go forward. So Mistrust and Timorous run down the hill, and Christian went on his way. But thinking again of what he heard from the man, he felt in his bosom for his roll, that he might read therein and be comforted; but he felt and found it not. Then was Christian in great distress, and knew not what to do; for he wanted that which used to relieve him, and that which should have been his pass into the Celestial City. Here, therefore, he began to be much perplexed, and knew not what to do. At last he bethought himself that he had slept in the arbor that is on the side of the hill; and falling down upon his knees, he asked God forgiveness for that his foolish act, and then went back to look for his roll. But all the way he went back, who can sufficiently set forth the sorrow of Christian's heart? Sometimes he sighed, sometimes he wept, and oftentimes he chid himself for being so foolish to fall asleep in that place, which was erected only for a little refreshment from his weariness. Thus, therefore, he went back, carefully looking on this side and on that, all the way as he went, if happily he might find his roll that had been his comfort so many times in his journey. He went thus till he came within sight of the arbor where he sat and slept; but that sight renewed his sorrow the more, by bringing again even afresh, his evil of sleeping unto his mind. Thus, therefore, he now went on, bewailing his sinful sleep, saying, Oh, wretched man that I am, that I should sleep in the daytime! that I should sleep in the midst of difficulty! that I should so indulge the flesh as to use that rest for ease to my flesh which the Lord of the hill hath erected only for the relief of the spirits of pilgrims! How many steps have I taken in vain! Thus it happened to Israel: for their sin they were sent back again by the way of the Red Sea; and I am made to tread those steps with sorrow, which I might have trod with delight had it not been for this sinful sleep. How far might I have been on my way by this time! I am made to tread those steps thrice over, which I needed not to have trod but once: yea, also now I am like to be benighted, for the day is almost spent. Oh, that I had not slept!

Now by this time he was come to arbor again, where for awhile he sat down and wept; but at last as Christian would have it, looking sorrowfully down under the settle, there he espied his roll, the which he with trembling and haste catched up, and put it into his bosom. But who can tell how joyful this man was when he had gotten his roll again? For this roll was the assurance of his life, and acceptance at the desired haven. Therefore he laid it up in his bosom, gave thanks to God for directing his eye to the place where it lay, and with joy and tears betook himself again to his journy. But oh, how nimbly now did he go up the rest of the hill! Yet, before he got up, the sun went down upon Christian; and this made him again recall the vanity of his sleeping to his remembrance; and thus he again began to condole with himself: O thou sinful sleep! how for thy sake am I like to be benighted in my journey! I must walk without the sun, darkness must cover the path of my feet, and I must hear the noise of the doleful creatures, because of my sinful sleep! Now also he remembered the story that Mistrust and Timorous told him, of how they were frighted with the sight of the lions. Then said Christian to himself again, These beasts range in the night for their prey, and if they should meet with me in the dark, how should I shift them? how should I escape being by them torn in pieces? Thus he went on his way. But while he was thus bewailing his unhappy miscarriage, he lift up his eyes, and behold there was a very stately palace before him, the name of which was Beautiful, and it stood just by the highway side.

So I saw in my dream, that he made haste, and went forward, that if possible he might get lodging there. Now before he had gone far he entered into a very narrow passage, which was about a furlong off the Porter's lodge; and looking very narrowly before him as he went, he espied two lions in the way. Now, thought he, I see the dangers that Mistrust and Timorous were driven back by. (The lions were chained, but he saw not the chains.) Then he was afraid, and thought also himself to go back after them; for he thought nothing but death was before him. But the Porter at the lodge, whose name is Watchful, perceiving that Christian made a halt, as if he would go back, cried unto him, saying, Is thy strength so small? Fear not the lions, for they are chained, and are placed there for trial of faith where it is, and for discovery of those that have none; keep in the midst of the path and no hurt shall come unto thee.

Then I saw that he went on trembling for fear of the lions; but taking good heed to the directions of the Porter, he heard them roar but they did him no harm. Then he clapped his hands and went on till he came and stood before the gate where the Porter was. Then said Christian to the Porter, Sir, what house is this? and may I lodge here to-night? The Porter answered, This house was built by the Lord of the hill, and he built it for the relief and security of pilgrims. The Porter also asked whence he was, and whither he was going.

Chr. I am come from the City of Destruction, and am going to Mount Zion; but because the sun is now set, I desire, if I may, to lodge here to-night.

Port. What is your name?

Chr. My name is now Christian, but my name at the first was Graceless; I came of the race of Japheth, whom God will persuade to dwell in the tents of Shem.

Port. But how doth it happen that you come so late? The sun is set.

Chr. I had been here sooner, but that, wretched man as I am, I slept in the arbor that stands on the hillside. Nay, I had, notwithstanding that, been here much sooner, but that in my sleep I lost my evidence, and came without it to the brow of the hill; and then feeling for it, and finding it not, I was forced with sorrow of heart to go back to the place where I slept my sleep, where I found it; and now I am come.

Port. Well, I will call out one of the virgins of this place, who will, if she likes your talk, bring you in to the rest of the family, according to the rules of the house. So Watchful, the Porter, rang a bell, at the sound of which came out of the door of the house a grave and beautiful damsel, named Discretion, and asked why she was called.

The Porter answered, This man is on a journey from the City of Destruction to Mount Zion, but being weary and benighted, he asked me if he might lodge here to-night; so I told him I would call for thee, who, after discourse had with him, mayest do as seemeth thee good, even according to the law of the house.

Then she asked him whence he was, and whither he was going; and he told her. She asked him also how he got into the way; and he told her. Then she asked him what he had seen and met with in the way, and he told her. And at last she asked his name. So he said, It is Christian; and I have so much the more a desire to lodge here to-night, because, by what I perceive, this place was built by the Lord of the hill for the relief and security of pilgrims. So she smiled, but the water stood in her eyes; and after a little pause she said, I will call forth two or three more of the family. So she ran to the door, and called out Prudence, Piety, and Charity, who, after a little more discourse with him, had him into the family; and many of them meeting him at the threshold of the house, said, Come in, thou blessed of the Lord; this house was built by the Lord of the hill on purpose to entertain such pilgrims in. Then he bowed his head, and followed them into the house. So when he was come in and sat down, they gave him something to drink, and consented together that, until supper was ready, some of them should have some particular discourse with Christian, for the best improvement of time; and they appointed Piety, Prudence, and Charity, to discourse with him.

Now I saw in my dream, that thus they sat talking together until supper was ready. So when they had made ready they sat down to meat. Now the table was furnished with fat things, and wine that was well refined; and all their talk at the table was about the Lord of the hill; as namely, what he had done, and wherefore he did what he did, and why he had builded that house; and by what they said, I perceived that he had been a great warrior, and had fought with and slain him that had the power of death, but not without great danger to himself, which made me love him the more.

For, as they said, and as I believe, said Christian, he did it with the loss of much blood. But that which put the glory of grace into all he did, was, that he did it out of pure love to this country. And besides, there was some of them of the household that said they had been and spoke with him since he did die on the cross; and they have attested, that they had it from his own lips, that he is such a lover of poor pilgrims, that the like is not to be found from the east to the west. They, moreover, gave an instance of what they affirmed, and that was, he had stripped himself of his glory that he might do this for the poor; and that they had heard him say and affirm, that he would not dwell in the mountain of Zion alone. They said, moreover, that he had made many pilgrims princes, though by nature they were beggars born, and their original had been the dunghill.

Thus they discoursed together till late at night: and after they had committed themselves to their Lord for protection, they betook themselves to rest. The pilgrim they laid in a large upper chamber, whose window opened toward the sunrising. The name of the chamber was Peace, where he slept till break of day, and then he awoke and sang:

Where am I now? Is this the love and care
Of Jesus, for the men that pilgrims are,

Thus to provide that I should be forgiven,
And dwell already the next door to heaven?

So in the morning they all got up; and after some more discourse, they told him that he should not depart till they had showed him the rarities of that place. And first they had him into the study, where they showed him records of the greatest antiquity; in which, as I remember my dream, they showed him the pedigree of the Lord of the hill, that he was the Son of the Ancient of days, and came by that eternal generation. Here also was more fully recorded the acts that he had done, and the names of many hundreds that he had taken into his service; and how he had placed them in such habitations, that could neither by length of days, nor decays of nature, be dissolved.

Then they read to him some of the worthy acts that some of his servants had done; as how they had subdued kingdoms, wrought righteousness, obtained promises, stopped the mouths of lions, quenched the violence of fire, escaped the edge of the sword, out of weakness were made strong, waxed valiant in fight, and turned to flight the armies of the aliens.

Then they read again another part of the records of the house, where it was shown how willing their Lord was to receive into his favor any, even any, though they in time past had offered great affronts to his person and proceedings. Here also were several other histories of many other famous things, of all which Christian had a view; as of things both ancient and modern, together with prophecies and predictions of things that have their certain accomplishment, both to the dread and amazement of enemies, and the comfort and solace of pilgrims.

The next day they took him, and had him into the armory, where they showed him all manner of furniture which their Lord had provided for pilgrims, as sword, shield, helmet, breastplate, all-prayer, and shoes that would not wear out. And there was here enough of this to harness out as many men for the service of their Lord as there be stars in heaven for multitude.

They also showed him some of the engines with which some of his servants had done wonderful things. They showed him Moses' rod; the hammer and nail with which Jael slew Sisera; the pitchers, trumpets, and lamps, too, with which Gideon put to flight the armies of Midian. Then they showed him the ox's goad wherewith Shamgar slew six hundred men. They showed him also the jaw-bone with which Samson did such mighty feats. They showed him, moreover, the sling and stone with which David slew Goliath of Gath, and the sword also with which their Lord will kill the Man of Sin, in the day that he shall rise up to the prey. They showed him besides many excellent things, with which Christian was much delighted. This done, they went to their rest again.

Then I saw in my dream, that on the morrow he got up to go forward, but they desired him to stay till the next day also; and then, said they, we will, if the day be clear, show you the Delectable Mountains; which, they said, would yet further add to his comfort, because they were nearer the desired haven than the place where at present he was; so he consented and stayed. When the morning was up, they had him to the top of the house, and bid him look south. So he did, and behold, at a great distance, he saw a most pleasant, mountainous country, beautified with woods, vineyards, fruit of all sorts, flowers also, with springs and fountains, very delectable to behold. Then he asked the name of the country. They said it was Immanuel's Land; and it is as common, said they, as this hill is, to and for all the pilgrims. And when thou comest there, from thence, said they, thou mayest see to the gate of the Celestial City, as the shepherds that live there will make appear.

Now he bethought himself of setting forward, and they were willing he should. But first, said they, let us go again into the armory. So they did, and when he came there they harnessed him from head to foot with what was of proof, lest perhaps he should meet with assaults in the way. He being therefore thus accoutred, walked out with his friends to the gate; and there he asked the Porter if he saw any pilgrim pass by. Then the Porter answered, Yes.

Chr. Pray, did you know him? said he.

Port. I asked his name, and he told me it was Faithful.

Chr. Oh, said Christian, I know him; he is my townsman, my dear neighbor; he comes from the place where I was born. How far do you think he may be before?

Port. He is got by this time below the hill.

Chr. Well, said Christian, good Porter, the Lord be with thee, and add to thy blessings much increase for the kindness thou hast shown to me.

Then he began to go forward; but Discretion, Piety, Chanty, and Prudence would accompany him down to the foot of the hill. So they went on together, reiterating their former discourses, till they came to go down the hill. Then said Christian, As it was difficult coming up, so, so far as I can see, it is dangerous going down. Yes, said Prudence, so it is; for it is a hard matter for a man to go down into the Valley of Humiliation, as thou art now, and to catch no slip by the way; therefore, said they, are we come out to accompany thee down the hill. So he began to go down, but very warily; yet he caught a slip or two.

Then I saw in my dream, that these good companions, when Christian was got down to the bottom of the hill, gave him a loaf of bread, a bottle of wine, and a cluster of raisins; and then he went his way.

But now, in this Valley of Humiliation, poor Christian was hard put to it; for he had gone but a little way before he espied a foul fiend coming over the field to meet him: his name is Apollyon. Then did Christian begin to be afraid, and to cast in his mind whether to go back, or to stand his ground. But he considered again that he had no armor for his back, and therefore thought that to turn the back to him might give him greater advantage with ease to pierce him with his darts; therefore he resolved to venture, and stand his ground; for, thought he, had I no more in mine eye than the saving of my life, it would be the best way to stand.

So he went on, and Apollyon met him. Now the monster was hideous to behold; he was clothed with scales like a fish, and they are his pride; he had wings like a dragon, and feet like a bear, and out of his belly came fire and smoke; and his mouth was as the mouth of a lion. When he came up to Christian he beheld him with a disdainful countenance, and thus began to question with him.

Apollyon. Whence come you, and whither are you bound?

Chr. I am come from the City of Destruction, which is the place of all evil, and I am going to the city of Zion.

Apol. By this I perceive that thou art one of my subjects; for all that country is mine, and I am the prince and god of it. How is it, then, that thou hast run away from thy king? Were it not that I hope thou mayst do me more service, I would strike thee now at one blow to the ground.

Chr. I was, indeed, born in your dominions, but your service was hard, and your wages such as a man could not live on: for the wages of sin is death; therefore when I was come to years, I did, as other considerate persons do, look out, if perhaps I might mend myself.

Apol. There is no prince that will thus lightly lose his subjects, neither will I as yet lose thee; but since thou complainest of thy service and wages, be content to go back, and what our country will afford I do here promise to give thee.

Chr. But I have let myself to another, even to the King of princes; and how can I with fairness go back with thee?

Apol. Thou hast done in this according to the proverb, "changed a bad for worse"; but it is ordinary for those that have professed themselves his servants, after awhile to give him the slip, and return again to me. Do thou so too, and all shall be well.

Chr. I have given him my faith, and sworn my allegiance to him; how then can I go back from this, and not be hanged as a traitor?

Apol. Thou didst the same to me, and yet I am willing to pass by all, if now thou wilt yet turn again and go back.

Chr. What I promised thee was in my nonage; and besides, I count that the Prince, under whose banner now I stand, is able to absolve me, yea, and to pardon also what I did as to my compliance with thee. And besides, O thou destroying Apollyon, to speak truth, I like his service, his wages, his servants, his government, his company, and country, better than thine; therefore leave off to persuade me further; I am his servant, and I will follow him.

Apol. Consider again, when thou art in cool blood, what thou art like to meet with in the way that thou goest. Thou knowest that for the most part his servants come to an ill end, because they are transgressors against me and my ways. How many of them have been put to shameful deaths! And besides, thou countest est his service better than mine; whereas he never came yet from the place where he is, to deliver any that serve him out of my hands; but as for me, how many times, as all the world very well knows, have I delivered, either by power or fraud, those that have faithfully served me, from him and his, though taken by them. And so I will deliver thee.

Chr. His forbearing at present to deliver them, is on purpose to try their love, whether they will cleave to him to the end; and as for the ill end thou sayest they come to, that is most glorious in their account. For, for the present deliverance, they do not much expect it; for they stay for their glory; and then they shall have it, when their Prince comes in his, and the glory of the angels.

Apol. Thou hast already been unfaithful in thy service to him; and how dost thou think to receive wages of him.

Chr. Wherein, O Apollyon, have I been unfaithful to him?

Apol. Thou didst faint at the first setting out, when thou wast almost choked in the Gulf of Despond. Thou didst attempt wrong ways to be rid of thy burden, whereas thou shouldst have stayed till thy Prince had taken it off. Thou didst sinfully sleep, and lose thy choice things. Thou wast almost persuaded to go back at the sight of the lions. And when thou talkest of thy journey, and of what thou hast seen and heard, thou art inwardly desirous of vain-glory in all that thou sayest or doest.

Chr. All this is true, and much more which thou hast left out; but the Prince whom I serve and honor is merciful and ready to forgive. But besides, these infirmities possessed me in thy country; for there I sucked them in, and I have groaned under them, been sorry for them, and have obtained pardon of my Prince.

Apol. Then Apollyon broke out into a grievous rage, saying, I am an enemy to this Prince; I hate his person, his laws, and people; I am come out on purpose to withstand thee.

Chr. Apollyon, beware what you do, for I am in the king's highway, the way of holiness; therefore take heed to yourself.

Then Apollyon straddled quite over the whole breadth of the way, and said, I am void of fear in this matter. Prepare thyself to die; for I swear by my infernal den, that thou shalt go no further; here will I spill thy soul. And with that he threw a naming dart at his breast: but Christian had a shield in his hand, with which he caught it, and so prevented the danger of that.

Then did Christian draw, for he saw it was time to bestir him; and Apollyon as fast made at him, throwing darts as thick as hail; by the which, notwithstanding all that Christian could do to avoid it, Apollyon wounded him in his head, his hand, and foot. This made Christian give a little back: Apollyon, therefore, followed his work amain, and Christian again took courage, and resisted as manfully as he could. This sore combat lasted for about half a day, even till Christian was almost quite spent. For you must know, that Christian, by reason of his wounds, must needs grow weaker and weaker.

Then, Apollyon, espying his opportunity, began to gather up close to Christian, wrestling with him, gave him a dreadful fall; and with that Christian's sword flew out of his hand. Then said Apollyon, I am sure of thee now. And with that he had almost pressed him to death; so that Christian began to despair of life. But, as God would have it, while Apollyon was fetching his last blow, thereby to make a full end of this good man, Christian nimbly reached out his hand for his sword, and caught it, saying, Rejoice not against me, O mine enemy; when I fall I shall arise; and with that gave him a deadly thrust, which made him give back, as one that had received his mortal wound. Christian perceiving that, made at him again, saying, Nay, in all these things we are more than conquerors through him that loved us. And with that Apollyon spread forth his dragon's wings, and sped him away, that Christian saw him no more.

In this combat no man can imagine, unless he had seen and heard as I did, what yelling and hideous roaring Apollyon made all the time of the fight; he spake like a dragon: and on the other side, what sighs and groans burst from Christian's heart. I never saw him all the while give so much as one pleasant look, till he perceived he had wounded Apollyon with his two-edged sword; then, indeed, he did smile, and look upward; but it was the dreadfulest fight that I ever saw.

So when the battle was over, Christian said, I will here give thanks to him that hath delivered me out of the mouth of the lion; to him that did help me against Apollyon. And so he did, saying:

Great Beelzebub, the captain of this fiend,
Design'd my ruin; therefore to this end
He sent him harness'd out, and he with rage,
That hellish was, did fiercely me engage:
But blessed Michael helped me, and I,
By dint of sword, did quickly make him fly.
Therefore to him let me give lasting praise,
And thank and bless his holy name always.

Then there came to him a hand, with some of the leaves of the tree of life, the which Christian took and applied to the wounds that he had received in the battle, and was healed immediately. He also sat down in that place to eat bread, and to drink of the bottle that was given to him a little before; so being refreshed, he addressed himself to his journey, with his sword drawn in his hand; for, he said, I know not but some other enemy may be at hand. But he met with no other affront from Apollyon quite through the valley.

Now at the end of this valley was another, called the Valley of the Shadow of Death; and Christian must needs go through it, because the way to the Celestial City lay through the midst of it. Now this valley is a very solitary place; the prophet Jeremiah thus describes it: "A wilderness, a land of deserts and pits, a land of drought, and of the shadow of death, a land that no man" (but a Christian) "passeth through, and where no man dwelt."

Now here Christian was worse put to it than in his fight with Apollyon, as by the sequel you shall see.

I saw then in my dream, that when Christian was got to the borders of the Shadow of Death, there met him two men, children of them that brought up an evil report of the good land—making haste to go back—to whom Christian spake as follows:

Chr. Whither are you going?

Men. They said, Back, back, and we would have you do so too, if either life or peace is prized by you.

Why, what's the matter? said Christian.

Men. Matter? said they; we were going that way as you are going, and went as far as we durst: and indeed we were almost past coming back; for had we gone a little further, we had not been here to bring the news to thee.

But what have you met with? said Christian.

Men. Why, we were almost in the Valley of the Shadow of Death, but that by good hap we looked before us, and saw the danger before we came to it.

But what have you seen? said Christian.

Men. Seen! why the valley itself, which is as dark as pitch: we also saw there the hobgoblins, satyrs, and dragons of the pit; we heard also in that valley a continual howling and yelling, as of a people under unutterable misery, who there sat bound in affliction and irons; and over that valley hangs the discouraging clouds of confusion: death also doth always spread his wings over it. In a word, it is every whit dreadful, being utterly without order.

Then, said Christian, I perceive not yet, by what you have said, but that this is my way to the desired haven.

Men. Be it thy way, we will not choose it for ours.

So they parted, and Christian went on his way, but still with his sword drawn in his hand, for fear lest he should be assaulted.

I saw then in my dream, so far as this valley reached, there was on the right hand a very deep ditch; that ditch is it, into which the blind have led the blind in all ages, and have both there miserably perished. Again, behold, on the left hand there was a very dangerous quag, into which, if even a good man falls, he finds no bottom for his foot to stand on: into that quag King David once did fall, and had no doubt therein been smothered, had not he that is able plucked him out.

The pathway was here also exceeding narrow, and therefore good Christian was the more put to it; for when he sought, in the dark, to shun the ditch on the one hand, he was ready to tip over into the mire on the other: also, when he sought to escape the mire, without great carefulness he would be ready to fall into the ditch. Thus he went on, and I heard him here sigh bitterly; for beside the danger mentioned above, the pathway was here so dark, that ofttimes, when he lifted up his foot to go forward, he knew not where or upon what he should set it next.

About the midst of this valley I perceived the mouth of hell to be, and it stood also hard by the wayside. Now, thought Christian, what shall I do? And ever and anon the flame and smoke would come out in such abundance, with sparks and hideous noises (things that cared not for Christian's sword, as did Apollyon before), that he was forced to put up his sword, and betake himself to another weapon, called All-prayer; so he cried, in my hearing, O Lord, I beseech thee, deliver my soul. Thus he went on a great while, yet still the flames would be reaching toward him; also he heard doleful voices, and rushings to and fro, so that sometimes he thought he should be torn in pieces, or trodden down like mire in the streets. This frightful sight was seen, and these dreadful noises were heard by him for several miles together: and coming to a place where he thought he heard a company of fiends coming forward to meet him, he stopped, and began to muse what he had best to do. Sometimes he had half a thought to go back; then, again, he thought he might be half way through the valley. He remembered, also, how he had already vanquished many a danger; and that the danger of going back might be much more than for to go forward. So he resolved to go on: yet the fiends seemed to come nearer and nearer. But when they were come even almost at him, he cried out with a most vehement voice, I will walk in the strength of the Lord God. So they gave back, and came no further.

One thing I would not let slip. I took notice that now poor Christian was so confounded that he did not know his own voice; and thus I perceived it. Just when he was come over against the mouth of the burning pit, one of the wicked ones got behind him, and stepped up softly to him, and whisperingly suggested many grievous blasphemies to him, which he verily thought had proceeded from his own mind. This put Christian more to it than anything that he met with before, even to think that he should now blaspheme him that he loved so much before. Yet if he could have helped it, he would not have done it; but he had not the discretion either to stop his ears, or to know from whence these blasphemies came.

When Christian had travelled in this disconsolate condition some considerable time, he thought he heard the voice of a man, as going before him, saying, Though I walk through the Valley of the Shadow of Death, I will fear no evil, for thou art with me.

Then was he glad, and that for these reasons:

First, Because he gathered from thence, that some who feared God were in this valley as well as himself.

Secondly, For that he perceived God was with them, though in that dark and dismal state. And why not, thought he, with me? though by reason of the impediment that attends this place, I cannot perceive it.

Thirdly, For that he hoped, could he overtake them, to have company by and by. So he went on, and called to him that was before; but he knew not what to answer, for that he also thought himself to be alone. And by and by the day broke: then said Christian, "He hath turned the shadow of death into the morning."

Now morning being come, he looked back, not out of desire to return, but to see, by the light of the day, what hazards he had gone through in the dark. So he saw more perfectly the ditch that was on the one hand, and the quag that was on the other; also how narrow the way was which led between them both. Also now he saw the hobgoblins, and satyrs, and dragons of the pit, but all afar off; for after break of day they came not nigh, yet they were discovered to him according to that which is written, "He discovereth deep things out of darkness, and bringeth out to light the shadow of death."

Now was Christian much affected with this deliverance from all the dangers of his solitary way; which dangers, though he feared them much before, yet he saw them more clearly now, because the light of the day made them conspicuous to him. And about this time the sun was rising, and this was another mercy to Christian; for you must note, that though the first part of the Valley of the Shadow of Death was dangerous, yet this second part, which he was yet to go, was, if possible, far more dangerous; for, from the place where he now stood, even to the end of the valley, the way was all along set so full of snares, traps, gins, and nets here, and so full of pits, pitfalls, deep holes, and shelvings down there, that had it now been dark, as it was when he came the first part of the way, had he had a thousand souls, they had in reason been cast away; but, as I said, just now the sun was rising. Then said he, "His candle shineth on my head, and by his light I go through darkness."

In this light, therefore, he came to the end of the valley. Now I saw in my dream, that at the end of the valley lay blood, bones, ashes, and mangled bodies of men, even of pilgrims that had gone this way formerly; and while I was musing what should be the reason, I espied a little before me a cave, where two giants, Pope and Pagan, dwelt in old time; by whose power and tyranny the men, whose bones, blood, ashes, etc., lay there, were cruelly put to death. But by this place Christian went without much danger, whereat I somewhat wondered; but I have learned since, that Pagan has been dead many a day; and as for the other, though he be yet alive, he is, by reason of age, and also of the many shrewd brushes that he met with in his younger days, grown so crazy and stiff in his joints, that he can now do little more than sit in his cave's mouth, grinning at pilgrims as they go by, and biting his nails because he cannot come at them.

So I saw that Christian went on his way; yet, at the sight of the old man that sat at the mouth of the cave, he could not tell what to think, especially because he spoke to him, though he could not go after him, saying, You will never mend till more of you be burned. But he held his peace, and set a good face on it, and so went by, and catched no hurt. Then sang Christian:

Oh, world of wonders (I can say no less),
That I should be preserved in that distress
That I have met with here! Oh, blessed be
That hand that from it hath deliver'd me!
Dangers in darkness, heaven, hell, and sin,
Did compass me, while I this vale was in;
Yea, snares, and pits, and traps, and nets did lie
My path about, that worthless, silly I
Might have been catch'd, entangled, and cast down,
But since I live, let Jesus wear the crown.

Now as Christian went on his way, he came to a little ascent, which was cast up on purpose that pilgrims might see before them; up there, therefore, Christian went; and looking forward, he saw Faithful before him upon his journey. Then said Christian aloud, Ho, ho; so-ho; stay, and I will be your companion. At that Faithful looked behind him; to whom Christian cried again, Stay, stay, till I come up to you. But Faithful answered, No, I am upon my life, and the avenger of blood is behind me.

At this Christian was somewhat moved, and putting to all his strength, he quickly got up with Faithful, and did also overrun him; so the last was first. Then did Christian vain-gloriously smile, because he had gotten the start of his brother; but not taking good heed to his feet, he suddenly stumbled and fell, and could not rise again until Faithful came up to help him.

Then I saw in my dream, they went very lovingly on together, and had sweet discourse of all things that had happened to them in their pilgrimage.

Then I saw in my dream, that when they were got out of the wilderness, they presently saw a town before them, and the name of that town is Vanity; and at the town there is a fair kept, called Vanity Fair. It is kept all the year long. It beareth the name of Vanity Fair because the town where it is kept is lighter than vanity, and also, because all that is there sold, or that cometh thither, is vanity; as is the saying of the wise, "All that cometh is vanity."

This fair is no new erected business, but a thing of ancient standing. I will show you the original of it.

Almost five thousand years ago there were pilgrims walking to the Celestial City, as these two honest persons are; and Beelzebub, Apollyon, and Legion, with their companions, perceiving by the path that the pilgrims made, that their way to the city lay through this town of Vanity, they contrived here to set up a fair; a fair wherein should be sold all sorts of vanity, and that it should last all the year long. Therefore at this fair are all such merchandise sold as houses, lands, trades, places, honors, preferments, titles, countries, kingdoms, lusts, pleasures; and delights of all sorts, such as harlots, wives, husbands, children, masters, servants, lives, blood, bodies, souls, silver, gold, pearls, precious stones, and what not.

And moreover, at this fair there are at all times to be seen jugglings, cheats, games, plays, fools, apes, knaves, and rogues, and that of every kind.

Here are to be seen, too, and that for nothing, thefts, murders, adulteries, false-swearers, and that of a blood-red color.

And as, in other fairs of less moment, there are the several rows and streets under their proper names, where such and such wares are vended: so here likewise you have the proper places, rows, streets, namely, countries and kingdoms, where the wares of this fair are soonest to be found. Here is the Britain Row, the French Row, the Italian Row, the Spanish Row, the German Row, where several sorts of vanities are to be sold. But as in other fairs some one commodity is as the chief of all the fair, so the ware of Rome and her merchandise is greatly promoted in this fair; only our English nation, with some others, have taken a dislike thereat.

Now, as I said, the way to the Celestial City lies just through this town where this lusty fair is kept; and he that would go to the city, and yet not go through this town, "must needs go out of the world." The Prince of princes himself, when here, went through this town to his own country, and that upon a fair-day, too; yea, and as I think, it was Beelzebub, the chief lord of this fair, that invited him to buy of his vanities, yea, would have made him lord of the fair, would he but have done him reverence as he went through the town. Yea, because he was such a person of honor Beelzebub had him from street to street, and showed him all the kingdoms of the world in a little time, that he might, if possible, allure that Blessed One to cheapen and buy some of his vanities; but he had no mind to the merchandise, and therefore left the town without laying out so much as one farthing upon these vanities. This fair, therefore, is an ancient thing of long standing, and a very great fair.

Now these pilgrims, as I said, must needs go through this fair. Well, so they did; but, behold, even as they entered into the fair, all the people in the fair were moved, and the town itself, as it were, in a hubbub about them, and that for several reasons: For,

First, The pilgrims were clothed with such kind of raiment as was diverse from the raiment of any that traded in that fair. The people, therefore, of the fair made a great gazing upon them; some said they were fools; some they were bedlams; and some they were outlandish men.

Secondly, And as they wondered at their apparel, so they did likewise at their speech; for few could understand what they said. They naturally spoke the language of Canaan; but they that kept the fair were the men of this world. So that from one end of the fair to the other they seemed barbarians each to the other.

Thirdly, But that which did not a little amuse the merchandisers was, that these pilgrims set very light by all their wares. They cared not so much as to look upon them; and if they called upon them to buy, they would put their fingers in their ears, and cry, "Turn away mine eyes from beholding vanity," and look upward, signifying that their trade and traffic was in heaven.

One chanced mockingly, beholding the carriage of the men, to say unto them, "What will ye buy?" But they looking gravely upon him, said, "We buy the truth." At that, there was an occasion taken to despise the men the more; some mocking, some taunting, some speaking reproachfully, and some calling upon others to smite them. At last things came to a hubbub and great stir in the fair, insomuch that all order was confounded. Now was word presently brought to the great one of the fair, who quickly came down, and deputed some of his most trusty friends to take those men into examination about whom the fair was almost overturned. So the men were brought to examination; and they that sat upon them asked whence they came, whither they went, and what they did there in such an unusual garb. The men told them that they were pilgrims and strangers in the world, and that they were going to their own country, which was the heavenly Jerusalem; and that they had given no occasion to the men of the town, nor yet to the merchandisers, thus to abuse them, and to let them in their journey, except it was for that when one asked them what they would buy, they said they would buy the truth. But they that were appointed to examine them did not believe them to be any other than bedlams and mad, or else such as came to put all things into a confusion in the fair. Therefore they took them and beat them, and besmeared them with dirt, and then put them into the cage, that they might be made a spectacle to all the men of the fair. There, therefore, they lay for some time, and were made the objects of any man's sport, or malice, or revenge; the great one of the fair laughing still at all that befell them. But the men being patient, and "not rendering railing for railing, but contrariwise blessing," and giving good words for bad, and kindness for injuries done, some men in the fair that were more observing and less prejudiced than the rest, began to check and blame the baser sort for their continual abuses done by them to the men. They, therefore, in angry manner, let fly at them again, counting them as bad as the men in the cage, and telling them that they seemed confederates and should be made partakers of their misfortunes. The others replied, that, for aught they could see, the men were quiet and sober, and intended nobody any harm; and that there were many that traded in their fair that were more worthy to be put into the cage, yea, and pillory too, than were the men that they had abused. Thus, after divers words had passed on both sides—the men behaving themselves all the while very wisely and soberly before them—they fell to some blows among themselves, and did harm one to another. Then were these two poor men brought before their examiners again, and there charged as being guilty of the late hubbub that had been in the fair. So they beat them pitifully, and hanged irons upon them, and led them in chains up and down the fair, for an example and terror to others, lest any should speak in their behalf, or join themselves unto them. But Christian and Faithful behaved themselves yet more wisely, and received the ignominy and shame that was cast upon them with so much meekness and patience, that it won to their side—though but few in comparison of the rest—several of the men in the fair. This put the other party yet into a greater rage, insomuch that they concluded the death of these two men. Wherefore they threatened that neither cage nor irons should serve their turn, but that they should die for the abuse they had done, and for deluding the men of the fair.

Then were they remanded to the cage again until further order should be taken with them. So they put them in, and made them fast in the stocks.

Here, therefore, they called again to mind what they had heard from their faithful friend Evangelist, and were the more confirmed in their way and sufferings, by what he told them would happen to them. They also now comforted each other, that whose lot it was to suffer, even he should have the best of it; therefore each man secretly wished that he might have that preferment. But committing themselves to the all-wise disposal of him that ruleth all things, with much content they abode in the condition in which they were until they should be otherwise disposed of.

Then a convenient time being appointed, they brought them forth to their trial, in order to their condemnation. When the time was come, they were brought before their enemies, and arraigned. The judge's name was Lord Hate-good; their indictment was one and the same in substance, though somewhat varying in form; the contents whereof was this: That they were enemies to, and disturbers of, the trade; that they had made commotions and divisions in the town, and had won a party to their own most dangerous opinions, in contempt of the law of their prince.

Then Faithful began to answer, that he had only set himself against that which had set itself against Him that is higher than the highest. And, said he, as for disturbance, I make none, being myself a man of peace: the parties that were won to us, were won by beholding our truth and innocence, and they are only turned from the worse to the better. And as to the king you talk of, since he is Beelzebub, the enemy of our Lord, I defy him and all his angels.

Then proclamation was made, that they that had aught to say for their lord the king against the prisoner at the bar, should forthwith appear, and give in their evidence. So there came in three witnesses, to wit, Envy, Superstition, and Pickthank. They were then asked, if they knew the prisoner at the bar; and what they had to say for their lord the king against him.

Then stood forth Envy, and said to this effect: My lord, I have known this man a long time, and will attest upon oath before this honorable bench, that he is—

Judge. Hold—give him his oath.

So they sware him. Then he said, My lord, this man, notwithstanding his plausible name, is one of the vilest men in our country; he neither regardeth prince nor people, law nor custom, but doeth all that he can to possess all men with certain of his disloyal notions, which he in the general calls principles of faith and holiness. And in particular, I heard him once myself affirm, that Christianity and the customs of our town of Vanity were diametrically opposite, and could not be reconciled. By which saying, my lord, he doth at once not only condemn all our laudable doings, but us in the doing of them.

Then did the judge say to him, Hast thou any more to say?

Envy. My lord, I could say much more, only I would not be tedious to the court. Yet if need be, when the other gentlemen have given in their evidence, rather than anything shall be wanting that will despatch him, I will enlarge my testimony against him. So he was bid to stand by.

Then they called Superstition, and bid him look upon the prisoner at the bar. They also asked, what he could say for their lord the king against him. Then they sware him; so he began:

Super. My lord, I have no great acquaintance with this man, nor do I desire to have further knowledge of him. However, this I know, that he is a very pestilent fellow, from some discourse I had with him, the other day, in this town; for then, talking with him, I heard him say, that our religion was naught, and such by which a man could by no means please God. Which saying of his, my lord, your lordship very well knows what necessarily thence will follow, to wit, that we still do worship in vain, are yet in our sins, and finally shall be damned: and this is that which I have to say.

Then was Pickthank sworn, and bid say what he knew in behalf of their lord the king against the prisoner at the bar.

Pick. My lord, and you gentlemen all, this fellow I have known of a long time, and have heard him speak things that ought not to be spoken; for he hath railed on our noble prince Beelzebub, and hath spoken contemptibly of his honorable friends, whose names are, the Lord Old Man, the Lord Carnal Delight, the Lord Luxurious, the Lord Desire of Vain Glory, my old Lord Lechery, Sir Having Greedy, with all the rest of our nobility; and he hath said, moreover, that if all men were of his mind, if possible, there is not one of these noblemen should have any longer a being in this town. Besides, he hath not been afraid to rail on you, my lord, who are now appointed to be his judge, calling you an ungodly villain, with many other suchlike vilifying terms, with which he hath bespattered most of the gentry of our town.

When this Pickthank had told his tale, the judge directed his speech to the prisoner at the bar, saying, Thou runagate, heretic, and traitor, hast thou heard what these honest gentlemen have witnessed against thee?

Faith. May I speak a few words in my own defence?

Judge. Sirrah, sirrah, thou deservest to live no longer, but to be slain immediately upon the place; yet that all men may see our gentleness toward thee, let us hear what thou hast to say.

Faith. 1. I say, then, in answer to what Mr. Envy hath spoken, I never said aught but this, that what rule, or laws, or customs, or people, were flat against the word of God, are diametrically opposite to Christianity. If I have said amiss in this, convince me of my error, and I am ready here before you to make my recantation.

2. As to the second, to wit, Mr. Superstition, and his charge against me, I said only this, that in the worship of God there is required a divine faith; but there can be no divine faith without a divine revelation of the will of God. Therefore, whatever is thrust into the worship of God, that is not agreeable to divine revelation, cannot be done but by a human faith, which faith will not be profitable to eternal life.

3. As to what Mr. Pickthank has said, I say—avoiding terms, as that I am said to rail, and the like—that the prince of this town, with all the rabblement, his attendants, by this gentleman named, are more fit for a being in hell than in this town and country. And so the Lord have mercy upon me.

Then the judge called to the jury—who all this while stood by to hear and observe—Gentlemen of the jury, you see this man about whom so great an uproar hath been made in this town; you have also heard what these worthy gentlemen have witnessed against him; also you have heard his reply and confession: it lieth now in your breast to hang him, or save his life; but yet I think meet to instruct you in our law.

There was an act made in the days of Pharaoh the Great, servant to our prince, that, lest those of a contrary religion should multiply, and grow too strong for him, their males should be thrown into the river. There was also an act made in the day of Nebuchadnezzar the Great, another of his servants, that whoever would not fall down and worship his golden image, should be thrown into a fiery furnace. There was also an act made in the days of Darius, that whoso for some time called upon any God but him, should be cast into the lions' den. Now, the substance of these laws this rebel has broken, not only in thought—which is not to be borne—but also in word and deed; which must, therefore, needs be intolerable.

For that of Pharaoh, his law was made upon a supposition, to prevent mischief, no crime being yet apparent; but here is a crime apparent. For the second and third, you see he disputeth against our religion; and for the treason that he hath confessed, he deserveth to die the death.

Then went the jury out, whose names were Mr. Blindman, Mr. No-good, Mr. Malice, Mr. Lovelust, Mr. Liveloose, Mr. Heady, Mr. High-mind, Mr. Enmity, Mr. Liar, Mr. Cruelty, Mr. Hatelight, and Mr. Implacable; who everyone gave in his private verdict against him among themselves, and afterward unanimously concluded to bring him in guilty before the judge. And first among themselves, Mr. Blindman, the foreman, said, I see clearly that this man is a heretic. Then said Mr. No-good, Away with such a fellow from the earth. Ay, said Mr. Malice, for I hate the very looks of him. Then said Mr. Lovelust, I could never endure him. Nor I, said Mr. Liveloose, for he would always be condemning my way. Hang him, hang him, said Mr. Heady. A sorry scrub, said Mr. High-mind. My heart riseth against him, said Mr. Enmity. He is a rogue, said Mr. Liar. Hanging is too good for him, said Mr. Cruelty. Let us despatch him out of the way, said Mr. Hatelight. Then said Mr. Implacable, Might I have all the world given me, I could not be reconciled to him; therefore, let us forthwith bring him in guilty of death.

And so they did; therefore he was presently condemned to be had from the place where he was, to the place from whence he came, and there to be put to the most cruel death that could be invented.

They, therefore, brought him out, to do with him according to their law: and first they scourged him, then they buffeted him, then they lanced his flesh with knives; after that they stoned him with stones; then pricked him with their swords; and last of all, they burned him to ashes at the stake. Thus came Faithful to his end.

Now I saw that there stood behind the multitude a chariot and a couple of horses, waiting for Faithful, who, so soon as his adversaries had despatched him, was taken up into it, and straightway was carried up through the clouds with sound of trumpet, the nearest way to the celestial gate.

But as for Christian, he had some respite, and was remanded back to prison; so he there remained for a space. But he who overrules all things, having the power of their rage in his own hand, so wrought it about, that Christian for that time escaped them, and went his way.

And as he went he sang, saying:

Well, Faithful, thou hast faithfully profest
Unto thy Lord, with whom thou shall be blest,
When faithless ones, with all their vain delights,
Are crying out under their hellish plights;
Sing, Faithful, sing, and let thy name survive,
For though they killed thee, thou art yet alive.

Now I saw in my dream that Christian went not forth alone; for there was one whose name was Hopeful—being so made by the beholding of Christian and Faithful in their words and behavior, in their sufferings at the fair—who joined himself unto him, and entering into a brotherly covenant, told him that he would be his companion. Thus one died to bear testimony to the truth, and another rises out of his ashes to be a companion with Christian in his pilgrimage. This Hopeful also told Christian, that there were many more of the men in the fair that would take their time and follow after.

I saw then that they went on their way to a pleasant river, which David the king called "the river of God," but John, "the river of the water of life." Now their way lay just upon the bank of this river; here, therefore, Christian and his companion walked with great delight; they drank also of the water of the river, which was pleasant and enlivening to their weary spirits. Besides, on the banks of this river, on either side, were green trees, with all manner of fruit; and the leaves they ate to prevent surfeits, and other diseases that are incident to those who heat their blood by travel. On either side of the river was also a meadow, curiously beautified with lilies; and it was green all the year long. In this meadow they lay down and slept, for here they might lie down safely. When they awoke, they gathered again of the fruit of the trees, and drank again of the water of the river, and then lay down again to sleep. Thus they did several days and nights. Then they sang:

Behold ye how these crystal streams do glide,
To comfort pilgrims by the highway-side,
The meadows green, besides their fragrant smell,
Yield dainties for them; and he who can tell

What pleasant fruit, yea, leaves, these trees do yield,
Will soon sell all, that he may buy this field.

So when they were disposed to go on — for they were not as yet at their journey's end — they ate and drank, and departed.

Now I beheld in my dream, that they had not journeyed far, but the river and the way for a time parted, at which they were not a little sorry; yet they durst not go out of the way. Now the way from the river was rough, and their feet tender by reason of their travels; so the souls of the pilgrims were much discouraged because of the way. Wherefore still as they went on, they wished for a better way. Now a little before them, there was on the left hand of the road a meadow, and a stile to go over into it, and that meadow is called By-path Meadow. Then said Christian to his fellow, If this meadow lieth along by our wayside, let's go over into it. Then he went to the stile to see, and behold a path lay along by the way on the other side of the fence. It is according to my wish, said Christian; here is the easiest going; come, good Hopeful, and let us go over.

Hope. But, how if this path should lead us out of the way?

That is not likely, said the other. Look, doth it not go along by the wayside? So Hopeful, being persuaded by his fellow, went after him over the stile. When they were gone over, and were got into the path, they found it very easy for their feet; and withal, they looking before them, espied a man walking as they did, and his name was Vain Confidence; so they called after him, and asked him whither that way led. He said, To the celestial gate. Look, said Christian, did not I tell you so? by this you may see we are right. So they followed, and he went before them. But behold the night came on, and it grew very dark; so that they that were behind lost the sight of him that went before.

He therefore that went before — Vain Confidence by name — not seeing the way before him, fell into a deep pit, which was on purpose there made, by the prince of those grounds, to catch vainglorious fools withal, and was dashed in pieces with his fall.

Now Christian and his fellow heard him fall. So they called to know the matter, but there was none to answer, only they heard a groaning. Then said Hopeful, Where are we now? Then was his fellow silent, as mistrusting that he had led him out of the way; and now it began to rain, and thunder and lighten in a most dreadful manner, and the water rose amain.

Then Hopeful groaned in himself, saying, Oh that I had kept on my way!

Chr. Who could have thought that this path should have led us out of the way?

Hope. I was afraid on it at the very first, and therefore gave you that gentle caution. I would have spoken plainer, but that you are older than I.

Chr. Good brother, be not offended; I am sorry I have brought thee out of the way, and that I have put thee into such imminent danger. Pray, my brother, forgive me; I did not do it of an evil intent.

Hope. Be comforted, my brother, for I forgive thee; and believe, too, that this shall be for our good.

Chr. I am glad I have with me a merciful brother; but we must not stand here; let us try to go back again.

Hope. But, good brother, let me go before.

Chr: No, if you please, let me go first, that if there be any danger, I may be first therein, because by my means we are both gone out of the way.

No, said Hopeful, you shall not go first, for your mind being troubled may lead you out of the way again. Then, for their encouragement, they heard the voice of one saying, "Let thine heart be toward the highway, even the way that thou wentest; turn again." But by this time the waters were greatly risen, by reason of which the way of going back was very dangerous. (Then I thought that it is easier going out of the way when we are in, than going in when we are out.) Yet they adventured to go back; but it was so dark, and the flood was so high, that in their going back they had like to have drowned nine or ten times.

Neither could they, with all the skill they had, get again to the stile that night. Wherefore at last, lighting under a little shelter, they sat down there until the day brake; but, being weary, they fell asleep. Now there was, not far from the place they lay, a castle, called Doubting Castle, the owner whereof was Giant Despair, and it was in his grounds they now were sleeping: wherefore he, getting up in the morning early, and walking up and down in his fields, caught Christian and Hopeful asleep in his grounds. Then with a grim and surly voice he bid them awake, and asked them whence they were, and what they did in his grounds. They told him they were pilgrims, and that they had lost their way. Then said the Giant, You have this night trespassed on me by trampling in and lying on my grounds, and therefore you must go along with me. So they were forced to go, because he was stronger than they. They also had but little to say, for they knew themselves in a fault. The Giant, therefore, drove them before him, and put them into his castle, in a very dark dungeon, nasty, and stinking to the spirits of these two men. Here, then, they lay from Wednesday morning till Saturday night, without one bit of bread, drop of drink, or light, or any to ask how they did; they were, therefore, here in evil case, and were far from friends and acquaintance. Now in this place Christian had double sorrow, because it was through his unadvised counsel that they were brought into this distress.

Now Giant Despair had a wife and her name was Diffidence: so when he was gone to bed he told his wife what he had done, to wit, that he had taken a couple of prisoners, and cast them into his dungeon for trespassing on his grounds. Then he asked her also what he had best to do further with them. So she asked him what they were, whence they came, and whither they were bound, and he told her. Then she counselled him, that when he arose in the morning he should beat them without mercy. So when he arose, he getteth him a grievous crabtree cudgel, and goes down into the dungeon to them, and there first falls to rating of them as if they were dogs, although they never gave him a word of distaste. Then he falls upon them, and beats them fearfully, in such sort that they were not able to help themselves, or to turn them upon the floor. This done, he withdraws and leaves them there to condole their misery, and to mourn under their distress: so all that day they spent their time in nothing but sighs and bitter lamentations. The next night she, talking with her husband further about them, and understanding that they were yet alive, did advise him to counsel them to make away with themselves. So when morning was come, he goes to them in a surly manner, as before, and perceiving them to be very sore with the stripes that he had given them the day before, he told them, that since they were never like to come out of that place, their only way would be forthwith to make an end of themselves, either with a knife, halter, or poison: for why, said he, should you choose to live, seeing it is attended with so much bitterness? But they desired him to let them go. With that he looked ugly upon them, and rushing to them, had doubtless made an end of them himself, but that he fell into one of his fits—for he sometimes in sunshiny weather fell into fits—and lost for a time the use of his hands; wherefore he withdrew, and left them as before to consider what to do. Then did the prisoners consult between themselves, whether it were best to take his counsel or no; and thus they began to discourse.

Brother, said Christian, what shall we do? The life that we now live is miserable. For my part, I know not whether it is best to live thus, or to die out of hand. My soul chooseth strangling rather than life, and the grave is more easy for me than this dungeon. Shall we be ruled by the Giant?

Hope. Indeed our present condition is dreadful, and death would be far more welcome to me than thus forever to abide; but yet let us consider, the Lord of the country to which we are going hath said, "Thou shalt do no murder," no, not to another man's person, much more then are we forbidden to take his counsel to kill ourselves. Besides, he that kills another, can but commit murder upon his body; but for one to kill himself, is to kill body and soul at once. And, moreover, my brother, thou talkest of ease in the grave, but hast thou forgotten the hell whither for certain the murderers go? for "no murderer hath eternal life," etc. And let us consider again, that all the law is not in the hand of Giant Despair; others, so far as I can understand, have been taken by him as well as we, and yet have escaped out of his hands. Who knows but that God, who made the world, may cause that Giant Despair may die; or that at some time or other he may forget to lock us in; or but he may, in a short time, have another of his fits before us, and he may lose the use of his limbs? And if ever that should come to pass again, for my part, I am resolved to pluck up the heart of a man, and to try my utmost to get from under his hand. I was a fool that I did not try to do it before. But however, my brother, let us be patient, and endure awhile; the time may come that may give us a happy release; but let us not be our own murderers. With these words Hopeful at present did moderate the mind of his brother; so they continued together in the dark that day, in their sad and doleful condition.

Well, toward evening the Giant goes down into the dungeon again, to see if his prisoners had taken his counsel. But when he came there he found them alive; and truly alive was all; for now, what for want of bread and water, and by reason of the wounds they received when he beat them, they could do little but breathe. But I say he found them alive; at which he fell into a grievous rage, and told them, that seeing they had disobeyed his counsel, it should be worse with them than if they had never been born.

At this they trembled greatly, and I think that Christian fell into a swoon; but coming a little to himself again, they renewed their discourse about the Giant's counsel, and whether yet they had best take it or no. Now Christian again seemed for doing it; but Hopeful made his second reply as followeth:

My brother, said he, rememberest thou not how valiant thou hast been heretofore? Apollyon could not crush thee, nor could all that thou didst hear, or see, or feel, in the Valley of the Shadow of Death. What hardship, terror, and amazement, hast thou already gone through! and art thou now nothing but fears? Thou seest that I am in the dungeon with thee, a far weaker man by nature than thou art. Also this Giant hath wounded me as well as thee, and also cut off the bread and water from my mouth, and with thee I mourn without the light. But let us exercise a little more patience. Remember how thou playedst the man at Vanity Fair, and wast neither afraid of the chain nor cage, nor yet of bloody death; wherefore let us—at least to avoid the shame that it becomes not a Christian to be found in—bear up with patience as well as we can.

Now night being come again, and the Giant and his wife in bed, she asked him concerning the prisoners, and if they had taken his counsel; to which he replied, They are sturdy rogues; they choose rather to bear all hardships than to make away with themselves. Then said she, Take them into the castle-yard to-morrow, and show them the bones and skulls of those that thou hast already despatched, and make them believe, ere a week comes to an end, thou wilt tear them in pieces, as thou hast done their fellows before them.

So when the morning was come, the Giant goes to them again, and takes them into the castle-yard, and shows them as his wife had bidden him. These, said he, were pilgrims, as you are, once, and they trespassed on my grounds as you have done; and when I thought fit I tore them in pieces, and so within ten days I will do you; go, get you down to your den again. And with that he beat them all the way thither. They lay, therefore, all day on Saturday in a lamentable case, as before. Now when night was come, and when Mrs. Diffidence and her husband, the Giant, were got to bed, they began to renew their discourse of their prisoners; and withal the old Giant wondered that he could neither by his blows nor counsel bring them to an end. And with that his wife replied, I fear, said she, that they live in hopes that some will come to relieve them; or that they have picklocks about them, by the means of which they hope to escape. And sayest thou so, my dear? said the Giant; I will therefore search them in the morning.

Well, on Saturday, about midnight, they began to pray, and continued in prayer till almost break of day.

Now, a little before it was day, good Christian, as one half amazed, broke out into this passionate speech: What a fool, quoth he, am I, to lie in a stinking dungeon, when I may as well walk at liberty! I have a key in my bosom, called Promise, that will, I am persuaded, open any lock in Doubting Castle. Then said Hopeful, That's good news; good brother, pluck it out of thy bosom, and try.

Then Christian pulled it out of his bosom, and began to try at the dungeon door, whose bolt, as he turned the key, gave back, and the door flew open with ease, and Christian and Hopeful both came out. Then he went to the outward door that leads into the castle-yard, and with his key opened that door also. After that he went to the iron gate, for that must be opened too, but that lock went desperately hard, yet the key did open it. Then they thrust open the gate to make their escape with speed; but that gate as it opened, made such a creaking that it waked Giant Despair, who hastily rising to pursue his prisoners, felt his limbs to fail; for his fits took him again, so that he could by no means go after them. Then they went on, and came to the King's highway again, and so were safe, because they were out of his jurisdiction.

Now, when they were gone over the stile, they began to contrive with themselves what they should do at that stile, to prevent those that shall come after from falling into the hands of Giant Despair. So they consented to erect there a pillar, and to engrave upon the side thereof this sentence: "Over this stile is the way to Doubting Castle, which is kept by Giant Despair, who despiseth the King of the Celestial Country, and seeks to destroy, his holy pilgrims." Many, therefore, that followed after, read what was written, and escaped the danger. This done, they sang as follows:

Out of the way we went, and then we found
What 'twas to tread upon forbidden ground;
And let them that come after have a care,
Lest they for trespassing, his pris'ners are,
Whose castle's Doubting, and whose name's Despair.

They then went till they came to the Delectable Mountains, which mountains belong to the Lord of that hill of which we have spoken before. So they went up to the mountains, to behold the gardens and orchards, the vineyards and fountains of water; where also they drank and washed themselves, and did freely eat of the vineyards. Now there were on the tops of these mountains shepherds feeding their flocks, and they stood by the highway-side. The pilgrims, therefore, went to them, and leaning upon their staffs—as is common with weary pilgrims when they stand to talk with any by the way—they asked, Whose Delectable Mountains are these, and whose be the sheep that feed upon them?

Shep. These mountains are Immanuel's Land, and they are within sight of his city; and the sheep also are his, and he laid down his life for them.

Chr. Is this the way to the Celestial City?

Shep. You are just in your way.

Chr. How far is it thither?

Shep. Too far for any but those who shall get thither, indeed.

Chr. Is the way safe, or dangerous?

Shep. Safe for those for whom it is to be safe; but transgressors shall fall therein.

Chr. Is there in this place any relief for pilgrims that are weary and faint in the way?

Shep. The Lord of these mountains hath given us a charge not to be forgetful to entertain strangers; therefore, the good of the place is before you.

I saw also in my dream, that when the Shepherds perceived that they were wayfaring men, they also put questions to them, to which they made answer as in other places, as, Whence came you? and, How got you into the way? and, By what means have you persevered therein? for but few of them that begin to come hither, do show their faces on these mountains. But when the Shepherds heard their answers, being pleased therewith, they looked very lovingly upon them, and said, Welcome to the Delectable Mountains.

The shepherds, I say, whose names were Knowledge, Experience, Watchful, and Sincere, took them by the hand, and had them to their tents, and made them partake of what was ready at present. They said, moreover, We would that you should stay here awhile, to be acquainted with us, and yet more to solace yourselves with the good of these Delectable Mountains. They then told them that they were content to stay. So they went to rest that night, because it was very late.

Then I saw in my dream, that in the morning the Shepherds called up Christian and Hopeful to walk with them upon the Mountains. So they went forth with them, and walked awhile, having a pleasant prospect on every side. Then said the Shepherds one to another, Shall we show these pilgrims some wonders? So when they had concluded to do it, they had them first to the top of a hill, called Error, which was very steep on the furthest side, and bid them look down to the bottom. So Christian and Hopeful looked down, and saw at the bottom several men dashed all to pieces by a fall they had from the top. Then said Christian, What meaneth this? The Shepherds answered, Have you not heard of them that were made to err, by hearkening to Hymeneus and Philetus, as concerning the faith of the resurrection of the body? They answered, Yes. Then said the Shepherds, Those that you see dashed in pieces at the bottom of this mountain are they; and they have continued to this day unburied, as you see, for an example to others to take heed how they clamber too high, or how they come too near the brink of this mountain.

Then I saw that they had them to the top of another mountain, and the name of that is Caution, and bid them look afar off; which, when they did, they perceived, as they thought, several men walking up and down among the tombs that were there; and they perceived that the men were blind, because they stumbled sometimes upon the tombs, and because they could not get out from among them. Then said Christian, What means this?

The Shepherds then answered, Did you not see a little below these mountains a stile that led into a meadow, on the left hand of this way? They answered, Yes. Then said the Shepherds, From that stile there goes a path that leads directly to Doubting Castle, which is kept by Giant Despair; and these men, pointing to them among the tombs, came once on pilgrimage, as you do now, even until they came to that same stile. And because the right way was rough in that place, they chose to go out of it into that meadow, and there were taken by Giant Despair, and cast into Doubting Castle, where, after they had awhile been kept in the dungeon, he at last did put out their eyes, and led them among those tombs, where he has left them to wander to this very day, that the saying of the wise man might be fulfilled, "He that wandereth out of the way of understanding shall remain in the congregation of the dead." Then Christian and Hopeful looked one upon another, with tears gushing out, but yet said nothing to the Shepherds.

Then I saw in my dream, that the Shepherds had them to another place in a bottom, where was a door on the side of a hill; and they opened the door, and bid them look in. They looked in, therefore, and saw that within it was very dark and smoky; they also thought that they heard there a rumbling noise, as of fire, and a cry of some tormented, and they smelled the scent of brimstone. Then said Christian, What means this? The Shepherds told them, This is a by-way to hell, a way that hypocrites go in at; namely, such as sell their birthright, with Esau; such as sell their Master, with Judas; such as blaspheme the gospel, with Alexander; and that lie and dissemble, with Ananias and Sapphira his wife.

Then said Hopeful to the Shepherds, I perceive that these had on them, even every one, a show of pilgrimage, as we have now; had they not?

Shep. Yes, and held it a long time too.

Hope. How far might they go on in pilgrimage in their day, since they, notwithstanding, were thus miserably cast away?

Shep. Some further, and some not so far as these mountains.

Then said the pilgrims one to another, We have need to cry to the Strong for strength.

Shep. Ay, and you will have need to use it, when you have it too.

By this time the pilgrims had a desire to go forward, and the Shepherds a desire they should; so they walked together toward the end of the mountains. Then said the Shepherds one to another, Let us here show the pilgrims the gate of the Celestial City, if they have skill to look through our perspective-glass. The pilgrims then lovingly accepted the motion; so they had them to the top of a high hill, called Clear, and gave them the glass to look.

Then they tried to look; but the remembrance of that last thing that the Shepherds had shown them made their hands shake, by means of which impediment they could not look steadily through the glass; yet they thought they saw something like the gate, and also some of the glory of the place. Thus they went away and sang:

Thus by the Shepherds secrets are reveal'd
Which from all other men are kept conceal'd:
Come to the Shepherds, then, if you would see
Things deep, things hid, and that mysterious be.

When they were about to depart, one of the Shepherds gave them a note of the way. Another of them bid them beware of the Flatterer. The third bid them take heed that they sleep not upon Enchanted Ground. And the fourth bid them God speed.

They went then till they came at a place where they saw a way put itself into their way, and seeming withal to lie as straight as the way which they should go; and here they knew not which of the two to take, for both seemed straight before them; therefore, here they stood still to consider. And as they were thinking about the way, behold, a man black of flesh, but covered with a very light robe, came to them, and asked them why they stood there. They answered, they were going to the Celestial City, but knew not which of these ways to take. Follow me, said the man; it is thither that I am going. So they followed him in the way that but now came into the road, which by degrees turned, and turned them so from the city that they desired to go to, that in a little time their faces were turned from it; yet they followed him. But by and by, before they were aware, he led them both within the compass of a net, in which they were both so entangled that they knew not what to do; and with that the white robe fell off the black man's back. Then they saw where they were. Wherefore there they lay crying some time, for they could not get themselves out.

Then said Christian to his fellow, Now do I see myself in an error. Did not the Shepherds bid us beware of the Flatterer? As is the saying of the wise man, so we have found it this day: "A man that flattereth his neighbor spreadeth a net for his feet."

Hope. They also gave us a note of directions about the way, for our more sure finding thereof; but therein we have also forgotten to read, and not kept ourselves from the paths of the destroyer. Here David was wiser than we, for, saith he, "Concerning the works of men, by the word of thy lips I have kept me from the paths of the destroyer." Thus they lay bewailing themselves in the net. At last they espied a Shining One coming toward them with a whip of small cords in his hand. When he was come to the place where they were, he asked them whence they came, and what they did there. They told him that they were poor pilgrims going to Zion, but were led out of their way by a black man clothed in white, who bid us, said they, follow him, for he was going thither too. Then said he with a whip, It Flatterer, a false apostle, that hath transformed himself into an angel of light. So he rent the net, and let the men out. Then said he to them, Follow me, that I may set you in your way again. So he led them back to the way which they had left to follow the Flatterer. Then he asked them, saying, Where did you lie the last night? They said, With the Shepherds upon the Delectable Mountains. He asked them if they had not a note of directions for the way. They answered, Yes. But did you not, said he, when you were at a stand, pluck out and read your note? They answered, No. He asked them, Why? They said they forgot. He asked, moreover, if the Shepherds did not bid them beware of the Flatterer. They answered, Yes; but we did not imagine, said they, this fine-spoken man had been he.

Then I saw in my dream, that he commanded them to lie down; which when they did, he chastised them sore, to teach them the good way wherein they should walk; and as he chastised them, he said, "As many as I love I rebuke and chasten; be zealous, therefore, and repent." This done, he bids them go on their way, and take good heed to the other directions of the Shepherds. So they thanked him for all his kindness, and went softly along the right way, singing:

Come hither, you that walk along the way,
See how the pilgrims fare that go astray:
They catched are in an entangled net,
'Cause they good counsel lightly did forget.
'Tis true they rescued were; but yet, you see,
They're scourg'd to boot: let this your caution be.

Now, after awhile, they perceived afar off one coming softly and alone, all along the highway to meet them. Then said Christian to his fellow, Yonder is a man with his back toward Zion, and he is coming to meet us.

Hope. I see him; let us take heed to ourselves now lest he should prove a flatterer also. So he drew nearer and nearer, and at last came up to them. His name was Atheist, and he asked them whither they were going.

Chr. We are going to the Mount Zion.

Then Atheist fell into a very great laughter.

Chr. What's the meaning of your laughter?

Atheist. I laugh to see what ignorant persons you are, to take upon you so tedious a journey, and yet are like to have nothing but your travel for your pains.

Chr. Why man, do you think we shall not be received?

Atheist. Received! There is no such place as you dream of in all this world.

Chr. But there is in the world to come.

Atheist. When I was at home in my own country, I heard as you now affirm, and from that hearing went out to see, and have been seeking this city these twenty years, but find no more of it than I did the first day I set out.

Chr. We have both heard, and believe, that there is such a place to be found.

Atheist. Had not I, when at home, believed, I had not come thus far to seek; but finding none—and yet I should had there been such a place to be found, for I have gone to seek it further than you—I am going back again, and will seek to refresh myself with the things that I then cast away for hopes of that which I now see is not.

Then said Christian to Hopeful his companion, Is it true which this man hath said?

Hope. Take heed, he is one of the flatterers. Remember what it hath cost us once already for hearkening to such kind fellows. What? no Mount Zion? Did we not see from the Delectable Mountains the gate of the city? Also, are we not now to walk by faith? Let us go on, lest the man with the whip overtake us again. You should have taught me that lesson, which I will round you in the ears withal: "Cease, my son, to hear the instruction that causeth to err from the words of knowledge." I say, my brother, cease to hear him, and let us believe to the saving of the soul.

Chr. My brother, I did not put the question to thee, for that I doubted of the truth of our belief myself, but to prove thee, and to fetch from thee a fruit of the honesty of thy heart. As for this man, I know that he is blinded by the god of this world. Let thee and me go on, knowing that we have belief of the truth, and no lie is of the truth.

Hope. Now do I rejoice in hope of the glory of God. So they turned away from the man, and he, laughing at them, went his way.

I then saw in my dream that they went on until they came into a certain country, whose air naturally tended to make one drowsy, if he came a stranger into it. And here Hopeful began to be very dull, and heavy to sleep;

wherefore he said unto Christian: I do now begin to grow so drowsy that I can scarcely hold open mine eyes; let us lie down and take one nap.

By no means, said the other, lest sleeping we never awake more.

Hope. Why, my brother? sleep is sweet to the laboring man; we may be refreshed if we take a nap.

Chr. Do you not remember that one of the Shepherds bid us to beware of the Enchanted Ground? He meant by that, that we should beware of sleeping: wherefore, "let us not sleep as others do, but let us watch and be sober."

Hope. I acknowledge myself in a fault; and had I been here alone, I had by sleeping run the danger of death. I see it is true that the wise man saith, "Two are better than one." Hitherto hath thy company been my mercy; and thou shalt have a good reward for thy labor.

Now then, said Christian, to prevent drowsiness in this place, let us fall into good discourse.

With all my heart, said the other.

Now I saw in my dream, that the pilgrims were got over the Enchanted Ground, and entering into the country of Beulah; whose air was very sweet and pleasant; the way lying directly through it, they solaced themselves there for a season. Yea, here they heard continually the singing of birds, and saw every day the flowers appear in the earth, and heard the voice of the turtle in the land. In this country the sun shineth night and day; wherefore this was beyond the Valley of the Shadow of Death, and also out of the reach of Giant Despair; neither could they from this place so much as see Doubting Castle. Here they were within sight of the city they were going to; also here met them some of the inhabitants thereof; for in this land the Shining Ones commonly walked, because it was upon the borders of heaven. In this land also the contract between the Bride and the Bridegroom was renewed; yea, here, "as the bridegroom rejoiceth over the bride, so doth their God rejoice over them." Here they had no want of corn and wine; for in this place they met with abundance of what they had sought for in all their pilgrimages. Here they heard voices from out of the city, loud voices, saying, "Say ye to the daughter of Zion, Behold thy salvation cometh! Behold, His reward is with him!" Here all the inhabitants of the country called them "the holy people, the redeemed of the Lord, sought out," etc.

Now, as they walked in this land, they had more rejoicing than in parts more remote from the kingdom to which they are bound; and drawing near to the city, they had yet a more perfect view thereof. It was builded of pearls and precious stones, also the streets thereof were paved with gold; so that, by reason of the natural glory of the city, and the reflection of the sunbeams upon it, Christian with desire fell sick; Hopeful also had a fit or two of the same disease: wherefore here they lay by it awhile, crying out because of their pangs, "If you see my Beloved, tell him that I am sick of love."

But, being a little strengthened, and better able to bear their sickness, they walked on their way, and came yet nearer and nearer, where were orchards, vineyards, and gardens, and their gates opened into the highway. Now, as they came up to these places behold the gardener stood in the way; to whom the pilgrims said, Whose goodly vineyards and gardens are these? He answered, They are the King's, and are planted here for his own delights, and also for the solace of pilgrims. So the gardener had them into the vineyards, and bid them refresh themselves with the dainties. He also showed them there the King's walks and the arbors where he delighteth to be: and here they tarried and slept.

Now, I beheld in my dream that they talked more in their sleep at this time than ever they did in all their journey, and being in a muse thereabout, the gardener said even to me, Wherefore musest thou at the matter: it is the nature of the fruit of the grapes of these vineyards "to go down so sweetly as to cause the lips of them that are asleep to speak."

So I saw that when they awoke they addressed themselves to go up to the city. But, as I said, the reflection of the sun upon the city—for the city was pure gold—was so extremely glorious that they could not as yet with open face behold it, but through an instrument made for that purpose. So I saw, that as they went on, there met them two men in raiment that shone like gold, also their faces shone as the light.

These men asked the pilgrims whence they came; and they told them. They also asked them where they had lodged, what difficulties and dangers, what comforts and pleasures, they had met in the way; and they told them. Then said the men that met them, You have but two difficulties more to meet with, and then you are in the city.

Christian then and his companion asked the men to go along with them: so they told them that they would: But, said they, you must obtain it by your own faith. So I saw in my dream that they went on together till they came in sight of the gate.

Now I further saw, that between them and the gate was a river: but there was no bridge to go over; and the river was very deep. At the sight therefore of this river the pilgrims were much stunned; but the men that went with them said, You must go through or you cannot come at the gate.

The pilgrims then began to inquire if there was no other way to the gate. To which they answered, Yes; but there hath not any, save two, to wit, Enoch and Elijah, been permitted to tread that path since the foundation of the world, nor shall until the last trumpet shall sound. The pilgrims then, especially Christian, began to despond in their minds, and looked this way and that, but no way could be found by them by which they might escape the river. Then they asked the men if the waters were all of a depth. They said, No; yet they could not help them in that case; for, said they, you shall find it deeper or shallower as you believe in the King of the place.

They then addressed themselves to the water, and entering, Christian began to sink, and crying out to his good friend Hopeful, he said, I sink in deep waters; the billows go over my head, all his waves go over me.

Then said the other, Be of good cheer, my brother: I feel the bottom, and it is good. Then said Christian, Ah, my friend, "the sorrows of death have compassed me about," I shall not see the land that flows with milk and honey. And with that a great darkness and horror fell upon Christian, so that he could not see before him. Also here he in a great measure lost his senses, so that he could neither remember nor orderly talk of any of those sweet refreshments that he had met with in the way of his pilgrimage. But all the words that he spoke still tended to discover that he had horror of mind, and heart-fears that he should die in that river, and never obtain entrance in at the gate. Here also, as they that stood by perceived, he was much in the troublesome thoughts of the sins that he had committed, both since and before he began to be a pilgrim. It was also observed, that he was troubled with apparitions of hobgoblins and evil spirits; for ever and anon he would intimate so much by words.

Hopeful therefore here had much ado to keep his brother's head above water; yea, sometimes he would be quite gone down, and then, ere awhile, he would rise up again half dead. Hopeful also would endeavor to comfort him, saying, Brother, I see the gate, and men standing by to receive us; but Christian would answer, It is you, it is you they wait for; you have been hopeful ever since I knew you. And so have you, said he to Christian. Ah, brother! said he, surely if I was right, he would now arise to help me; but for my sins he hath brought me into the snare, and hath left me. Then said Hopeful, My brother, you have quite forgot the text where it is said of the wicked, "There are no bands in their death, but their strength is firm; they are not troubled as other men, neither are they plagued like other men." These troubles and distresses that you go through in these waters, are no sign that God hath forsaken you; but are sent to try you, whether you will call to mind that which heretofore you have received of his goodness, and live upon him in your distresses.

Then I saw in my dream, that Christian was in a muse awhile. To whom also Hopeful added these words, Be of good cheer, Jesus Christ maketh thee whole. And with that Christian brake out with a loud voice, Oh, I see him again; and he tells me "When thou passest through the waters, I shall be with thee; and through the rivers, they shall not overflow thee." Then they both took courage, and the enemy was, after that, as still as a stone, until they were gone over. Christian, therefore, presently found ground to stand upon, and so it followed that the rest of the river was but shallow. Thus they got over.

Now upon the bank of the river, on the other side, they saw the two shining men again, who there waited for them. Wherefore being come out of the river, they saluted them, saying, We are ministering spirits, sent forth to minister for those that shall be heirs of salvation. Thus they went along toward the gate.

Now you must note, that the city stood upon a mighty hill; but the pilgrims went up that hill with ease, because they had these two men to lead them up by the arms: they had likewise left their mortal garments behind them in the river; for though they went in with them, they came out without them. They therefore went up here with much agility and speed, though the foundation upon which the city was framed was higher than the clouds; they therefore went up through the regions of the air, sweetly talking as they went, being comforted because they safely got over the river, and had such glorious companions to attend them.

The talk that they had with the Shining Ones was about the glory of the place; who told them that the beauty and glory of it was inexpressible. There, said they, is "the Mount Zion, the heavenly Jerusalem, the innumerable company of angels, and the spirits of just men made perfect." You are going now, said they, to the paradise of God, where you shall see the tree of life, and eat of the never fading fruits thereof: and when you come there you shall have white robes given you, and your walk and talk shall be every day with the King, even all the days of eternity. There you shall not see again such things as you saw when you were in the lower region upon the earth; to wit, sorrow, sickness, affliction, and death; "For the former things are passed away." You are going now to Abraham, to Isaac, and Jacob, and to the prophets, men that God hath taken away from the evil to come, and that are now "resting upon their beds, each one walking in his righteousness." The men then asked, What must we do in the holy place? To whom it was answered, You must there receive the comfort of all your toil, and have joy for all your sorrow; you must reap what you have sown, even the fruit of all your prayers, and tears, and sufferings for the King by the way. In that place you must wear crowns of gold, and enjoy the perpetual sight and vision of the Holy One; for "there you shall see him as he is." There also you shall serve him continually with praise, with shouting and thanksgiving, whom you desired to serve in the world, though with much difficulty, because of the infirmity of your flesh. There your eyes shall be delighted with seeing, and your ears with hearing the pleasant voice of the Mighty One. There you shall enjoy your friends again that are gone hither before you; and there you shall with joy receive even every one that follows into the holy place after you. There also you shall be clothed with glory and majesty, and put in an equipage fit to ride out with the King of Glory. When he shall come with sound of trumpet in the clouds, as upon the wings of the wind, you shall come with him; and when he shall sit upon the throne of judgment, you shall sit by him; yea, and when he shall pass sentence upon all the workers of iniquity, let them be angels or men, you also shall have a voice in that judgment, because they were his and your enemies. Also, when he shall again return to the city, you shall go too with sound of trumpet, and be ever with him.

Now, while they were thus drawing toward the gate, behold a company of the heavenly host came out to meet them; to whom it was said by the other two Shining Ones, These are the men that have loved our Lord, when they were in the world, and that have left all for his holy name; and he has sent us to fetch them, and we have brought them thus far on their desired journey, that they may go in and look their Redeemer in the face with joy. Then the heavenly host gave a great shout, saying, "Blessed are they that are called to the marriage supper of the Lamb." There came out also at this time to meet them several of the King's trumpeters, clothed in white and shining raiment, who with melodious voices and loud, made even the heavens to echo with their sound. These trumpeters saluted Christian and his fellow with ten thousand welcomes from the world; and this they did with shouting and sound of trumpet.

This done, they compassed them round on every side; some went before, some behind, and some on the right hand, and some on the left—as it were to guard them through the upper regions—continually sounding as they went, with melodious noise, in notes on high; so that the very sight was to them that could behold it as if heaven itself was come down to meet them. Thus therefore they walked on together; and, as they walked, ever and anon these trumpeters, even with joyful sound, would, by mixing their music with looks and gestures, still signify to Christian, and his brother, how welcome they were into their company, and with what gladness they came to meet them. And now were these two men, as it were, in heaven, before they came at it, being swallowed up with the sight of angels, and with hearing of their melodious notes. Here also they had the city itself in view; and thought they heard all the bells therein to ring, to welcome them thereto. But, above all, the warm and joyful thoughts that they had about their own dwelling there with such company, and that for ever and ever, oh, by what tongue or pen can their glorious joy be expressed!—Thus they came up to the gate.

Now when they were come up to the gate, there was written over it in letters of gold, "BLESSED ARE THEY THAT DO HIS COMMANDMENTS, THAT THEY MAY HAVE RIGHT TO THE TREE OF LIFE, AND MAY ENTER IN THROUGH THE GATES INTO THE CITY."

Then I saw in my dream that the shining men bid them call at the gate: the which when they did, some from above looked over the gate, to wit, Enoch, Moses, and Elijah, etc., to whom it was said, These pilgrims are come from the City of Destruction, for the love that they bear to the King of this place: and then the pilgrims gave in unto them each man his certificate, which they had received in the beginning; those, therefore, were carried in to the King, who, when he had read them, said, Where are the men? To whom it was answered, They are standing without the gate. The King then commanded to open the gate, "That the righteous nation," said he, "that keepeth truth may enter in."

Now I saw in my dream that these two men went in at the gate; and lo! as they entered, they were transfigured; and they had raiment put on that shone like gold. There were also that met them with harps and crowns, and gave them to them: the harps to praise withal, and the crowns in token of honor. Then I heard in my dream that all the bells in the city rang again for joy, and that it was said unto them, "ENTER YE INTO THE JOY OF OUR LORD." I also heard the men themselves, that they sang with a loud voice, saying, "BLESSING, AND HONOR, AND GLORY, AND POWER, BE UNTO HIM THAT SITTETH UPON THE THRONE, AND UNTO THE LAMB, FOR EVER AND EVER."

Now, just as the gates were opened to let in the men, I looked in after them, and behold the city shone like the sun; the streets also were paved with gold; and in them walked many men, with crowns on their heads, palms in their hands, and golden harps, to sing praises withal.

They were also of them that had wings, and they answered one another without intermission, saying, "Holy, holy, holy, is the Lord." And after that they shut up the gates: which, when I had seen, I wished myself among them.

Now while I was gazing upon all these things, I turned my head to look back, and saw Ignorance come up to the river side; but he soon got over, and that without half the difficulty which the other two men met with. For it happened that there was then in the place one Vain-hope, a ferry-man, that with his boat helped him over; so he, as the others I saw, did ascend the hill, to come up to the gate; only he came alone; neither did any meet him with the least encouragement. When he was come up to the gate, he looked up to the writing that was above, and then began to knock, supposing that entrance should have been quickly administered to him; but he was asked by the men that looked over the top of the gate, Whence came you? and what would you have? He answered, I have ate and drank in the presence of the King, and he has taught in our streets. Then they asked him for his certificate, that they might go in and show it to the King: so he fumbled in his bosom for one, and found none. Then said they, Have you none? but the man answered never a word. So they told the King, but he would not come down to see him, but commanded the two Shining Ones, that conducted Christian and Hopeful to the city, to go out, and take Ignorance, and bind him, hand and foot, and have him away. Then they took him up, and carried him through the air, to the door that I saw in the side of the hill, and put him in there. Then I saw that there was a way to hell, even from the gate of heaven, as well as from the City of Destruction. So I awoke, and behold it was a dream.

THE PILGRIM

Who would true valor see
  Let him come hither!
One here will constant be,
  Come wind, come weather;
There's no discouragement
  Shall make him once relent
His first-avow'd intent
  To be a Pilgrim.

Whoso beset him round
  With dismal stories,
Do but themselves confound;
  His strength the more is.
No lion can him fright;
  He'll with a giant fight;
But he will have a right
  To be a Pilgrim.

Nor enemy, nor fiend,
  Can daunt his spirit;
He knows he at the end
  Shall Life inherit:—
Then, fancies, fly away;
  He'll not fear what men say;
He'll labor, night and day,
  To be a Pilgrim.

—*J. Bunyan*

THE GREAT STONE FACE

By Nathaniel Hawthorne

One afternoon, when the sun was going down, a mother and her little boy sat at the door of their cottage, talking about the Great Stone Face. They had but to lift their eyes, and there it was plainly to be seen, though miles away, with the sunshine brightening all its features.

And what was the Great Stone Face?

Embosomed among a family of lofty mountains, there was a valley so spacious that it contained many thousand inhabitants. Some of these good people dwelt in log huts, with the black forest all around them, on the steep and difficult hillsides. Others had their homes in comfortable farmhouses, and cultivated the rich soil on the gentle slopes or level surfaces of the valley. Others, again, were congregated into populous villages, where some wild, highland rivulet, tumbling down from its birthplace in the upper mountain region, had been caught and tamed by human cunning, and compelled to turn the machinery of cotton factories. The inhabitants of this valley, in short, were numerous, and of many modes of life. But all of them, grown people and children, had a kind of familiarity with the Great Stone Face, although some possessed the gift of distinguishing this grand natural phenomenon more perfectly than many of their neighbors.

The Great Stone Face, then, was a work of Nature in her mood of majestic playfulness, formed on the perpendicular side of a mountain by some immense rocks, which had been thrown together in such a position as, when viewed at a proper distance, precisely to resemble the features of the human countenance. It seemed as if an enormous giant, or a Titan, had sculptured his own likeness on the precipice. There was the broad arch of the forehead, a hundred feet in height; the nose, with its long bridge; and the vast lips, which, if they could have spoken, would have rolled their thunder accents from one end of the valley to the other. True it is, that if the spectator approached too near, he lost the outline of the gigantic visage, and could discern only a heap of ponderous and gigantic rocks, piled in chaotic ruin one upon another. Retracing his steps, however, the wondrous features would again be seen; and the further he withdrew from them, the more like a human face, with all its original divinity intact, did they appear;

until, as it grew dim in the distance, with the clouds and glorified vapor of the mountains clustering about it, the Great Stone Face seemed positively to be alive.

It was a happy lot for children to grow up to manhood or womanhood with the Great Stone Face before their eyes, for all the features were noble, and the expression was at once grand and sweet, as if it were the glow of a vast, warm heart, that embraced all mankind in its affections, and had room for more. It was an education only to look at it. According to the belief of many people, the valley owed much of its fertility to this benign aspect that was continually beaming over it, illuminating the clouds, and infusing its tenderness into the sunshine.

As we began with saying, a mother and her little boy sat at their cottage-door, gazing at the Great Stone Face, and talking about it. The child's name was Ernest.

"Mother," said he, while the Titanic visage smiled on him, "I wish that it could speak, for it looks so very kindly that its voice must needs be pleasant. If I were to see a man with such a face, I should love him dearly."

"If an old prophecy should come to pass," answered his mother, "we may see a man, some time or other, with exactly such a face as that."

"What prophecy do you mean, dear mother?" eagerly inquired Ernest. "Pray tell me all about it!"

So his mother told him a story that her own mother had told to her, when she herself was younger than little Ernest; a story, not of things that were past, but of what was yet to come; a story, nevertheless, so very old, that even the Indians, who formerly inhabited this valley, had heard it from their forefathers, to whom, as they affirmed, it had been murmured by the mountain streams, and whispered by the wind among the tree-tops. The purport was, that, at some future day, a child should be born hereabouts, who was destined to become the greatest and noblest personage of his time, and whose countenance, in manhood, should bear an exact resemblance to the Great Stone Face. Not a few old-fashioned people, and young ones likewise, in the ardor of their hopes, still cherished an enduring faith in this old prophecy. But others, who had seen more of the world, had watched and waited till they were weary, and had beheld no man with such a face, nor any man that proved to be much greater or nobler than his neighbors, concluded it to be nothing but an idle tale. At all events, the great man of the prophecy had not yet appeared.

"O mother, dear mother!" cried Ernest, clapping his hands above his head, "I do hope that I shall live to see him!"

His mother was an affectionate and thoughtful woman, and felt that it was wisest not to discourage the generous hopes of her little boy. So she only said to him, "Perhaps you may."

And Ernest never forgot the story that his mother told him. It was always in his mind, whenever he looked upon the Great Stone Face. He spent his childhood in the log-cottage where he was born, and was dutiful to his mother, and helpful to her in many things, assisting her much with his little hands, and more with his loving heart. In this manner, from a happy yet often pensive child, he grew up to be a mild, quiet, unobtrusive boy, and sun-browned with labor in the fields, but with more intelligence brightening his aspect than is seen in many lads who have been taught at famous schools. Yet Ernest had had no teacher, save only that the Great Stone Face became one to him. When the toil of the day was over, he would gaze at it for hours, until he began to imagine that those vast features recognized him, and gave him a smile of kindness and encouragement, responsive to his own look of veneration. We must not take upon us to affirm that this was a mistake, although the Face may have looked no more kindly at Ernest than at all the world besides. But the secret was, that the boy's tender and confiding simplicity discerned what other people could not see; and thus the love, which was meant for all, became his peculiar portion.

About this time, there went a rumor throughout the valley, that the great man, foretold from ages ago, who was to bear a resemblance to the Great Stone Face, had appeared at last. It seems that, many years before, a young man had migrated from the valley and settled at a distant seaport, where, after getting together a little money, he had set up as a shopkeeper. His name—but I could never learn whether it was his real one, or a nickname that had grown out of his habits and success in life—was Gathergold. Being shrewd and active, and endowed by Providence with that inscrutable faculty which develops itself in what the world calls luck, he became an exceedingly rich merchant, and owner of a whole fleet of bulky-bottomed ships. All the countries of the globe appeared to join hands for the mere purpose of adding heap after heap to the mountainous accumulation of this one man's wealth. The cold regions of the north, almost within the gloom and shadow of the Arctic Circle, sent him their tribute in the shape of furs; hot Africa sifted for him the golden sands of her rivers, and gathered up the ivory tusks of her great elephants out of the forests; the East came bringing him the rich shawls, and spices, and teas, and the effulgence of diamonds, and the gleaming purity of large pearls. The ocean, not to be behindhand with the earth, yielded up her mighty whales, that Mr. Gathergold might sell their oil, and make a profit on it. Be the original commodity what it might, it was gold within his grasp. It might be said of him, as of Midas in the fable, that whatever he touched with his finger immediately glistened, and grew yellow, and was changed at once into sterling metal, or, which suited him still better, into piles of coin. And, when Mr. Gathergold had become so very rich that it would have taken him a hundred years only to count his wealth, he bethought himself of his native valley, and resolved to go back thither, and end his days where he was born. With this purpose in view, he sent a skilful architect to build him such a palace as should be fit for a man of his vast wealth to live in.

As I have said above, it had already been rumored in the valley that Mr. Gathergold had turned out to be the prophetic personage so long and vainly looked for, and that his visage was the perfect and undeniable similitude of the Great Stone Face. People were the more ready to believe that this must needs be the fact, when they beheld the splendid edifice that rose, as if by enchantment, on the site of his father's old weather-beaten farmhouse. The exterior was of marble, so dazzlingly white that it seemed as though the whole structure might melt away in the sunshine, like those humbler ones which Mr. Gathergold, in his young play-days, before his fingers were gifted with the touch of transmutation, had been accustomed to build of snow. It had a richly ornamented portico, supported by tall pillars, beneath which was a lofty door, studded with silver knobs, and made of a kind of variegated wood that had been brought from beyond the sea. The windows, from the floor to the ceiling of each stately apartment, were composed, respectively, of but one enormous pane of glass, so transparently pure that it was said to be a finer medium than even the vacant atmosphere. Hardly anybody had been permitted to see the interior of this palace; but it was reported, and with good semblance of truth, to be far more gorgeous than the outside, insomuch that whatever was iron or brass in other houses was silver or gold in this; and Mr. Gathergold's bedchamber, especially, made such a glittering appearance that no ordinary man would have been able to close his eyes there. But, on the other hand, Mr. Gathergold was now so inured to wealth, that perhaps he could not have closed his eyes unless where the gleam of it was certain to find its way beneath his eyelids.

In due time, the mansion was finished; next came the upholsterers, with magnificent furniture; then, a whole troop of black and white servants, the harbingers of Mr. Gathergold, who, in his own majestic person, was expected to arrive at sunset. Our friend Ernest, meanwhile, had been deeply stirred by the idea that the great man, the noble man, the man of prophecy, after so many ages of delay, was at length to be made manifest to his native valley. He knew, boy as he was, that there were a thousand ways in which Mr. Gathergold, with his vast wealth, might transform himself into an angel of beneficence, and assume a control over human affairs as wide and benignant as the smile of the Great Stone Face. Full of faith and hope, Ernest doubted not that what the people said was true, and that now he was to behold the living likeness of those wondrous features on the mountain side. While the boy was still gazing up the valley, and fancying, as he always did, that the Great Stone Face returned his gaze and looked kindly at him, the rumbling of wheels was heard, approaching swiftly along the winding road.

"Here he comes!" cried a group of people who were assembled to witness the arrival. "Here comes the great Mr. Gathergold!"

A carriage, drawn by four horses, dashed round the turn of the road. Within it, thrust partly out of the window, appeared the physiognomy of a little old man, with a skin as yellow as if his own Midas-hand had transmuted it. He had a low forehead, small, sharp eyes, puckered about with innumerable wrinkles, and very thin lips, which he made still thinner by pressing them forcibly together.

"The very image of the Great Stone Face!" shouted the people. "Sure enough, the old prophecy is true; and here we have the great man come, at last!"

And, what greatly perplexed Ernest, they seemed actually to believe that here was the likeness which they spoke of. By the roadside there chanced to be an old beggar-woman and two little beggar-children, stragglers from some far-off region, who, as the carriage rolled onward, held out their hands and lifted up their doleful voices, most piteously beseeching charity. A yellow claw—the very same that had clawed together so much wealth— poked itself out of the coach window, and dropped some copper coins upon the ground; so that, though the great man's name seems to have been Gathergold, he might just as suitably have been nicknamed Scattercopper. Still, nevertheless, with an earnest shout, and evidently with as much good faith as ever, the people bellowed—

"He is the very image of the Great Stone Face!"

But Ernest turned sadly from the wrinkled shrewdness of that sordid visage, and gazed up the valley, where, amid a gathering mist, gilded by the last sunbeams, he could still distinguish those glorious features which had impressed themselves into his soul. Their aspect cheered him. What did the benign lips seem to say?

"He will come! Fear not, Ernest; the man will come!"

The years went on, and Ernest ceased to be a boy. He had grown to be a young man now. He attracted little notice from the other inhabitants of the valley; for they saw nothing remarkable in his way of life, save that, when the labor of the day was over, he still loved to go apart and gaze and meditate upon the Great Stone Face. According to their idea of the matter, it was a folly, indeed, but pardonable, inasmuch as Ernest was industrious, kind, and neighborly, and neglected no duty for the sake of indulging this idle habit. They knew not that the Great Stone Face had become a teacher to him, and that the sentiment which was expressed in it would enlarge the young man's heart, and fill it with wider and deeper sympathies than other hearts. They knew not that thence would come a better wisdom than could be learned from books, and a better life than could be molded on the defaced example of other human lives. Neither did Ernest know that the thoughts and affections which came to him so naturally, in the fields and at the fireside, and wherever he communed with himself, were of a higher tone than those which all men shared with him. A simple soul—simple as when his mother first taught him the old prophecy—he beheld the marvellous features beaming adown the valley, and still wondered that their human counterpart was so long in making his appearance.

By this time poor Mr. Gathergold was dead and buried; and the oddest part of the matter was, that his wealth, which was the body and spirit of his existence, had disappeared before his death, leaving nothing of him but a living skeleton, covered over with a wrinkled, yellow skin. Since the melting away of his gold, it had been very generally conceded that there was no such striking resemblance, after all, between the ignoble features of the ruined merchant and that majestic face upon the mountain-side. So the people ceased to honor him during his lifetime, and quietly consigned him to forgetfulness after his decease. Once in a while, it is true, his memory was brought up in connection with the magnificent palace which he had built, and which had long ago been turned into a hotel for the accommodation of strangers, multitudes of whom came, every summer, to visit that famous natural curiosity, the Great Stone Face. Thus, Mr, Gathergold being discredited and thrown into the shade, the man of prophecy was yet to come.

It so happened that a native-born son of the valley, many years before, had enlisted as a soldier, and, after a great deal of hard fighting, had now become an illustrious commander. Whatever he may be called in history, he was known in camps and on the battle-field under the nickname of Old Blood-and-Thunder. This war-worn veteran, being now infirm with age and wounds, and weary of the turmoil of a military life, and of the roll of the drum and the clangor of the trumpet, that had so long been ringing in his ears, had lately signified a purpose of returning to his native valley, hoping to find repose where he remembered to have left it. The inhabitants, his old neighbors and their grown-up children, were resolved to welcome the renowned warrior with a salute of cannon and a public dinner; and all the more enthusiastically, it being affirmed that now, at last, the likeness of the Great Stone Face had actually appeared. An aid-de-camp of Old Blood-and-Thunder, travelling through the valley, was said to have been struck with the resemblance. Moreover the schoolmates and early acquaintances of the general were ready to testify, on oath, that, to the best of their recollection, the aforesaid general had been exceedingly like the majestic image, even when a boy, only that the idea had never occurred to them at that period. Great, therefore, was the excitement throughout the valley; and many people, who had never once thought of glancing at the Great Stone Face for years before, now spent their time in gazing at it, for the sake of knowing exactly how General Blood-and-Thunder looked.

On the day of the great festival, Ernest, with all the other people of the valley, left their work, and proceeded to the spot where the sylvan banquet was prepared. As he approached, the loud voice of the Rev. Dr. Battleblast was heard, beseeching a blessing on the good things set before them, and on the distinguished friend of peace in whose honor they were assembled. The tables were arranged in a cleared space of the woods, shut in by the surrounding trees, except where a vista opened eastward, and afforded a distant view of the Great Stone Face. Over the general's chair, which was a relic from the home of Washington, there was an arch of verdant boughs, with the laurel profusely intermixed, and surmounted by his country's banner, beneath which he had won his victories. Our friend Ernest raised himself on his tiptoes, in hopes to get a glimpse of the celebrated guest; but there was a mighty crowd about the tables anxious to hear the toasts and speeches, and to catch any word that might fall from the general in reply; and a volunteer company, doing duty as a guard, pricked ruthlessly with their bayonets at any particularly quiet person among the throng. So Ernest, being of an unobtrusive character, was thrust quite into the background, where he could see no more of Old Blood-and-Thunder's physiognomy than if it had been still blazing on the battle-field. To console himself, he turned toward the Great Stone Face, which, like a faithful and long-remembered friend, looked back and smiled upon him through the vista of the forest. Meantime, however, he could overhear the remarks of various individuals, who were comparing the features of the hero with the face on the distant mountain-side.

"'Tis the same face, to a hair!" cried one man, cutting a caper for joy.

"Wonderfully like, that's a fact!" responded another.

"Like! why, I call it Old Blood-and-Thunder himself, in a monstrous looking-glass!" cried a third. "And why not? He's the greatest man of this or any other age, beyond a doubt."

And then all three of the speakers gave a great shout, which communicated electricity to the crowd, and called forth a roar from a thousand voices, that went reverberating for miles among the mountains, until you might have supposed that the Great Stone Face had poured its thunder-breath into the cry. All these comments, and this vast enthusiasm, served the more to interest our friend; nor did he think of questioning that now, at length, the mountain-visage had found its human counterpart. It is true, Ernest had imagined that this long-looked-for personage would appear in the character of a man of peace, uttering wisdom, and doing good, and making people happy. But, taking an habitual breadth of view, with all his simplicity, he contended that Providence should choose its own method of blessing mankind, and could conceive that this great end might be effected even by a warrior and a bloody sword, should inscrutable wisdom see fit to order matters so.

"The general! the general!" was now the cry. "Hush! silence! Old Blood-and-Thunder's going to make a speech."

Even so; for, the cloth being removed, the general's health had been drunk amid shouts of applause, and he now stood upon his feet to thank the company. Ernest saw him. There he was, over the shoulders of the crowd, from the two glittering epaulets and embroidered collar upward, beneath the arch of green boughs with intertwined laurel, and the banner drooping as if to shade his brow! And there, too, visible in the same glance, through the vista of the forest, appeared the Great Stone Face! And was there, indeed, such a resemblance as the crowd had testified? Alas, Ernest could not recognize it! He beheld a war-worn and weather-beaten countenance, full of energy, and expressive of an iron will; but the gentle wisdom, the deep, broad, tender sympathies, were altogether wanting in Old Blood-and-Thunder's visage; and even if the Great Stone Face had assumed his look of stern command, the milder traits would still have tempered it.

"This is not the man of prophecy," sighed Ernest, to himself, as he made his way out of the throng. "And must the world wait longer yet?"

The mists had congregated about the distant mountain-side, and there were seen the grand and awful features of the Great Stone Face, awful but benignant, as if a mighty angel were sitting among the hills, and enrobing himself in a cloud-vesture of gold and purple. As he looked, Ernest could hardly believe but that a smile beamed over the whole visage, with a radiance still brightening, although without motion of the lips. It was probably the effect of the western sunshine, melting through the thinly diffused vapors that had swept between him and the object that he gazed at. But—as it always did—the aspect of his marvellous friend made Ernest as hopeful as if he had never hoped in vain.

"Fear not, Ernest," said his heart, even as if the Great Face were whispering him—"fear not, Ernest; he will come."

More years sped swiftly and tranquilly away. Ernest still dwelt in his native valley, and was now a man of middle age. By imperceptible degrees, he had become known among the people. Now, as heretofore, he labored for his bread, and was the same simple-hearted man that he had always been. But he had thought and felt so much, he had given so many of the best hours of his life to unworldly hopes for some great good to mankind, that it seemed as though he had been talking with the angels, and had imbibed a portion of their wisdom unawares. It was visible in the calm and well-considered beneficence of his daily life, the quiet stream of which had made a wide green margin all along its course. Not a day passed by, that the world was not the better because this man, humble as he was, had lived. He never stepped aside from his own path, yet would always reach a blessing to his neighbor. Almost involuntarily, too, he had become a preacher. The pure and high simplicity of his thought, which, as one of its manifestations, took shape in the good deeds that dropped silently from his hand, flowed also forth in speech. He uttered truths that wrought upon and molded the lives of those who heard him. His auditors, it may be, never suspected that Ernest, their own neighbor and familiar friend, was more than an ordinary man; least of all did Ernest himself suspect it; but, inevitably as the murmur of a rivulet, came thoughts out of his mouth that no other human lips had spoken.

When the people's minds had had a little time to cool, they were ready enough to acknowledge their mistake in imagining a similarity between General Blood-and-Thunder's truculent physiognomy and the benign visage on the mountain-side. But now, again, there were reports and many paragraphs in the newspapers, affirming that the likeness of the Great Stone Face had appeared upon the broad shoulders of a certain eminent statesman. He, like Mr. Gathergold and Old Blood-and-Thunder, was a native of the valley, but had left it in his early days, and taken up the trades of law and politics. Instead of the rich man's wealth and the warrior's sword, he had but a tongue, and it was mightier than both together. So wonderfully eloquent was he, that whatever he might choose to say, his auditors had no choice but to believe him; wrong looked like right, and right like wrong; for when it pleased him, he could make a kind of illuminated fog with his mere breath, and obscure the natural daylight with it. His tongue, indeed, was a magic instrument: sometimes it rumbled like the thunder; sometimes it warbled like the sweetest music. It was the blast of war—the song of peace; and it seemed to have a heart in it, when there was no such matter. In good truth, he was a wondrous man; and when his tongue had acquired him all other imaginable success,—when it had been heard in halls of state, and in the courts of princes and potentates—after it had made him known all over the world, even as a voice crying from shore to shore—it finally persuaded his countrymen to select him for the Presidency. Before this time—indeed, as soon as he began to grow celebrated—his admirers had found out the resemblance between him and the Great Stone Face; and so much were they struck by it, that throughout the country this distinguished gentleman was known by the name of Old Stony Phiz. The phrase was considered as giving a highly favorable aspect to his political prospects; for, as is likewise the case with the Popedom, nobody ever becomes President without taking a name other than his own.

While his friends were doing their best to make him President, Old Stony Phiz, as he was called, set out on a visit to the valley where he was born. Of course, he had no other object than to shake hands with his fellow-citizens, and neither thought nor cared about any effect which his progress through the country might have upon the election. Magnificent preparations were made to receive the illustrious statesman; a cavalcade of horsemen set forth to meet him at the boundary line of the State, and all the people left their business and gathered along the wayside to see him pass. Among these was Ernest. Though more than once disappointed, as we have seen, he had such a hopeful and confiding nature, that he was always ready to believe in whatever seemed beautiful and good. He kept his heart continually open, and thus was sure to catch the blessing from on high, when it should come. So now again, as buoyantly as ever, he went forth to behold the likeness of the Great Stone Face.

The cavalcade came prancing along the road, with a great clattering of hoofs and a mighty cloud of dust, which rose up so dense and high that the visage of the mountain-side was completely hidden from Ernest's eyes. All the great men of the neighborhood were there on horseback: militia officers, in uniform; the member of Congress; the sheriff of the county; the editors of newspapers; and many a farmer, too, had mounted his patient steed, with his Sunday coat upon his back. It really was a very brilliant spectacle, especially as there were numerous banners flaunting over the cavalcade, on some of which were gorgeous portraits of the illustrious statesman and the Great Stone Face, smiling familiarly at one another, like two brothers. If the pictures were to be trusted, the mutual resemblance, it must be confessed, was marvellous. We must not forget to mention that there was a band of music, which made the echoes of the mountains ring and reverberate with the loud triumph of its strains; so that airy and soul-thrilling melodies broke out among all the heights and hollows, as if every nook of his native valley had found a voice, to welcome the distinguished guest. But the grandest effect was when the far-off mountain precipice flung back the music; for then the Great Stone Face itself seemed to be swelling the triumphant chorus, in acknowledgment that, at length, the man of prophecy was come.

All this while the people were throwing up their hats and shouting, with enthusiasm so contagious that the heart of Ernest kindled up, and he likewise threw up his hat, and shouted, as loudly as the loudest, "Huzza for the great man! Huzza for Old Stony Phiz!" But as yet he had not seen him.

"Here he is, now!" cried those who stood near Ernest. "There! There! Look at Old Stony Phiz and then at the Old Man of the Mountain, and see if they are not as like as two twin-brothers!"

In the midst of all this gallant array, came an open barouche, drawn by four white horses; and in the barouche, with his massive head uncovered, sat the illustrious statesman, Old Stony Phiz himself.

"Confess it," said one of Ernest's neighbors to him, "the Great Stone Face has met its match at last!"

Now, it must be owned that, at his first glimpse of the countenance which was bowing and smiling from the barouche, Ernest did fancy that there was a resemblance between it and the old familiar face upon the mountain-side. The brow, with its massive depth and loftiness, and all the other features, indeed, were boldly and strongly hewn, as if in emulation of a more than heroic, of a Titanic model. But the sublimity and stateliness, the grand expression of a divine sympathy, that illuminated the mountain visage, and etherealized its ponderous granite substance into spirit, might here be sought in vain. Something had been originally left out, or had departed. And therefore the marvellously gifted statesman had always a weary gloom in the deep caverns of his eyes, as of a child that has outgrown its playthings, or a man of mighty faculties and little aims, whose life, with all its high performances, was vague and empty, because no high purpose had endowed it with reality.

Still, Ernest's neighbor was thrusting his elbow into his side, and pressing him for an answer.

"Confess! confess! Is not he the very picture of your Old Man of the Mountain?"

"No!" said Ernest, bluntly, "I see little or no likeness."

"Then so much the worse for the Great Stone Face!" answered his neighbor; and again he set up a shout for Old Stony Phiz.

But Ernest turned away, melancholy, and almost despondent: for this was the saddest of his disappointments, to behold a man who might have fulfilled the prophecy, and had not willed to do so. Meantime, the cavalcade, the banners, the music, and the barouches swept past him, with the vociferous crowd in the rear, leaving the dust to settle down, and the Great Stone Face to be revealed again, with the grandeur that it had worn for untold centuries.

"Lo, here I am, Ernest!" the benign lips seemed to say. "I have waited longer than thou, and am not yet weary. Fear not; the man will come."

The years hurried onward, treading in their haste on one another's heels. And now they began to bring white hairs, and scatter them over the head of Ernest; they made reverend wrinkles across his forehead, and furrows in his cheeks. He was an aged man. But not in vain had he grown old: more than the white hairs on his head were the sage thoughts in his mind; his wrinkles and furrows were inscriptions that Time had graved, and in which he had written legends of wisdom that had been tested by the tenor of a life. And Ernest had ceased to be obscure. Unsought for, undesired, had come the fame which so many seek, and made him known in the great world, beyond the limits of the valley in which he had dwelt so quietly. College professors, and even the active men of cities, came from far to see and converse with Ernest; for the report had gone abroad that this simple husbandman had ideas unlike those of other men, not gained from books, but of a higher tone—a tranquil and familiar majesty, as if he had been talking with the angels as his daily friends. Whether it were sage, statesman, or philanthropist, Ernest received these visitors with the gentle sincerity that had characterized him from boyhood, and spoke freely with them of whatever came uppermost, or lay deepest in his heart or their own. While they talked together, his face would kindle, unawares, and shine upon them, as with a mild evening light. Pensive with the fulness of such discourse, his guests took leave and went their way; and passing up the valley, paused to look at the Great Stone Face, imagining that they had seen its likeness in a human countenance, but could not remember where.

While Ernest had been growing up and growing old, a bountiful Providence had granted a new poet to this earth. He, likewise, was a native of the valley, but had spent the greater part of his life at a distance from that romantic region, pouring out his sweet music amid the bustle and din of cities. Often, however, did the mountains which had been familiar to him in his childhood lift their snowy peaks into the clear atmosphere of his poetry. Neither was the Great Stone Face forgotten, for the poet had celebrated it in an ode, which was grand enough to have been uttered by its own majestic lips. This man of genius, we may say, had come down from heaven with wonderful endowments. If he sang of a mountain, the eyes of all mankind beheld a mightier grandeur reposing on its breast, or soaring to its summit, than had before been seen there. If his theme were a lovely lake, a celestial smile had now been thrown over it, to gleam forever on its surface. If it were the vast old sea, even the deep immensity of its dread bosom seemed to swell the higher, as if moved by the emotions of the song. Thus the world assumed another and a better aspect from the hour that the poet blessed it with his happy eyes. The Creator had bestowed him, as the last best touch to his own handiwork. Creation was not finished till the poet came to interpret, and so complete it.

The effect was no less high and beautiful, when his human brethren were the subject of his verse. The man or woman, sordid with the common dust of life, who crossed his daily path, and the little child who played in it, were glorified if he beheld them in his mood of poetic faith. He showed the golden links of the great chain that intertwined them with an angelic kindred; he brought out the hidden traits of a celestial birth that made them worthy of such kin. Some, indeed, there were, who thought to show the soundness of their judgment by affirming that all the beauty and dignity of the natural world existed only in the poet's fancy. Let such men speak for themselves, who undoubtedly appear to have been spawned forth by Nature with a contemptuous bitterness; she having plastered them up out of her refuse stuff, after all the swine were made. As respects all things else, the poet's ideal was the truest truth.

The songs of this poet found their way to Ernest. He read them after his customary toil, seated on the bench before his cottage-door, where for such a length of time he had filled his repose with thought, by gazing at the Great Stone Face. And now as he read stanzas that caused the soul to thrill within him, he lifted his eyes to the vast countenance beaming on him so benignantly.

"O majestic friend," he murmured, addressing the Great Stone Face, "is not this man worthy to resemble thee?"

The Face seemed to smile, but answered not a word.

Now it happened that the poet, though he dwelt so far away, had not only heard of Ernest, but had meditated much upon his character, until he deemed nothing so desirable as to meet this man, whose untaught wisdom walked hand in hand with the noble simplicity of his life. One summer morning, therefore, he took passage by the railroad, and, in the decline of the afternoon, alighted from the cars at no great distance from Ernest's cottage. The great hotel, which had formerly been the palace of Mr. Gathergold, was close at hand, but the poet, with his carpet-bag on his arm, inquired at once where Ernest dwelt, and was resolved to be accepted as his guest.

Approaching the door, he there found the good old man, holding a volume in his hand, which alternately he read, and then, with a finger between the leaves, looked lovingly at the Great Stone Face.

"Good evening," said the poet. "Can you give a traveller a night's lodging?"

"Willingly," answered Ernest; and then he added, smiling, "Methinks I never saw the Great Stone Face look so hospitably at a stranger."

The poet sat down on the bench beside him, and he and Ernest talked together. Often had the poet held intercourse with the wittiest and the wisest, but never before with a man like Ernest, whose thoughts and feelings gushed up with such a natural freedom, and who made great truths so familiar by his simple utterance of them. Angels, as had been so often said, seemed to have wrought with him at his labor in the fields; angels seemed to have sat with him by the fireside; and, dwelling with angels as friend with friends, he had imbibed the sublimity of their ideas, and imbued it with the sweet and lowly charm of household words. So thought the poet. And Ernest, on the other hand, was moved and agitated by the living images which the poet flung out of his mind, and which peopled all the air about the cottage-door with shapes of beauty, both gay and pensive. The sympathies of these two men instructed them with a profounder sense than either could have attained alone. Their minds accorded into one strain, and made delightful music which neither of them could have claimed as all his own, nor distinguished his own share from the other's. They led one another, as it were, into a high pavilion of their thoughts, so remote, and hitherto so dim, that they had never entered it before, and so beautiful that they desired to be there always.

As Ernest listened to the poet, he imagined that the Great Stone Face was bending forward to listen too. He gazed earnestly into the poet's glowing eyes.

"Who are you, my strangely gifted guest?" he said.

The poet laid his finger on the volume that Ernest had been reading.

"You have read these poems," said he. "You know me, then—for I wrote them."

Again, and still more earnestly than before, Ernest examined the poet's features; then turned toward the Great Stone Face; then back, with an uncertain aspect, to his guest. But his countenance fell; he shook his head, and sighed.

"Wherefore are you sad?" inquired the poet.

"Because," replied Ernest, "all through life I have awaited the fulfilment of a prophecy; and, when I read these poems, I hoped that it might be fulfilled in you."

"You hoped," answered the poet, faintly smiling, "to find in me the likeness of the Great Stone Face. And you are disappointed, as formerly with Mr. Gathergold, and Old Blood-and-Thunder, and Old Stony Phiz. Yes, Ernest, it is my doom. You must add my name to the illustrious three, and record another failure of your hopes. For—in shame and sadness do I speak it, Ernest—I am not worthy to be typified by yonder benign and majestic image."

"And why?" asked Ernest. He pointed to the volume. "Are not those thoughts divine?"

"They have a strain of the Divinity," replied the poet. "You can hear in them the far-off echo of a heavenly song. But my life, dear Ernest, has not corresponded with my thought. I have had grand dreams, but they have been only dreams, because I have lived—and that, too, by my own choice—among poor and mean realities. Sometimes even—shall I dare to say it?—I lack faith in the grandeur, the beauty, and the goodness, which my own works are said to have made more evident in nature and in human life. Why, then, pure seeker of the good and true, shouldst thou hope to find me, in yonder image of the divine?"

The poet spoke sadly, and his eyes were dim with tears. So, likewise, were those of Ernest.

At the hour of sunset, as had long been his frequent custom, Ernest was to discourse to an assemblage of the neighboring inhabitants in the open air. He and the poet, arm in arm, still talking together as they went along, proceeded to the spot. It was a small nook among the hills, with a gray precipice behind, the stern front of which was relieved by the pleasant foliage of many creeping plants, that made a tapestry for the naked rock, by hanging their festoons from all its rugged angles. At a small elevation above the ground, set in a rich framework of verdure, there appeared a niche, spacious enough to admit a human figure, with freedom for such gestures as spontaneously ascompany earnest thought and genuine emotion. Into this natural pulpit Ernest ascended, and threw a look of familiar kindness around upon his audience. They stood, or sat, or reclined upon the grass, as seemed good to each, with the departing sunshine falling obliquely over them, and mingling its subdued cheerfulness with the solemnity of a grove of ancient trees, beneath and amid the boughs of which the golden rays were constrained to pass. In another direction was seen the Great Stone Face, with the same cheer, combined with the same solemnity, in its benignant aspect.

Ernest began to speak, giving to the people of what was in his heart and mind. His words had power, because they accorded with his thoughts; and his thoughts had reality and depth, because they harmonized with the life which he had always lived. It was not mere breath that this preacher uttered; they were the words of life, because a life of good deeds and holy love was melted into them. Pearls, pure and rich, had been dissolved into this precious draught. The poet, as he listened, felt that the being and character of Ernest were a nobler strain of poetry than he had ever written. His eyes glistening with tears, he gazed reverentially at the venerable man, and said within himself that never was there an aspect so worthy of a prophet and a sage as that mild, sweet, thoughtful countenance, with the glory of white hair diffused about it. At a distance, but distinctly to be seen, high up in the golden light of the setting sun, appeared the Great Stone Face, with hoary mists around it, like the white hairs around the brow of Ernest. Its look of grand beneficence seemed to embrace the world.

At that moment, in sympathy with a thought which he was about to utter, the face of Ernest assumed a grandeur of expression, so imbued with benevolence, that the poet, by an irresistible impulse, threw his arms aloft, and shouted:

"Behold! Behold! Ernest is himself the likeness of the Great Stone Face!"

Then all the people looked, and saw that what the deep-sighted poet said was true. The prophecy was fulfilled. But Ernest, having finished what he had to say, took the poet's arm, and walked slowly homeward, still hoping that some wiser and better man than himself would by and by appear, bearing a resemblance to the GREAT STONE FACE.

THE GENTLE BOY

By NATHANIEL HAWTHORNE

In the course of the year 1656, several of the people called Quakers, led, as they professed, by the inward movement of the spirit, made their appearance in New England. Their reputation, as holders of mystic and pernicious principles, having spread before them, the Puritans early endeavored to banish, and to prevent the further intrusion of the rising sect. But the measures by which it was intended to purge the land of heresy, though more than sufficiently vigorous, were entirely unsuccessful. The Quakers, esteeming persecution as a divine call to the post of danger, laid claim to a holy courage, unknown to the Puritans themselves, who had shunned the cross, by providing for the peaceable exercise of their religion in a distant wilderness. Though it was the singular fact, that every nation of the earth rejected the wandering enthusiasts who practiced peace toward all men, the place of greatest uneasiness and peril, and therefore, in their eyes, the most eligible, was the province of Massachusetts Bay.

The fines, imprisonments, and stripes, liberally distributed by our pious forefathers, the popular antipathy, so strong that it endured nearly a hundred years after actual persecution had ceased, were attractions as powerful for the Quakers as peace, honor, and reward would have been for the wordly-minded. Every European vessel brought new cargoes of the sect, eager to testify against the oppression which they hoped to share; and, when shipmasters were restrained by heavy fines from affording them passage, they made long and circuitous journeys through the Indian country, and appeared in the province as if conveyed by a supernatural power. Their enthusiasm, heightened almost to madness by the treatment which they received, produced actions contrary to the rules of decency, as well as of rational religion, and presented a singular contrast to the calm and staid deportment of their sectarian successors of the present day. The command of the spirit, inaudible except to the soul, and not to be controverted on grounds of human wisdom, was made a plea for most indecorous exhibitions, which, abstractedly considered, well deserved the moderate chastisement of the rod. These extravagances, and the persecution which was at once their cause and consequence, continued to increase, till, in the year 1659, the government of Massachusetts Bay indulged two members of the Quaker sect with the crown of martyrdom.

An indelible stain of blood is upon the hands of all who consented to this act, but a large share of the awful responsibility must rest upon the person then at the head of the government. He was a man of narrow mind and imperfect education, and his uncompromising bigotry was made hot and mischievous by violent and hasty passions; he exerted his influence indecorously and unjustifiably to compass the death of the enthusiasts; and his whole conduct, in respect to them, was marked by brutal cruelty.

The Quakers, whose revengeful feelings were not less deep because they were inactive, remembered this man and his associates, in after times. The historian of the sect affirms that, by the wrath of Heaven, a blight fell upon the land in the vicinity of the "bloody town" of Boston, so that no wheat would grow there; and he takes his stand, as it were, among the graves of the ancient persecutors, and triumphantly recounts the judgments that overtook them, in old age or at the parting hour. He tells us that they died suddenly, and violently, and in madness; but nothing can exceed the bitter mockery with which he records the loathsome disease, and "death by rottenness," of the fierce and cruel governor.

On the evening of the autumn day, that had witnessed the martyrdom of two men of the Quaker persuasion, a Puritan settler was returning from the metropolis to the neighboring country town in which he resided. The air was cool, the sky clear, and the lingering twilight was made brighter by the rays of a young moon, which had now nearly reached the verge of the horizon. The traveller, a man of middle age, wrapped in a gray frieze cloak, quickened his pace when he had reached the outskirts of the town, for a gloomy extent of nearly four miles lay between him and his home. The low, straw-thatched houses were scattered at considerable intervals along the road, and the country having been settled but about thirty years, the tracts of original forest still bore no small proportion to the cultivated ground. The autumn wind wandered among the branches, whirling away the leaves from all except the pine-trees, and moaning as if it lamented the desolation of which it was the instrument. The road had penetrated the mass of woods that lay nearest to the town, and was just emerging into an open space, when the traveller's ears were saluted by a sound more mournful than even that of the wind. It was like the wailing of some one in distress, and it seemed to proceed from beneath a tall and lonely fir-tree, in the centre of a cleared, but uninclosed and uncultivated field. The Puritan could not but remember that this was the very spot which had been made accursed a few hours before by the execution of the Quakers, whose bodies had been thrown together into one hasty grave, beneath the tree on which they suffered. He struggled, however, against the superstitious fears which belonged to the age, and compelled himself to pause and listen.

"The voice is most likely mortal, nor have I cause to tremble if it be otherwise," thought he, straining his eyes through the dim moonlight. "Methinks it is like the wailing of a child; some infant, it may be, which has strayed from its mother, and chanced upon this place of death. For the ease of mine own conscience, I must search this matter out."

He therefore left the path, and walked somewhat fearfully across the field. Though now so desolate, its soil was pressed down and trampled by the thousand footsteps of those who had witnessed the spectacle of that day, all of whom had now retired, leaving the dead to their loneliness. The traveller at length reached the fir-tree, which from the middle upward was covered with living branches, although a scaffold had been erected beneath, and other preparations made for the work of death. Under this unhappy tree, which in after times was believed to drop poison with its dew, sat the one solitary mourner for innocent blood. It was a slender and light-clad little boy, who leaned his face upon a hillock of fresh-turned and half-frozen earth, and wailed bitterly, yet in a suppressed tone, as if his grief might receive the punishment of crime. The Puritan, whose approach had been unperceived, laid his hand upon the child's shoulder, and addressed him compassionately.

"You have chosen a dreary lodging, my poor boy, and no wonder that you weep," said he. "But dry your eyes, and tell me where your mother dwells. I promise you if the journey be not too far, I will leave you in her arms to-night."

The boy had hushed his wailing at once, and turned his face upward to the stranger. It was a pale, bright-eyed countenance, certainly not more than six years old, but sorrow, fear, and want had destroyed much of its infantile expression. The Puritan, seeing the boy's frightened gaze, and feeling that he trembled under his hand, endeavored to reassure him.

"Nay, if I intended to do you harm, little lad, the readiest way were to leave you here. What! you do not fear to sit beneath the gallows on a new-made grave, and yet you tremble at a friend's touch. Take heart, child, and tell me what is your name, and where is your home!"

"Friend," replied the little boy, in a sweet, though faltering voice, "they call me Ilbrahim, and my home is here."

The pale, spiritual face, the eyes that seemed to mingle with the moonlight, the sweet airy voice, and the outlandish name almost made the Puritan believe that the boy was in truth a being which had sprung up out of the grave on which he sat. But perceiving that the apparition stood the test of a short mental prayer, and remembering that the arm which he had touched was life-like, he adopted a more rational supposition. "The poor child is stricken in his intellect," thought he, "but verily his words are fearful, in a place like this." He then spoke soothingly, intending to humor the boy's fantasy.

"Your home will scarce be comfortable, Ilbrahim, this cold autumn night, and I fear you are ill provided with food. I am hastening to a warm supper and bed, and if you will go with me, you shall share them!"

"I thank thee, friend, but though I be hungry, and shivering with cold, thou wilt not give me food nor lodging," replied the boy, in the quiet tone which despair had taught him, even so young. "My father was of the people whom all men hate. They have laid him under this heap of earth, and here is my home."

The Puritan, who had laid hold of little Ilbrahim's hand, relinquished it as if he were touching a loathsome reptile. But he possessed a compassionate heart, which not even religious prejudice could harden into stone.

"God forbid that I should leave this child to perish, though he comes of the accursed sect," said he to himself. "Do we not all spring from an evil root? Are we not all in darkness till the light doth shine upon us? He shall not perish, neither in body, nor, if prayer and instruction may avail for him, in soul." He then spoke aloud and kindly to Ilbrahim, who had again hid his face in the cold earth of the grave. "Was every door in the land shut against you, my child, that you have wandered to this unhallowed spot?"

"They drove me forth from the prison when they took my father thence," said the boy, "and I stood afar off, watching the crowd of people; and when they were gone, I came hither, and found only this grave. I knew that my father was sleeping here, and I said, This shall be my home."

"No, child, no; not while I have a roof over my head, or a morsel to share with you!" exclaimed the Puritan, whose sympathies were now fully excited. "Rise up and come with me, and fear not any harm."

The boy wept afresh, and clung to the heap of earth, as if the cold heart beneath it were warmer to him than any in a living breast. The traveller, however, continued to entreat him tenderly, and seeming to acquire some degree of confidence, he at length arose. But his slender limbs tottered with weakness, his little head grew dizzy, and he leaned against the tree of death for support.

"My poor boy, are you so feeble?" said the Puritan. "When did you taste food last?"

"I ate of bread and water with my father in the prison," replied Ilbrahim, "but they brought him none neither yesterday nor to-day, saying that he had eaten enough to bear him to his journey's end. Trouble not thyself for my hunger, kind friend, for I have lacked food many times ere now."

The traveller took the child in his arms and wrapped his cloak about him, while his heart stirred with shame and anger against the gratuitous cruelty of the instruments in this persecution. In the awakened warmth of his feelings, he resolved that, at whatever risk, he would not forsake the poor little defenceless being whom Heaven had confided to his care. With this determination, he left the accursed field, and resumed the homeward path from which the wailing of the boy had called him. The light and motionless burden scarcely impeded his progress, and he soon beheld the fire rays from the windows of the cottage which he, a native of a distant clime, had built in the Western wilderness. It was surrounded by a considerable extent of cultivated ground, and the dwelling was situated in the nook of a wood-covered hill, whither it seemed to have crept for protection.

"Look up, child," said the Puritan to Ilbrahim, whose faint head had sunk upon his shoulder, "there is our home."

At the word "home," a thrill passed through the child's frame, but he continued silent. A few moments brought them to the cottage-door, at which the owner knocked; for at that early period, when savages were wandering everywhere among the settlers, bolt and bar were indispensable to the security of a dwelling. The summons was answered by a bond-servant, a coarse-clad and dull-featured piece of humanity, who, after ascertaining that his master was the applicant, undid the door, and held a flaring pine-knot torch to light him in. Further back in the passageway, the red blaze discovered a matronly woman, but no little crowd of children came bounding forth to greet their father's return. As the Puritan entered, he thrust aside his cloak, and displayed Ilbrahim's face to the female.

"Dorothy, here is a little outcast whom Providence hath put into our hands," observed he. "Be kind to him, even as if he were of those dear ones who have departed from us."

"What pale and bright-eyed little boy is this, Tobias?" she inquired. "Is he one whom the wilderness folk have ravished from some Christian mother?"

"No, Dorothy, this poor child is no captive from the wilderness," he replied. "The heathen savage would have given him to eat of his scanty morsel, and to drink of his birchen cup; but Christian men, alas! had cast him out to die."

Then he told her how he had found him beneath the gallows, upon his father's grave; and how his heart had prompted him, like the speaking of an inward voice, to take the little outcast home, and be kind unto him. He acknowledged his resolution to feed and clothe him, as if he were his own child, and to afford him the instruction which should counteract the pernicious errors hitherto instilled into his infant mind. Dorothy was gifted with even a quicker tenderness than her husband, and she approved of all his doings and intentions.

"Have you a mother, dear child?" she inquired.

The tears burst forth from his full heart, as he attempted to reply; but Dorothy at length understood that he had a mother, who, like the rest of her sect, was a persecuted wanderer. She had been taken from the prison a short time before, carried into the uninhabited wilderness, and left to perish there by hunger or wild beasts. This was no uncommon method of disposing of the Quakers, and they were accustomed to boast, that the inhabitants of the desert were more hospitable to them than civilized man.

"Fear not, little boy, you shall not need a mother, and a kind one," said Dorothy, when she had gathered this information. "Dry your tears, Ilbrahim, and be my child, as I will be your mother."

The good woman prepared the little bed, from which her own children had successively been borne to another resting-place. Before Ilbrahim would consent to occupy it, he knelt down, and as Dorothy listened to his simple and affecting prayer, she marvelled how the parents that had taught it to him could have been judged worthy of death. When the boy had fallen asleep, she bent over his pale and spiritual countenance, pressed a kiss upon his white brow, drew the bedclothes up about his neck, and went away with a pensive gladness in her heart.

Tobias Pearson was not among the earliest emigrants from the old country. He had remained in England during the first years of the civil war, in which he had borne some share as a cornet of dragoons, under Cromwell. But when the ambitious designs of his leader began to develop themselves, he quitted the army of the Parliament, and sought a refuge from the strife, which was no longer holy, among the people of his persuasion in the colony of Massachusetts. A more worldly consideration had perhaps an influence in drawing him thither; for New England offered advantages to men of unprosperous fortunes, as well as to dissatisfied religionists, and Pearson had hitherto found it difficult to provide for a wife and increasing family. To this supposed impurity of motive, the more bigoted Puritans were inclined to impute the removal by death of all the children, for whose earthly good the father had been over-thoughtful. They had left their native country blooming like roses, and like roses they had perished in a foreign soil. Those expounders of the ways of Providence, who had thus judged their brother, and attributed his domestic sorrows to his sin, were not more charitable when they saw him and Dorothy endeavoring to fill up the void in their hearts by the adoption of an infant of the accursed sect. Nor did they fail to communicate their disapprobation to Tobias; but the latter, in reply, merely pointed at the little, quiet, lovely boy, whose appearance and deportment were indeed as powerful arguments as could possibly have been adduced in his own favor. Even his beauty, however, and his winning manners, sometimes produced an effect ultimately unfavorable; for the bigots, when the outer surfaces of their iron hearts had been softened and again grew hard, affirmed that no merely natural cause could have so worked upon them.

Their antipathy to the poor infant was also increased by the ill success of divers theological discussions, in which it was attempted to convince him of the errors of his sect. Ilbrahim, it is true, was not a skilful controversialist; but the feeling of his religion was strong as instinct in him, and he could neither be enticed nor driven from the faith which his father had died for. The odium of this stubbornness was shared in a great measure by the child's protectors, insomuch that Tobias and Dorothy very shortly began to experience a most bitter species of persecution, in the cold regards of many a friend whom they had valued. The common people manifested their opinions more openly. Pearson was a man of some consideration, being a representative to the General Court, and an approved lieutenant in the trainbands; yet within a week after his adoption of Ilbrahim, he had been both hissed and hooted. Once, also, when walking through a solitary piece of woods, he heard a loud voice from some invisible speaker; and it cried, "What shall be done to the backslider? Lo! the scourge is knotted for him, even the whip of nine cords, and every cord three knots!" These insults irritated Pearson's temper for the moment; they entered also into his heart, and became imperceptible but powerful workers toward an end which his most secret thought had not yet whispered.

On the second Sabbath after Ilbrahim became a member of their family, Pearson and his wife deemed it proper that he should appear with them at public worship. They had anticipated some opposition to this measure from the boy, but he prepared himself in silence, and at the appointed hour was clad in the new mourning suit which Dorothy had wrought for him. As the parish was then, and during many subsequent years, unprovided with a bell, the signal for the commencement of religious exercises was the beat of a drum. At the first sound of that martial call to the place of holy and quiet thoughts, Tobias and Dorothy set forth, each holding a hand of little Ilbrahim, like two parents linked together by the infant of their love. On their path through the leafless woods, they were overtaken by many persons of their acquaintance, all of whom avoided them, and passed by on the other side; but a severer trial awaited their constancy when they had descended the hill, and drew near the pine-built and undecorated house of prayer. Around the door, from which the drummer still sent forth his thundering summons, was drawn up a formidable phalanx, including several of the oldest members of the congregation, many of the middle aged, and nearly all the younger males. Pearson found it difficult to sustain their united and disapproving gaze; but Dorothy, whose mind was differently circumstanced, merely drew the boy closer to her, and faltered not in her approach. As they entered the door, they overheard the muttered sentiments of the assemblage, and when the reviling voices of the little children smote Ilbrahim's ear, he wept.

The interior aspect of the meeting-house was rude. The low ceiling, the unplastered walls, the naked woodwork, and the undraperied pulpit offered nothing to excite the devotion, which, without such external aids, often remains latent in the heart. The floor of the building was occupied by rows of long, cushionless benches, supplying the place of pews, and the broad aisle formed a sexual division, impassable except by children beneath a certain age.

Pearson and Dorothy separated at the door of the meeting-house, and Ilbrahim, being within the years of infancy, was retained under the care of the latter. The wrinkled beldams involved themselves in their rusty cloaks as he passed by; even the mild-featured maidens seemed to dread contamination; and many a stern old man arose, and turned his repulsive and unheavenly countenance upon the gentle boy, as if the sanctuary were polluted by his presence. He was a sweet infant of the skies, that had strayed away from his home, and all the inhabitants of this miserable world closed up their impure hearts against him, drew back their earth-soiled garments from his touch, and said, "We are holier than thou."

Ilbrahim, seated by the side of his adopted mother, and retaining fast hold of her hand, assumed a grave and decorous demeanor, such as might befit a person of matured taste and understanding, who should find himself in a temple dedicated to some worship which he did not recognize, but felt himself bound to respect. The exercises had not yet commenced, however, when the boy's attention was arrested by an event, apparently of trifling interest. A woman, having her face muffled in a hood, and a cloak drawn completely about her form, advanced slowly up the broad aisle, and took a place upon the foremost bench. Ilbrahim's faint color varied, his nerves fluttered, he was unable to turn his eyes from the muffled female.

When the preliminary prayer and hymn were over, the minister arose, and having turned the hour-glass which stood by the great Bible, commenced his discourse. He was now well stricken in years, a man of pale, thin countenance, and his gray hairs were closely covered by a black velvet skull cap. In his younger days he had practically learned the meaning of persecution from Archbishop Laud, and he was not now disposed to forget the lesson against which he had murmured then. Introducing the often-discussed subject of the Quakers, he gave a history of that sect, and a description of their tenets, in which error predominated, and prejudice distorted the aspect of what was true. He adverted to the recent measures in the province, and cautioned his hearers of weaker parts against calling in question the just severity which God-fearing magistrates had at length been compelled to exercise. He spoke of the danger of pity, in some cases a commendable and Christian virtue, but inapplicable to this pernicious sect. He observed that such was their devilish obstinacy in error, that even the little children, the sucking babes, were hardened and desperate heretics. He affirmed that no man, without Heaven's especial warrant, should attempt their conversion, lest while he lent his hand to draw them from the slough, he should himself be precipitated into its lowest depths.

The sands of the second hour were principally in the lower half of the glass when the sermon concluded. An approving murmur followed, and the clergyman, having given out a hymn, took his seat with much self-congratulation, and endeavored to read the effect of his eloquence in the visages of the people. But while voices from all parts of the house were tuning themselves to sing, a scene occurred, which, though not very unusual at that period in the province, happened to be without precedent in this parish.

The muffled female, who had hitherto sat motionless in the front rank of the audience, now arose, and with slow, stately, and unwavering step ascended the pulpit stairs. The quiverings of incipient harmony were hushed, and the divine sat in speechless and almost terrified astonishment, while she undid the door, and stood up in the sacred desk from which his maledictions had just been thundered. She then divested herself of the cloak and hood, and appeared in a most singular array. A shapeless robe of sackcloth was girded about her waist with a knotted cord; her raven hair fell down upon her shoulders, and its blackness was defiled by pale streaks of ashes, which she had strewn upon her head. Her eyebrows, dark and strongly defined, added to the deathly whiteness of a countenance, which, emaciated with want, and wild with enthusiasm and strange sorrows, retained no trace of earlier beauty. This figure stood gazing earnestly on the audience, and there was no sound, nor any movement, except a faint shuddering which every man observed in his neighbor, but was scarcely conscious of in himself. At length, when her fit of inspiration came, she spoke, for the first few moments in a low voice and not invariably distinct utterance. Her discourse gave evidence of an imagination hopelessly entangled with her reason; it was a vague and incomprehensible rhapsody, which, however, seemed to spread its own atmosphere round the hearer's soul, and to move his feelings by some influence unconnected with the words. As she proceeded, beautiful but shadowy images would sometimes be seen, like bright things moving in a turbid river; or a strong and singularly shaped idea leaped forth, and seized at once on the understanding or the heart. But the course of her unearthly eloquence soon led her to the persecutions of her sect, and from thence the step was short to her own peculiar sorrows. She was naturally a woman of mighty passions, and hatred and revenge now wrapped themselves in the garb of piety; the character of her speech was changed, her images became distinct though wild, and her denunciations had an almost hellish bitterness.

"The governor and his mighty men," she said, "have gathered together, taking counsel among themselves and saying, 'What shall we do unto this people—even unto the people that have come into this land to put our iniquity to the blush?' And lo! the Devil entereth into the council-chamber, like a lame man of low stature and gravely apparelled, with a dark and twisted countenance, and a bright, downcast eye. And he standeth up among the rulers; yea, he goeth to and fro, whispering to each; and every man lends his ear, for his word is, 'Slay, slay!' But I say unto ye, Woe to them that slay! Woe to them that shed the blood of saints! Woe to them that have slain the husband, and cast forth the child, the tender infant, to wander homeless, and hungry, and cold, till he die; and have saved the mother alive, in the cruelty of their tender mercies! Woe to them in their lifetime, cursed are they in the delight and pleasure of their hearts! Woe to them in their death-hour, whether it come swiftly with blood and violence, or after long and lingering pain! Woe, in the dark house, in the rottenness of the grave, when the children's children shall revile the ashes of the fathers! Woe, woe, woe, at the judgment, when all the persecuted and all the slain in this bloody land, and the father, the mother, and the child shall await them in a day that they cannot escape! Seed of the faith, seed of the faith, ye whose hearts are moving with a power that ye know not, arise, wash your hands of this innocent blood! Lift your voices, chosen ones, cry aloud, and call down a woe and a judgment with me!"

Having thus given vent to the flood of malignity which she mistook for inspiration, the speaker was silent. Her voice was succeeded by the hysteric shrieks of several women, but the feelings of the audience generally had not been drawn onward in the current with her own. They remained stupefied, stranded as it were, in the midst of a torrent, which deafened them by its roaring, but might not move them by its violence. The clergyman, who could not hitherto have ejected the usurper of his pulpit otherwise than by bodily force, now addressed her in the tone of just indignation and legitimate authority.

"Get you down, woman, from the holy place which you profane," he said. "Is it to the Lord's house that you came to pour forth the foulness of your heart, and the inspiration of the Devil? Get you down, and remember that the sentence of death is on you, yea, and shall be executed, were it but for this day's work!"

"I go, friend, I go, for the voice hath had its utterance," replied she, in a depressed and even mild tone. "I have done my mission unto thee and to thy people. Reward me with stripes, imprisonment, or death, as ye shall be permitted."

The weakness of exhausted passion caused her steps to totter as she descended the pulpit stairs. The people, in the meanwhile, were stirring to and fro on the floor of the house, whispering among themselves, and glancing toward the intruder. Many of them now recognized her as the woman who had assaulted the governor with frightful language, as he passed by the window of her prison; they knew, also, that she was adjudged to suffer death, and had been preserved only by an involuntary banishment into the wilderness. The new outrage, by which she had provoked her fate, seemed to render further lenity impossible; and a gentleman in military dress, with a stout man of inferior rank, drew toward the door of the meeting-house, and awaited her approach. Scarcely did her feet press the floor, however, when an unexpected scene occurred. In that moment of her peril, when every eye frowned with death, a little timid boy pressed forth, and threw his arms round his mother.

"I am here, mother, it is I, and I will go with thee to prison," he exclaimed.

She gazed at him with a doubtful and almost frightened expression, for she knew that the boy had been cast out to perish, and she had not hoped to see his face again. She feared, perhaps, that it was but one of the happy visions, with which her excited fancy had often deceived her, in the solitude of the desert or in prison. But when she felt his hand warm within her own, and heard his little eloquence of childish love, she began to know that she was yet a mother.

"Blessed art thou, my son," she sobbed. "My heart was withered; yea, dead with thee and with thy father; and now it leaps as in the first moment when I pressed thee to my bosom."

She kneeled down and embraced him again and again, while the joy that could find no words expressed itself in broken accents, like the bubbles gushing up to vanish at the surface of a deep fountain. The sorrows of past years, and the darker peril that was nigh, cast not a shadow on the brightness of that fleeting moment. Soon, however, the spectators saw a change upon her face, as the consciousness of her sad estate returned, and grief supplied the fount of tears which joy had opened. By the words she uttered, it would seem that the indulgence of natural love had given her mind a momentary sense of its errors, and made her know how far she had strayed from duty, in following the dictates of a wild fanaticism.

"In a doleful hour art thou returned to me, poor boy," she said, "for thy mother's path has gone darkening onward, till now the end is death. Son, son, I have borne thee in my arms when my limbs were tottering, and I have fed thee with the food that I was fainting for; yet I have ill performed a mother's part by thee in life, and now I leave thee no inheritance but woe and shame. Thou wilt go seeking through the world, and find all hearts closed against thee, and their sweet affections turned to bitterness for my sake. My child, my child, how many a pang awaits thy gentle spirit and I the cause of all!"

She hid her face on Ilbrahim's head, and her long raven hair, discolored with the ashes of her mourning, fell down about him like a veil. A low and interrupted moan was the voice of her heart's anguish, and it did not fail to move the sympathies of many who mistook their involuntary virtue for a sin. Sobs were audible in the female section of the house, and every man who was a father drew his hand across his eyes. Tobias Pearson was agitated and uneasy, but a certain feeling like the consciousness of guilt oppressed him, so that he could not go forth and offer himself as the protector of the child. Dorothy, however, had watched her husband's eye. Her mind was free from the influence that had begun to work on his, and she drew near the Quaker woman, and addressed her in the hearing of all the congregation.

"Stranger, trust this boy to me, and I will be his mother," she said, taking Ilbrahim's hand. "Providence has signally marked out my husband to protect him, and he has fed at our table and lodged under our roof, now many days, till our hearts have grown very strongly unto him. Leave the tender child with us, and be at ease concerning his welfare."

The Quaker rose from the ground, but drew the boy closer to her, while she gazed earnestly in Dorothy's face. Her mild, but saddened features, and neat matronly attire harmonized together, and were like a verse of fireside poetry. Her very aspect proved that she was blameless, so far as mortal could be so, in respect to God and man; while the enthusiast, in her robe of sackcloth and girdle of knotted cord, had as evidently violated the duties of the present life and the future, by fixing her attention wholly on the latter. The two females, as they held each a hand of Ilbrahim, formed a practical allegory; it was rational piety and unbridled fanaticism contending for the empire of a young heart.

"Thou art not of our people," said the Quaker, mournfully.

"No, we are not of your people," replied Dorothy, with mildness, "but we are Christians, looking upward to the same Heaven with you. Doubt not that your boy shall meet you there, if there be a blessing on our tender and prayerful guidance of him. Thither, I trust, my own children have gone before me, for I also have been a mother; I am no longer so," she added, in a faltering tone, "and your son will have all my care."

"But will ye lead him in the path which his parents have trodden?" demanded the Quaker. "Can ye teach him the enlightened faith which his father has died for, and for which I, even I, am soon to become an unworthy martyr? The boy has been baptized in blood; will ye keep the mark fresh and ruddy upon his forehead?"

"I will not deceive you," answered Dorothy. "If your child become our child, we must breed him up in the instruction which Heaven has imparted to us; we must pray for him the prayers of our own faith; we must do toward him according to the dictates of our own consciences, and not of yours. Were we to act otherwise, we should abuse your trust, even in complying with your wishes."

The mother looked down upon her boy with a troubled countenance, and then turned her eyes upward to Heaven. She seemed to pray internally, and the contention of her soul was evident.

"Friend," she said at length to Dorothy, "I doubt not that my son shall receive all earthly tenderness at thy hands. Nay, I will believe that even thy imperfect lights may guide him to a better world; for surely thou art on the path thither. But thou hast spoken of a husband. Doth he stand here among this multitude of people? Let him come forth, for I must know to whom I commit this most precious trust."

She turned her face upon the male auditors, and after a momentary delay, Tobias Pearson came forth from among them. The Quaker saw the dress which marked his military rank, and shook her head; but then she noted the hesitating air, the eyes that struggled with her own, and were vanquished; the color that went and came, and could find no resting-place. As she gazed, an unmirthful smile spread over her features, like sunshine that grows melancholy in some desolate spot. Her lips moved inaudibly, but at length she spake.

"I hear it, I hear it. The voice speaketh within me and saith, 'Leave thy child, Catharine, for his place is here, and go hence, for I have other work for thee. Break the bonds of natural affection, martyr thy love, and know that in all these things eternal wisdom hath its ends.' I go, friends, I go. Take ye my boy, my precious jewel. I go hence, trusting that all shall be well, and that even for his infant hands there is a labor in the vineyard."

She knelt down and whispered to Ilbrahim, who at first struggled and clung to his mother, with sobs and tears, but remained passive when she had kissed his cheek and arisen from the ground. Having held her hands over his head in mental prayer, she was ready to depart.

"Farewell, friends in mine extremity," she said to Pearson and his wife; "the good deed ye have done me is a treasure laid up in Heaven, to be returned a thousand-fold hereafter. And farewell ye, mine enemies, to whom it is not permitted to harm so much as a hair of my head, nor to stay my footsteps even for a moment. The day is coming when ye shall call upon me to witness for ye to this one sin uncommitted, and I will rise up and answer."

She turned her steps toward the door, and the men, who had stationed themselves to guard it, withdrew, and suffered her to pass. A general sentiment of pity overcame the virulence of religious hatred. Sanctified by her love and her affliction, she went forth, and all the people gazed after her till she had journeyed up the hill, and was lost behind its brow. She went, the apostle of her own unquiet heart, to renew the wanderings of past years. For her voice had been already heard in many lands of Christendom; and she had pined in the cells of a Catholic Inquisition before she felt the lash and lay in the dungeons of the Puritans. Her mission had extended also to the followers of the Prophet, and from them she had received the courtesy and kindness which all the contending sects of our purer religion united to deny her. Her husband and herself had resided many months in Turkey, where even the Sultan's countenance was gracious to them; in that pagan land, too, was Ilbrahim's birthplace, and his Oriental name was a mark of gratitude for the good deeds of an unbeliever.

When Pearson and his wife had thus acquired all the rights over Ilbrahim that could be delegated, their affection for him became, like the memory of their native land, or their mild sorrow for the dead, a piece of the immovable furniture of their hearts. The boy, also, after a week or two of mental disquiet, began to gratify his protectors, by many inadvertent proofs that he considered them as parents, and their house as home. Before the winter snows were melted, the persecuted infant, the little wanderer from a remote and heathen country, seemed native in the New England cottage, and inseparable from the warmth and security of its hearth. Under the influence of kind treatment, and in the consciousness that he was loved, Ilbrahim's demeanor lost a premature manliness which had resulted from his earlier situation; he became more childlike, and his natural character displayed itself with freedom. It was in many respects a beautiful one, yet the disordered imaginations of both his father and mother had perhaps propagated a certain unhealthiness in the mind of the boy. In his general state, Ilbrahim would derive enjoyment from the most trifling events, and from every object about him; he seemed to discover rich treasures of happiness, by a faculty analogous to that of the witch-hazel, which points to hidden gold where all is barren to the eye. His airy gayety, coming to him from a thousand sources, communicated itself to the family, and Ilbrahim was like a domesticated sunbeam, brightening moody countenances, and chasing away the gloom from the dark corners of the cottage.

On the other hand, as the susceptibility of pleasure is also that of pain, the exuberant cheerfulness of the boy's prevailing temper sometimes yielded to moments of deep depression. His sorrows could not always be followed up to their original source, but most frequently they appeared to flow, though Ilbrahim was young to be sad for such a cause, from wounded love. The flightiness of his mirth rendered him often guilty of offences against the decorum of a Puritan household, and on these occasions he did not invariably escape rebuke. But the slightest word of real bitterness, which he was infallible in distinguishing from pretended anger, seemed to sink into his heart and poison all his enjoyments, till he became sensible that he was entirely forgiven. Of the malice which generally accompanies a superfluity of sensitiveness, Ilbrahim was altogether destitute; when trodden upon, he would not turn; when wounded, he could but die. His mind was wanting in the stamina for self-support; it was a plant that would twine beautifully round something stronger than itself, but if repulsed, or torn away, it had no choice but to wither on the ground. Dorothy's acuteness taught her that severity would crush the spirit of the child, and she nurtured him with the gentle care of one who handles a butterfly. Her husband manifested an equal affection, although it grew daily less productive of familiar caresses.

The feelings of the neighboring people, in regard to the Quaker infant and his protectors, had not undergone a favorable change, in spite of the momentary triumph which the desolate mother had obtained over their sympathies. The scorn and bitterness, of which he was the object, were very grievous to Ilbrahim, especially when any circumstance made him sensible that the children, his equals in age, partook of the enmity of their parents. His tender and social nature had already overflowed in attachments to everything about him, and still there was a residue of unappropriated love, which he yearned to bestow upon the little ones who were taught to hate him. As the warm days of spring came on, Ilbrahim was accustomed to remain for hours silent and inactive within hearing of the children's voices at their play; yet, with his usual delicacy of feeling, he avoided their notice, and would flee and hide himself from the smallest individual among them. Chance, however, at length seemed to open a medium of communication between his heart and theirs; it was by means of a boy about two years older than Ilbrahim, who was injured by a fall from a tree in the vicinity of Pearson's habitation. As the sufferer's own home was at some distance, Dorothy willingly received him under her roof, and became his tender and careful nurse.

Ilbrahim was the unconscious possessor of much skill in physiognomy, and it would have deterred him, in other circumstances, from attempting to make a friend of this boy. The countenance of the latter immediately impressed a beholder disagreeably, but it required some examination to discover that the cause was a very slight distortion of the mouth, and the irregular, broken line and near approach of the eyebrows. Analogous, perhaps, to these trifling deformities was an almost imperceptible twist of every joint, and the uneven prominence of the breast; forming a body, regular in its general outline, but faulty in almost all its details. The disposition of the boy was sullen and reserved, and the village schoolmaster stigmatized him as obtuse in intellect; although, at a later period of life, he evinced ambition and very peculiar talents. But whatever might be his personal or moral irregularities, Ilbrahim's heart seized upon, and clung to him, from the moment that he was brought wounded into the cottage; the child of persecution seemed to compare his own fate with that of the sufferer, and to feel that even different modes of misfortune had created a sort of relationship between them. Food, rest, and the fresh air, for which he languished, were neglected; he nestled continually by the bedside of the little stranger, and, with a fond jealousy, endeavored to be the medium of all the cares that were bestowed upon him. As the boy became convalescent, Ilbrahim contrived games suitable to his situation, or amused him by a faculty which he had perhaps breathed in with the air of his barbaric birthplace. It was that of reciting imaginary adventures, on the spur of the moment, and apparently in inexhaustible succession. His tales were of course monstrous, disjointed, and without aim; but they were curious on account of a vein of human tenderness which ran through them all, and was like a sweet, familiar face, encountered in the midst of wild and unearthly scenery. The auditor paid much attention to these romances, and sometimes interrupted them by brief remarks upon the incidents, displaying shrewdness above his years, mingled with a moral obliquity which grated very harshly against Ilbrahim's instinctive rectitude.

Nothing, however, could arrest the progress of the latter's affection, and there were many proofs that it met with a response from the dark and stubborn nature on which it was lavished. The boy's parents at length removed him, to complete his cure under their own roof.

Ilbrahim did not visit his new friend after his departure; but he made anxious and continual inquiries respecting him, and informed himself of the day when he was to reappear among his playmates. On a pleasant summer afternoon, the children of the neighborhood had assembled in the little forest-crowned amphitheatre behind the meeting-house, and the recovering invalid was there, leaning on a staff. The glee of a score of untainted bosoms was heard in light and airy voices, which danced among the trees like sunshine become audible; the grown men of this weary world, as they journeyed by the spot, marvelled why life, beginning in such brightness, should proceed in gloom; and their hearts, or their imaginations, answered them and said, that the bliss of childhood gushes from its innocence. But it happened that an unexpected addition was made to the heavenly little band. It was Ilbrahim, who came toward the children with a look of sweet confidence on his fair and spiritual face, as if, having manifested his love to one of them, he had no longer to fear a repulse from their society. A hush came over their mirth the moment they beheld him, and they stood whispering to each other while he drew nigh; but, all at once, the devil of their fathers entered into the unbreeched fanatics, and sending up a fierce, shrill cry, they rushed upon the poor Quaker child. In an instant, he was the centre of a brood of baby-fiends, who lifted sticks against him, pelted him with stones, and displayed an instinct of destruction far more loathsome than the blood-thirstiness of manhood.

The invalid, in the meanwhile, stood apart from the tumult, crying out with a loud voice, "Fear not, Ilbrahim, come hither and take my hand"; and his unhappy friend endeavored to obey him. After watching the victim's struggling approach with a calm smile and unabashed eye, the foul-hearted little villain lifted his staff, and struck Ilbrahim on the mouth, so forcibly that the blood issued in a stream. The poor child's arms had been raised to guard his head from the storm of blows; but now he dropped them at once. His persecutors beat him down, trampled upon him, dragged him by his long, fair locks, and Ilbrahim was on the point of becoming as veritable a martyr as ever entered bleeding into heaven. The uproar, however, attracted the notice of a few neighbors, who put themselves to the trouble of rescuing the little heretic, and of conveying him to Pearson's door.

Ilbrahim's bodily harm was severe, but long and careful nursing accomplished his recovery; the injury done to his sensitive spirit was more serious, though not so visible. Its signs were principally of a negative character, and to be discovered only by those who had previously known him. His gait was thenceforth slow, even, and unvaried by the sudden bursts of sprightlier motion, which had once corresponded to his overflowing gladness; his countenance was heavier, and its former play of expression, the dance of sunshine reflected from moving water, was destroyed by the cloud over his existence; his notice was attracted in a far less degree by passing events, and he appeared to find greater difficulty in comprehending what was new to him, than at a happier period. A stranger, founding his judgment upon these circumstances, would have said that the dulness of the child's intellect widely contradicted the promise of his features; but the secret was in the direction of Ilbrahim's thoughts, which were brooding within him when they should naturally have been wandering abroad. An attempt of Dorothy to revive his former sportiveness was the single occasion on which his quiet demeanor yielded to a violent display of grief; he burst into passionate weeping, and ran and hid himself, for his heart had become so miserably sore that even the hand of kindness tortured it like fire. Sometimes, at night and probably in his dreams, he was heard to cry, "Mother! mother!" as if her place, which a stranger had supplied while Ilbrahim was happy, admitted of no substitute in his extreme affliction. Perhaps, among the many life-weary wretches then upon the earth, there was not one who combined innocence and misery like this poor, broken-hearted infant, so soon the victim of his own heavenly nature.

While this melancholy change had taken place in Ilbrahim, one of an earlier origin and of different character had come to its perfection in his adopted father. The incident with which this tale commences found Pearson in a state of religious dulness, yet mentally disquieted, and longing for a more fervid faith than he possessed. The first effect of his kindness to Ilbrahim was to produce a softened feeling, and incipient love for the child's whole sect; but joined to this, and resulting perhaps from self-suspicion, was a proud and ostentatious contempt of their tenets and practical extravagances. In the course of much thought, however, for the subject struggled irresistibly into his mind, the foolishness of the doctrine began to be less evident, and the points which had particularly offended his reason assumed another aspect, or vanished entirely away. The work within him appeared to go on even while he slept, and that which had been a doubt, when he laid down to rest, would often hold the place of a truth, confirmed by some forgotten demonstration, when he recalled his thoughts in the morning. But while he was thus becoming assimilated to the enthusiasts, his contempt, in no wise decreasing toward them, grew very fierce against himself; he imagined, also, that every face of his acquaintance wore a sneer, and that every word addressed to him was a gibe. Such was his state of mind at the period of Ilbrahim's misfortune; and the emotions consequent upon that event completed the change, of which the child had been the original instrument.

In the meantime, neither the fierceness of the persecutors, nor the infatuation of their victims, had decreased. The dungeons were never empty; the streets of almost every village echoed daily with a lash; the life of a woman, whose mild and Christian spirit no cruelty could imbitter, had been sacrificed; and more innocent blood was yet to pollute the hands that were so often raised in prayer. Early after the Restoration, the English Quakers represented to Charles II. that a "vein of blood was open in his dominions"; but though the displeasure of the voluptuous king was roused, his interference was not prompt. And now the tale must stride forward over many months, leaving Pearson to encounter ignominy and misfortune; his wife to a firm endurance of a thousand sorrows; poor Ilbrahim to pine and droop like a cankered rosebud; his mother to wander on a mistaken errand, neglectful of the holiest trust which can be committed to a woman.

A winter evening, a night of storm, had darkened over Pearson's habitation, and there were no cheerful faces to drive the gloom from his broad hearth. The fire, it is true, sent forth a glowing heat and a ruddy light, and large logs, dripping with half-melted snow, lay ready to be cast upon the embers. But the apartment was saddened in its aspect by the absence of much of the homely wealth which had once adorned it; for the exaction of repeated fines, and his own neglect of temporal affairs, had greatly impoverished the owner. And with the furniture of peace, the implements of war had likewise disappeared; the sword was broken, the helm and cuirass were cast away forever; the soldier had done with battles, and might not lift so much as his naked hand to guard his head. But the Holy Book remained, and the table on which it rested was drawn before the fire, while two of the persecuted sect sought comfort from its pages.

He who listened, while the other read, was the master of the house, now emaciated in form, and altered as to the expression and healthiness of his countenance; for his mind had dwelt too long among visionary thoughts, and his body had been worn by imprisonment and stripes. The hale and weather-beaten old man, who sat beside him, had sustained less injury from a far longer course of the same mode of life. In person he was tall and dignified, and, which alone would have made him hateful to the Puritans, his gray locks fell from beneath the broad-brimmed hat, and rested on his shoulders. As the old man read the sacred page, the snow drifted against the windows, or eddied in at the crevices of the door, while a blast kept laughing in the chimney, and the blaze leaped fiercely up to seek it. And sometimes, when the wind struck the hill at a certain angle, and swept down by the cottage across the wintry plain, its voice was the most doleful that can be conceived; it came as if the Past were speaking, as if the Dead had contributed each a whisper, as if the Desolation of Ages were breathed in that one lamenting sound.

The Quaker at length closed the book, retaining however his hand between the pages which he had been reading, while he looked steadfastly at Pearson. The attitude and features of the latter might have indicated the endurance of bodily pain; he leaned his forehead on his hands, his teeth were firmly closed, and his frame was tremulous at intervals with a nervous agitation.

"Friend Tobias," inquired the old man, compassionately, "hast thou found no comfort in these many blessed passages of Scripture?"

"Thy voice has fallen on my ear like a sound afar off and indistinct," replied Pearson, without lifting his eyes. "Yea, and when I have hearkened carefully, the words seemed cold and lifeless, and intended for another and a lesser grief than mine. Remove the book," he added, in a tone of sullen bitterness. "I have no part in its consolations, and they do but fret my sorrow the more."

"Nay, feeble brother, be not as one who hath never known the light," said the elder Quaker, earnestly, but with mildness. "Art thou he that wouldst be content to give all, and endure all, for conscience' sake; desiring even peculiar trials, that thy faith might be purified, and thy heart weaned from worldly desires? And wilt thou sink beneath an affliction which happens alike to them that have their portion here below, and to them that lay up treasure in heaven? Faint not, for thy burden is yet light."

"It is heavy! It is heavier than I can bear!" exclaimed Pearson, with the impatience of a variable spirit. "From my youth upward I have been a man marked out for wrath; and year by year, yea, day after day, I have endured sorrows, such as others know not in their lifetime. And now I speak not of the love that has been turned to hatred, the honor to ignominy, the ease and plentifulness of all things to danger, want, and nakedness. All this I could have borne, and counted myself blessed. But when my heart was desolate with many losses, I fixed it upon the child of a stranger, and he became dearer to me than all my buried ones; and now he too must die, as if my love were poison. Verily, I am an accursed man, and I will lay me down in the dust, and lift up my head no more."

"Thou sinnest, brother, but it is not for me to rebuke thee; for I also have had my hours of darkness, wherein I have murmured against the cross," said the old Quaker. He continued, perhaps in the hope of distracting his companion's thoughts from his own sorrows. "Even of late was the light obscured within me, when the men of blood had banished me on pain of death, and the constables led me onward from village to village, toward the wilderness. A strong and cruel hand was wielding the knotted cords; they sunk deep into the flesh, and thou mightst have tracked every reel and totter of my footsteps by the blood that followed. As we went on—"

"Have I not borne all this; and have I murmured?" interrupted Pearson, impatiently.

"Nay, friend, but hear me," continued the other. "As we journeyed on, night darkened on our path, so that no man could see the rage of the persecutors, or the constancy of my endurance, though Heaven forbid that I should glory therein. The lights began to glimmer in the cottage windows, and I could discern the inmates as they gathered in comfort and security, every man with his wife and children by their own evening hearth. At length we came to a tract of fertile land; in the dim light, the forest was not visible around it; and behold! there was a straw-thatched dwelling, which bore the very aspect of my home, far over the wild ocean, far in our own England. Then came bitter thoughts upon me; yea, remembrances that were like death to my soul. The happiness of my early days was painted to me; the disquiet of my manhood, the altered faith of my declining years. I remembered how I had been moved to go forth a wanderer, when my daughter, the youngest, the dearest of my flock, lay on her dying bed, and—"

"Couldst thou obey the command at such a moment?" exclaimed Pearson, shuddering.

"Yea, yea," replied the old man, hurriedly. "I was kneeling by her bedside when the voice spoke loud within me; but immediately I rose, and took my staff, and gat me gone. O, that it were permitted me to forget her woful look, when I thus withdrew my arm, and left her journeying through the dark valley alone! for her soul was faint, and she had leaned upon my prayers. Now in that night of horror I was assailed by the thought that I had been an erring Christian, and a cruel parent; yea, even my daughter, with her pale, dying features, seemed to stand by me and whisper, 'Father, you are deceived; go home and shelter your gray head.' O Thou, to whom I have looked in my furthest wanderings," continued the Quaker, raising his agitated eyes to Heaven, "inflict not upon the bloodiest of our persecutors the unmitigated agony of my soul, when I believed that all I had done and suffered for thee was at the instigation of a mocking fiend! But I yielded not; I knelt down and wrestled with the tempter, while the scourge bit more fiercely into the flesh. My prayer was heard, and I went on in peace and joy toward the wilderness."

The old man, though his fanaticism had generally all the calmness of reason, was deeply moved while reciting this tale; and his unwonted emotion seemed to rebuke and keep down that of his companion. They sat in silence, with their faces to the fire, imagining perhaps, in its red embers, new scenes of persecution yet to be encountered. The snow still drifted hard against the windows, and sometimes, as the blaze of the logs had gradually sunk, came down the spacious chimney and hissed upon the hearth. A cautious footstep might now and then be heard in a neighboring apartment, and the sound invariably drew the eyes of both Quakers to the door which led thither. When a fierce and riotous gust of wind had led his thoughts, by a natural association, to homeless travellers on such a night, Pearson resumed the conversation.

"I have well-nigh sunk under my own share of this trial," observed he, sighing heavily; "yet I would that it might be doubled to me, if so the child's mother could be spared. Her wounds have been deep and many, but this will be the sorest of all."

"Fear not for Catharine," replied the old Quaker, "for I know that valiant woman, and have seen how she can bear the cross. A mother's heart, indeed, is strong in her, and may seem to contend mightily with her faith; but soon she will stand up and give thanks that her son has been thus early an accepted sacrifice. The boy hath done his work, and she will feel that he is taken hence in kindness both to him and her. Blessed, blessed are they that with so little suffering can enter into peace!"

The fitful rush of the wind was now disturbed by a portentous sound; it was a quick and heavy knocking at the outer door. Pearson's wan countenance grew paler, for many a visit of persecution had taught him what to dread; the old man, on the other hand, stood up erect, and his glance was firm as that of the tried soldier who awaits his enemy.

"The men of blood have come to seek me," he observed, with calmness. "They have heard how I was moved to return from banishment; and now am I to be led to prison, and thence to death. It is an end I have long looked for. I will open unto them, lest they say, 'Lo, he feareth!'"

"Nay, I will present myself before them," said Pearson, with recovered fortitude. "It may be that they seek me alone, and know not that thou abidest with me."

"Let us go boldly, both one and the other," rejoined his companion. "It is not fitting that thou or I should shrink."

They therefore proceeded through the entry to the door, which they opened, bidding the applicant, "Come in, in God's name!" A furious blast of wind drove the storm into their faces, and extinguished the lamp; they had barely time to discern a figure, so white from head to foot with the drifted snow, that it seemed like Winter's self, come in human shape to seek refuge from its own desolation.

"Enter, friend, and do thy errand, be it what it may," said Pearson. "It must needs be pressing, since thou comest on such a bitter night."

"Peace be with this household," said the stranger, when they stood on the floor of the inner apartment.

Pearson started, the elder Quaker stirred the slumbering embers of the fire, till they sent up a clear and lofty blaze; it was a female voice that had spoken; it was a female form that shone out, cold and wintry, in that comfortable light.

"Catharine, blessed woman," exclaimed the old man, "art thou come to this darkened land again? art thou come to bear a valiant testimony as in former years? The scourge hath not prevailed against thee, and from the dungeon hast thou come forth triumphant; but strengthen, strengthen now thy heart, Catharine, for Heaven will prove thee yet this once, ere thou go to thy reward."

"Rejoice, friends!" she replied. "Thou who hast long been of our people, and thou whom a little child hath led to us, rejoice! Lo! I come, the messenger of glad tidings, for the day of persecution is overpast. The heart of the king, even Charles, hath been moved in gentleness toward us, and he hath sent forth his letters to stay the hands of the men of blood. A ship's company of our friends hath arrived at yonder town, and I also sailed joyfully among them."

As Catharine spoke, her eyes were roaming about the room, in search of him for whose sake security was dear to her. Pearson made a silent appeal to the old man, nor did the latter shrink from the painful task assigned him.

"Sister," he began, in a softened yet perfectly calm tone, "thou tellest us of His love, manifested in temporal good; and now must we speak to thee of that selfsame love, displayed in chastenings. Hitherto, Catharine, thou hast been as one journeying in a darksome and difficult path, and leading an infant by the hand; fain wouldst thou have looked heavenward continually, but still the cares of that little child have drawn thine eyes and thy affections to the earth. Sister! go on rejoicing, for his tottering footsteps shall impede thine own no more."

But the unhappy mother was not thus to be consoled; she shook like a leaf, she turned white as the very snow that hung drifted into her hair. The firm old man extended his hand and held her up, keeping his eye upon hers, as if to repress any outbreak of passion.

"I am a woman, I am but a woman; will He try me above my strength?" said Catharine very quickly, and almost in a whisper. "I have been wounded sore; I have suffered much; many things in the body, many in the mind; crucified in myself, and in them that were dearest to me. Surely," added she, with a long shudder, "He hath spared me in this one thing." She broke forth with sudden and irrepressible violence, "Tell me, man of cold heart, what has God done to me? Hath he cast me down, never to rise again? Hath he crushed my very heart in his hand? And thou, to whom I committed my child, how hast thou fulfilled thy trust? Give me back the boy, well, sound, alive, alive; or earth and Heaven shall avenge me!"

The agonized shriek of Catharine was answered by the faint, the very faint voice of a child.

On this day it had become evident to Pearson, to his aged guest, and to Dorothy that Ilbrahim's brief and troubled pilgrimage drew near its close. The two former would willingly have remained by him, to make use of the prayers and pious discourses which they deemed appropriate to the time, and which, if they be impotent as to the departing traveller's reception in the world whither it goes, may at least sustain him in bidding adieu to earth. But though Ilbrahim uttered no complaint, he was disturbed by the faces that looked upon him; so that Dorothy's entreaties, and their own conviction that the child's feet might tread heaven's pavement and not soil it, had induced the two Quakers to remove. Ilbrahim then closed his eyes and grew calm, and, except for now and then a kind and low word to his nurse, might have been thought to slumber. As nightfall came on, however, and the storm began to rise, something seemed to trouble the repose of the boy's mind, and to render his sense of hearing active and acute. If a passing wind lingered to shake the casement, he strove to turn his head toward it; if the door jarred to and fro upon its hinges, he looked long and anxiously thitherward; if the heavy voice of the old man, as he read the Scriptures, rose but a little higher, the child almost held his dying breath to listen; if a snowdrift swept by the cottage, with a sound like the trailing of a garment, Ilbrahim seemed to watch that some visitant should enter.

But, after a little time, he relinquished whatever secret hope had agitated him, and, with one low, complaining whisper, turned his cheek upon the pillow. He then addressed Dorothy with his usual sweetness, and besought her to draw near him; she did so, and Ilbrahim took her hand in both of his, grasping it with a gentle pressure, as if to assure himself that he retained it. At intervals, and without disturbing the repose of his countenance, a very faint trembling passed over him from head to foot, as if a mild but somewhat cool wind had breathed upon him, and made him shiver. As the boy thus led her by the hand, in his quiet progress over the borders of eternity, Dorothy almost imagined that she could discern the near, though dim delightfulness of the home he was about to reach; she would not have enticed the little wanderer back, though she bemoaned herself that she must leave him and return. But just when Ilbrahim's feet were pressing on the soil of Paradise, he heard a voice behind him, and it recalled him a few, few paces of the weary path which he had travelled. As Dorothy looked upon his features, she perceived that their placid expression was again disturbed; her own thoughts had been so wrapped in him, that all sounds of the storm, and of human speech, were lost to her; but when Catharine's shriek pierced through the room, the boy strove to raise himself.

"Friend, she is come! Open unto her!" cried he.

In a moment, his mother was kneeling by the bedside; she drew Ilbrahim to her bosom, and he nestled there, with no violence of joy, but contentedly, as if he were hushing himself to sleep. He looked into her face, and, reading its agony, said, with feeble earnestness, "Mourn not, dearest mother. I am happy now." And with these words, the gentle boy was dead.

The king's mandate to stay the New England persecutors was effectual in preventing further martyrdoms; but the colonial authorities, trusting in the remoteness of their situation, and perhaps in the supposed instability of the royal government, shortly renewed their severities in all other respects. Catharine's fanaticism had become wilder by the sundering of all human ties; and wherever a scourge was lifted, there was she to receive the blow; and whenever a dungeon was unbarred, thither she came, to cast herself upon the floor. But in process of time, a more Christian spirit—a spirit of forbearance, though not of cordiality or approbation—began to pervade the land in regard to the persecuted sect. And then, when the rigid old Pilgrims eyed her rather in pity than in wrath; when the matrons fed her with the fragments of their children's food, and offered her a lodging on a hard and lowly bed; when no little crowd of schoolboys left their sports to cast stones after the roving enthusiast—then did Catharine return to Pearson's dwelling, and made that her home.

As if Ilbrahim's sweetness yet lingered round his ashes, as if his gentle spirit came down from heaven to teach his parent a true religion, her fierce and vindictive nature was softened by the same griefs which had once irritated it. When the course of years had made the features of the unobtrusive mourner familiar in the settlement, she became a subject of not deep, but general interest; a being on whom the otherwise superfluous sympathies of all might be bestowed. Every one spoke of her with that degree of pity which it is pleasant to experience, every one was ready to do her the little kindnesses, which are not costly, yet manifest good-will; and when at last she died, a long train of her once bitter persecutors followed her, with decent sadness and tears that were not painful, to her place by Ilbrahim's green and sunken grave.

THE ANGEL

By HANS CHRISTIAN ANDERSEN

Whenever a good child dies, an angel from heaven comes down to earth, and takes the dead child in his arms, spreads out his great white wings, and flies away over all the places the child has loved, and picks quite a handful of flowers, which he carries up to the Almighty, that they may bloom in heaven more brightly than on earth. And the Father presses all the flowers to His heart; but He kisses the flower that pleases him best, and the flower is then endowed with a voice, and can join in the great chorus of praise!

"See"—this is what an angel said, as he carried a dead child up to heaven, and the child heard, as if in a dream, and they went on over the regions of home where the little child had played, and they came through gardens with beautiful flowers—"which of these shall we take with us to plant in heaven?" asked the angel.

Now there stood near them a slender, beautiful rose bush; but a wicked hand had broken the stem, so that all the branches, covered with half-opened buds, were hanging drooping around, quite withered.

"The poor rose bush!" said the child. "Take it, that it may bloom up yonder."

And the angel took it, and kissed the child, and the little one half opened his eyes. They plucked some of the rich flowers, but also took with them the despised buttercup and the wild pansy.

"Now we have flowers," said the child.

And the angel nodded, but he did not yet fly upward to heaven. It was night and quite silent. They remained in the great city; they floated about there in a small street, where lay whole heaps of straw, ashes, and sweepings, for it had been removal-day. There lay fragments of plates, bits of plaster, rags, and old hats, and all this did not look well. And the angel pointed amid all this confusion to a few fragments of a flower-pot, and to a lump of earth which had fallen out, and which was kept together by the roots of a great dried field flower, which was of no use, and had therefore been thrown out into the street.

"We will take that with us," said the angel. "I will tell you why, as we fly onward.

"Down yonder in the narrow lane, in the low cellar, lived a poor sick boy; from his childhood he had been bedridden. When he was at his best he could go up and down the room a few times, leaning on crutches; that was the utmost he could do. For a few days in summer the sunbeams would penetrate for a few hours to the ground of the cellar, and when the poor boy sat there and the sun shone on him, and he looked at the red blood in his three fingers, as he held them up before his face, he would say, 'Yes, to-day he has been out.' He knew the forest with its beautiful vernal green only from the fact that the neighbor's son brought him the first green branch of a beech-tree, and he held that up over his head, and dreamed he was in the beech wood where the sun shone and the birds sang. On a spring day the neighbor's boy also brought him field flowers, and among these was, by chance, one to which the root was hanging; and so it was planted in a flower-pot, and placed by the bed, close to the window. And the flower had been planted by a fortunate hand; and it grew, threw out new shoots, and bore flowers every year. It became as a splendid flower-garden to the sickly boy—his little treasure here on earth. He watered it, and tended it, and took care that it had the benefit of every ray of sunlight, down to the last that struggled in through the narrow window; and the flower itself was woven into his dreams, for it grew for him and gladdened his eyes, and spread its fragrance about him; and toward it he turned in death when the Father called him. He has now been with the Almighty for a year; for a year the flower has stood forgotten in the window, and is withered; and thus, at the removal, it has been thrown out into the dust of the street. And this is the flower, the poor withered flower, which we have taken into our nosegay; for this flower has given more joy than the richest flower in a Queen's garden!"

"But how do you know all this?" asked the child which the angel was carrying to heaven.

"I know it," said the angel, "for I myself was that little boy who walked on crutches! I know my flower well!"

And the child opened his eyes and looked into the glorious, happy face of the angel; and at the same moment they entered the regions where there is peace and joy. And the Father pressed the dead child to His bosom, and then it received wings like the angel, and flew hand in hand with him. And the Almighty pressed all the flowers to His heart; but He kissed the dry withered field flower, and it received a voice and sang with all the angels hovering around—some near, and some in wider circles, and some in infinite distance, but all equally happy. And they all sang, little and great, the good happy child, and the poor field flower that had lain there withered, thrown among the dust, in the rubbish of the removal-day, in the narrow, dark lane.

THE RED SHOES

By HANS CHRISTIAN ANDERSEN

There once was a little girl; a very nice pretty little girl. But in summer she had to go barefoot, because she was poor, and in winter she wore thick wooden shoes, so that her little instep became quite red, altogether red.

In the middle of the village lived an old shoemaker's wife; she sat, and sewed, as well as she could, a pair of little shoes, of old strips of red cloth; they were clumsy enough, but well meant, and the little girl was to have them. The little girl's name was Karen.

On the day when her mother was buried she received the red shoes and wore them for the first time. They were certainly not suited for mourning; but she had no others, and therefore thrust her little bare feet into them and walked behind the plain deal coffin.

Suddenly a great carriage came by, and in the carriage sat an old lady; she looked at the little girl and felt pity for her and said to the clergyman:

"Give me the little girl and I will provide for her."

Karen thought this was for the sake of the shoes; but the old lady declared they were hideous; and they were burned. But Karen herself was clothed neatly and properly: she was taught to read and to sew, and the people said she was agreeable. But her mirror said, "You are much more than agreeable; you are beautiful."

Once the Queen travelled through the country, and had her little daughter with her; and the daughter was a Princess. And the people flocked toward the castle, and Karen too was among them; and the little Princess stood in a fine white dress at a window, and let herself be gazed at. She had neither train nor golden crown, but she wore splendid red morocco shoes; they were certainly far handsomer than those the shoemaker's wife had made for little Karen. Nothing in the world can compare with red shoes!

Now Karen was old enough to be confirmed: new clothes were made for her, and she was to have new shoes. The rich shoemaker in the town took the measure of her little feet; this was done in his own house, in his little room, and there stood great glass cases with neat shoes and shining boots. It had quite a charming appearance, but the old lady could not see well, and therefore took no pleasure in it. Among the shoes stood a red pair, just like those which the princess had worn. How beautiful they were! The shoemaker also said they had been made for a Count's child, but they had not fitted.

"That must be patent leather," observed the old lady, "the shoes shine so!"

"Yes, they shine!" replied Karen; and they fitted her, and were bought. But the old lady did not know that they were red; for she would never have allowed Karen to go to the confirmation in red shoes; and that is what Karen did.

Every one was looking at her shoes. And when she went across the church porch, toward the door of the choir, it seemed to her as if the old pictures on the tombstones, the portraits of clergymen and clergymen's wives, in their stiff collars and long black garments, fixed their eyes upon her red shoes. And she thought of her shoes only, when the priest laid his hand upon her head and spoke holy words. And the organ pealed solemnly, the children sang with their fresh sweet voices, and the old preceptor sang too; but Karen thought only of her red shoes.

In the afternoon the old lady was informed by everyone that the shoes were red; and she said it was naughty and unsuitable, and that when Karen went to church in future, she should always go in black shoes, even if they were old.

Next Sunday was sacrament Sunday. And Karen looked at the black shoes, and looked at the red ones—looked at them again—and put on the red ones.

The sun shone gloriously; Karen and the old lady went along the footpath through the fields, and it was rather dusty.

By the church door stood an old invalid soldier with a crutch and a long beard; the beard was rather red than white, for it was red altogether; and he bowed down almost to the ground, and asked the old lady if he might dust her shoes. And Karen also stretched out her little foot.

"Look, what pretty dancing shoes!" said the old soldier. "Fit so tightly when you dance!"

And he tapped the soles with his hand. And the old lady gave the soldier an alms, and went into the church with Karen.

And every one in the church looked at Karen's red shoes, and all the pictures looked at them. And while Karen knelt in the church she only thought of her red shoes; and she forgot to sing her psalm, and forgot to say her prayer.

Now all the people went out of church, and the old lady stepped into her carriage. Karen lifted up her foot to step in too; then the old soldier said:

"Look, what beautiful dancing shoes!"

And Karen could not resist: she was obliged to dance a few steps; and when she once began, her legs went on dancing. It was just as though the shoes had obtained power over her. She danced round the corner of the church—she could not help it; the coachman was obliged to run behind her and seize her; he lifted her into the carriage, but her feet went on dancing, so that she kicked the good old lady violently. At last they took off her shoes, and her legs became quiet.

At home the shoes were put away in a cupboard; but Karen could not resist looking at them.

Now the old lady became very ill, and it was said she would not recover. She had to be nursed, and waited on: and this was no one's duty so much as Karen's. But there was to be a great ball in the town, and Karen was invited. She looked at the old lady who could not recover; she looked at the red shoes, and thought there would be no harm in it. She put on the shoes, and that she might very well do; but they went to the ball and began to dance.

But when she wished to go to the right hand, the shoes danced to the left, and when she wanted to go upstairs the shoes danced downward, down into the street and out at the town gate. She danced, and was obliged to dance, till she danced straight out into the dark wood.

There was something glistening up among the trees, and she thought it was the moon, for she saw a face. But it was the old soldier with the red beard: he sat and nodded, and said:

"Look, what beautiful dancing-shoes!"

Then she was frightened, and wanted to throw away the red shoes; but they clung fast to her. And she tore off her stockings; but the shoes had grown fast to her feet. And she danced and was compelled to go dancing over field and meadow, in rain and sunshine, by night and by day; but it was most dreadful at night.

She danced out into the open churchyard; but the dead there do not dance; they have far better things to do. She wished to sit down on the poor man's grave, where the bitter fern grows; but there was no peace nor rest for her. And when she danced toward the open church door, she saw there an angel in long white garments, with wings that reached from his shoulders to his feet; his countenance was serious and stern, and in his hand he held a sword that was broad and gleaming.

"Thou shalt dance!" he said—"dance on thy red shoes, till thou art pale and cold, and till thy body shrivels to a skeleton. Thou shalt dance from door to door, and where proud, haughty children dwell, shalt thou knock, that they may hear thee, and be afraid of thee! Thou shalt dance, dance!"

"Mercy!" cried Karen.

But she did not hear what the angel answered, for the shoes carried her away—carried her through the door on to the field, over stock and stone, and she was always obliged to dance.

One morning she danced past a door which she knew well. There was a sound of psalm-singing within, and a coffin was carried out, adorned with flowers. Then she knew that the old lady was dead, and she felt that she was deserted by all, and condemned by the angel of heaven.

She danced, and was compelled to dance—to dance in the dark night. The shoes carried her on over thorn and brier; she scratched herself till she bled; she danced away across the heath to a little lonely house. Here she knew the executioner dwelt; and she tapped with her fingers on the panes, and called:

"Come out, come out! I cannot come in for I must dance!"

And the executioner said:

"You probably don't know who I am? I cut off the bad people's heads with my axe, and mark how my axe rings!"

"Do not strike off my head," said Karen, "for if you do I cannot repent of my sin. But strike off my feet with the red shoes!"

And then she confessed all her sin, and the executioner cut off her feet with the red shoes; but the shoes danced away with the little feet over the fields and into the deep forest.

And he cut her a pair of wooden feet, with crutches, and taught her a psalm, which the criminals always sing; and she kissed the hand that had held the axe, and went away across the heath.

"Now I have suffered pain enough for the red shoes," said she. "Now I will go into the church, that they may see me."

And she went quickly toward the church door, but when she came there the red shoes danced before her, so that she was frightened, and turned back.

The whole week through she was sorrowful, and wept many bitter tears; but when Sunday came she said:

"Now I have suffered and striven enough! I think that I am just as good as many of those who sit in the church and carry their heads high."

And then she went boldly on; but she did not get further than the churchyard gate before she saw the red shoes dancing along before her; then she was seized with terror, and turned back, and repented of her sin right heartily.

And she went to the parsonage, and begged to be taken there as a servant. She promised to be industrious, and to do all she could; she did not care for wages, and only wished to be under a roof and with good people. The clergyman's wife pitied her, and took her into her service. And she was industrious and thoughtful. Silently she sat and listened when in the evening the pastor read the Bible aloud. All the little ones were very fond of her; but when they spoke of dress and splendor and beauty, she would shake her head.

Next Sunday they all went to church, and she was asked if she wished to go too, but she looked sadly, with tears in her eyes, at her crutches. And then the others went to hear God's word; but she went alone into her little room, which was only large enough to contain her bed and a chair. And here she sat with her hymn-book; and as she read it with a pious mind, the wind bore the notes of the organ over to her from the church; and she lifted up her face, wet with tears, and said:

"O Lord, help me!"

Then the sun shone so brightly; and before her stood the angel in the white garments, the same as she had seen that night at the church door. But he no longer grasped the sharp sword; he held a green branch covered with roses; and he touched the ceiling, and it rose up high, and wherever he touched it a golden star gleamed forth; and he touched the walls, and they spread forth widely, and she saw the organ which was pealing its rich sounds; and she saw the old pictures of clergymen and their wives; and the congregation sat in the decorated seats, and sang from their hymn-books.

The church had come to the poor girl in her narrow room, or her chamber had become a church. She sat in the chair with the rest of the clergyman's people; and when they had finished the psalm, and looked up, they nodded and said:

"That was right that you came here, Karen."

"It was mercy!" said she.

And the organ sounded its glorious notes; and the children's voices singing in the chorus sounded sweet and lovely; the clear sunshine streamed so warm through the window upon the chair in which Karen sat; and her heart became so filled with sunshine, peace, and joy, that it broke. Her soul flew on the sunbeams to heaven; and there was nobody who asked after the RED SHOES.

THE LOVLIEST ROSE IN THE WORLD

By HANS CHRISTIAN ANDERSEN

Once there reigned a Queen, in whose garden were found the most glorious flowers at all seasons and from all the lands in the world; but especially she loved roses, and therefore she possessed the most various kinds of this flower, from the wild dog-rose, with the apple-scented green leaves, to the most splendid Provence rose. They grew against the earth walls, wound themselves round pillars and window-frames, into the passages, and all along the ceiling in all the halls. And the roses were various in fragrance, form, and color.

But care and sorrow dwelt in these halls: the Queen lay upon a sick-bed, and the doctors declared that she must die.

"There is still one thing that can serve her," said the wisest of them. "Bring her the loveliest rose in the world, the one which is the expression of the brightest and purest love; for if that is brought before her eyes ere they close, she will not die."

And young and old came from every side with roses, the loveliest that bloomed in each garden; but they were not the right sort. The flower was to be brought out of the garden of Love; but what rose was it there that expressed the highest and purest love?

And the poets sang of the loveliest rose in the world, and each one named his own; and intelligence was sent far round the land to every heart that beat with love, to every class and condition, and to every age.

"No one has till now named the flower," said the wise man. "No one has pointed out the place where it bloomed in its splendor. They are not the roses from the coffin of Romeo and Juliet, or from the Walburg's grave, though these roses will be ever fragrant in song. They are not the roses that sprouted forth from Winkelried's blood-stained lances, from the blood that flows in a sacred cause from the breast of the hero who dies for his country; though no death is sweeter than this, and no rose redder than the blood that flows then. Nor is it that wondrous flower, to cherish which man devotes, in a quiet chamber, many a sleepless night, and much of his fresh life—the magic flower of science."

"I know where it blooms," said a happy mother, who came with her pretty child to the bedside of the Queen. "I know where the loveliest rose of the world is found! The rose that is the expression of the highest and purest love springs from the blooming cheeks of my sweet child when, strengthened by sleep, it opens its eyes and smiles at me with all its affection!"

"Lovely is this rose; but there is still a lovelier," said the wise man.

"Yes, a far lovelier one," said one of the women. "I have seen it, and a loftier, purer rose does not bloom. I saw it on the cheeks of the Queen. She had taken off her golden crown, and in the long dreary night she was carrying her sick child in her arms: she wept, kissed it, and prayed for her child as a mother prays in the hour of her anguish."

"Holy and wonderful in its might is the white rose of grief; but it is not the one we seek."

"No, the loveliest rose of the world I saw at the altar of the Lord," said the good old Bishop. "I saw it shine as if an angel's face had appeared. The young maidens went to the Lord's Table, and renewed the promise made at their baptism, and roses were blushing, and pale roses shining on their fresh cheeks. A young girl stood there; she looked with all the purity and love of her young spirit up to heaven: that was the expression of the highest and purest love."

"May she be blessed," said the wise man; "but not one of you has yet named to me the loveliest rose of the world."

Then there came into the room a child, the Queen's little son. Tears stood in his eyes and glistened on his cheeks; he carried a great open book, and the binding was of velvet, with great silver clasps.

"Mother!" cried the boy, "only hear what I have read."

And the child sat by the bedside, and read from the book of Him who suffered death on the cross to save men, and even those who were not yet born.

"Greater love there is not" —

And a roseate hue spread over the cheeks of the Queen, and her eyes gleamed, for she saw that from the leaves of the book there bloomed the loveliest rose, that sprang from the blood of Christ shed on the cross.

"I see it!" she said: "he who beholds this, the loveliest rose on earth, shall never die."

A VISION OF THE LAST DAY

By HANS CHRISTIAN ANDERSEN

Of all the days of our life the greatest and most solemn is the day on which we die. Hast thou ever tried to realize that most sure, most portentous hour, the last hour we shall spend on earth?

There was a certain man, an upholder of truth and justice, a Christian man and orthodox, so the world esteemed him. And, in sooth, it may be that some good thing was found in him, since in sleep, amid the visions of the night, it pleased the Father of spirits to reveal him to himself, making manifest to him what he was in truth, namely, one of those who trust in themselves that they are righteous and despise others.

He went to rest, secure that his accounts were right with all men, that he had paid his dues and wrought good works that day; of the secret pride of his heart, of the harsh words that had passed his lips, he took no account at all. And so he slept, and in his sleep Death stood by his bedside, a glorious Angel, strong, spotless, beautiful, but unlike every other angel, stern, unsmiling, pitiless of aspect.

"Thine hour is come, and thou must follow me!" spake Death. And Death's cold finger touched the man's feet, whereupon they became like ice, then touched his forehead, then his heart. And the chain that bound the immortal soul to clay was riven asunder, and the soul was free to follow the Angel of Death.

But during those brief seconds, while yet that awful touch thrilled through feet, and head, and heart, there passed over the dying man, as in great, heaving, ocean waves, the recollection of all that he had wrought and felt in his whole life; just as one shuddering glance into a whirlpool suffices to reveal in thought rapid as lightning, the entire unfathomable depth; just as in one momentary glance at the starry heavens we can conceive the infinite multitude of that glorious host of unknown orbs.

In such a retrospect the terrified sinner shrinks back into himself, and finding there no stay by which to cling, must feel shrinking into infinite nothingness; while the devout soul raises its thoughts to the Almighty, yielding itself up to Him in childlike trust, and praying, "Thy will be done in me!"

But this man had not the childlike mind, neither did he tremble like the sinner; his thoughts were still the self-praising thoughts in which he had fallen asleep. His path, he believed, must lead straight heavenward, and Mercy, the promised Mercy, would open to him the gates.

And, in his dream, the Soul followed the Angel of Death, though not without first casting one wistful glance at the couch where lay, in its white shroud, the lifeless image of clay, still, as it were, bearing the impress of the soul's own individuality. And now they hovered through the air, now glided along the ground. Was it a vast decorated hall they were passing through, or a forest? It seemed hard to tell; Nature, it appeared, was formally set out for show, as in the artificial old French gardens, and amid its strange, carefully arranged scenes, passed and repassed troops of men and women, all clad as for a masquerade.

"Such is human life!" said the Angel of Death.

The figures seemed more or less disguised; those who swept by in the glories of velvet and gold were not all among the noblest or most dignified-looking, neither were all those who wore the garb of poverty insignificant or vulgar. It was a strange masquerade! But most strange it was to see how one and all carefully concealed under their clothing something they would not have others perceive, but in vain, for each was bent upon discovering his neighbor's secret, and they tore and snatched at one another till, now here, now there, some part of an animal was revealed. In one was found the grinning head of an ape, in another the cloven foot of a goat, in a third the poison-fang of a snake, in a fourth the clammy fin of a fish.

All had in them some token of the animal—the animal which is fast rooted in human nature, and which here was seen struggling to burst forth. And, however closely a man might hold his garment over it, the others would never rest till they had rent the hiding veil, and all kept crying out, "Look here! look now! here he is! there she is!"—and every one mockingly laid bare his fellow's shame.

"And what was the animal in me?" inquired the disembodied Soul; and the Angel of Death pointed to a haughty form, around whose head shone a bright, widespread glory of rainbow-colored rays, but at whose heart might be seen lurking, half-hidden, the feet of the peacock; the glory was, in fact, merely the peacock's gaudy tail.

And as they passed on, large, foul-looking birds shrieked out from the boughs of the trees; with clear, intelligible, though harsh, human voices they shrieked, "Thou that walkest with Death, dost remember me?" All the evil thoughts and desires that had nestled within him from his birth until his death now called after him, "Rememberest thou me?"

And the Soul shuddered, recognizing the voices; it could not deny knowledge of the evil thoughts and desires that were now rising up in witness against it.

"In our flesh, in our evil nature, dwelleth no good thing," cried the Soul; "but, at least, thoughts never with me ripened into actions; the world has not seen the evil fruit." And the Soul hurried on to get free from the accusing voices; but the great black fowls swept in circles round, and screamed out their scandalous words louder and louder, as though they would be heard all over the world. And the Soul fled from them like the hunted stag, and at every step stumbled against sharp flint stones that lay in the path. "How came these sharp stones here? They look like mere withered leaves lying on the ground."

"Every stone is for some incautious word thou hast spoken, which lay as a stumbling-block in thy neighbor's path, which wounded thy neighbor's heart far more sorely and deeply than these sharp flints now wound thy feet."

"Alas! I never once thought of that," sighed the Soul.

And those words of the gospel rang through the air, "Judge not, that ye be not judged."

"We have all sinned," said the Soul, recovering from its momentary self-abasement. "I have kept the Law and the Gospel, I have done what I could, I am not as others are!"

And in his dream this man now stood at the gates of heaven, and the Angel who guarded the entrance inquired, "Who art thou? Tell me thy faith, and show it to me in thy works."

"I have faithfully kept the Commandments, I have humbled myself in the eyes of the world, I have preserved myself free from the pollution of intercourse with sinners, I have hated and persecuted evil, and those who practice it, and I would do so still, yea, with fire and sword, had I the power."

"Then thou art one of Mohammed's followers?" said the Angel.

"I? a Mohammedan?—never!"

"'He who strikes with the sword shall perish by the sword,' thus spake the Son; His religion thou knowest not. It may be that thou art one of the children of Israel, whose maxim is, 'An eye for an eye, a tooth for a tooth'—art thou such?"

"I am a Christian."

"I see it not in thy faith or in thine actions. The law of Christ is the law of forgiveness, love, and mercy."

"Mercy!" The gracious echo of that sweet word thrilled through infinite space, the gates of heaven opened, and the Soul hovered toward the realms of endless bliss.

But the flood of light that streamed forth from within was so dazzlingly bright, so transcendently white and pure, that the Soul shrank back as from a two-edged sword, and the hymns and harp-tones of Angels mingled in such exquisite celestial harmony as the earthly mind has not power either to conceive or to endure. And the Soul trembled and bowed itself deeper and deeper, and the heavenly light penetrated it through and through, and it felt to the quick, as it had never truly felt before, the burden of its own pride, cruelty, and sin.

"What I have done of good in the world, that did I because I could not otherwise, but the evil that I did—that was of myself!"

The confession was wrung from him; more and more the man felt dazzled and overpowered by the pure light of heaven; he seemed falling into a measureless abyss, the abyss of his own nakedness and unworthiness. Shrunk into himself, humbled, cast out, unripe for the kingdom of heaven, shuddering at the thought of the just and holy God—hardly dared he to gasp out, "Mercy!"

And the face of the Angel at the portal was turned toward him in softening pity. "Mercy is for them who implore it, not claim it; there is Mercy also for thee. Turn thee, child of man, turn thee back the way thou camest to thy clayey tabernacle; in pity is it given thee to dwell in dust yet a little while. Be no longer righteous in thine own eyes, copy Him who with patience endured the contradiction of sinners, strive and pray that thou mayest become poor in spirit, and so mayest thou yet inherit the Kingdom."

"Holy, loving, glorious forever shalt thou be, O, erring human spirit!"—thus rang the chorus of Angels. And again overpowered by those transcendent melodies, dazzled and blinded by that excess of purest light, the Soul again shrank back into itself. It seemed to be falling an infinite depth; the celestial music grew fainter and fainter, till common earthly sights and sounds dispelled the vision. The rays of the early morning sun falling full on his face, the cheerful crow of the vigilant cock, called the sleeper up to pray.

Inexpressibly humbled, yet thankful, he arose and knelt beside his bed. "Thou, who hast shown me to myself, help me now, that I may not only do justly, but love mercy, and walk humbly with my God. Thou, who hast convicted me of sin, now purify me, strengthen me, that, though ever unworthy of Thy presence, I may yet, supported by Thy Love, dare to ascend into Thine ever lasting light!"

The Vision was his; be the lesson, the prayer, also ours.

THE OLD GRAVESTONE

By HANS CHRISTIAN ANDERSEN

In one of our small trading towns, at that time of year when folk say "The evenings grow long," a whole family was assembled together. The air was still mild and warm; the lamp was lighted, the long curtains hung down before the windows, and bright moonlight prevailed without. They were talking about a big old stone that lay down in the yard, close by the kitchen door, where the servants often placed the kitchen utensils, after they had been cleaned, to dry in the sun, and where the children were fond of playing; it was, in fact, an old gravestone.

"Yes," said the master of the house, "I believe it comes from the old ruined convent chapel; pulpit and gravestones, with all their epitaphs, were sold; my late father bought several of these; the others were broken into paving-stones, but this one was left unused, lying in the yard."

"It is easy to know it for a gravestone," said the eldest of the children. "You can still see on it an mountain-sides and a piece of an angel, but the inscription is almost quite worn out, except the name 'Preben,' and a capital 'S' a little further on, and underneath it 'Martha,' but it is impossible to make out any more, and that you can only read after if has been raining, or when we have washed it."

"Why, then, it must be the gravestone of Preben Swan and his wife!" exclaimed an old man, who by his age might appear the grandfather of everybody in the room. "To be sure, they were among the last that were buried in the old convent churchyard—the grand old couple! Everybody knew them, everybody loved them; they were like king and queen in the town. Folk said they had more than a barrelful of gold, and yet they went about simply clad, in the coarsest cloth, only their linen was always of dazzling whiteness. Yes, that was a charming old pair, Preben and Martha. One was always so glad to see them, sitting together on the bench at the top of their stone staircase, under the old lime-tree's shade. They were so good to the poor! they feasted them, clothed them, and there was good sense and a true Christian spirit in all their benevolence.

"The wife died first; I remember the day quite well; I was then a little boy, and went with my father to see old Preben: the old man was so grieved, he cried like a child. The corpse still lay in her bedroom, close to the chamber where we sat; she looked as if she had just fallen asleep. And the old man told my father how he should now be so lonely, and how many years, they had spent together, and how they had first made acquaintance and came to love each other. As I said before, I was a child, but it moved me strangely to listen to the old man, and watch how he grew more animated as he went on speaking, a faint color coming into his cheeks as he talked of their youthful days, how pretty she had been, how many little innocent tricks he had played, in order to meet her. And when he spoke of his wedding-day his eyes quite sparkled; he seemed to be living his happy time over again—and all the while she was lying dead in the next chamber, an old lady, and he was an old man—ah, how time passes! I was a child then, and now I am as old as Preben Swan. Yes, time and change come to all. I remember as well as possible the funeral-day, and Preben Swan following the coffin. They had had their gravestone carved with names and inscriptions, all except the dates of their death, some years before; that same evening the stone was taken to the grave, and put into its place. The next year the grave had to be reopened, and old Preben rejoined his wife. They did not turn out to be so rich as people had fancied, and what they did leave went to distant relations very far off. The old wooden house, with the bench at the top of the high stone staircase under the lime-tree, was ordered to be pulled down, for it was too ruinous to stand any longer. And afterward, when the convent chapel and cemetery were destroyed, the gravestone of Preben and Martha was sold, like others, to whomsoever chose to buy it. And so now it lies in the yard for the little ones to roll over, and to make a shelf for the kitchen pots and pans. And the paved street now covers the resting-place of old Preben and his wife, and nobody thinks of them any more."

And the old man who related all this shook his head sadly. "Forgotten! All things are forgotten!"

And the rest began to speak of other matters; but the youngest boy, a child with large, grave eyes, crept up on a chair behind the curtains, and looked out into the yard, where the moon shone brightly on the big stone that before had seemed to him flat and uninteresting enough, but now had become to him like a page of a large-sized story-book. For all that the boy had heard concerning Preben and his wife, the stone seemed to contain within it; and he looked first at the stone, and then at the brilliant moon, which looked to him like a bright kind face looking down through the pure still air upon the earth.

"Forgotten! all shall be forgotten!" these words came to his ears from the room; but at that very moment an invisible angel kissed the boy's forehead and softly whispered, "Keep the seed carefully, keep it till the time for ripening. Through thee, child as thou art, shall the half-erased inscription, the crumbling gravestone, stand out in clear, legible characters for generations to come! Through thee shall the old couple again walk arm-in-arm through the ancient gateways, and sit with smiling faces on the bench under the lime tree, greeting rich and poor. The good and the beautiful perish never; they live eternally in tale and song."

"GOOD-FOR-NOTHING"

By HANS CHRISTIAN ANDERSEN

The sheriff stood at the open window; he wore ruffles, and a dainty breastpin decorated the front of his shirt; he was neatly shaven, and a tiny little strip of sticking-plaster covered the little cut he had given himself during the process. "Well, my little man?" quoth he.

The "little man" was no other than the laundress's son, who respectfully took off his cap in passing. His cap was broken in the rim, and adapted to be put into the pocket on occasion; his clothes were poor, but clean, and very neatly mended, and he wore heavy wooden shoes. He stood still when the sheriff spoke, as respectfully as though he stood before the king.

"Ah, you're a good boy, a well-behaved boy!" said the sheriff. "And so your mother is washing down at the river; she isn't good for much. And you're going to her, I see. Ah, poor child!—well, you may go."

And the boy passed on, still holding his cap in his hand, while the wind tossed to and fro his waves of yellow hair. He went through the street, down a little alley to the brook, where his mother stood in the water, at her washing-stool, beating the heavy linen. The water-mill's sluices were opened, and the current was strong; the washing-stool was nearly carried away by it, and the laundress had hard work to strive against it.

"I am very near taking a voyage," she said, "and it is so cold out in the water; for six hours have I been standing here. Have you anything for me?"—and the boy drew forth a phial, which his mother put to her lips. "Ah, that is as good as warm meat, and it is not so dear. O, the water is so cold—but if my strength will but last me out to bring you up honestly, my sweet child!"

At that moment approached an elderly woman, poorly clad, blind of one eye, lame on one leg, and with her hair brushed into one large curl to hide the blind eye—but in vain, the defect was only the more conspicuous. This was "Lame Maren," as the neighbors called her, a friend of the washerwoman's. "Poor thing, slaving and toiling away in the cold water!

it is hard that you should be called names"—for Maren had overheard the sheriff speaking to the child about his own mother— "hard that your boy should be told you are good-for-nothing."

"What! did the sheriff really say so, child?" said the Laundress, and her lips quivered. "So you have a mother who is good-for-nothing! Perhaps he is right, only he should not say so to the child—but I must not complain, for good things have come to me from that house."

"Why yes, you were in service there once, when the sheriff's parents were alive, many years since. There is a grand dinner at the sheriff's to-day," went on Maren; "it would have been put off, though, had not everything been prepared. I heard it from the porter. News came in a letter, an hour ago, that the sheriff's younger brother, at Copenhagen, is dead."

"Dead!" repeated the Laundress, and she turned as white as a corpse.

"What do you care about it?" said Maren. "To be sure, you must have known him, since you served in the house."

"Is he dead? he was the best, the kindest of creatures! indeed, there are not many like him," and the tears rolled down her cheeks. "O, the world is turning round, I feel so ill!" and she clung to the washing-stool for support.

"You are ill, indeed!" cried Maren. "Take care, the stool will overturn. I had better get you home at once."

"But the linen?"

"I will look after that—only lean on me. The boy can stay here and watch it till I come back and wash what is left; it is not much."

The poor laundress's limbs trembled under her. "I have stood too long in the cold water; I have had no food since yesterday. O, my poor child!" and she wept.

The boy cried too, as he sat alone beside the brook, watching the wet linen. Slowly the two women made their way up the little alley and through the street, past the sheriff's house. Just as she reached her humble home, the laundress fell down on the paving-stones, fainting. She was carried upstairs and put to bed. Kind Maren hastened to prepare a cup of warm ale—that was the best medicine in this case, she thought—and then went back to the brook and did the best she could with the linen.

In the evening she was again in the laundress's miserable room. She had begged from the sheriff's cook a few roasted potatoes and a little bit of bacon, for the sick woman. Maren and the boy feasted upon these, but the patient was satisfied with the smell of them—that, she declared, was very nourishing.

Supper over, the boy went to bed, lying crosswise at his mother's feet, with a coverlet made of old carpet-ends, blue and red, sewed together.

The Laundress now felt a little better; the warm ale had strengthened her, the smell of the meat had done her good.

"Now, you good soul," said she to Maren, "I will tell you all about it, while the boy is asleep. That he is already; look at him, how sweetly he looks with his eyes closed; he little thinks how his mother has suffered. May he never feel the like! Well, I was in service with the sheriff's parents when their youngest son, the student, came home; I was a wild young thing then, but honest—that I must say for myself. And the student was so pleasant and merry, a better youth never lived. He was a son of the house, I only a servant, but we became sweethearts—all in honor and honesty—and he told his mother that he loved me; she was like an angel in his eyes, so wise, kind, and loving! And he went away, but his gold ring of betrothal was on my finger. When he was really gone, my mistress called me in to speak to her; so grave, yet so kind she looked, so wisely she spoke, like an angel, indeed. She showed me what a gulf of difference in tastes, habits, arid mind lay between her son and me. 'He sees you now to be good-hearted and pretty, but will you always be the same in his eyes? You have not been educated as he has been; intellectually you cannot rise to his level. I honor the poor,' she continued, 'and I know that in the kingdom of heaven many a poor man will sit in a higher seat than the rich; but that is no reason for breaking the ranks in this world, and you two, left to yourselves, would drive your carriage full tilt against all obstacles till it toppled over with you both. I know that a good honest handicraftsman, Erik, the glove-maker, has been your suitor; he is a widower without children, he is well off; think whether you cannot be content with him.' Every word my mistress spoke went like a knife through my heart, but I knew she was right; I kissed her hand, and shed such bitter tears! But bitterer tears still came when I went into my chamber and lay upon my bed. O, the long, dreary night that followed! Our Lord alone knows what I suffered. Not till I went to church on Sunday did a light break upon my darkness. It seemed providential that as I came out of church I met Erik the glove-maker. There were no more doubts in my mind; he was a good man, and of my own rank. I went straight to him, took his hand, and asked, 'Art thou still in the same mind toward me?'—'Yes, and I shall never be otherwise minded,' he replied.—'Dost thou care to have a girl who likes and honors thee, but does not love thee?'—'I believe love will come,' he said, and so he took my hand. I went home to my mistress; the gold ring that her son had given to me, that I wore all day next my heart, and on my finger at night in bed, I now drew forth; I kissed it till my mouth bled, I gave it to my mistress, and said that next week the bans would be read for me and the glove-maker. My mistress took me in her arms and kissed me; she did not tell me I was good-for-nothing; I was good for something then, it seems, before I had known so much trouble. The wedding was at Candlemastide, and our first year all went well; my husband had apprentices, and you, Maren, helped me in the housework."

"O, and you were such a good mistress!" exclaimed Maren. "Never shall I forget how kind you and your husband were to me."

"Ah, you were with us during our good times! We had no children then. The student I never saw again—yes, once I saw him, but he did not see me. He came to his mother's funeral; I saw him standing by her grave, looking so sad, so ashy pale—but all for his mother's sake. When afterward his father died, he was abroad and did not come to the funeral. Nor has he been here since; he is a lawyer, that I know, and he has never married. But he thought no more of me, and had he seen me, he would certainly have never recognized me, so ugly as I am now. And it is right it should be so."

Then she went on to speak of the bitter days of adversity, when troubles had come upon them in a flood. They had five hundred rix-dollars, and as in their street a house could be bought for two hundred, it was considered a good investment to buy it, take it down, and build it anew. The house was bought; masons and carpenters made an estimate that one thousand and twenty rix-dollars more would be required. Erik arranged to borrow this sum from Copenhagen, but the ship that was to bring him the money was lost, and the money with it. "It was just then that my sweet boy, who lies sleeping here, was born. Then his father fell sick; for three-quarters of a year I had to dress and undress him every day. We went on borrowing and borrowing; all our things had to be sold, one by one; at last Erik died. Since then I have toiled and moiled for the boy's sake, have gone out cleaning and washing, done coarse work or fine, whichever I could get; but I do everything worse and worse; my strength will never return any more; it is our Lord's will! He will take me away, and find better provision for my boy."

She fell asleep. In the morning she seemed better, and fancied she was strong enough to go to her work again. But no sooner did she feel the cold water than a shivering seized her, she felt about convulsively with her hands, tried to step forward, and fell down. Her head lay on the dry bank, but her feet were in the water of the brook, her wooden shoes were carried away by the stream. Here she was found by Maren.

A message had been taken to her lodging that the sheriff wanted her, had something to say to her. It was too late; the poor washerwoman was dead. The letter that had brought the sheriff news of his brother's death also gave an abstract of his will; among other bequests he had left six hundred rix-dollars to the glove-maker's widow, who had formerly served his parents. "There was some love-nonsense between my brother and her," quoth the sheriff. "It is all as well she is out of the way; now it will all come to the boy, and I shall apprentice him to honest folk who will make him a good workman." For whatever the sheriff might do, were it ever so kind an action, he always spoke harshly and unkindly. So he now called the boy to him, promised to provide for him, and told him it was a good thing his mother was dead; she was good-for-nothing!

She was buried in the paupers' churchyard. Maren planted a little rose-tree over the grave; the boy stood by her side the while.

"My darling mother!" he sighed, as the tears streamed down from his eyes. "It was not true that she was good-for-nothing!"

"No, indeed!" cried her old friend, looking up to heaven. "Let the world say she was good-for-nothing; our Lord in his heavenly kingdom will not say so."

"IN THE UTTERMOST PARTS OF THE SEA"

By HANS CHRISTIAN ANDERSEN

Some large ships were sent up toward the North Pole, for the purpose of discovering the boundaries of land and sea, and of trying how far men could make their way.

A year and a day had elapsed; amid mist and ice had they, with great difficulty, steered further and further; the winter had now begun; the sun had set, one long night would continue during many, many weeks. One unbroken plain of ice spread around them; the ships were all fast moored to it; the snow lay about in heaps, and had even shaped itself into cubiform houses, some as big as our barrows, some only just large enough for two or three men to find shelter within. Darkness they could not complain of, for the Northern Lights—Nature's fireworks—now red, now blue, flashed unceasingly, and the snow glistened so brightly.

At times when it was brightest came troops of the natives, strange-looking figures, clad in hairy skins, and with sledges made out of hard fragments of ice; they brought skins to exchange, which the sailors were only too glad to use as warm carpets inside their snow houses, and as beds whereon they could rest under their snowy tents, while outside prevailed an intensity of cold such as we never experience during our severest winters. But the sailors remembered that at home it was still autumn; and they thought of the warm sunbeams and the leaves still clinging to the trees in varied glories of crimson and gold. Their watches told them it was evening, and time for rest, and in one of the snow houses two sailors had already lain down to sleep; the youngest of these two had with him his best home-treasure, the Bible that his grandmother had given him at parting. Every night it lay under his pillow; he had known its contents from childhood, and every day he read a portion; and often as he lay on his couch, he recalled to mind those holy words of comfort, "If I should take the wings of the morning, and remain in the uttermost parts of the sea, even there should Thy hand lead me, and Thy right hand should hold me."

These sublime words of faith were on his lips as he closed his eyes, when sleep came to him, and dreams with sleep—busy, swift-winged dreams, proving that though the body may rest, the soul must ever be awake. First he seemed to hear the melodies of songs dear to him in his home; a mild summer breeze seemed to breathe upon him, and a light shone upon his couch, as though the snowy dome above him had become transparent; he lifted his head, and behold! the dazzling white light was not the white of a snow wall, it came from the large wings of an angel stooping over him, an angel with eyes beaming with love. The angel's form seemed to spring from the pages of the Bible, as from the pitcher of a lily-blossom; he extended his arms, and lo! the narrow walls of the snow-hut sank back like a mist melting before the daylight. Once again the green meadows and autumnal-tinted woods of the sailor's home lay around him, bathed in quiet sunshine; the stork's nest was empty, but the apples still clung to the wild apple-tree; though leaves had fallen, the red hips glistened, and the blackbird whistled in the little green cage that hung in the lowly window of his childhood's home; the blackbird whistled the tune he had taught him, and the old grandmother wound chickweed about the bars of the cage, as her grandson had been wont to do. And the smith's pretty young daughter stood drawing water from the well, and as she nodded to the grandmother, the latter beckoned to her, and held up a letter to show her, a letter that had come that morning from the cold northern lands, from the North Pole itself, where the old woman's grandson now was—safe under God's protecting hand. And the two women, old and young, laughed and wept by turns—and he the while, the young sailor whose body was sleeping amid ice and snow, his spirit roaming in the world of dreams, under the angel's wings, saw and heard it all, and laughed and wept with them. And from the letter these words were read aloud, "Even in the uttermost parts of the sea, His right hand shall hold me fast": and a sweet, solemn music was wafted round him, and the angel drooped his wings; like a soft protecting veil they fell closer over the sleeper.

The dream was ended; all was darkness in the little snow-hut, but the Bible lay under the sailor's head, faith and hope abode in his heart. God was with him, and his home was with him, "even in the uttermost parts of the sea."

"SOMETHING"

By HANS CHRISTIAN ANDERSEN

"I will be Something," declared the eldest of five brothers; "I will be of use in the world; be it ever so humble a position that I may hold, let me be but useful, and that will be Something. I will make bricks; folk cannot do without them, so I shall at least do Something."

"Something very little, though," replied the second brother. "Why, it is as good as nothing! it is work that might be done by a machine. Better be a mason, as I intend to be. Then one belongs to a guild, becomes a citizen, has a banner of one's own. Nay, if all things go well, I may become a master, and have apprentices and workmen under me. That will be Something!"

"It will be nothing at all then, I can tell you that!" rejoined the third. "Think how many different ranks there are in a town far above that of a master-mason. You may be an honest sort of a man, but you will never be a gentleman; gentle and simple; those are the two grand divisions, and you will always be one of the 'simple.' Well, I know better than that. I will be an architect; I will be one of the thinkers, the artists; I will raise myself to the aristocracy of intellect. I may have to begin from the very lowest grade; I may begin as a carpenter's boy, and run about with a paper-cap on my head, to fetch ale for the workmen; I may not enjoy it, but I shall try to imagine it is only a masquerade. 'To-morrow,' I shall say, 'I will go my own way, and others shall not come near me.' Yes, I shall go to the Academy, learn to draw, and be called an architect. That will be Something! I may get a title, perhaps; and I shall build and build, as others before me have done. Yes, that will be Something!"

"But it is Something that I care nothing about," said the fourth. "I should not care to go on, on, in the beaten track, to be a mere copyist; I will be a genius, cleverer than all of you put together; I will create a new style, provide ideas for buildings suited to the climate and materials of our country, suited to our national character, and the requirements of the age."

"But supposing the climate and the materials don't agree," suggested the fifth, "how will you get on then, if they won't co-operate? As for our national character, to be following out that in architecture will be sheer affectation, and the requirements of modern civilization will drive you perfectly mad. I see you will none of you ever be anything, though of course you won't believe me. But do as you please, I shall not be like you. I shall reason over what you execute; there is something ridiculous in everything; I shall find it out, show you yeur faults—that will be Something!"

And he kept his word; and folk said of this fifth brother, "There is something in him, certainly; he has plenty of brains! but he does nothing." But he was content, he was Something.

But what became of the five brothers? We will hear the whole.

The eldest brother, the brickmaker, found that every brick he turned out whole yielded him a tiny copper coin—only copper—but a great many of these small coins, added together, could be converted into a bright silver dollar, and through the power of this, wheresoever he knocked, whether at baker's, butcher's, or tailor's, the door flew open, and he received what he wanted. Such was the virtue of his bricks; some, of course, got broken before they were finished, but a use was found even for these. For up by the trench would poor Mother Margaret fain build herself a little house, if she might; she took all the broken bricks, ay, and she got a few whole ones besides, for a good heart had the eldest brother, though only a brickmaker. The poor thing built her house with her own hands; it was very narrow, its one window was all on one side, the door was too low, and the thatch on the roof might have been laid on better, but it gave her shelter and a home, and could be seen far over the sea, which sometimes burst over the trench in its might, and sprinkled a salt shower over the little house, which kept its place there years after he who made the bricks was dead and gone.

As for the second brother, he learned to build after another fashion, as he had resolved. When he was out of his apprenticeship, he buckled on his knapsack and started, singing as he went, on his travels. He came home again, and became a master in his native town; he built, house after house, a whole street of houses; there they stood, looked well, and were a credit to the town; and these houses soon built him a little house for himself. How? Ask the houses, and they will give you no answer; but the people will answer you and say, "Why, of course, the street built him his house!" It was small enough, and had only a clay floor, but when he and his bride danced over it, the floor grew as smooth as if it had been polished, and from every stone in the wall sprung a flower, that looked as gay as the costliest tapestry. It was a pretty house and a happy wedded pair. The banner of the Masons' Guild waved outside, and workmen and apprentices shouted "Hurra!" Yes, that was Something! and at last he died—that, too, was Something!

Next comes the architect, the third brother. He began as a carpenter's apprentice, and ran about the town on errands, wearing a paper-cap; but he studied industriously at the Academy, and rose steadily upward. If the street full of houses had built a house for his brother the mason, the street took its name from the architect; the handsomest house in the whole street was his—that was Something, and he was Something! His children were gentlemen, and could boast of their "birth"; and when he died, his widow was a widow of condition—that is Something—and his name stood on the corner of the street, and was in everybody's lips—that is Something, too!

Now for the genius, the fourth brother, who wanted to invent something new, something original. Somehow the ground gave way beneath his feet; he fell and broke his neck. But he had a splendid funeral, with music and banners, and flowery paragraphs in the newspapers; and three eulogiums were pronounced over him, each longer than the last, and this would have pleased him mightily, for he loved speechifying of all things. A monument was erected over his grave, only one story high—but that is Something!

So now he was dead, as well as his three elder brothers; the youngest, the critic, outlived them all, and that was as it should be, for thus he had the last word, which to him was a matter of the greatest importance. "He had plenty of brains," folk said. Now his hour had struck, he died, and his soul sought the gates of heaven. There it stood side by side with another soul— old Mother Margaret from the trenches.

"It is for the sake of contrast, I suppose, that I and this miserable soul should wait here together," thought the critic. "Well now, who are you, my good woman?" he inquired.

And the old woman replied, with as much respect as though St. Peter himself were addressing her—in fact, she took him for St. Peter, he gave himself such grand airs—"I am a poor old soul, I have no family, I am only old Margaret from the house near the trenches."

"Well, and what have you done down below?"

"I have done as good as nothing in the world! nothing whatever! It will be mercy, indeed, if such as I am suffered to pass through this gate."

"And how did you leave the world?" inquired the critic, carelessly. He must talk about something; it wearied him to stand there, waiting.

"Well, I can hardly tell how I left it; I have been sickly enough during these last few years, and could not well bear to creep out of bed at all during the cold weather. It has been a severe winter, but now that is all past. For a few days, as your highness must know, the wind was quite still, but it was bitterly cold; the ice lay over the water as far as one could see. All the people in the town were out on the ice; there was dancing, and music, and feasting, and sledge-racing, I fancy; I could hear something of it all as I lay in my poor little chamber. And when it was getting toward evening, the moon was up, but was not yet very bright; I looked from my bed through the window, and I saw how there rose up over the sea a strange white cloud; I lay and watched it, watched the black dot in it, which grew bigger and bigger, and then I knew what it foreboded; that sign is not often seen, but I am old and experienced. I knew it, and I shivered with horror. Twice before in my life have I seen that sign, and I knew that there would be a terrible storm and a spring flood; it would burst over the poor things on the ice, who were drinking and dancing and merry-making. Young and old, the whole town was out on the ice; who was to warn them, if no one saw it, or no one knew what I knew? I felt so terrified, I felt all alive, as I had not felt for years! I got out of bed, forced the window open; I could see the folk running and dancing over the ice; I could see the gay-colored flags, I could hear the boys shout 'Hurra!' and the girls and lads a-singing. All were so merry; and all the time the white cloud with its black speck rose higher and higher! I screamed as loud as I could; but no one heard me, I was too far off. Soon would the storm break loose, the ice would break in pieces, and all that crowd would sink and drown. Hear me they could not; get out to them I could not; what was to be done? Then our Lord sent me a good thought; I could set fire to my bed; better let my house be burned to the ground than that so many should miserably perish. So I kindled a light; I saw the red flame mount up; I got out at the door, but then I fell down; I lay there, I could not get up again. But the flames burst out through the window and over the roof; they saw it down below, and they all ran as fast as they could to help me; the poor old crone they believed would be burned; there was not one who did not come to help me. I heard them come, and I heard, too, such a rustling in the air, and then a thundering as of heavy cannon-shots, for the spring-flood was loosening the ice, and it all broke up. But the folk were all come off it to the trenches, where the sparks were flying about me; I had them all safe. But I could not bear the cold and the fright, and that is how I have come up here. Can the gates of heaven be opened to such a poor old creature as I? I have no house now at the trenches; where can I go, if they refuse me here?"

Then the gates opened, and the Angel bade poor Margaret enter. As she passed the threshold, she dropped a blade of straw—straw from her bed—that bed which she had set alight to save the people on the ice, and lo! it had changed into gold! dazzling gold! yet flexible withal, and twisting into various forms.

"Look, that was what yonder poor woman brought," said the Angel. "But what dost thou bring? Truly, I know well that thou hast done nothing, not even made bricks. It is a pity thou canst not go back again to fetch at least one brick—not that it is good for anything when it is made, no, but because anything, the very least, done with a good will, is Something. But thou mayst not go back, and I can do nothing for thee."

Then poor Margaret pleaded for him thus: "His brother gave me all the bricks and broken bits wherewith I built my poor little house—that was a great kindness toward a poor old soul like me! May not all those bits and fragments, put together, be reckoned as one brick for him? It will be an act of mercy; he needs it, and this is the home of mercy."

"To thy brother, whom thou didst despise," said the Angel, "to him whose calling, in respect of worldly honor, was the lowest, shalt thou owe this mite of heavenly coin. Thou shalt not be sent away; thou shalt have leave to stand here without, and think over thy manner of life down below. But within thou canst not enter, until thou hast done something that is good—Something!"

"I fancy I could have expressed that better," thought the critic; but he did not say it aloud, and that was already—Something!

THE JEWISH GIRL

By HANS CHRISTIAN ANDERSEN

There was in the charity-school among the other children a little Jewish girl, so clever and good; the best, in fact, of them all; but one of the lessons she could not attend—the one when religion was taught, for this was a Christian school.

Then she held her geography book before her to learn from it, or she did her sum; but the lesson was quickly learned, the sum was soon done; the book might be there open before her, but she did not read, she was listening; and the teacher soon noticed that she was attending more intently, even, than any of the rest.

"Read your book," the teacher urged, mildly and earnestly; but she looked at him with her black sparkling eyes, and when he put questions to her also, she knew more than all the others. She had listened, understood, and kept his words.

Her father was a poor honest man, and when first he brought her to the school, he had made the stipulation that she should not be taught the Christian faith. To let her go away during the Scripture lesson might, however, have given offence, and raised thoughts of various kinds in the minds of the other children, and so she stayed; but this could not go on any longer.

The teacher went to her father, and told him that either he must take his daughter away from the school, or consent to her becoming a Christian.

"I cannot bear to see those burning eyes, that yearning, that thirst of the soul, as it were, after the words of the gospel," said the teacher.

And the father burst into tears. "I know but little myself of our own religion, but her mother was a daughter of Israel, of strong and firm faith, and on her dying bed I made a vow that our child should never receive Christian baptism; that vow I must keep; it is to me as a convenant with God."

And the little Jewish girl was taken away from the school of the Christians.

Years rolled by.

In one of the smallest towns of Jutland served as maid in a plain burgher's house a poor girl of the Mosaic faith; this was Sarah. Her hair was black as ebony, her eyes dark, and yet brilliant and full of light, such as you see among the daughters of the East; and the expression in the countenance of the grown-up girl was still that of the child who sat on the school-room bench, listening with thoughtful and wistful eye.

Each Sunday sounded from the church the pealing of the organ to the song of the congregation, and the tones floated over the street, into the house, where the Jewish girl attended to her work, diligent and faithful in her calling. "Remember the Sabbath day to keep it holy," this was her law; but her Sabbath was a day of labor to the Christians, and only in her heart could she keep it holy; and that was not enough for her. But when the thought arose in her soul, "What matters it before God about days and hours?" and on the Sunday of the Christians her hour of devotion remained undisturbed. If, then, the organ's peal and the psalm-tunes reached over to her, where she stood in the kitchen, even this became a quiet and consecrated spot. She would read then the treasure and peculiar property of her people, the Old Testament, and this alone; for she kept deep in her heart what her father had told the teacher and herself when she was taken from the school—the vow made to her dying mother, "that Sarah should not be baptized, not forsake the faith of her fathers." The New Testament was, and should remain forever, a sealed book to her; and yet she knew much of it; it shone to her through the recollections of childhood.

One evening she sat in a corner of the parlor, and heard her master reading aloud. She might listen, she thought, for this was not the gospel; nay! 'twas out of an old story-book he read: she might stay. And he read of a Hungarian knight, taken captive by a Turkish pasha, who had him yoked with oxen to the plow; and he was driven with lashes, and had to suffer pain and ignominy beyond endurance.

But at home the knight's wife sold all her jewels, and mortgaged castle and lands, and his friends contributed large sums, for enormous was the ransom demanded; still it was raised, and he was delivered out of thraldom and disgrace. Sick and suffering, he came to his home. But soon resounded far and near the summons to war against the foe of Christianity. The sick man heard the call, and had neither peace nor rest any longer; he was placed on his charger; the blood came again to his cheeks, his strength seemed to return, and he rode forth to victory. The very pasha who had him yoked to the plow, and made him suffer pain and scorn, became his captive. He was carried home to the castle dungeon, but before his first hour had elapsed the knight came, and asked the prisoner, "What dost thou think awaiteth thee?"

"I know," said the Turk; "retribution."

"Yes, the Christian's retribution," said the knight. "Christ taught us to forgive our enemies, to love our fellow-men. God is love! Depart in peace to thy home and thy dear ones, and be gentle and good to those who suffer."

Then the prisoner burst into tears.

"How could I believe such a thing could be possible? Torments and sufferings I looked forward to as a certainty, and I took poison, which must kill me; within a few hours I shall die. There is no remedy. But before I die make known to me the faith that embraces such an amount of love and mercy; it is great and divine! In it let me die; let me die a Christian!" and his prayer was granted.

This was the legend, the history which was read; they all listened to it with attention, but deepest sank it into the heart of her who sat alone in the corner—the servant maid—Sarah, the Jewess. Heavy tears stood in her black sparkling eyes while she sat here, as once on the school-bench, and felt the greatness of the gospel. The tears rolled down her cheeks.

"Let not my child become a Christian!" were the mother's last words on her dying bed, and they rang through her soul with those of the law, "Honor thy father and thy mother!"

"Still I have not been baptized! they call me 'the Jewess'; the neighbors' boys did so, hooting at me last Sunday as I stood outside the open church door, and looked in where the altar-lights burned and the congregation sang. Ever since my school-days, up to this hour—even though I have tried to close my eyes against it—a power from Christianity has like a sunbeam shone into my heart. But, my mother, I will not give thee sorrow in thy grave! I will not betray the vow my father made to thee; I will not read the Christian's Bible. Have not I the God of my fathers? On Him let me rest my head!"

And years rolled by.

The husband died, the wife was left behind in hard plight. Now she could no longer afford to have a maid; but Sarah did not forsake the widow; she became her help in distress, and kept the household together; she worked till late in the night, and got bread for the house by the labor of her hands. There were no near relatives to help a family where the mother grew weaker each day, lingering for months on a bed of sickness. Sarah, gentle and pious, watched, nursed, and worked, and became the blessing of the poor home.

"There lies the Bible," said the invalid; "read to me this wearisome evening; I sadly want to hear God's word."

And Sarah bowed her head; she folded her hands round the Bible, which she opened, and read aloud to the sick woman; now and again the tears welled forth, but her eyes shone clearer, even as the darkness cleared from her soul. "Mother, thy child shall not receive the baptism of the Christians, shall not be named in their communion; in this we will be united here on earth, but above this there is—is a greater unity—even in God. 'He goes with us beyond the grave'; 'It is He who pours water upon him that is thirsty, and floods upon the dry ground.' I understand it! I do not know myself how I came to it! through Him it is—in Him—Christ!"

And she trembled as she named the holy name; a baptism of fire streamed through her, stronger than her frame could bear, and she bent down, more powerless even than she by whom she watched.

"Poor Sarah!" they said; "she is worn out with labor and watching."

They took her to the hospital for the poor; there she died; thence she was borne to her grave; not to the Christians' graveyard; that was not the place for the Jewish girl: no, outside, by the wall, her grave was dug.

And God's sun, which shone upon the graves of the Christians, shines also upon that of the Jewish girl; and the hymns which are sung by the graves of the Christians resound by her grave beyond the wall; thither, too, reaches the promise: "There is resurrection in Christ, in Him, the Saviour, who said to his disciples, 'John truly baptized with water; but ye shall be baptized with the Holy Ghost.'"

THE STORY OF A MOTHER

By HANS CHRISTIAN ANDERSEN

A mother sat by her little child: she was very sorrowful, and feared that it would die. Its little face was pale, and its eyes were closed. The child drew its breath with difficulty, and sometimes so deeply as if it were sighing; and then the mother looked more sorrowfully than before on the little creature.

Then there was a knock at the door, and a poor old man came in, wrapped up in something that looked like a great horse-cloth, for that keeps warm; and he required it, for it was cold winter. Without, everything was covered with ice and snow, and the wind blew so sharply that it cut one's face.

And as the old man trembled with cold, and the child was quiet for a moment, the mother went and put some beer on the stove in a little pot, to warm it for him. The old man sat down and rocked the cradle, and the mother seated herself on an old chair by him, looked at her sick child that drew its breath so painfully, and seized the little hand.

"You think I shall keep it, do you not?" she asked. "The good God will not take it from me!"

And the old man—he was *Death*—nodded in such a strange way, that it might just as well mean *yes* as *no*. And the mother cast down her eyes, and tears rolled down her cheeks. Her head became heavy: for three days and three nights she had not closed her eyes; and now she slept, but only for a minute; then she started up and shivered with cold.

"What is that?" she asked, and looked round on all sides; but the old man was gone, and her little child was gone; he had taken it with him. And there in the corner the old clock was humming and whirring; the heavy leaden weight ran down to the floor—plump!—and the clock stopped.

But the poor mother rushed out of the house crying for her child.

Out in the snow sat a woman in long black garments, and she said, "Death has been with you in your room; I saw him hasten away with your child: he strides faster than the wind, and never brings back what he has taken away."

"Only tell me which way he has gone," said the mother. "Tell me the way, and I will find him."

"I know him," said the woman in the black garments; "but before I tell you, you must sing me all the songs that you have sung to your child. I love those songs; I have heard them before. I am Night, and I saw your tears when you sang them."

"I will sing them all, all!" said the mother. "But do not detain me, that I may overtake him, and find my child."

But Night sat dumb and still. Then the mother wrung her hands, and sang and wept. And there were many songs, but yet more tears, and then Night said, "Go to the right into the dark fir wood; for I saw Death take that path with your little child."

Deep in the forest there was a cross road, and she did not know which way to take. There stood a Blackthorn Bush, with not a leaf nor a blossom upon it; for it was in the cold winter time, and icicles hung from the twigs.

"Have you not seen Death go by, with my little child?"

"Yes," replied the Bush, "but I shall not tell you which way he went unless you warm me on your bosom. I'm freezing to death here; I'm turning to ice."

And she pressed the Blackthorn Bush to her bosom, quite close, that it might be well warmed. And the thorns pierced into her flesh, and her blood oozed out in great drops. But the Blackthorn shot out fresh green leaves, and blossomed in the dark winter night: so warm is the heart of a sorrowing mother! And the Blackthorn Bush told her the way that she should go.

Then she came to a great Lake, on which there were neither ships nor boat. The Lake was not frozen enough to carry her, nor sufficiently open to allow her to wade through, and yet she must cross it if she was to find her child. Then she laid herself down to drink the Lake; and that was impossible for any one to do. But the sorrowing mother thought that perhaps a miracle might be wrought.

"No, that can never succeed," said the Lake. "Let us rather see how we can agree. I'm fond of collecting pearls, and your eyes are the two clearest I have ever seen: if you will weep them out into me I will carry you over into the great greenhouse, where Death lives and cultivates flowers and trees; each of these is a human life."

"Oh, what would I not give to get my child!" said the afflicted mother; and she wept yet more, and her eyes fell into the depths of the Lake, and became two costly pearls. But the Lake lifted her up, as if she sat in a swing, and she was wafted to the opposite shore, where stood a wonderful house, miles in length. One could not tell if it was a mountain containing forests and caves, or a place that had been built. But the poor mother could not see it, for she had wept her eyes out.

"Where shall I find Death, who went away with my little child?" she asked.

"He has not arrived here yet," said an old gray-haired Woman, who was going about and watching the hothouse of Death. "How have you found your way here, and who helped you?"

"The good God has helped me," she replied. "He is merciful, and you will be merciful too. Where shall I find my little child?"

"I do not know it," said the old Woman, "and you cannot see. Many flowers and trees have faded this night, and Death will soon come and transplant them. You know very well that every human being has his tree of life, or his flower of life, just as each is arranged. They look like other plants, but their hearts beat. Children's hearts can beat too. Think of this. Perhaps you may recognize the beating of your child's heart. But what will you give me if I tell you what more you must do?"

"I have nothing more to give," said the afflicted mother. "But I will go for you to the ends of the earth."

"I have nothing for you to do there," said the old Woman, "but you can give me your long black hair. You must know yourself that it is beautiful, and it pleases me. You can take my white hair for it, and that is always something."

"Do you ask for nothing more?" asked she. "I will give you that gladly." And she gave her beautiful hair, and received in exchange the old Woman's white hair.

And then they went into the great hothouse of Death, where flowers and trees were growing marvellously intertwined. There stood the fine hyacinths under glass bells, some quite fresh, others somewhat sickly; water snakes were twining about them, and black crabs clung tightly to the stalks. There stood gallant palm-trees, oaks, and plantains, and parsley and blooming thyme. Each tree and flower had its name; each was a human life: the people were still alive, one in China, another in Greenland, scattered about in the world. There were great trees thrust into little pots, so that they stood quite crowded, and were nearly bursting the pots; there was also many a little weakly flower in rich earth, with moss round about it, cared for and tended. But the sorrowful mother bent down over all the smallest plants, and heard the human heart beating in each, and out of millions she recognized that of her child.

"That is it!" she cried, and stretched out her hands over a little crocus flower, which hung down quite sick and pale.

"Do not touch the flower," said the old dame; "but place yourself here; and when Death comes—I expect him every minute—then don't let him pull up the plant, but threaten him that you will do the same to the other plants; then he'll be frightened. He has to account for them all; not one may be pulled up till he receives commission from Heaven."

And all at once there was an icy cold rush through the hall, and the blind mother felt that Death was arriving.

"How did you find your way hither?" said he. "How have you been able to come quicker than I?"

"I am a mother," she answered.

And Death stretched out his long hands toward the little delicate flower; but she kept her hands tight about it, and held it fast; and yet she was full of anxious care lest he should touch one of the leaves. Then Death breathed upon her hands, and she felt that his breath was colder than the icy wind; and her hands sank down powerless.

"You can do nothing against me," said Death.

"But the merciful God can," she replied.

"I only do what He commands," said Death. "I am his gardener. I take all his trees and flowers, and transplant them into the great Paradise gardens, in the unknown land. But how they will flourish there, and how it is there, I may not tell you."

"Give me back my child," said the mother; and she implored and wept. All at once she grasped two pretty flowers with her two hands, and called to Death, "I'll tear off all your flowers, for I am in despair."

"Do not touch them," said Death. "You say you are so unhappy, and now you would make another mother just as unhappy!"

"Another mother?" said the poor woman; and she let the flowers go.

"There are your eyes for you," said Death. "I have fished them up out of the Lake; they gleamed up quite brightly. I did not know that they were yours. Take them back—they are clearer now than before—and then look down into the deep well close by. I will tell you the names of the two flowers you wanted to pull up, and you will see what you were about to frustrate and destroy."

And she looked down into the well, and it was a happiness to see how one of them became a blessing to the world, how much joy and gladness she diffused around her. And the woman looked at the life of the other, and it was made up of care and poverty, misery and woe.

"Both are the will of God," said Death.

"Which of them is the flower of misfortune, and which the blessed one?" she asked.

"That I may not tell you," answered Death; "but this much you shall hear, that one of these two flowers is that of your child. It was the fate of your child that you saw—the future of your own child."

Then the mother screamed aloud for terror.

"Which of them belongs to my child? Tell me that. Release the innocent child! Let my child free from all that misery! Rather carry it away! Carry it into God's kingdom! Forget my tears, forget my entreaties, and all that I have done!"

"I do not understand you," said Death. "Will you have your child back, or shall I carry it to that place that you know not?"

Then the mother wrung her hands, and fell on her knees, and prayed to the good God.

"Hear me not when I pray against Thy will, which is at all times the best! Hear me not! hear me not!" And she let her head sink down on her bosom.

And Death went away with her child into the unknown land.

THE LITTLE MATCH GIRL

By HANS CHRISTIAN ANDERSEN

It was terribly cold; it snowed and was already almost dark, and evening came on, the last evening of the year. In the cold and gloom a poor little girl, bareheaded and barefoot, was walking through the streets. When she left her own house she certainly had had slippers on; but of what use were they? They were very big slippers, and her mother had used them till then, so big were they. The little maid lost them as she slipped across the road, where two carriages were rattling by terribly fast. One slipper was not to be found again, and a boy had seized the other, and run away with it. He thought he could use it very well as a cradle, some day when he had children of his own. So now the little girl went with her little naked feet, which were quite red and blue with the cold. In an old apron she carried a number of matches, and a bundle of them in her hand. No one had bought anything of her all day, and no one had given her a farthing.

Shivering with cold and hunger she crept along, a picture of misery, poor little girl! The snowflakes covered her long fair hair, which fell in pretty curls over her neck; but she did not think of that now. In all the windows lights were shining, and there was a glorious smell of roast goose, for it was New Year's Eve. Yes, she thought of that!

In a corner formed by two houses, one of which projected beyond the other, she sat down, cowering. She had drawn up her little feet, but she was still colder, and she did not dare to go home, for she had sold no matches, and did not bring a farthing of money. From her father she would certainly receive a beating, and besides, it was cold at home, for they had nothing over them but a roof through which the wind whistled, though the largest rents had been stopped with straw and rags.

Her little hands were almost benumbed with the cold. Ah, a match might do her good, if she could only draw one from the bundle, and rub it against the wall, and warm her hands at it. She drew one out. R-r-atch! how it spluttered and burned! It was a warm bright flame, like a little candle, when she held her hands over it; it was a wonderful little light! It really seemed to the little girl as if she sat before a great polished stove, with bright brass feet and a brass cover. How the fire burned! how comfortable it was! but the little flame went out, the stove vanished, and she had only the remains of the burned match in her hand.

A second was rubbed against the wall. It burned up, and when the light fell upon the wall it became transparent like a thin veil, and she could see through it into the room. On the table a snow-white cloth was spread; upon it stood a shining dinner service; the roast goose smoked gloriously, stuffed with apples and dried plums. And what was still more splendid to behold, the goose hopped down from the dish, and waddled along the floor, with a knife and fork in its breast, to the little girl. Then the match went out, and only the thick, damp, cold wall was before her. She lighted another match. Then she was sitting under a beautiful Christmas tree; it was greater and more ornamented than the one she had seen through the glass door at the rich merchant's. Thousands of candles burned upon the green branches, and colored pictures like those in the print shops looked down upon them. The little girl stretched forth her hand toward them; then the match went out. The Christmas lights mounted higher. She saw them now as stars in the sky: one of them fell down, forming a long line of fire.

"Now some one is dying," thought the little girl, for her old grandmother, the only person who had loved her, and who was now dead, had told her that when a star fell down a soul mounted up to God.

She rubbed another match against the wall; it became bright again, and in the brightness the old grandmother stood clear and shining, mild and lovely.

"Grandmother!" cried the child, "O! take me with you! I know you will go when the match is burned out. You will vanish like the warm fire, the warm food, and the great, glorious Christmas tree!"

And she hastily rubbed the whole bundle of matches, for she wished to hold her grandmother fast. And the matches burned with such a glow that it became brighter than in the middle of the day; grandmother had never been so large or so beautiful. She took the little girl in her arms, and both flew in brightness and joy above the earth, very, very high, and up there was neither cold, nor hunger, nor care—they were with God.

But in the corner, leaning against the wall, sat the poor girl with red cheeks and smiling mouth, frozen to death on the last evening of the Old Year. The New Year's sun rose upon a little corpse! The child sat there, stiff and cold, with the matches, of which one bundle was burned. "She wanted to warm herself," the people said. No one imagined what a beautiful thing she had seen, and in what glory she had gone in with her grandmother to the New Year's Day.

FLOWERS WITHOUT FRUIT

Prune thou thy words; the thoughts control
  That o'er thee swell and throng:—
They will condense within thy soul,
  And change to purpose strong.

But he who lets his feelings run
  In soft luxurious flow,
Shrinks when hard service must be done,
  And faints at every woe.

Faith's meanest deed more favor bears,
  Where hearts and wills are weigh'd,
Than brightest transports, choicest prayers,
  Which bloom their hour, and fade.

—*J. H. Newman*

CONTENTMENT

My mind to me a kingdom is;
  Such perfect joy therein I find,
As far exceeds all earthly bliss
  That world affords, or grows by kind:
Though much I want what most men have,
Yet doth my mind forbid me crave.

Content I live—this is my stay;
  I seek no more than may suffice:
I press to bear no haughty sway;
  Look—what I lack, my mind supplies!
Lo! thus I triumph like a king,
Content with that my mind doth bring.

I see how plenty surfeits oft,
  And hasty climbers soonest fall;
I see how those that sit aloft
  Mishap doth threaten most of all;
These get with toil, and keep with fear:
Such cares my mind could never bear.

I laugh not at another's loss;
  I grudge not at another's gain;
No worldly wave my mind can toss;
  I brook that is another's pain.
I fear no foe: I scorn no friend:
I dread no death: I fear no end.

Some have too much, yet still they crave;
  I little have, yet seek no more:
They are but poor, though much they have,
  And I am rich, with little store.
They poor, I rich: they beg, I give:
They lack, I lend: they pine, I live.

I wish but what I have at will:
　　I wander not to seek for more:
I like the plain; I climb no hill:
　　In greatest storm I sit on shore,
And laugh at those that toil in vain,
To get what must be lost again.
—This is my choice; for why?—I find
No wealth is like a quiet mind.

—*Unknown*

THE SEARCH FOR PEACE

Sweet Peace, where dost thou dwell? I humbly crave,
　Let me once know.
　I sought thee in a secret cave,
　　And ask'd, if Peace were there?
A hollow wind did seem to answer, "No:—
　Go seek elsewhere."

I did; and going did a rainbow note:
　Surely, thought I,
　This is the lace of Peace's coat:
　　I will search out the matter.
But while I look'd, the clouds immediately
　Did break and scatter.

Then went I to a garden, and did spy
　A gallant flower,
　The Crown Imperial: Sure, said I,
　　Peace at the root must dwell.
But when I digg'd, I saw a worm devour
　What show'd so well.

At length I met a reverend good old man:
　Whom when for Peace
　I did demand, he thus began:
　　"There was a Prince of old
At Salem dwelt, who lived with good increase
　Of flock and fold.

"He sweetly lived; yet sweetness did not save
　His life from foes.
　But after death, out of his grave
　　There sprang twelve stalks of wheat:
Which many wondering at, got some of those
　To plant and set.

"It prosper'd strangely, and did soon disperse
　Through all the earth:

For they that taste it do rehearse,
    That virtue lies therein;
A secret virtue, bringing peace and mirth
    By flight of sin.

"Take of this grain, which in my garden grows,
    And grows for you;
    Make bread of it:—and that repose
    And peace, which everywhere
With so much earnestness you do pursue,
    Is only there."

—*G. Herbert*

A SONG OF PRAISE

To God, ye choir above, begin
  A hymn so loud and strong
That all the universe may hear
  And join the grateful song.

Praise Him, thou sun, Who dwells unseen
  Amidst transcendent light,
Where thy refulgent orb would seem
  A spot, as dark as night.

Thou silver moon, 'ye host of stars,
  The universal song
Through the serene and silent night
  To listening worlds prolong.

Sing Him, ye distant worlds and suns,
  From whence no travelling ray
Hath yet to us, through ages past,
  Had time to make its way.

Assist, ye raging storms, and bear
  On rapid wings His praise,
From north to south, from east to west,
  Through heaven, and earth, and seas.

Exert your voice, ye furious fires
  That rend the watery cloud,
And thunder to this nether world
  Your Maker's words aloud.

Ye works of God, that dwell unknown
  Beneath the rolling main;
Ye birds, that sing among the groves,
  And sweep the azure plain;

Ye stately hills, that rear your heads,
  And towering pierce the sky;
Ye clouds, that with an awful pace
  Majestic roll on high;

Ye insects small, to which one leaf
  Within its narrow sides
A vast extended world displays,
  And spacious realms provides;

Ye race, still less than these, with which
  The stagnant water teems,
To which one drop, however small,
  A boundless ocean seems;

Whate'er ye are, where'er ye dwell,
  Ye creatures great or small,
Adore the wisdom, praise the power,
  That made and governs all.

—*P. Skelton*

THE TRAVELLER

How are thy servants blest, O Lord!
  How sure is their defence!
Eternal wisdom is their guide,
  Their help, Omnipotence.

In foreign realms, and lands remote,
  Supported by Thy care,
Through burning climes I pass'd unhurt,
  And breathed in tainted air.

Thy mercy sweeten'd every soil,
  Made every region please;
The hoary Alpine hills it warm'd,
  And smoothed the Tyrrhene seas.

Think, O my soul, devoutly think,
  How, with affrighted eyes,
Thou saw'st the wide-extended deep
  In all its horrors rise.

Confusion dwelt in every face,
  And fear in every heart;
When waves on waves, and gulfs on gulfs,
  O'ercame the pilot's art.

Yet then from all my griefs, O Lord,
  Thy mercy set me free;
Whilst, in the confidence of prayer,
  My soul took hold on Thee.

For though in dreadful whirls we hung
  High on the broken wave,
I knew Thou wert not slow to hear,
  Nor impotent to save.

—The storm was laid; the winds retired,
  Obedient to Thy will;
The sea that roar'd at Thy command,
  At Thy command was still.

—J. Addison

TRUE GREATNESS

The fairest action of our human life
  Is scorning to revenge an injury:
For who forgives without a further strife
  His adversary's heart to him doth tie:
And 'tis a firmer conquest truly said
  To win the heart, than overthrow the head.

If we a worthy enemy do find,
  To yield to worth, it must be nobly done:—
But if of baser metal be his mind,
  In base revenge there is no honor won.
Who would a worthy courage overthrow?
  And who would wrestle with a worthless foe?

We say our hearts are great, and cannot yield;
  Because they cannot yield, it proves them poor:
Great hearts are task'd beyond their power but seld:
  The weakest lion will the loudest roar.
Truth's school for certain does this same allow,
  High-heartedness doth sometimes teach to bow.

—*Lady E. Carew*

CHARACTER OF A HAPPY LIFE

How happy is he born and taught
  That serveth not another's will;
Whose armor is his honest thought,
  And simple truth his utmost skill!

Whose passions not his masters are,
  Whose soul is still prepared for death,
Not tied unto the world with care
  Of public fame, or private breath;

Who envies none that chance doth raise
  Or vice; who never understood
How deepest wounds are given by praise;
  Nor rules of state, but rules of good;

Who hath his life from rumors freed;
  Whose conscience is his strong retreat;
Whose state can neither flatterers feed,
  Nor ruin make accusers great;

Who God doth late and early pray
  More of His grace than gifts to lend;
And entertains the harmless day
  With a well-chosen book or friend;

—This man is freed from servile bands
  Of hope to rise, or fear to fall;
Lord of himself, though not of lands;
  And having nothing, yet hath all.

—*Sir H. Wotton*

A THANKSGIVING TO GOD, FOR HIS HOUSE

Lord, thou hast given me a cell,
  Wherein to dwell;
A little house, whose humble roof
  Is weather-proof;
Under the spars of which I lie
  Both soft and dry;
Where thou, my chamber for to ward,
  Hast set a guard
Of harmless thoughts, to watch and keep
  Me, while I sleep.
Low is my porch, as is my fate:
  Both void of state;
And yet the threshold of my door
  Is worn by th' poor,
Who thither come, and freely get
  Good words, or meat.
Like as my parlor, so my hall
  And kitchen's small;
A little buttery, and therein
  A little bin,
Which keeps my little loaf of bread
  Unchipt, unflead;
Some brittle sticks of thorn or briar
  Make me a fire,
Close by whose living coal I sit,
  And glow like it.
Lord, I confess too, when I dine,
  The pulse is thine,
And all those other bits that be
  There placed by thee;
The worts, the purslain, and the mess
  Of water-cress,
Which of thy kindness thou hast sent;
  And my content

Makes those, and my beloved beet,
  To be more sweet.
'Tis thou that crown'st my glittering hearth
  With guiltless mirth,
And giv'st me wassail-bowls to drink,
  Spiced to the brink.
Lord, 'tis thy plenty-dropping hand
  That soils my land,
And giv'st me, for my bushel sown,
  Twice ten for one;
Thou mak'st my teeming hen to lay
  Her egg each day;
Besides my healthful ewes to bear
  Me twins each year;
The while the conduits of my kine
  Run cream, for wine:
All these, and better, thou dost send
  Me—to this end,
That I should render, for my part,
  A thankful heart.

    —R. Herrick

FRIENDS DEPARTED

They are all gone into the world of light!
  And I alone sit lingering here!
Their very memory is fair and bright,
  And my sad thoughts doth clear.

It glows and glitters in my cloudy breast
  Like stars upon some gloomy grove,
Or those faint beams in which this hill is drest
  After the Sun's remove.

I see them walking in an air of glory,
  Whose light doth trample on my days;
My days, which are at best but dull and hoary,
  Mere glimmerings and decays.

O holy hope! and high humility!
  High as the Heavens above!
These are your walks, and you have show'd them me,
  To kindle my cold love.

Dear, beauteous Death; the jewel of the just!
  Shining nowhere but in the dark;
What mysteries do lie beyond thy dust,
  Could man outlook that mark!

He that hath found some fledged birdes nest may know
  At first sight if the bird be flown;
But what fair dell or grove he sings in now,
  That is to him unknown.

And yet, as Angels in some brighter dreams
  Call to the soul when man doth sleep,
So some strange thoughts transcend our wonted themes,
  And into glory peep.

       —*H. Vaughan*

THE LAND OF DREAMS

"Awake, awake, my little boy!
Thou wast thy mother's only joy;
Why dost thou weep in thy gentle sleep?
O wake! thy father does thee keep."

—"O what land is the Land of Dreams?
What are its mountains, and what are its streams?
O father! I saw my mother there
Among the lilies by waters fair.

"Among the lambs, clothed in white,
She walk'd with her Thomas in sweet delight:
I wept for joy; like a dove I mourn:—
O when shall I again return!"

—"Dear child! I also by pleasant streams
Have wander'd all night in the Land of Dreams:—
But, though calm and warm the waters wide,
I could not get to the other side."

—"Father, O father! what do we here,
In this land of unbelief and fear?—
The Land of Dreams is better far,
Above the light of the morning star."

—W. Blake

ADORATION

Sweet is the dew that falls betimes,
And drops upon the leafy limes;
  Sweet Hermon's fragrant air:
Sweet is the lily's silver bell,
And sweet the wakeful tapers smell
  That watch for early prayer.

Sweet the young nurse, with love intense,
Which smiles o'er sleeping innocence;
  Sweet when the lost arrive;
Sweet the musician's ardor beats,
While his vague mind's in quest of sweets,
  The choicest flowers to hive.

Strong is the horse upon his speed;
Strong in pursuit the rapid glede,
  Which makes at once his game:
Strong the tall ostrich on the ground;
Strong through the turbulent profound
  Shoots xiphias to his aim.

Strong is the lion—like a coal
His eyeball—like a bastion's mole
  His chest against the foes:
Strong the gier-eagle on his sail;
Strong against tide the enormous whale
  Emerges as he goes.

But stronger still, in earth and air,
And in sea, the man of prayer,
  And far beneath the tide:
And in the seat to Faith assign'd,
Where ask is, have; where seek is, find;
  Where knock is, open wide.

—*C. Smart*